# FOCUS ON WORLD FESTIVALS

## CONTEMPORARY CASE STUDIES AND PERSPECTIVES

Edited by

**Chris Newbold and Jennie Jordan**

(G) Goodfellow Publishers Ltd

(G) Published by Goodfellow Publishers Limited,
Woodeaton, Oxford, OX3 9TJ
http://www.goodfellowpublishers.com

British Library Cataloguing in Publication Data: a catalogue record for this title is available from the British Library.

Library of Congress Catalog Card Number: on file.

ISBN: 978-1-910158-56-2



Design and typesetting by P.K. McBride, www.macbride.org.uk

Cover design by Cylinder

Printed by Marston Book Services, www.marston.co.uk

Cover photo: "Joy to the World," by Minshall, from his mas presentation HALLELUJAH (Trinidad Carnival, 1995). Performed by Alyson Brown. Photo by Butch Limchoy.

# Contents

# List of figures

# Notes on contributors

**Robyn Archer** is a singer, writer, artistic director and public advocate for the arts. She is Artistic Director of *The Light in Winter* (which she created for Federation Square, Melbourne), Deputy Chair of *The Australia Council* (the Australian Government's arts funding and advisory body) and Strategic Advisor to Gold Coast Arts and Culture. She is a member of the *European House of Culture* and a mentor in the European Festivals Association's *Atelier* programme. Robyn is an *Officer of the Order of Australia*, and has been awarded the *Chevalier de l'Ordre des Arts et des Lettres* (France) and Belgium's *Order of the Crown*.

**Rachel Bowditch** is a theatre director and performance studies scholar. She is an assistant professor in the Arizona State University School of Theatre and Film, and has a PhD in Performance Studies from NYU. Her main areas of research are invented ritual practices and the festival as a site for utopic/dystopic social transformation, she is also interested in experimental and avant-garde theatre and the application of digital technology in performance. Her published work includes, *On the Edge of Utopia: Performance and Ritual at Burning Man, Festive Performance: Staging Identity, Politics and Utopia in the Americas* (co-edited with Pegge Vissicaro). She is currently co editing *Crossing the Line: Rasaboxes Source Book* with Paula Murray Cole.

**Emily Bradfield** is Grants and Community Engagement Manager for Cambridgeshire Community Foundation, she lectures part time at De Montfort University and has an MSc in Cultural Events Management. She has spent seven years teaching English Language in Italy. Her interest in Mexico and *Dia de los Muertos* developed after traveling extensively in the country.

**Simon Brown** has spent 12 years as Festivals and Events Officer in Leicester City Council directly managing and supporting on a variety of events. He is currently carrying out a temporary strategic role as Cultural Programme Coordinator for the local authority. He is also a part time lecturer, De Montfort University, and he has an MSc. in Cultural Events Management.

**Eve Carroll-Dwyer** is an independent researcher. Eve is a casual lecturer in American history in the faculty of Arts and Social Sciences at the University of New South Wales, Australia.

**Roberta Comunian** is Lecturer in the Department of Culture, Media and Creative Industries at King's College London. Her work focuses on the relationship between arts, cultural regeneration projects and the cultural and creative industries.

**Aurélien Djakouane** has a PhD in Sociology and is Associate Researcher at CEPEL, University of Montpellier. His research focuses on cultural practices and public policies. He is the author of several books: *Les publics des festivals, (dir.)* (2010); *Un territoire de rock. Le(s) public(s) des Eurockéennes de Belfort. Logiques Sociales,* (2012); *L'enseignement des danses du monde et des danses traditionnelles. Logiques Sociales,* (2013).

**Elena Elkanova** is currently a PhD student in National Research University Higher School of Economics (Saint Petersburg) researching cultural organisations operations management (including events). She contributed to research projects of Cultural Economics Laboratory: hospitality and events studies, joint research project of HSE and University of Turku 'Socioeconomic impact of arts festivals' (*Pori Jazz Festival* survey). She is also involved within creative project group in Museum Quarter development project in Saint Petersburg.

**Carmel Foley** is a Senior Lecturer in the Management Discipline Group at the UTS Business School, University of Technology, Sydney. She is a Research Associate of the Australian Centre for Event Management (ACEM) and a core member of Cosmopolitan Civil Societies Research Centre.

**Lydia Fraser-Ward** is a freelance producer, choreographer and artist specialising in creating live performances and interactive installations in unusual spaces. She is the founder and Creative Director of Fantasy High Street, a not-for-profit arts organisation specialising in creating magical, interactive arts projects in high street spaces and town centres.

**Floriane Gaber** is a writer, researcher, journalist, teacher and cultural consultant. She is also a lecturer at the University of Paris III where she coordinated the Association of Research on Street Arts. She is a well-travelled European commentator and critic of street theatre, mime, circus and spoken/written word performance.

**Silvia Guglielmini** has successfully completed her *viva voce* discussion at the School of Art History and Cultural Policy in University College Dublin. Her research project has investigated the relationship between tourism and festivals, paying particular attention to the dynamics of cultural production in the case of *Galway International Arts Festival* in Ireland. She has guest-lectured in several Irish universities including University College Dublin, University of Limerick and National University of Ireland, Galway.

**Alison Shin-Yi Huang** has an MSc. in Cultural Events Management from De Montfort University, and been organizing and consulting for the festival and event industry since 2000, including performing arts festivals, *International Flora Expo* and *Taiwan Lantern Festival*.

**Silvie Jacobi** is a joint-PhD candidate at the Department of Culture, Media and Creative Industries at King's College London and Geographisches Institut at Humboldt University Berlin. Trained as visual artist, she holds an MSc in Creative Cities from King's and currently works as an independent consultant at the intersection between social science and cultural practice.

**Jennie Jordan** is Senior Lecturer in Arts and Festivals Management, De Montfort University Leicester, where she focuses on cultural leadership, cultural policy and audience engagement. Jennie has a significant track record as a consultant, having worked for the Department of Cultural Media and Sport, the Department of Food and Rural Affairs and national bodies such as Youth Music, Capacity Builders and Arts Council England. She is currently undertaking a PhD researching festivals and has written an Arts Council funded research paper as part of the *Discussion Papers in Arts and Festivals Management series,* which she co-edits with Chris Newbold. Jennie is one of the co-editors of *Focus on Festivals* (2015).

**Arkotong Longkumer** is Lecturer in Religious Studies in the University of Edinburgh. He has written widely on the Northeast of India and has produced a major monograph, *Reform, Identity and Narratives of Belonging* (Bloomsbury, 2010), and an article, *"As our ancestors once lived": Representation, Performance, and Constructing a National Culture amongst the Nagas of India* (Himalaya, 2015). He is very much interested in the performance of identity and the way religion, culture, and politics constantly shape and challenge notions of belonging. He is on the editorial board of *Himalaya* and *The South Asianist.*

**Maurice Maguire** is an experienced arts manager with specialist skills in public art, arts and regeneration projects, commissions and artist-led programmes. He was the lead artist and curator for the *Transform* project at Snibston Museum, Coalville 2010-14 and teaches at De Montfort University. He has authored significant reports for local authorities and other public bodies. In 2001 he established the artist group pro/POSIT with David Patten (2001 – 05) and as a team they undertook significant studies in arts and cultural regeneration.

**Vanessa Martin** is Visiting Professor at SEBRAE and other Brazilian universities. She has almost 30 years' experience managing international, national and regional events, and acts as a consultant for companies in the areas of events and corporate revitalisation.

**Christopher Maughan** worked as an academic and researcher at De Montfort University for over 25 years. In 2002-3 he co-authored a major report on the economic and social impact of ten cultural festivals in the East Midlands of England. Since then he has contributed to the development of two festivals' tool-kits and published related work on festivals' life cycles, festivals and public authorities. Chris is one of the co-editors of *Focus on Festivals* (2015).

**Emmanuel Négrier** is a CNRS senior research fellow in political science at CEPEL, University of Montpellier I (France). He dedicates a notable part of his investigations to festivals and public policies. He is the author or co-author of the following books: *Les Musiques du monde et leurs publics*, Le Mot et le Reste, (2014); *Music Festivals : a Changing World*, Michel de Maule ed. (2013);*Un territoire de rock*, L'Harmattan (2012); *Les publics des festivals*, Michel de Maule (2010).

**Chris Newbold** is Senior Lecturer in Arts and Cultural Industries Management, and Programme Leader for the MSc. Cultural Events Management De Montfort University Leicester. He has published on culture, media and research methods, Chris is one of the co-editors of *Focus on Festivals* (2015), and has produced two major media text books in *Approaches to Media* (1995) and *The Media Book* (2002). He is joint series editor with Jennie Jordan of the *Discussion Papers in Arts and Festivals Management* series.

**Daniel Nordgård** has a background in music, originally as musician, but later working as a project manager; in the period 2007-2008 as the festival manager for the *Quart-Festival* in Norway. Nordgård currently works as researcher and teaches music business at Agder Research in Norway. In 2013 he was appointed by the Norwegian Government to lead their committee on digital changes in the music industry. Nordgård is currently finishing his doctorate on digital change in the international music industry.

**Samuel Aniegye Ntewusu** is a social historian and holds a PhD in History from the University of Leiden, The Netherlands and an MPhil in African Studies from the University of Ghana. Since August 2011 Ntewusu, has worked as Research Fellow at the Institute of African Studies, University of Ghana, Legon. He is currently the University of Ghana Coordinator of the Gonja-Dagomba project.

**Svetlana Puchkova** is Associate Professor of The Institute of Economics and Social Technologies of St Petersburg State University of Technology and Design. She successfully participated in several educational marketing programmes at De Montfort University (UK), Manchester Business School (UK), Open Society University (Hungary). Her PhD thesis was on the research and modelling of consumer behaviour in Fashion industry. She contributed to research projects of the Cultural Economics Laboratory: hospitality and events studies and the HSE/University of Turku 'Socioeconomic impact of arts festivals' (*Pori Jazz Festival* survey).

**Ljiljana Radošević** is a doctoral candidate in the Department of Art and Culture Studies in the University of Jyväskylä in Finland. For three years she was a researcher in the department's Research Centre for Contemporary Culture and a member of the Popular Culture Studies Programme coordinated by Turku University. She has worked as a researcher in the Centre for the Study of Cultural Development and in the Museum of African Arts both in Belgrade, and completed an internship at the *International Festival of Comics* in Angoulême, France in 2006/07.

**Milla Cozart Riggio** is James J. Goodwin Professor of English, Trinity College, Hartford, Connecticut. She received her PhD from Harvard University. Since 1995, she has focused on Trinidad Carnival and culture. Among her edited books and monographs are *Ta`ziyeh: Ritual and Drama in Iran* (1988), *The Play of Wisdom: Its Text and Contexts* (1990), a special issue of TDR: The Drama Review on Trinidad and Tobago Carnival (1998), and *Carnival: Culture in Action—the Trinidad Experience (2004)*. She co-edited *Renegades: The History of the Renegades Steel Orchestra* (2002) and *In Trinidad: Photographs by Pablo Delano* (2008). She has also written on Hindu Ramleela performances in Trinidad. *Festive Devils of the Americas* is forthcoming in 2015.

**Monica Sassatelli** is a cultural sociologist with a particular interest on cultural events and institutions, and has a focus on Europe. She is a Lecturer in the Sociology Department at Goldsmiths, University of London, where she is also co-director of the Centre for Urban and Community research. She co-edited the volume *Festivals and the Cultural Public Sphere* (2011, with L. Giorgi and G. Delanty).

**Katie Schlenker** is a Senior Lecturer in the Management Discipline Group at the UTS Business School, University of Technology, Sydney. Katie teaches in the Event Management programs at both the undergraduate and postgraduate levels. Her research interests and publications are in the areas of event evaluation, particularly the social impacts of events on host communities. Katie's research is industry linked, with recent projects including inscope expenditure studies for the *Sydney Entertainment Centre* and *Business Events Sydney*.

**Jen Snowball** is a full professor of Economics at Rhodes University, with a PhD in Economics from the same university. She is also a research strategist at the National Cultural Observatory in South Africa. She has more than 40 articles published in national and international journals. Her book, *Measuring the Value of Culture: Methods and Economics in Cultural Economics* (2008), was well received both locally and internationally. She is a member of the executive board of the Association of Cultural Economics International. Her research in cultural economics has focused on the use of market and non-market valuation methods for cultural economics, especially as they apply to cultural festivals.

**János Zoltán Szabó** is a guest lecturer at Eötvös Loránd University, Budapest, and senior adviser at the Ministry of Human Resources, Hungary. Formerly he worked as a research officer at the Budapest Observatory (2003-2012), independent expert (2000-2003) and theatre manager at Csokonai Theatre, Debrecen (1995-2000). He obtained his PhD on Educational Sciences from Debrecen University (2012).

**Mathilda van Niekerk** is assistant professor at the University of Central Florida's Rosen College of Hospitality Management. She has a PhD in tourism management from the North West University in South Africa. She has extensive experience in leadership positions and of managing organisational budgets and events, and 15 years of university teaching experience in the USA and South Africa. She is the author or co-author of more than 78 academic publications, and is the Associate Editor of the *International Journal of Contemporary Hospitality Management* (IJCHM).

**Paolo Vignolo** is associate professor of history and humanities at the National University of Colombia, Bogotá. His fields of research and creation deal with public history, cultural heritage and memory studies with a focus on live arts, play and performance. He holds a PhD in history at the School for Advanced Studies in the Social Sciences of Paris, and was 2012-13 Santo Domingo Visiting Scholar of the David Rockefeller Center for Latin American Studies at Harvard. He is director and co-founder of the research group 'Play, Fiesta and Power' of the Hemispheric Institute of Performance and Politics (New York University) and co-founder of the Colombian chapter of the Cultural Agents Initiative (Harvard University).

**Meng Xiang** is responsible for promotion and branding of the international exchange programme at Shanghai University of finance and economics, she has an MSc in Cultural Events Management and a BA in Radio and Television Editing and Directing from Nanjing University of the Arts. She has worked in newspaper editing and has volunteered at independent festivals in China.

# Preface

## Chris Newbold and Jennie Jordan

*Focus on World Festivals* has been written and produced to be a companion volume to *Focus on Festivals*, to expand its contemporary case studies and perspectives approach from Europe to festivals around the world. It is hoped that together they will form a major resource for practitioners, scholars and students alike. When we first embarked on this project it was with the intention of providing much needed examples and case studies to the field of festivals study, for at that time many of the issues and debates were clearly extant, but concrete examples and illustrations were hard to come by. Together these two books provide over fifty case studies of contemporary festivals for the reader to refer to.

On the Monday morning following the launch of *Focus on Festivals*, the previous Friday, we sat down and began to discuss potential themes and perspectives, debates and issues that had arisen during the editing process, and to create a wish list of festivals across the globe we would like to be included in a book entitled *Focus on World Festivals*. It was then, with some trepidation that we sent out the first batch of e-mails asking for potential contributions. We need not have concerned ourselves, for the response was instant and overwhelming. Colleagues from around the globe were enthusiastic about the project, and they wanted to be part of it. Thanks to the involvement of an inspiring and insightful group of contributors, including academics, practitioners and festival managers, all of whom think very deeply about their own festivals and the place of festivals in society, this book has been a joy to produce, driven as it has by these colleagues' enthusiasm, dedication and belief in the project.

We hope that readers enjoy engaging with the case studies and theoretical perspectives presented, and that they will find that both these books have achieved their aim of deepening understanding of the festivals sector and its benefits both locally and internationally.

# Acknowledgements

The work of compiling a book such as this represents many challenges that are different to the writing of an authored text. The acts of organising, collating and editing a variety of material from a variety of authors presents many and varied challenges, inevitably the endeavour overall owes a great deal to team effort and team support. With this in mind the editors would like to thank all those who have been involved in both *Focus on…* books. It is a truism that without their practical and moral support these books would not have been completed in the timely and efficient manner that they have, and certainly would not have been the enjoyable experience to produce that they have been. As academics, we find that our students play a major role in stimulating our thoughts and discussions, thus we would also like to thank all our students from all over the world who have inevitably played a part in the construction of this book.

We would like to thank the British Arts and Science Festivals Association (BAFA), particularly Kim Hart, for her support and encouragement, and we would also like to acknowledge the European Festivals Association for their help and involvement in both book projects.

Special thanks go to Todd Gulick of the Callaloo Company in Trinidad and Tobago and Peter Minshall the author of the mas character 'Joy to the World' which is the image on the front of the book.

Finally, we would like to thank Goodfellow publishers, Tim and his team, Sally and Mac, for their work and their unhesitating and unwavering support of the whole *Focus on Festivals* project.

# Introduction: focusing on world festivals

Chris Newbold and Jennie Jordan

Festivals are found in every society, on every continent and throughout history. The urge to communal celebration and rapturous experiences is ubiquitous, as the case studies in this book illustrate. Festivity is found in rich and poor societies, quietly under repressive regimes, or exuberantly in state-sanctioned festivals. The irrepressibility of festival causes us to question the belief that festivals are marginal, liminal, at the edges of society. If all societies invest precious resources in this kind of activity – and festivals are, let us not forget, events that are planned over months (Getz, 2010), with costumes made, food prepared, bands rehearsed, parades organised – it would seem that festivity answers a central social or human need. There is not space in this introduction to do more than speculate on what these needs might be, but the chapters in this book provide some hints and indications: tradition, reaffirming shared identity; religion, celebrating the divine through communal experience; and continuity reaffirming social structure and order.

This book brings together 35 different authors drawn from 18 different countries considering festivals in 20 places around the globe; it has over 30 different festival case studies. The contributions from around the world speak to us in authentic voices of their experience of running and reflecting on festivals in their own country. The reader will find that this book has many themes and debates that are similar and familiar regardless of wherever in the world these case studies take place. Thus the book can be used in several ways: first, to examine the variety of festival incarnations that occur across the globe, from those rooted in cultural and religious beliefs and traditions, to those developed to establish a tourist market, or as a promoter of local and national identities; second, to understand the organisational and management processes involved in running different types of festivals; and third, to discuss different types of festivals from ritualistic festivals, art and performance festivals, music festivals, and carnival.

In *Focus on Festivals* (Newbold et al., 2015) we were keen to demonstrate that festivals did not take place in a vacuum, and again we encourage the reader in this more world-based book to consider the importance of context in assessing each of the festivals discussed; as we said "they are the result of a range of social and cultural pressures, organisational and management decisions, and artist and audience expectations" (2015: xv). Alongside this, many of the examples in this book are subject to more national, political and economic considerations as well. By the same token, festival studies itself does not take place in an academic vacuum, and this book can also be used to engage debates and theoretical issues that are current within the field.

In *Focus on Festivals* we identified festivalisation as a key debate in understanding the role of festivals in contemporary society, we particularly drew attention to the role of local authorities and their festivalisation strategies (xxi), and in a major chapter Négrier (2015) reminded us that the process was "deeply differentiated in the events market", and should not be seen as a "monolithic and linear movement" (25-26). Beginning with the first chapter by Jordan we continue the engagement with festivalisation in this book, since its world focus allows us to consider it alongside globalisation and 'glocalisation' debates, as well as in various specific world contexts. The research by Sassatelli (Chapter 5) on the rise of biennials is closely allied to notions of festivalisation. The process of festivalisation can be broadly seen as the process by which festivals have become the favoured vehicle for the delivery of cultural products and a variety of other types of events ranging from food and produce to nostalgia and vintage. Hauptfleisch (2007) talks about how festivals eventify everyday life events turning them into significant cultural events. As he says:

> The arguments for the festivalisation of culture in the world today [Kaptein 1996] seems to suggest that the arts festival circuit may actually in some cases have come to represent the theatrical 'season' [...] the festivals *are* where plays, performances and other arts events are effectively launched and displayed for the public today. Slogans like 'As seen at the *Melbourne Festival*', 'Newly from the *Edinburgh Festival*' or 'The hit show of the *Grahamstown Festival*' have become a standard and effective part of marketing (39).

The process of festivalisation, as we shall see, is not only concerned with the delivery of the arts, traditional culture and community; festivalisation has become a key element in the endeavours of local governments to act out community cohesion policies and give cultural voices and diversity a platform. Along with urban regeneration and the economic restructuring of cities, the belief in the power and role of festivals to deliver a whole range of social outcomes seems to have continued unabashed.

Connected to the process of festivalisation, it is clear that since the early 1980s a change has been observed (Holbrook and Hirschman 1982) in consumer appetites, where the role of experiences in consumption patterns has come to the fore. In their conception of the 'experience economy', Pine and Gilmore (1998) discuss experiences as being active or passive, immersive or absorbing, or creating a balance of all four. Their further work (1999) on retail entertainment districts (RED) cites Las Vegas and Disneyland as examples of the experience economy where everything is designed to create the complete experience and the most important elements are interactivity and the immersive environment. Clearly the large multi-day on-site festivals such as *Glastonbury*, *Exit* or *Burning Man* (see Chapter 6) can come close to achieving a RED-like situation, however most festivals of a local or traditional nature would probably like to think of their event as at least being an immersive or transformational experience.

The rise of the experience economy can be seen to be a result of contemporary life being lived in and through a mediated and mass mediatised world where people come to desire 'real' experiences, physical sensations, and contact with human beings and like-minded people. Festivals can be seen as the perfect deliverers of such 'experiences', as Richards and Palmer say:

> ...events are excellent vehicles for experience production because they are limited in time and imply co-presence, not just between producers and consumers, but also the co-presence of fellow consumers. The shared experience of cultural events is often what makes them special... (2010: 22)

Co-presence and shared experience, particularly those that are immersive, demands active participation, a point that can be seen to be central to a number of the case studies in this book. Costuming, event production and volunteering are all evident and place the audience at the centre of festivals, as both active participants and part of the experience for others. Such active participation helps to create a sense of community and deepen the memories that are taken away (Pine and Gilmore, 1999, Poulsson and Kale, 2001).

The growing demand for festivals and their success as deliverers of multiple societal functions means inevitably that they can become commodified and have a market value in the 'experience economy'. The pressure to manufacture or stage-manage experiences as part of the festival 'package' is intense, and as we shall see in many of the festivals represented in this book this leads to debates on authenticity and to the consequences of festivalisation. The connection here with the consumer society and consumption is important; festivals are not only single sites of consumption, but through various retail outlets and opportunities provide multiple sites of consumption. It is tempting to recall Marx's work on commodity fetishism (1963) and Adorno's on exchange values in the realm of cultural goods (1991), by recalling his observation that in the world of popular music the price of the ticket becomes more venerated than the concert itself, suggesting that the long cherished wristband, becomes *the* fetishised commodity long after the festival experience has been forgotten. Whilst accepting the wristband as status symbol, we would argue that it is also a personal souvenir, a reminder of the experience that reinforces memories and a marker of shared identity amongst those who were there.

Questions about the societal and personal value of culture have become major issues in public policy in recent years, as governments have sought to rethink their role, often with a view to withdrawing from areas that could be considered non-essential, and commercial cultural activity has become established and legitimated. New Public Management introduced rationality into the funding process, and the requirement to prove and measure the benefit that subsidy produced (Belfiore, 2004). The arts in general have sought to find ways to define and capture their effects, although many of these efforts have been allied to instrumental projects driven by the need to access funding for cultural activities that are not directly cultural such as health and well-being, urban regeneration or tourism (Gray, 2004, 2007). In 2014 the Arts and Humanities Research Council (AHRC) in the UK launched a major research project to "establish a framework that will advance the way in which we talk about the value of cultural engagement and the methods by which we evaluate that value" (Arts and Humanities Research Council, 2014: 3).

In 2015 one of its projects concluded that, "culture and creativity exist in a distinct ecosystem. They feed and depend on each other. The points of connection [...] are where the potential for greatest value creation resides – culturally, socially and economically" (The University of Warwick, 2015: 9). The need to prove the cultural value of festivals, in particular to find a language to express their significance beyond the number of visitors attracted or jobs secured, can be found in the number of chapters concerned with impact in a variety of forms. Although primarily economic, the studies here are also concerned with the wider community and the effects that festivals have on residents' well-being, whether or not they attend; on social cohesion; and on perceptions of place and place development.

Debates around cultural participation are twofold: definitions, and consideration of who and who does not participate. UNESCO (2006) identifies three types of participation: reception, production and interaction. Reception refers to attendance at theatre, music and dance performances or exhibitions. Production refers to making creative work, often on a voluntary or amateur basis. Interaction refers to the co-creation of work or dialogue between professional arts organisations and individual participants or groups. There are examples of festivals that engage with their communities in each of these ways throughout this book.

Questions of access and engagement have become thorny political issues in many countries as questions have been raised about who is benefiting from public subsidies and whether or not these are a fair reflection of the wider community. Discourse around participation has for the most part centred on the deficit model, which identifies lack of participation in subsidised cultural activity as problematic (Jancovich and Bianchini, 2013; Miles, 2007; Belfiore et al., 2011) and encourages publically funded arts organisations to engage 'hard to reach' individuals and communities. As David Stevenson (2015) points out, cultural participation might include all sorts of commercial and community activity that is not publically funded, raising questions about whether or not public authorities should rethink their rationales for funding.

Within these discussions we see an increase in public support for festivals, often justified because of their ability to reach out to communities who do not usually attend arts programmes. Research by the Independent Streets Arts Network in the UK, for example, found that one in ten of the participants at the outdoor events surveyed had not taken part in any other arts events in the previous 12 months, not even the cinema (The Audience Agency, 2015: 11). Whether it is participating in making costumes, taking part in a parade or volunteering to drive artists to and from the airport, the practicalities of festival production and their tradition of community involvement, make festivals a more egalitarian and open environment that encompass each of UNESCO's participation types.

Clearly participation is a key element in the success and growth of the festival phenomenon across the world, especially at the community level, Picard and Robinson state that:

> The explanation for the recent proliferation of festivals is complex, but in part relates to a response from communities seeking to re-assert their identities in the face of a feeling of cultural dislocation brought about by rapid structural change, social mobility and globalisation processes (2006: 2).

Community and identity are central to the discussion of place in festival studies. The idea of the 'local' and 'local identity' being strengthened by events is important (Richards and Palmer, 2010), however the relationship to place is also important to both the resident and the 'visitor', and this may be an ideal of authenticity that both share as part of their expectations of the event. For Richards and Palmer there is a symbiotic relationship with the location where events are held: "the event should strengthen the sense of place of that location, and the location should help to distinguish the event" (2010: 418). The role of the artists in this process is important. Maguire (Chapter 4) in his people-place-purpose triad sees engagement with these elements as central to a festival successfully engaging with and animating a place.

A danger to the connectedness of place and festivals may well be a consequence of the movements towards festivalisation, tourism growth and globalisation, where there becomes a disconnection between the 'local' and the event, as MacLeod says:

> a consequent trend towards spectacle and the carnivalesque has become observable, creating festivals that are global in appeal, ungrounded in local identity and demonstrate the characteristics of placelessness (2006: 229).

Connectedness to place is clearly important in the success of festivals and their continued growth. As they are increasingly the arbiters of festivals, it is incumbent on local authorities and municipal governments to ensure that festivals retain their role in place making and do not become pre-packaged consumables driven by place marketing imperatives. There is a role for the touring companies such as *Artichoke* and their spectacular animated creations, in that they bring a global experience to the locality, and as such they are part of the phenomenon of 'glocalisation' that can be observed in much contemporary festival provision.

This book is about how the form and nature of contemporary festivals crosses national borders, and how their role and function is generally recognised in most locations and cultures. It is reasonable to describe festivals as a worldwide cultural activity, indeed much discussion recognises the 'glocal' nature of festivals. Robertson's adaptation of the Japanese phrase is useful for considering the apparent dichotomy that festivals take place within specific localities *and* increasingly within globalised, some might argue homogenising, cultural industries. The term was coined to

> transcend the tendency to cast the idea of globalisation as inevitably in tension with the idea of localisation. I have instead maintained that globalisation – in the broadest sense, the compression of the world – has involved and increasingly involves the creation and the incorporation of locality, processes which themselves largely shape, in turn, the compression of the world as a whole. Even though we are, for various reasons, likely to continue to use the concept of globalisation, it might well be preferable to replace it for certain purposes with the concept of glocalisation. The latter concept has the definite advantage of making the concern with space as important as the focus upon temporal issues (Robertson, 1995: 40).

The notion of glocalisation describes the local interpretation of globalised cultural goods and experiences, and the transmission of local cultures around the world and cultural hybridity, in which local cultures collide and create something new. As the *Galway International Arts Festival* (Chapter 9) illustrates, festivals can therefore be both local and global, authentic or commodified at the same time, depending on who is having the experience.

As part of the 'glocal' dimension, festival imagery with local roots and currency can become iconographic of specific festivals, and indeed of festivals or festivalisation worldwide. An under-discussed aspect of festival studies that appears throughout the book is festival aesthetics or the aesthetics of festivals. Undoubtedly carnival is dominated by the aesthetic and aesthetic experiences – the cover of this book shows how these can be instantly recognisable and instantly attributed to a particular event. Huang in her chapter (8) on the *Taiwanese Lantern Festival* talks about the image of the Chinese festive lantern standing as an icon for the Chinese people around the world. *Dia de los Muertos* and the *Tuscon All Souls Parade* (Chapters 23 and 24) feature images of the skull and the aesthetics of death throughout their event, and indeed, these have become the central image motif for these festivals and other Carnivals and events throughout the Americas (see Figure 27.3 for an image of the 'death' at the *Trinidad and Tobago Carnival*). The iconography of *Dia de los Muertos* is so striking that it now features in the opening sequence of the new James Bond film *Spectre*. Clearly the film-makers wanted to use this spectacular festival for its connotations to Bond as an assassin and a bringer of death, but also the iconographic construction and scopophilic nature of film means that the *Dia de los Muertos* festival is perfect for the medium. It could be argued that this is another aspect of the commodification of festivals, where the iconography of events is packaged and sold. As we will see this is undoubtedly the case in tourism marketing, where the aesthetics of the *Hornbill Festival* and the *Songkran Festival* (Chapters 18 and 19) are used to package and market the events.

Yet festival aesthetics are not always inauthentic, as Debord (1983) argued when he contrasted spectacular with festival. The participatory and experimental nature of festivals demands certain sorts of aesthetic responses: large scale artworks and costumes; immersive sensory environments; participatory events; and site-specific productions that respond to local places and myths. Festivalisation means that there is an increasing familiarity amongst artists and audiences with festival-style culture, which, in turn, is shaping the work being produced. Festival aesthetics can be seen to be influencing theatre, visual arts and music, not just because there is a growing market for these new works, although that is a factor, but also because artists are finding inspiration and engagement in working with and within these forms (Jordan, 2015).

The world festival context in which this book is set can be understood with reference to a number of dimensions. First, there are the festivals and festival organisations with a global reach, *WOMAD*, *Rock in Rio* (Chapter 10), *Burning Man* (Chapter 6) and *Electric Daisies* are all part of an expanding market of festivals with international editions. The second dimension is the globalised formats such as Glastonbury, Woodstock in music festivals and biennials and triennials (Chapter 5) in art festivals. Third, festivals that have 'travelled' via diaspora across the globe, such as *mela* and *Chinese New Year* (see *Focus on Festivals* Chapters 17 and 18) and, as we shall see *Dia de los Muertos* (Chapter 23). Then there are the festivals that are settled in their context. These tend to be rooted in local traditions, but their function can be recognised worldwide, be it seasonal festivals, religious ones and indeed cultural events. Finally there are the 'rehabilitated' festivals and the 'newly created' festivals, that is either older and traditional festivals that have been given a new lease of life by tourist authorities and local government, and the festivals that have been created to meet various impact 'targets'. The idea of the rehabilitation of festivals is introduced in connection to the discussion on Chinese festivals (Chapter 20), however, we would argue that in recent times festivals have been rehabilitated by many societies and cultures. The debates on impact (economic, social and cultural) are central drivers of this rehabilitation, and this acceptance has led to festivity, both traditional and contemporary in origin, becoming more visible and overt.

Journalist and social critic Barbara Ehrenreich (2006) develops the argument that festivity was supressed throughout the western world in the fifteenth and sixteenth centuries as a result of the Protestant Reformation. Communal celebrations were perceived as undermining the developing Protestant work ethic and as potential threats to the emerging national power structures. This starts in the west and is exported around the world by colonial authorities that perceived the rites and rituals they found as evidence of a lack of civilisation and self-control, and therefore would attempt to repress it wherever they found it. As we shall see in Chapter 27, *Carnival* in Trinidad and Tobago emerges as a response to attempts to supress Afro-Trinidadian celebrations in the 1880s, and that 'playing mas' was related to the role reversal of the *Feast of Fools*, in which planation slaves would mock theirs master through masquerading and creating caricatures of the whites and their behaviour. Post-colonial governments, particularly in Africa, attempted to rehabilitate and revive festivals as part of their endeavour to create national identities *FESTAC 77 – The second world Black and African festival of Arts and Culture* held in Lagos Nigeria is an example of this.

In Europe in the 18th and 19th centuries rationality is entangled with notions of class and civilisation that still inform our concepts of art, and comes someway to explaining the gap found in European cultural policies in relation to festivals. Rehabilitation comes at a price, and the need to rationalise festival subsidies in terms of economics can be seen in the interest in festival impacts reflected in a number of chapters in this book, including Brown (Chapter 7), Snowball (Chapter 14), and van Niekerk (Chapter 15). Rehabilitation comes in many forms. If one of the elements of traditional festivals was the reversal of the established order, albeit temporarily, then we can understand carnival and mela in this light, where the streets are, briefly, handed over to 'others' before being returned to the normative order. In this way, it could be argued the social cultural impact of these festivals has led to their rehabilitation and acceptance on many of the streets of the UK and elsewhere. Undoubtedly the rehabilitation of festivals can be seen as part of the festivalisation process throughout the world, whether it be related to tourism and place marketing, impacts and identity, or simply cultural democracy.

Structurally, *Focus on World Festivals* is divided into three sections, each reflecting the main themes of the author's discussion. The three sections are *Understanding Festivals, Managing Festivals: policy, impact and people,* and *Using Festivals: culture and identity.*

In Section 1 we introduce and engage with some key theoretical insights into festivals, looking at the festivalisation of culture, the internationalisation and eventalisation of the music industry and the consequences for festivals; biennialisation of visual art; place-making; participatory festivals and immersive experiences.

Section 2 is concerned with the organising and managing of festivals, looking at local government and festivals; internationalisation; festival team making and volunteering; impacts; audiences and communities.

Section 3 looks broadly at how festivals around the world are used by particular societies, communities, authorities, and individuals for social and cultural purposes. The main themes are festivals and tradition; tourism; festivals in situations of social strife and repression; festivals and healing; festivals and play; and festivals and identity.

Case studies illuminate and add depth to the many viewpoints in this book, but it would be a mistake to think that their particularity means that these examples are not more widely relevant. The emergence of similar themes in chapters considering festivals on various continents highlights the validity and relevance of the analyses and insights for a wider audience. From the discussion of festivalisation and the use of techniques of festivity throughout society in the early chapters, through to the turbulence within the music industry and the challenges of identity facing communities in an increasingly globalised and marketised world in the later chapters, it is clear that festivals reflect many of the issues found within contemporary life. Yet, festivals are also spaces in which new forms of society can be played with, tested, debated and explored. The utopian dream may not survive unscathed, but elements can be seen to be influencing cultural forms, political engagement and social practices, placing festivals at the forefront of contemporary global society.

## Bibliography

Adorno, T. (1991) *The Culture Industry*, London: Routledge.

Belfiore, E. (2004) Auditing culture: the subsidised cultural sector and the New Public Management, in *International Journal of Cultural Policy*, **10**(2), 183-202.

Belfiore, E., Bunting, C., Gibson, L., Gilmore, A., James, F., Miles, A., Milling, J., Stannage, S. and Schaefer, K. (2011) *AHRC Communities, Culture and Creative Economies Development Project "Understanding Everyday Participation - Articulating Cultural Values" Literature Review*, Centre for Economic and Sociocultural Change, Manchester.

Debord, G. (1983) *Society of the Spectacle.* Detroit: Black & Red.

Ehrenreich, B. (2006) *Dancing in the Streets: A history of collective joy*, New York: Metropolitan Books.

Getz, D. (2010) The Nature and Scope of Festival Studies . *International Journal of Event Management Research,* **5**(1), 1-47.

Gray, C. (2007) Commodification and instrumentality in cultural policy, *International Journal of Cultural Policy,* **13**(2), 203-215.

Gray, C. (2004) Joining-up or tagging on? The arts, cultural planning and the view from below, *Public Policy and Administration,* **19**(2), 38-49.

Hauptfleisch, T. (2007) Festivals as eventifying systems, in T. Hauptfleisch, S. Lev-Aladgem, J. Martin., W. Sauter, H. Schoenmakers, *Festivalising!: Theatrical Events, Politics and Culture,* Amsterdam: Rodopi

Holbrook, M. and Hirschman, E. (1982) The experiential aspects of consumption: consumer fantisies, feelings and fun, in *Journal of Consumer Research*, **9**(2), 132-140.

Jancovich, L. and Bianchini, F. (2013) Problematising participation, in *Cultural Trends,* **22**(2), 63-66.

Jordan, J. (2015) Festivalisation of cultural production, ENCACT, ed. In: *The Ecology of Culture: Community Engagement, Co-creation, Cross Fertilization, Conference Proceedings of the 6th Annual ENCACT Research Session,* 21-23 October 2015, ENCACT, 244-255.

Kaptein, P. (1996) De beginperiode van het Holland Festival. Festivals en festivalisering, in R. L. Erenstein (ed.) *Een Theater Geschiedenis de Nederlande,* Amsterdam: Amsterdam University Press, 672-680.

MacLeod, N. (2006) The placeless festival: identity and place in the post-modern festival, in D. Picard, and M. Robinson (eds.), *Festivals, Tourism and Social Change: remaking worlds,* Clevedon: Channel View.

Marx, K. (1963) *Selected Writings in Sociology and Social Philosophy,* T. Bottomore and M. Rubel (eds.), Harmondsworth: Penguin.

Miles, A. (2007) *Taking part in the North West: Understanding engagement and participation in culture,* Culture Northwest, Manchester.

Négrier, E. (2015) Festivalisation: Patterns and limits, in C. Newbold, C. Maughan, J. Jordan and F. Bianchini, (eds.) *Focus on Festivals: Contemporary European Case Studies and Perspectives*. Oxford: Goodfellow, 18-27.

Newbold, C., Maughan, C., Jordan, J., and Bianchini, F. (eds.) (2015) *Focus on Festivals: Contemporary European Case Studies and Perspectives*. Oxford: Goodfellow.

Picard, D., and Robinson, M. (eds.) (2006) *Festivals, Tourism and Social Change: Remaking Worlds,* Clevedon: Channel View.

Pine, J. and Gilmore, J. (1998) Welcome to the Experience Economy, in *Harvard Business Review,* July–August, 97–105.

Pine, J. and Gilmore, J. (1999) *The Experience Economy: work is theatre and everyday business a stage,* Boston: Harvard Business School Press.

Poulsson, S.H.G. and Kale, S.H., (2001) The experience economy and commercial experiences. *Marketing review,* **4**(3), 267-277.

Richards, G., and Palmer, R. (2010) *Eventful Cities: Cultural management and urban revitalisation,* Oxford: Butterworth Heinemann.

Robertson, R., (1995) Glocalisation: time-space and homogeneity-heterogeneity. In: M. Featherstone, S. Lash and R. Robertson, eds, *Global Modernities* . London: Sage, 25-44.

Stevenson, D. (2015) *Cultural policy is about more than the arts*. The Scotsman, http://www.scotsman.com/news/cultural-policy-is-about-more-than-the-arts-1-3849442#axzz3oiAkcQ7C, accessed 15 October 2015.

The Audience Agency (2015) *Audience Finder: Outdoor Arts Year 2 Report (May – November 2014),* The Audience Agency, London.

UNESCO (2006) *Guidelines for Measuring Cultural Participation,* UNESCO Institute for Statistics, Montreal.

# FOCUS ON WORLD FESTIVALS

## SECTION 1
## UNDERSTANDING FESTIVALS

# Introduction

## Jennie Jordan

What does 'understanding festivals' mean? The chapters in this section explore festivalisation in the international music industry and the visual arts, in place-making, international tourism and wider aspects of contemporary life such as global brand sponsorships and the experience economy. Festivals are both in and out of society, proscribed in time and space, intensified and idealised versions of contemporary life. The authors in this section have all, in various and wide-ranging ways, seized upon this to explore changes in communities, and the artistic and cultural responses these changes are eliciting. The title of this section is Understanding Festivals, yet in many ways the chapters here are using festivals as lenses through which to see society, too.

Chapter 1 introduces the concept of festivalisation. It asks why there is such a growth in festivals across the world and why it is happening now. It argues that it is more than simply an increase in the number of festivals, rather that key principles associated with festival production can be seen to be growing factors in commercial and political fields as well as cultural production. The five festival dimensions of festivity, experimentation, spectacularisation, theming and participation are defined and seen to be responses to digitisation and on-line retail, globalisation and transformations in politics, commerce and culture itself.

Examples of festivity are found in social campaigning and charitable fundraising, as well as in festivals themselves. Experimentation in innovative partnerships between tech companies and festivals is leading to new product developments. Spectacularisation is seen in city marketing and the growth of site specific performances. Theming is identified in the digital world as a navigational tool signposting users to content that might otherwise be lost in the crowd, adding meaning just as it does at a large festival. Participation and immersion, central festival practices, are growing aspects of both the cultural market and the commercial sphere as producers, retailers and cities seek to differentiate themselves from the virtual world by creating 'you have to be there' moments within the experience economy (Pine and Gilmore, 1999). The ubiquity of these five dimensions within wider society points to the importance of core aspects of festivals and, perhaps, provides a useful framework for understanding why festivals have becomes so pervasive and popular in contemporary society.

Djakouane and Négrier (Chapter 2) consider festivals as privileged spaces, a crucible in which cultural changes can be identified and explored. In particular they are interested in the concept of 'glocal' (Robertson 1995), the collision of local identities and audiences with the globalised music industry and consumer brands. Both they and Nordgård (Chapter 3) detect the influence of increased competition on non-classical music festivals' programming. For Djakouane and Négrier, the increase in events with similar headliners is an explanation for the increase they detect in audiences from the local region. Why travel to see an act that is performing a few nights later at a festival much closer to home? Legendary music promoter Harvey Goldsmith discussed the impact of digitisation and changing consumption practices in the music business on festivals at the *Hay Festival*:

> The festival circuit has peaked. There's too many of them and there are not enough big acts to headline them. [...] most rock bands built a reputation on a body of work – they might take three albums to really hone their art, to become great, but young people don't want that. They home in on a track, a sound, then ping off again to the next one (McVeigh, 2015).

Nordgård perceives increasing global competition to be the cause behind the problems music festivals in Norway are experiencing in booking crowd pleasing headliners who are guaranteed to attract a mass audience. As with Finkel's (2009) survey of urban arts festivals, both of these studies contend that the festivalisation of culture is seen to be reducing choice as the market consolidates around well-known, often global, brands.

In contrast, Maguire (Chapter 5) explores the relationship between festivals, artists and particular places. Focusing on the *Wirkswork Festival*, the *Lumiere* project in Durham and the *Setouchi Trienniale* in Japan, he explores the use of commissions inspired by the locality to help (re)shape, (re)define and celebrate places so that they express the local community's values, traditions and identity. The importance of community participation and work that is responsive to residents' values lies at the heart of local festivals that value tradition, yet find ways to renew shared local meanings and make them relevant to contemporary society. Developing the concept of folk-work-place (Geddes, 1949), he argues that successful global events are rooted in the local, and have to have authentic meaning for residents as well as visitors (a point also noted by van Niekerk in Section 2). His framework of people-place-purpose proposes a democratic artistic animation process that engages local communities with their place, and enables them to critically examine it and (re)define its purpose. Festivals in this paradigm are an essential part of the cultural public sphere (McGuigan 2009, Giorgi, Sassatelli and Delanty 2011) as they provide a uniquely engaging environment in which communities and artists participate and explore their responses to each other and place, reframing and changing perceptions in the process.

While Maguire is interested in festivals for their roles in community identity and place-making, Sassatelli (Chapter 4) traces the rise of visual art biennials and explores their roles in defining and shaping the global art market. She identifies a number of stages in biennial development, which she relates to global trends and influences. The genesis of the national pavilions of the *Venice Biennale* are traced back to *The Great Exhibition* in London in 1851. As with that event, the *Biennale* was established for city and national marketing purposes and Sassatelli notes themes that will be familiar to those who have studied mega-events or the European Capitals of Culture; economic rationalisations and national rivalries (Garcia 2005, O'Brien 2011).

Globalisation throughout the late 20th century saw both a growth in the number of biennials, triennials and quadrennials and new differentiation strategies. Themes emerged as a guiding curatorial framework, rather than the survey of the best of world art, which improvements in transport and increases in international travel was making redundant. Biennials are now found in over 50 countries, and are themselves addressing issues associated with globalisation such as hybridisation, neoliberal capitalism and urbanisation. Where the original biennials provided an overview of national cultures, and many still provide this, biennials in non-Western cities are offering critiques of contemporary culture and Western paradigms, and giving the format a distinctly glocal (Robertson 1995) flavour.

*Burning Man*, Bowditch's case study (Chapter 6), is a radical participatory festival that takes place in Nevada's Black Rock Desert. Place is an important factor in the festival's 'no spectators' ethos. With no pre-existing services, everyone in this temporary community has to participate to survive in the desert. Bennett (2015) maintains that place is a taken-for-granted and often overlooked basis for traditional behaviours. The particular nature of a shared environment tangibly influences the performance of everyday life and, consequently, the sense of belonging that is at the heart of community. While Bennett's research concerns life in an established town, it is clear that the hardship of desert life is an influential factor in the sense of mutual obligation found at *Burning Man*, while the scale of the landscape is fundamentally spectacular.

Despite, or perhaps because of, the theatricality of its setting, there is no main stage at *Burning Man*. This is a totally immersive experience. Participants are performers, organisers, citizens of a temporary, but isolated world, often described as utopian, where categories such as work and play, performer and audience, are elided.

Yet, behind this apparently spontaneous 'collective effervescence' (Bakhtin 1994 [1965]) sits an organisation that is increasingly having to respond to external commercial and corporate life. Wealthy Burners now book in to ready-made camps and pay artists to make work. The radical equality of early festival editions is being challenged as *Burning Man* grows into a global brand, the gold-standard of immersive experiences.

The chapters in this section introduce a range of themes that are expanded on throughout this collection: the relationship between globalisation and the local; place; uncertainty about the effects of new technologies on the structure of the music industry, including music festivals; biennialisation and festivalisation of cultural production; the nature of participation, belonging and identity. The studies explore and elucidate festival-specific matters, but often as a route into wider societal and cultural change.

## Bibliography

Bakhtin, M. (1994 [1965]) Rabelais and his world', in P. Morris (ed.), *The Bakhtin Reader: Selected Writings of Bakhtin, Medvedev, Voloshninov*, London: Arnold, 194-244.

Bennett, J. (2015) Snowed in! Offbeat rhythms and belonging as everyday practice, *Sociology*, **49**(5), 955-967.

Finkel, R. (2009) A picture of the contemporary combined arts festival landscape, *Cultural Trends*, **18**(1), 3-21.

Garcia, B. (2005) De-constructing the City of Culture: the long term cultural legacies of Glasgow 1990, *Urban Studies*, **42**(5/6), 1-28.

Geddes, P. (1949) *Cities in Evolution*, London: Williams and Northgate.

Giorgi, L., Sassatelli, M. and Delanty, G. (eds.) (2011) *Festivals and the Cultural Public Sphere*, Abingdon: Routledge.

McGuigan, J. (2009) The cultural public sphere - a critical measure of public culture? *Euro-Festivals Consortium: Public Culture and Festivals* Euro-Festivals Consortium, 26-27 February 2009.

McVeigh, T. (2015) Move over, Glastonbury: promoter says the age of the music festival is passing, in *The Guardian* (30 May 2015).

O'Brien, D. (2011) Who is in charge? Liverpool, European Captial of Culture 2008 and the governance of cultural planning, *Town Planning Review*, **82**(1), 45-59.

Pine, J. B., and Gilmore, J. H. (1999) *The Experience Economy*, Boston, MA: Harvard Business School Press.

Robertson, R. (1995) Glocalisation: time-space and homogeneity-heterogeneity, in M. Featherstone, S. Lash and R. Robertson (eds.) *Global Modernities*, London: Sage, 25-44.

# 1 The Festivalisation of Contemporary Life

Jennie Jordan

## Introduction

Driving home from work a few days ago, I passed through a sequence of villages, all with fluorescent roadside posters. The first was for a flower festival on the following Saturday in the church hall. The second promoted a steam festival at a local stately home. The third was for a festival of local food in a nearby gastro pub. It started me thinking about the increasing number of things that are being labelled and defined as festivals; things that don't fit neatly into Négrier's conception of festivalisation as 'the process by which cultural activity, previously presented in a regular, on-going pattern or season, is reconfigured to form a 'new' event, e.g. a regular series of jazz concerts is reconfigured as a jazz festival' (2015: 18). Whilst accepting this as one dimension – part of a wider festivalisation of the ways in which culture is produced, distributed and consumed – this chapter seeks to understand the wider festivalisation of contemporary life by identifying key principles associated with festival production. In addition to the changes to the cultural sector presentation practices noted by Négrier and discussed later, festivalisation processes can increasingly be seen in brand and city marketing strategies.

This chapter will argue that the festivalisation of contemporary life can be considered to be the instrumental use of techniques found in the production dimensions of festivals to achieve cultural and non-cultural outcomes within social, economic and policy fields.

The five key dimensions of festivalisation proposed in this analysis are:

- **Festivity**: a time and space for celebration and play that is distinct from everyday life.
- **Experimentation**: opportunities for audiences, producers and artists to try out new personas or artistic approaches.
- **Spectacularisation**: highly visual or sensual, surprising and often large-scale art works and performances.
- **Theming**: a method for establishing an intelligible identity for disparate activities.
- **Participation**: experiences that are immersive or co-created by audiences.

This chapter will highlight areas where these key elements can be used to identify and understand changes in society or cultural production that may help explain the extraordinary growth in the number of festivals worldwide.

# Festivity

The easiest way to conceive of festivity is to contrast the festive period and the festival site with the everyday world of work (Pieper 1999, 1963). Without the mundane world there cannot be the festive world. Shields conceives of leisure as 'controlled and legitimated breaks from routines of everyday, proper behaviour' (in Rojek 1995: 88); places beyond the control of the authorities, places where one can be 'authentic', free from the demands of contemporary modernity.

Yet festivity is not simply the opposite of everyday life. It is associated with moments of sensual excess, feasts for all of the senses (Newbold et al. 2015) and a time of 'collective effervescence' (Durkheim 1995, 1912) in which societies commemorate traditions, create utopian dreams or reaffirm social ties. The power of festivity lies in its ability to dazzle, to appeal directly to the emotions rather than sophisticated aesthetic judgements. Bowditch's example of the *Tuscon All Souls' Procession* later in this volume highlights the power of festive rituals in communal healing and community identity. Participants feel part of a genuinely emotional collective experience.

Falassi (1987) argues that, unlike traditional religious or seasonal festivals, urban festivals are inauthentic traditions invented to celebrate economic success. Such events manipulate the rituals associated with festivals, such as decorating the site, fencing it off or opening it up at new times, removing as many reminders of the humdrum transactions as possible. The message is that this space will for a limited time obey different rules, welcome different people, symbolise something new or other. Festivity can be seen to be in 'binary opposition' to the rational everyday world, thus adjectives such as fun, amusement, merriment, joy are used to define it, and as such festivity is desirable and has value.

## Festivity and the experience economy

The experience economy conceptualises 'experiences' as a source of competitive advantage in a global market that has evolved from selling bulk raw goods to anonymous markets to personalising experiences for guests (Pine and Gilmore 1998: 98). Engaging experiences can be used to sell more products or services, as well as being a product themselves, in the form of memories, for the guest to take home. Disney's theme parks add value to the thrill rides or annual holiday by providing a feeling of belonging to the Disney 'family'.

Experiences are intensely personal and involve participation, either passively as an audience member, or actively as a co-creator in a workshop, performance or sports event. Yet passive spectators are also actively involved in creating a sense of occasion and atmosphere for others and Pine and Gilmore (1999) argue that this sense of connection is an important element in making experiences enjoyable. Equally important in creating memorable experiences is the engagement of the senses. Poulsson and Kale consider that an experience has to involve the customer, who must feel that the encounter was either personally relevant, novel, surprising, gave them the opportunity to learn or was engaging and involving. The more elements that are involved, the more intense and memorable the experience (2001: 271-272). The distinguishing feature of experiences is the fact that the participant has to be there (physically or virtually) for the event to happen. The scale and variety of 'spaces' and stages in both urban and greenfield festivals means that audiences and participants can choose the experiences that are personally relevant and desired. Increasingly the new digital technologies provide audience-led engagement opportunities with participants able to co-create events and make and maintain social relationships associated with the festival online.

Although the live cultural sector, including festivals, has experiences at its core, the experience economy thesis argues that experiences can also have cultural, lifestyle and identity associations that can be used as add-ons to other kinds of products and services, as selling propositions or to develop brand loyalty. Commercial sponsorship of festivals has been widely used since the 1980s as a method of developing awareness of a product amongst festival audiences and associating a brand with the festival's values and lifestyle, at a time when the audience was relaxed and receptive. Anderton argues that simply adding a logo to a festival's marketing materials is ineffective and that sponsors have begun to develop events specifically for the festivals they are involved with (2015). The relaxed mood of a truly festive event ensures that the sponsor's brand is associated with happy memories, and the immersion in a stimulating multi-sensory environment ensures that the memories are strong and long lasting.

The idea of the experience economy does raise questions, though, about the authenticity of the festivity within a strategically planned contemporary festival. Jay considers that events are experiences that 'happen without intentionality or preparation' (in Knudsen and Christensen 2015: 120) and have catalysing and paradigm-shifting potential for the individual. If we accept this, then it raises the question of whether any festival produced for economic or policy purposes can truly be considered authentically festive?

## Festivalisation of place marketing

That question aside, their essential 'you have to be there' nature makes using experiences for marketing appealing to those tasked with attracting people to particular places. This is not a new phenomenon; McGuigan quotes Raymond

Williams as saying that during 'arguments about public funding of the arts people mentioned tourism rather early' (2004: 62), but the scale and scope is new. Shopping centres, heritage properties, campaign groups and cities are increasingly looking to festive experiences, to help them compete against online shopping, virtual gaming, social media and low cost airlines. As Knudsen and Christensen maintain, people 'like being part of the thing' (2015: 117).

*Amsterdam Light Festival* (*ALF*) was launched in December 2012, primarily to boost city tourism during the winter months. Festival producer Frans von Konijnenburg (interview, January 2014) explained that a light festival was selected as a six or seven week event would maximise its economic impact in terms of hotels beds filled, canal tours booked and to avoid swamping the city centre with visitors and upsetting local residents. *ALF*, approached canal tour operators with the proposition that, if the festival increased visitor numbers, they would support it financially. The boating companies agreed immediately that for each €15.00 trip, they would donate €2.50 to *ALF*.

Festival's ability to drive footfall and increase visitor numbers can be seen in the festivalisation of retail marketing. In the UK, hard-pressed independent music retailers stage the annual *Record Store Day* festival to encourage people to visit their local record shops. Unique vinyl and CD releases are produced and hundreds of musicians make special appearances and give in-store performances (Entertainment Retailers Association 2015). Queues for some shops start the day before as fans seek to secure a release by a favourite band or ensure a good spot from which to see them play.

## Festivalisation of social campaigning

In his interpretation of Habermas' concept of communicative action, in which humans attempt to achieve mutual understanding, McGuigan (1996) argues that culture may offer more freedom for political debate because it is less likely to be blocked by dominant and powerful vested interests within the political and economic systems. The history of censorship and urge of nation states to control new technologies such as television that provide a means by which communities can be represented and narratives developed is a good example of the potential power of culture to communicate ideas, facilitate debate and define identities and notions of citizenship.

Dahlgren (1995) contends that no representational form is ever fully rational, despite the claims to full and fair reporting of some news producers – an argument that is increasing supported by psychological research into emotions and decision-making. Incidental emotions and feelings that are carried over from another situation, are fundamental to the choices that people make (including political choices). People who are relaxed and happy make more optimistic judgements about outcomes than people who are in a worse mood. Emotions are also inherently social and help individuals to maintain healthy relationships by signalling beliefs and intentions, and evoking similar emotions in others (Lerner et al. 2015). For a campaigning organisation, and for commercial sponsors, festivals are particularly conducive social environments in which to canvass support.

Some campaigning organisations use pre-existing festivals as opportunities to create affinity with a target audience in much the same way as commercial sponsors. The Green Messengers at Festival Republic's *Leeds, Reading* and *Latitude* festivals raise awareness of environmental issues by encouraging recycling and sustainable travel to the event. Face Your Elephant is an organisation that tours music festivals to 'engage festival-goers in the science and engineering of reducing their carbon dioxide emissions' (2015) as part of the Royal Academy of Engineering's public engagement strategy. The purpose is to engage audiences on affective, personal and social levels that have a longer-term impact.

Other campaigns create their own festivals. Cancer Research UK's well established campaign strand, *Race for Life,* encourages women to run 5 or 10 kilometre whilst wearing pink to fund-raise for breast cancer research. The events are promoted as festivals, with on-stage entertainment, stalls and refreshments to keep supporters amused and reward runners when they finish (Cancer Research UK 2015). The scale of the events and the festive atmosphere increases awareness and encourages participation as the event is both social and fun.

In Poland, *Woodstock Festival,* a free music festival attended by over 750,000 in 2014 was created as a thank you party for supporters and volunteers who took part in a national fundraising campaign organised by the Great Orchestra of Christmas charity. The music stages were complemented by a programme of talks, amounting to a festival of ideas, that the organisers claim are a crucial element and which reinforce the charity's messages about social responsibility (Great Orchestra of Christmas Charity Foundation 2015).

As sites in which the public meet, whether or not their purpose is explicitly or implicitly political, festivals are a form of active citizen engagement that encourages and reinforces allegiances and social identities. It is in the cultural public sphere that individuals realise that their personal political concerns are or are not widely shared communal concerns.

Festivity, the creation of a world away from everyday concerns, is potentially transformative. Periods of change are exciting and offer opportunities and dangers for participants as old ways of thinking and behaving are swept away and new norms have not yet become established. Caught up in a festive atmosphere, participants may suspend their critical faculties, becoming more open to new influences.

## Festivals and experimentation

The ephemeral nature of festivals provides an environment in which audiences are able to play and experiment. Fancy dress and carnival costumes, disguise and masquerade are common festival behaviours. Less common, but still present are "experimentation and sensation-seeking along and across the edges of experience in order to achieve a sense of transportation and reconfiguring of self" (O'Grady 2015: 158). The other worldliness of the festival environment provides a safe space in which to try out different personas or activities that can either be incorporated into or be rejected on return to everyday life. Audiences at festivals are more adventurous with their artistic choices than at other times (Morgan 2007, Kim et al. 2001, Mohr et al. 1993), making them good places for new acts to be launched and for artists to experiment with new material.

The experimentation dimension also attracts innovation companies. Rogier van der Heide, former Chief Design Officer of Philips Lighting, is a co-founder and artistic director of the *Amsterdam Light Festival*. Philips is at the forefront of LED technology and immediately saw the synergies between the creativity of the artists pushing the boundaries of what can be achieved with light to make spectacular new works, and its own advances. Rogier van der Heide believes that it is essential for designers to work with experts from other disciplines such as the arts in order to drive innovation (James 2015).

The potential to use festivals as social and spatial laboratories has also been embraced by some urban planners. City planner David Dooghe, for example, has been using Rotterdam's festivals to test out innovative city development ideas that are informing its plans (2015, 2008). Elsewhere, festivals have been innovative early exploiters of spaces that go on to become, first bohemian and then gentrified. The *Flow Festival* in Helsinki has taken place in three sites, each of which has followed this pattern (Silvanto 2015).

The opportunity to experiment has also made festivals important commissioners of cultural products, a factor that can be seen to be influencing the work that is produced. Festivals are increasingly important structures with cultural production; sometimes run by independent organisations, either not-for-profit or commercial, and sometimes as one event in larger programme of work by a theatre or local council. The increase in festival numbers is a response to a variety of factors. Increasing 'noise' in a globalised market place means that cultural producers have to have a bigger and better, more intense offer in order to be noticed. Cultural events such as festivals have symbolic and affective value for individuals and social groups that adds to their intensity (Lash and Lury 2007, Lash 2010). Grouping events in one place or over a limited period provides economies of scale in marketing and production and makes an event more attractive to sponsors than a season of work spread out over a few months. Competition from online gaming, social media, music and film sites mean that live events have to differentiate themselves, too, and the sensations associated with immersion in a festive environment are, as yet, not available in the digital world. The participatory nature of many festivals where audiences are involved in creating the environment, and in some cases the work itself has been noted by Fabiani (2011), Chen (2009, 2011) and Robinson (2015) amongst others. Festivals are also environments where audiences can experiment, safe in the knowledge that they can alleviate the risk of seeing new work or unknown acts as they know that they like the headliners they will be seeing later (Morgan 2007). These factors are influencing the nature and scale of the works that some artists are making, with a marked increase in spectacular, eye catching, site-specific and immersive works.

## Spectacularisation

Since its year as European Capital of Culture in 2008, Liverpool has staged two events with French company Royal de Luxe in which 50 foot high puppets parade the streets followed by enormous crowds (Liverpool City Council 2014). The *Liverpool Giant Spectacular* events combine instrumental city marketing with a communal impetus of encouraging audiences to engage with the city's streets and public spaces in new and different ways. In Coventry, UK, Imagineer Productions have used a 20 foot puppet of local legend Lady Godiva created for the 2012 Cultural Olympiad as the basis for the *Festival of Imagineers*, an outdoor showcase of street arts, design, engineering, technology that aims to celebrate the city's creativity and support its design industries (Arts Council England 2014).

**Figure 1.1:** The Little Girl parading at *Liverpool Giant Spectacular* 2014 (author's photograph)

Spectacular elements, in these cases surprisingly large puppets, animatronics and parades, are eye-catching and unusual. Roads that are normally dominated by traffic are closed and pedestrians wander along the carriageway. Food stalls appear on the roadside or in parks, musicians play and crowds of people come out to watch or follow, giving the festival a rich sensory environment that makes the event highly memorable and distinct from everyday life. The normal rules of society are suspended in a way that has more in common with carnival (Bakhtin 1994, 1965) than the urban arts festival model of events taking place in theatres and concert halls that dominated in the second half of the twentieth century.

Debord distinguishes between the 'society of spectacle' (1983, thesis 127), in which the highly visual is used for the sole purpose of selling products, and festivals, which he considers to be "the moment of a community's participation in the luxurious expenditure of life" (1983, thesis 154). Festivals for Debord are authentic expressions of community values and traditions that are unsullied by instrumental market purposes. The festivalisation of so much of contemporary life identified in this chapter indicates that this distinction is one that is increasingly blurred. Visual artist Christo, for example, makes large scale outdoor aesthetically driven works that reimagine buildings and landscapes and, by temporarily changing visual aspects of a place, encourage audiences to feel and engage with it differently. This does not stop the installations becoming tourist attractions that boost the local economy.

Festivals are sites that encourage a particular kind of engagement with art that is more active than the traditional expectations of spectators at art galleries or museums (Richards 2015). They also offer a different set of opportunities for artists that can be seen to generate innovative practices (Kill 2015) and an increasing number of festivals in the UK are moving outside the concert hall on to the streets (the *City of London Festival*) and commissioning site-specific pieces (*Norwich and Norfolk Festival, Kendal Calling, Latitude, Beacons Festival*) that are spectacular, immersive and relational responses to both the place and the particular temporality (Kill 2015) and sociability of the festive environment. The ripples of this can be seen in the increasing popularity of immersive theatre such as that produced by Punchdrunk, Ontroerend Goed or Look Left Look Right. The influence of festival's limited time frame and site-specific nature can be found in the *Fortnight Project*, in which a small group of city residents who probably don't know each other are selected to enjoy "daily explorations of what it means to be here now" (Proto-type 2015) over a two week period. Each day participants receive a text or email inviting them to meet in a surprising place or to try something new and unexpected that encourages them to see their city anew. Originally commissioned for *Mayfest* in Bristol, Fortnight is now a touring production that has curated themed experiences in six cities across the UK since 2011.

## Theming

Bryman (1999) highlights theming as a method used within the entertainment sector for establishing an intelligible identity for disparate activities and this is a technique that arts festivals have used since Earl Harewood introduced a Russian theme to the *Edinburgh Festival* in 1962. It can now also be found in the proliferation of cultural and creative quarters in many cities, each with their own symbolic narratives, some traditional and some invented. Festivals are increasingly being used to add to the layers of meaning and create value for the residents, workers and visitors who inhabit these areas, in addition to their useful ability to drive footfall.

Theming is increasingly being used as a navigational tool in the digital world. In an environment of sometimes overwhelmingly abundant information, themes are a source of guidance, much as they are in a busy festival setting. And, whether it's a YouTube channel on a niche musical genre, or a board on social media site Pintrest that highlights shoe design, themes provide a basis for individuals with a particular expertise or enthusiasm to select and share the work they value; to curate and validate their cultural choices.

## Participation

The final dimension of the festivalisation of contemporary life is the participatory nature of festivals. Fabiani (2011) argues that there is a distinctive relationship between audiences and artists at festivals. Artists become part of the audience for other people's shows and mingle with spectators in a way that the notions of front and backstage in theatres and concert halls militate against. Whilst protected VIP and sponsor-funded exclusive access areas have become a feature of mainstream music festival (Anderton 2015), the tradition of audience participation in and co-creation of carnivals and festivals can still be found. Winkelhorn's (2015) case study of *Holstebro Festive Week* in Denmark, claims that the festival's success is due to the role plays by that the city's professional company, Odin Theatre. Rather than producing and showing its own experimental work, Odin engages Holstebro's residents in the production of new performances, concerts and exhibitions that play with the city's expectations and values, encourage unexpected encounters and restages everyday life (Bakhtin 1994, 1965), thereby altering the reality that is returned to.

For Richards "collective participation can perform an act of symbolic integration" (2015: 250), particularly where communities are involved in producing the work. For Bowditch (2010) the 'no spectators' ethos of *Burning Man* in the Nevada desert, which has no main stage or big-name artists, is the archetype of a contemporary co-created, participatory festival. Unlike concert-style festivals that are reliant for ticket sales on the headline bands, *Burning Man* and an increasing number of festivals in the UK including *Shambala*, *Boomtown Fair* and

*Secret Garden Party* ask festival attenders to collectively produce the event. Participants propose ideas and a selection produce themed performances, events or areas within the site and tend to dress in costume (Robinson 2015). The festival here is a stage on which all of the festival attenders are both performers and audience members, fully immersed in the experience.

Artist and producer Gavin Kroeber is interested in the experiences that can be created for audiences if the "operating principle is not about presenting art as a moment onstage... but, rather, crafting an audience's experiential arc – from the moment they walk in the door (or sometimes before) to the moment they leave" (Sellar 2014: 126) and identifies a "wider turn of the economy at large toward the manufacture of ephemeral experiences, and the specific turn of theaters and museums toward participation and immersion" (126). Festivals that tap into the tradition of participation found in carnivals and community festivals are at the forefront of this trend and provide a useful testing ground for works that can later be found on the touring circuit.

## Conclusions

This chapter has argued that the festivalisation of contemporary life can be considered to be the instrumental use of techniques found in the production of festivals to achieve cultural and non-cultural outcomes within social, economic and policy fields. The interaction of festivity, spectacularisation, participation, theming and experimentation make festivals singular events that provide audiences with unforgettable 'experiences'. Festivals are designed to enchant, to encourage participants to feel a sense of community, to experiment with new societal forms and social identities, to involve themselves in activities that are new to them and to immerse themselves in a sensually stimulating environment. Increasingly, the five festival dimensions – festivity, participation, spectacle, themes and experimentation – are being selectively employed by a range of actors in contemporary life to achieve non-festival objectives, ranging from selling beer to marketing whole cities, from urban planning to political campaigning, from designing new consumer products to creating different art forms.

The increase in the number of festivals and festival-like events can be seen as a logical response to societal and market changes such as digitisation, which has encouraged the music industry to invest in live performance, and the fact that greenfield sites can be found with larger capacities than most venues. Having paid to attend, audiences also take more risks on the acts they are willing to see, so festivals become good places to launch a new band or experiment with new material. And, as festivals become more numerous, artists and producers have responded by creating artwork that is more spectacular, more catchy and more immersive – w ork that helps to build a festive atmosphere and provides truly memorable experiences.

The increasing noise in the wider market place means that brands have to work harder to be noticed and, in an era of social networking, want to develop personal relationships with their customers. The social and symbolic aspects of festivals create sites that appear to be authentic, to diverge from the capitalist consumer world of everyday life. Audiences and participants are relaxed and more willing to engage than at other times, and the brands that were part of their festival experience become associated with that pleasurable time.

Governmental institutions, charities and firms employing festivalisation strategies in place marketing, political and charity campaigns and brand development can be seen to be trying to create a more or less authentic emotional connection and commitment to the product being sold. Festivals have been a traditional part of the enchanted world associated with celebrations and religious holidays. Arguably, governments and religious authorities have always harnessed festivals ability to manage meaning, create communal attachments and reinforce irrational power structures, and now companies and other organisations are starting to understand the potential of festive enchantment too.

## Bibliography

Anderton, C. (2015) Branding, sponsorship and the music festival, in: G. McKay (ed.) *The Pop Festival: History, music, media, culture*, London: Bloomsbury, 199-212.

Arts Council England, (2014) Coventry hosts brand new Festival of Imagineers, July 15 2014. Available: http://www.artscouncil.org.uk/news/arts-council-news/coventry-hosts-brand-new-festival-imagineers/, June 26, 2015.

Bakhtin, M. (1994, 1965) Rabelais and his world, in P. Morris, (ed.) *The Bakhtin Reader: Selected Writings of Bakhtin, Medvedev, Voloshninov*. London: Arnold, 194-244.

Bowditch, R. (2010) *On The Edge of Utopia: Performance and Ritual at Burning Man. London,* New York and Calcutta: Seagull Books.

Bryman, A. (1999) The Disneyization of society, in *The Sociological Review*, **47**(1), 25-47.

Cancer Research UK, (2015) Race for Life, Cancer Research UK: Find Your Event, Cambridge 10k. Available: http://raceforlife.cancerresearchuk.org/choose-your-event/events/cambridge-10k-2015-07-19-1100.html, June 8, 2015.

Chen, K. (2011) Artistic prosumption: cocreative destruction at Burning Man, in *American Behavioural Scientist*, **56**(4), 570-595.

Chen, K. (2009) *Enabling Creative Chaos: The Organization Behind the Burning Man Event.* Chicago: The University of Chicago Press.

Dahlgren, P. (1995) *Television and the Public Sphere – Citizenship, Democracy and the Media,* London: Sage.

Debord, G. (1983) *Society of the Spectacle*, Detroit: Black & Red.

Dooghe, D. (2015) Festival City – Rotterdam, in C. Newbold, C. Maughan, J. Jordan and F. Bianchini, (eds.) *Focus on Festivals: Contemporary European Case Studies and Perspectives*. Oxford: Goodfellow, 147-158.

Dooghe, D. (2008) *The urban impact of artistic festivals*. Available: http://www.daviddooghe.com/article/4718 June 2013.

Durkheim, E. (1995, 1912) *The Elementary Forms of the Religious Life*. Glencoe USA: Free Press.

Entertainment Retailers Association, (2015) *Record Store Day: celebrating the UK's independent record shops* July 14 2015. Available: http://recordstoreday.co.uk/, July 14, 2015.

Fabiani, J. (2011) Festivals, local and global: Critical interventions, in L. Giorgi, M. Sassatelli and G. Delanty, (eds.) *Festivals and the Cultural Public Sphere*, London: Routledge, 92-107.

Face Your Elephant, (2015) *Face Your Elephant: Home*. Available: http://faceyourelephant.org, June 8, 2015.

Falassi, A. (1987) Festival: definition and morphology, in A. Falassi, (ed.) *Time Out of Time: Essays on the Festival*, Albuquerque: University of New Mexico Press, 1-10.

Great Orchestra of Christmas Charity Foundation, (2015) *Woodstock Festival Poland*. Available: http://woodstockfestival.pl/en/woodstock_festival/about, June 8, 2015.

James, P. (2015) Rogier van der Heide. Mondo*arc: *The International Magazine for Designers with Light*, 83(January / February 2015), pp. http://www.mondoarc.com/interviews/2750696/rogier_van_der_heide.html-7 July 2015.

Kill, R. (2015) The artist at the music festival, in: G. McKay, (ed.), *The Pop Festival: History, music, media, culture*, London: Bloomsbury, 75-86.

Kim, K., Uysal, M., and Chen, J. S. (2001) Festival visitor motivation from the organizer's point of view. in *Event Management*, **7**(2), 127-34.

Knudsen, B. T. and Christensen, D. R. (2015) Eventful events: event-making strategies in contemporary culture, in B.T. Knudsen, D. R. Christensen and P. Blenker, (eds.), *Enterprising Initiatives in the Experience Economy: Transforming social worlds*, Abingdon: Routledge, 117-154.

Lash, S. (2010) *Intensive Culture: Social theory, religion & contemporary capitalism*, Los Angeles: Sage.

Lash, S. and Lury, C. (2007) *Global Culture Industry: The mediation of things*, Oxford: Polity.

Lerner, J.S., Li, Y., Valdesolo, P. and Kassam, K. S. (2015) Emotion and decision-making, in *Annual Review of Psychology*, **66**, 799-823.

Liverpool City Council, (2014) *Memories of August 2014*. Available: http://www.giantspectacular.com/royal-de-luxe, June 24, 2015.

McGuigan, J. (2004) *Rethinking Cultural Policy*. Maidenhead: Open University Press.

McGuigan, J. (1996) *Culture and the Public Sphere*, London: Routledge.

Mohr, K., Backman, K., Gahan, l. and Backman, S. (1993) An investigation of festival motivations and event satisfaction by visitor type, in *Festival Management and Event Tourism*, **1**(3), 89-97.

Morgan, M. (2007) What makes a good festival? Understanding the event experience, *Event Management*, **12**, 81-93.

Négrier, E. (2015) Festivalistion: patterns and limits, in: C. Newbold, C. Maughan, J.Jordan and F. Bianchini, (eds.) *Focus on Festivals: Contemporary European Case Studies and Perspectives*, Oxford: Goodfellow, 18-27.

Newbold, C., Jordan, J., Bianchini, F. and Maughan, C. (2015) Introduction: focusing on festivals, in: C. Newbold, C. Maughan, J. Jordan and F. Bianchini, (eds.) *Focus on Festivals: Contemporary European Case Studies and Perspectives*. Oxford: Goodfellow, xv-xxvi.

O'Grady, A. (2015) Alternative playworlds: Psytrance festivals, deep play and creative zones of transcendence, in G. McKay, (ed.) *The Pop Festival: history, music, media, culture*, London: Bloomsbury, 151-164.

Pieper, J. (1999, 1963) *In Tune with the World: A Theory of Festivity*. Indiana: St. Augustine's Press.

Pine II, J. and Gilmore, J.H. (1999) *The Experience Economy*, Boston, MA: Harvard Business School Press.

Poulsson, S.H.G., and Kale, S.H. (2001) The experience economy and commercial experiences, in *Marketing Review*, **4**(3), 267-277.

Proto-Type, (2015) *Fortnight: About*. Available: http://www.fortnightproject.com/about/, June 26, 2015.

Richards, G. (2015) Festivals in the network society, in C. Newbold, C. Maughan, J. Jordan and F. Bianchini, (eds.) *Focus on Festivals: contemporary European case studies and perspectives*, Oxford: Goodfellow, 245-254.

Ritzer, G. (2004) *The McDonaldization of Society*, (2nd edn.) London: Sage Publications.

Robinson, R. (2015) No Spectators! The art of participation, from Burning Man to boutique festivals in Britain, in G. McKay, (ed.) *The Pop Festival: history, music, media, culture*, London: Bloomsbury, 165-181.

Rojek, C. (1995) *Decentring Leisure: Rethinking Leisure Theory*, London: Sage Publications.

Sellar, T. (2014) Economies of experience: interview with Gavin Kroeber, in *Theater*, **44**(2), 124-141.

Silvanto, S. (2015) How to Flow, in C. Newbold, C. Maughan, J. Jordan, and F. Bianchini, (eds.) *Focus on Festivals: Contemporary European Case Studies and Perspectives*, Oxford: Goodfellow, 88-97.

Winklehorn, K. (2015) The Enchanted City: Hostelbro Festive Week - an experiential and social cultural space, in C. Newbold, C. Maughan, J. Jordan and F. Bianchini, (eds.) *Focus on Festivals: Contemporary European Case Studies and Perspectives*. Oxford: Goodfellow, 168-179.

# 2 The Place to be... global! The 'glocal' configuration of world festivals: The case of *Les Eurockéennes de Belfort*

Aurélien Djakouane and Emmanuel Négrier

## Introduction: world festivals and 'glocalisation'

The simple aim throughout this book is to ask questions of world festivals, as evidenced in recent advances in research about festivals. The 'festivalisation of culture' (Négrier, 2015) approach has seen an expansion in both qualitative and quantitative research in recent years. A few years ago, the research on festivals was going in three directions: a monographic approach (Autissier, 2008); an approach dominated by economic issues, management (Maughan and Bianchini, 2004; Bonet and Schargorodsky, 2012) or tourist attractiveness (Anderson and Getz, 2009); and an approach considering the festivals as peripheral, or exceptional, items of cultural policies. More recently, new opportunities emerged with the crossing of these three approaches with more artistic or aesthetic issues, as we can see in *Focus on Festivals* (Newbold et al, 2015). At the same time, the interest in the multi-dimensional nature of festivals opens up new questions about the relationship between festivals and public space (Giorgi et al, 2011).

The identification of a world category of festival is both logical and paradoxical. It is logical, because, by their history, festivals, more than other cultural enterprises, were the levers for artistic exchange beyond national borders and beyond daily life (Falassi, 1987). Rather than the local and national institutions permanently installed in cities and artistic seasons, the programming of festival is still a powerful tool for the circulation of artists, for sharing tastes, and for cooperation between actors. The global nature of festivals is a substantial element of their dynamics, even if not all of them have the same degree of international openness. That's why festivals seem to be not only in perfect harmony with the contemporary anthropological moment, but also a response to several ongoing issues of cultural policies: cultural democratisation (Négrier et al, 2010), the legitimisation of local authorities (Watermann, 1998), the transformation of artistic genres (Dowd et al, 2004), cultural diversity or European identity (Maggauda and Solaroli, 2011) or, more generally, territorial identity. The development of mega-events, as a new strategy of distinction for towns and cities, has become a particular research topic (Gold and Gold, 2005; Quinn, 2005; Van Aalst and Van Melik, 2012), not without a causing a critical current (Rojek, 2013).

However the world category of festivals can also be paradoxical. Indeed, alongside the considerable growth of these events, the balance of studies about many of them shows how each festival has a singular story, and is always singularly local. Here we have the opportunity to illustrate this from the perspective of a particular event, the *Eurockéennes de Belfort*. But on this point, the example is widely generalisable.

The research discussed in this chapter is based on a dual survey conducted four years apart (2010 and 2014), using the same quantitative and qualitative methods. It is part of a research programme about festivals that began, in France then in Europe, in 2006.

## From local to 'glocal'

Three factors lead thinking about the 'localisation' of global festivals (or their 'glocalisation'): public and volunteers, private partnerships, public support.

As for the public, it is clear that global festivals can be charactised by having a higher proportion of people coming from other countries. Everyone knows the extent of foreign spectators – sometimes above the average – declared by festivals like *Sziget* in Hungary, *Glastonbury* in England, *Sonar* or *Primavera Sound System* in Barcelona. But the trend observed in these festivals is growth in regional audiences due to the increase in the number of festivals in neighbouring artistic niches, especially in the world of rock and electronic music. The competition between these festivals for major headliners makes it less attractive to make a long trip to see a particular artist. Of course, the attraction of the show is not the only motivation for participating in world festivals, and some people, attracted by the atmosphere or the legend of this or that event, choose the experience of distance as an adventure per se. But let's say the regionalisation (partial) of the audience for festivals is a consequence of the increased supply. Volunteering, an important resource for festivals and a new way to participate in the event, is generally higher amongst citizens living near the festival.

As for private partnerships, it is clear that patrons and sponsors of global festivals are mostly large global enterprises, mirroring the global nature of the event itself. But in practice, this concerns only a part of the private partners. A very high proportion of private support for a festival comes from within its region – much more than is generally believed. The reason is the reluctance of business patrons to invest in culture without, depending on the country, incentives such as tax incentives. Regionally based sponsors are more likely to be influenced by arguments of local 'politico-economic' socialisation, making the tax bonus less important. Regional sponsorship is, therefore, a major resource for global festivals.

As for political support, local and regional powers cannot be indifferent to the benefits (economic, symbolic) that can be reaped from the presence and energy of international events. Reciprocally, cultivating good relations with the local government provides important guarantees: facilitation of the authorisation procedures, security, location, accessibility, as well as access to a local elite, which includes potential patrons and sponsors and getting indirect support in kind or public subsidy.

Of course, these events take place within national frameworks, which have some influence on festivals' configurations. In our international comparison of music festivals (Négrier et al., 2013), we found that festivals shared more things beyond borders than is often said. But some characteristics continue to make a difference between countries: the cultures of public support or sponsorship, the social practice of volunteering or micro-wage labour; and the intensity of partnerships with the cultural and social actors of the territory.

All these factors explain the dual global and local nature of world events. There is still a phenomenon that needs to be understood. How do artistic and cultural dynamics interact with a festival's local identity? Audiences (local, regional, international) have a global understanding and expectations of artistic references and tastes. Globalisation of the event also occurs in the other direction: from the demands of the local audience for the event to achieve global standards. That is why the neologism 'glocalisation' (Robertson, 1995) seems entirely appropriate to describe the sociology of these events, both inserted into the flow of global benchmarks and rooted in economic configurations and local cultural policies.

This double glocal side does not occur without tension, especially between the most mainstream dimensions of globalisation, which are sometimes considered excessively standardised, and local dimensions of the culture of proximity often label amateurish in return. Glocalisation then also refers to events that are in nature both global and unique, like the *Belfort Eurockéennes*, and those who try to reproduce or replicate their unique appeal in new spaces. This is the case of *Sonar* in Barcelona (Spain), which creates an event under the same brand in other Spanish cities and New York; and the *Folle Journée de Nantes* (France), which replicates in Bilbao, Warsaw and Tokyo. In an interesting way for our idea of glocalisation, *La Folle Journée* led both a duplication process and international relocation strategy within the French region within a network of 11 mid-sized cities.

In any case, if the international character of an event depends on several specific criteria (financial, public, programming), its global reach also refers to more territorial dimensions. We can point to five criteria: (1) economic impact, (2) duration, (3) the area where the event takes place, (4) ways of experiencing the event for the public, and (5) changes in relation to culture. But before considering these five dimensions in detail, we will present the case study on which we have worked to develop our comparative temporal analysis.

## Origin and evolution of *Les Eurockéennes de Belfort*

The festival *Les Eurockéennes de Belfort* was born in 1989. The birth itself illustrates the combination of local and global motivations. Indeed, this festival was a local government response to a double motivation: create an event that is open to new currents of youth culture (globalisation), and that transforms the identity of the region (location). This festival provides an offer (70 concerts), a device (5 stages) and a capacity (80,000-120,000 spectators) very different from local festivals, which represent the most common type of event offer. However, this festival shape is not unique in France. *Rock en Seine*, near Paris, the *Vieilles Charrues* in Brittany, or the *Francofolies* in La Rochelle are based on a same device. More broadly, this kind of festival, inspired by the great Anglo-Saxon popular gathering from in the 60s and the 70s, is everywhere in Europe.

Moreover, this kind of 'grand format' festival (multiple stages, abundant supply, mass audience) is representative of an offering dedicated to popular music (rock, electronic music, rap, hip hop, world music, etc.) that is difficult to export to other kinds of music. Since 1989, the festival has experienced several phases. The developmental (more or less amateur) at the beginning, gives way, in the 90s, to a headliner race strategy, and then the model that still applies today, a hybrid between headliners and discoveries, between artistic supply and festive event.

From its beginnings, the festival contributed to the local economy, particularly in certain sectors. However, its contribution is also symbolic: from international media coverage to local media attention, including identification and territorial belonging through participation in the event. This allows links between individuals to be created; links that few economic actions can trigger. From the economic perspective, patronage plays a role in local economic dynamics that exceeds, with the sponsorship, one million euros. Furthermore, the festival is also a place for business meetings and partnerships. 650 journalists cover the event and 151 companies support it. There is therefore a double date for music lovers and professionals, in a triple environment of finance, arts and culture.

On the financial side, *Eurockéennes* operate in a pressurised performance economy. Inflation of artistic expenditure (headliners, emerging scene or local groups) objectively increases the cost of a festival. Furthermore, at European level, this development is part of a increasingly open competition among a growing number of events as the rise of the *Main Square Festival* in Arras (North of France) attests. It is owned by the multinational company Live Nation Entertainment, and takes place at the same time of year (early July). In fact, the identity of the festival as it arises today is radically different from how it was at the time of its creation, when it was the only 'game in town'. Early July now sees dates for more than 50 other European music festivals.

# Five comparative lessons

It is a considerable advantage to have been able, four years after a first research (Négrier et al., 2012), to return to the same place in order to carry out a second survey. Indeed, few research projects can compare the same cultural institutions and their audience. Outside the emblematic case of *Avignon* (Ethis, 2002, Ethis et al., 2008), such a research perspective remains infrequent. Perhaps it is significant that 'grand format' festivals are subject to this type of approach, partly because of their dual local and global dimension. We can draw five general lessons from this longitudinal comparison.

## Retain and renew

The first lesson concerns the evolution of the audience year after year and the way that festival crosses time. We see it through a double movement of renewal / loyalty. Our data show that *Eurockéennes* displayed a 34% renewal rate, which is very important for a festival that is more than 25 years old. Over the years, however, this renewal follows a slightly downward trend reflecting a growing loyalty since 2000. This trend contradicts the idea that an ever-increasing festival offer would atomise the audience and encourage a more occasional consumption of the events following a particular programming appeal. The interviews show forcefully that it is the music and programming that explain the success of *Eurockéennes*, festival goers are mainly looking for both a more global atmosphere and a dual social and aesthetic experience. It is also one of the constants of comparison over time. Although important, the public renewal marginally changes the sociological composition of the public.

Two elements, however, need to be pointed out: some ageing and feminisation of the audience. The second phenomenon is a trend that can be more generally observed about amplified music festivals, reflecting a gendered democratisation of rock. However, ageing raises questions about the dynamic of renewal of the *Eurockéennes* public; over ten years, the average age of the public has steadily increased from 24 to 29 years. While continuing to attract a young population that is renewed, the festival also manages to retain a significant portion of its audience that grow older with it. This phenomenon is explained by the persistence of a commitment to musical aesthetic discovery during adolescence. This is also true about the social experience at the *Eurockéennes*, even if the interviews show us that audiences experience this differently as they age. In addition, fidelity to the festival does not necessarily mean regularity or frequency. The gap between the year of the first attendance and the number of editions experienced (6 on average) reflects increasingly intermittent participation as festival goers grow older. The older we get, the more difficult it is to attend each *Eurockéennes*, particularly for reasons of domestic organisation. This intermittent participation often sets in after an intense period of attendance related to youth and monitoring music news.

Finally, observation of social classes also shows a great demographic stability despite some minor variations. At first glance, renewal does not foster social widening of a public that is already diverse. However, observation of the occupational position of festival goer's parents shows that categories are changing. About 60% of the now upper classes come from middle and lower classes families. The relative increase of the upper classes in the *Eurockéennes'* public is more evidence of a social mobility than an increased presence of 'heirs'. That is reflecting, through time, the sociological capacity of a musical style (i.e. amplified music) to expand its audience. This is, for us, a special skill of glocal festivals.

## Local roots and national outreach

The second lesson is about another phenomenon, apparently paradoxical but also concomitant, the local roots of the festival on the one hand, and its wider regional attractiveness on the other. Between 2010 and 2014, the share of the local public remained stable at around 18%. However, a movement took place in favour of a broad regional audience (northeast quarter of France) that increased from 38% to 57%, to the detriment of the audience from outside the region. This regionalisation of the audience took place in a context of increased competition between festivals. It is also important to contextualize this, because, comparatively, *Eurockéennes* attract twice as many people from outside the region as most of other festivals (see Figure 2.1 below).

<table>
<tr><td></td><td colspan="3">Eurockéennes</td><td colspan="2">Festivals in Europe and Quebec</td></tr>
<tr><td></td><td>2004</td><td>2010</td><td>2014</td><td></td><td>2008</td></tr>
<tr><td>Local</td><td>20%</td><td>19%</td><td>19%</td><td>Local</td><td>54%</td></tr>
<tr><td>Area</td><td rowspan="2">} 39%</td><td>19%</td><td>26%</td><td>Area</td><td>16%</td></tr>
<tr><td>Northeast quarter of France</td><td>18%</td><td>28%</td><td rowspan="2">Rest of France</td><td rowspan="2">} 26%</td></tr>
<tr><td>Rest of France</td><td>35%</td><td>37%</td><td>23%</td></tr>
<tr><td>Foreign</td><td>6%</td><td>7%</td><td>4%</td><td>Foreign</td><td>4%</td></tr>
<tr><td>Total</td><td>100%</td><td>100%</td><td>100%</td><td>Total</td><td>100%</td></tr>
</table>

**Figure 2.1:** The geographical origin of spectators

Beyond the national scope, the increasing number of international festivals based on similar musical programming can only strengthen the regional and interregional composition of their audiences. For this type of event, the geographical home of its audience is not antagonistic with its extension. Two pieces of data illustrate this. First, the loyalty to the festival. 29% of the *Greater East* festival goers took part in more than 6 editions of the festival (against 42% for people living in the festival city), 51% of them came for the very first time before 2008 (against 49% for the local population). Certainly geographical remoteness makes regular attendance more difficult. But the enthusiasm it generates stands the test of time. Second, the renewal. On one hand, local origin is measured by the small percentage of local festival goers who had never been to the festival before (12%). On the other hand, its regional (39%) and extra-regional (49%) attractiveness is not undermined. The campsite plays, on this level as on the previous one, a decisive role.

## Between 'patrimonialisation' and new trends

The third lesson illustrates the changing tastes of the *Eurockéennes*' audience. It refers to the ability of glocal festivals to follow transformations in the relationship with culture. Three factors are important. First, the rise of a positive appreciation for classical music. Second, the persistence of certain taste profiles, the disappearance of other ones, and the emergence of new ones. Third, the contingent relationship between taste profiles and festivals' programming. In four years, the overall hierarchy of musical aesthetics remained unchanged. Rock outclasses all the other musical genres. Electronic music ranks second while other music genres are around the average. None has a strong and broad rejection. At the same time, this trend is confirmed because classical music (while maintaining the lowest ranking) increased from 7/20 to 9/20.

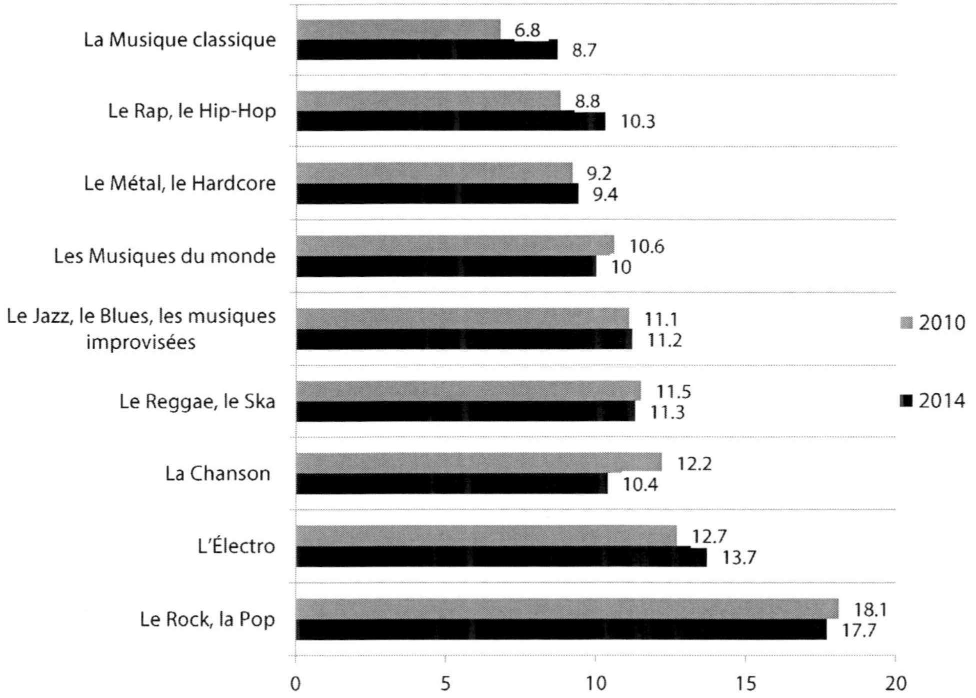


**Figure 2.2:** Graph of musical tastes – 2010-2014 (mark /20)

This reflects a stable form of appreciation and tolerance for all music. The rise of classic taste might be attributed to the influx of retirees, university graduates, students and executives in 2014. These trends are so low that it would be wrong to impute to them such an explanatory power. More probably the expansion of the eclectic spectrum refers to a plurality of social configurations, age or education levels. The arrival of new demographic groups, parallel to the maintenance of others already present in 2010, also marks the singular identity of the *Eurockéennes'* audience's musical tastes in 2014. For instance, the disappearance of the 'chanson' lovers and the emergence of eclectic profiles were certainly no surprise to the programmers of this edition. However, across all profiles, the analysis of social determinants continues to surprise. Some associations are expected: the appeal of classical music to the upper classes and older people or rap and electro for youth and working classes. In the most eclectic profiles where sociology often sees the most elite social groups, we find, for example, as much middle and working classes as in the general public. These eclectic profiles are more common at the campsite as if the liberal and friendly atmosphere found there was associated with tolerance and openness, as many festival goers claimed.

| Where are... | Profiles |
|---|---|
| Women? | B: Jazz and Classic / A: Electro-Rock / D: Everything but...rap! |
| Graduates? | D: Everything but...rap! / B: Jazz & Classic |
| The upper classes? | D: Everything but...rap! |
| The working classes? | C: Rap-Electro / E: Reggae, Rap, Electro, World music |
| Campers? | C: Rap-Electro / G: Eclectic |
| Young people? | C: Rap-Electro /E: Reggae, Rap, Electro, World music |
| The elderly? | D: Everything but...rap! / B: Jazz & Classic |
| Students? | C: Rap-Electro |
| Amateur musicians? | G: Eclectic / B: Jazz & Classic |
| Local people? | E: Reggae, Rap, Electro, World music / F: Heavy Metal |
| Newcomers? | C: Rap-Electro / B: Jazz & Classic |
| The old followers? | D: Everything but...rap! / G: Eclectic |

**Figure 2.3:** Variables and taste profiles

Once again, we end up with an ambivalent conclusion. On the one hand, the link between musical preferences and sociological identity still exists but this link is becoming weaker and no longer precludes the influence of other factors, including the way that festival goers made their 'own' festival. Basically, the influence of demographic determinants is constantly being challenged by the life course. This is true for cultural practices and tastes (Djakouane 2005 and 2011) as for all social practices. As such, the glocal festivals are ideal places to observe the contemporary transformations of the relation to culture.

## Total experience and transformation of the relationship to culture

The fourth lesson is about the cohabitation of populations with very different demographic backgrounds and musical tastes sharing the *Eurockéennes* experience. Our investigation did not reveal heterogeneous feelings about the lived experience during this festival but several shared values. No doubt we touch here the limits of socio-ethnographic investigations in the festive ground where vindictiveness and sadness disappear. However, it does not mean that all festival goers live this event in the same way. On the contrary, the ways to participate are very different; from camping or not, to come for one day or more, etc. These behaviours also refer to several ways to get involved in the collective life of the festival. Thus, the surprising result about the crowd-funding (18%) – including projects in culture 50%, social 22%, environment 19% – emphasizes a new relationship with culture where the public is more involved in the supply chain. Similarly, the uses of digital tools, though still mainly advisory, show a transformation of the relationship with the cultural offering, with the status of artists and with the representation of institutions. These elements emphasize the new active nature of the audience faced with cultural content in the digital age. Behind these behaviours, festival goers agree on the values of the *Eurockéennes* experience: tolerance, critical benevolence, curiosity, sharing and relationship with others.

| | Attended before | | Newcomers | |
|---|---|---|---|---|
| | **2014** | **2010** | **2014** | **2010** |
| For the festival in general | 79% | 76% | 66% | 72% |
| For some artists | 21% | 24% | 34% | 28% |
| Came alone or in pairs | 29% | 27% | 29% | 22% |
| Came with friends | 53% | 57% | 56% | 66% |
| Came with family | 9% | - | 8% | - |
| Came in groups | 9% | - | 8% | - |
| Remained for the whole festival | 64% | 63% | 54% | 52% |

**Figure 2.4:** Why and how does one come to the festival?

The success of a festival is based on a fragile alchemy where the search for music programming, that mixes airtime, headliners and new discoveries, adjusts to a special atmosphere, including the environment, camping and festive atmosphere. In short, festival goers value the importance of the double aesthetic and social dimension that makes the *Eurockéennes* experience. The explanation comes from a unique intersection each year between two vectors: programming and sociability. It is this last point that the survey allows us to objectify. This may seem obvious, but like many cultural outings, attending a festival usually takes place collectively. The experience lived there, the way it takes place, the way it is prepared, require the involvement and participation of others. Participating in a festival is an experience where the many dimensions compared to others (familiar or unknown) play a key role alongside the musical experience. It explains the memory we hold, the desire to return we have, and the parenthetical character of the moment we live there. We will not however conclude that the aesthetic experience is socially universal. The sociological examination shows that people, their careers, their social origin and their relationship with music are differentiated. But it would seem that the human dimension is as important as the musical dimension. Because it makes coming to the festival an event, both individually and collectively, but also because it drives navigation around the festival: choice of concerts, moment of conviviality, meetings… This encourages us to talk about the *Eurockéennes* as a 'total social experience', in which several dimensions (economic, cultural, symbolic, social, etc.) interact with each other. The case of the *Eurockéennes* shows that the practice of such a festival is a taste experience, a social relationship, something like a little tolerant republic. That commonality is the fragility of the ephemeral and the strength of fidelity, pretty much what Spinoza called the 'joyful passions'.

## Global market and local economic benefits

The fifth lesson focuses on the economic impact of the festival. The calculation of the economic impact of festivals, and more generally culture, is the subject of much debate (Kancel et al., 2013). The various calculation methods lead to very different results that require a great deal of caution ( , 2009).

| | 2010 | 2014 | Gap |
|---|---|---|---|
| Direct impact | 1,380,000 € | 1,790,000 € | +29.7% |
| Indirect impact | 5,903,796 € | 7,636,457 € | +29.3% |
| Total impact | 7,283,96 € | 9,426,457 € | + 29.4% |
| Impact for 1€ of subsidy | 8.1 € | 12.0 € | + 48.1% |

**Figure 2.5:** Territorial economic impact

At four-year intervals, this impact increases significantly; more than 30% in absolute terms, and if subsidies are included, it increases by approximately 50%. This result invites us to a deeper reflection about the ambivalent discourse on the economic value of culture. The first logic that explains the increasing economic impact is the success of the festival in 2014 that was not the case in 2010. The difference in profit caused by the increased attendance is obviously considerable. Compared to the grant, it is even more so, because the level of public support does not follow the volume of expenditure.

The second logic is a trend towards regionalisation of festival companies. This was already the case in 2010, but it is now increasingly obvious. The more a festival is rooted in a territory, the more it creates direct employment, the more it builds economic partnerships (industry, services, marketing, communication). Yes it's true that some festivals are still rootless; they arrive in the territory only a few days before the event and leave as soon as it completed. This is not the case for the *Eurockéennes* that have real local roots. That is what explains the high level of its direct impact: 40% of total expenditures are made in its territory. This is an important figure because the artistic expenses of an international art event are not generally local.

Finally, we would like to indicate here that the economic value of *Eurockéennes* to its territory may be too diffuse to be appreciated by economic accounting alone. Impact calculations generally do not take into account the image effects, territorial enhancement, qualification or requalification of living spaces. Our investigation shows that such a festival acts both on an interregional and international map of Rock (in this case), but it is also rooted in the life of the people of the territory. There is an 'age' to *Eurockéennes*. It is going there to the campsite, even when you live close by. It is discovering there new music and groups. It is finding there, friends from here or elsewhere. It is celebrating there his results or his entry into professional life. Cultivated there is an ephemeral republic then linked in to social networks.

## Conclusions

From a study of the audience of a large format festival undertaken four years apart, the purpose of this research was to consider festivals in their local and global double dimension. For us, this question seemed crucial when the analysis of world festivals is growing in connection with the globalisation of the economy and music, and also with eventalisation and festivalisation of culture. With reference to the second phenomenon, the study of festival audiences allows us to highlight the local and anthropological dimension of festival activity. By observing closely the nature of the festival experience, this approach also allows us to recall how festivals are privileged spaces to report on contemporary changes in culture; active ways of involving citizens in the public space; and economic and political issues of culture. The interest in the ambivalent category of *glocal* festival, also allows us to move beyond economic tropism. Certainly, culture needs economic expertise. But the example of the economic benefits shows how those calculations are foreign to the social and cultural dynamics of festivals, their ability to mobilise a mass audience, to animate the public space and foster the encounter between art and the public. In short, everything that makes the fragility and the strength of these small businesses, mid-way between private and public, often dependent on the active involvement of many volunteers and still dependent on the vagaries of traffic, climate and political arbitration. This viewpoint is not contradictory with the fact that festivals are now increasingly involved in a global economy. Finally at the turn of this research, festival enterprise is becoming more global but still local. Glocal basically.

## Bibliography


Andersson, T., and Getz, D. (2009) Tourism as a mixed industry: Differences between private, public and not-for-profit festivals, in *Tourism Management,* **30**(6), 847-856.

Autissier, A. M. (2008) *L'Europe des Festivals,* Paris: Éditions de l'Attribut.

Bonet, L., and Schargorodsky, H. (eds.) (2012) *La gestion de festivals por sus protagonistas,* Barcelona: Gescénic.

Djakouane, A. (2005) De l'espace incertain des pratiques culturelles à l'espace négocié des carrières de spectateurs : une épreuve pour la notion de milieu social, in *Carnet de bord,* no.8, 35-45.

Djakouane, A. (2011) La carrière du spectateur. Une approche relationnelle des temps de la réception, in *Temporalités,* no. 14: https://temporalites.revues.org/1939

Dowd, T.J., Liddle K., and Nelson, K. (2004) Music festivals as scenes, in A. Bennett, R. A. Peterson, (eds.) *Music Scenes. Local, Translocal and Virtual,* Nashville: Vandebilt University Press, 149-167

Ethis, E. (ed.) (2002) *Avignon, Le public réinventé. Le festival sous le regard des sciences sociales,* Paris: La Documentation Française.

Ethis, E., Fabiani, J. L., and Malinas, D. (2008) *Avignon, le public participan*t, Montpellier: L'Entretemps.

Falassi, A. (1987) Festival: definition and morphology, in A. Falassi, (ed.) *Time Out of Time: Essays on the Festival,* Albuquerque: University of New Mexico Press, 1-10.

Giorgi, L., Sassatelli M. and Delante, G. (eds.) (2011) *Festivals and the Cultural Public Sphere,* London: Routledge.

Gold, M., and Gold, J. R. (2005) *Cities of Culture: Staging International Festivals and the Urban Agenda 1951-2000,* Aldershot: Ashgate.

Kancel, S., Itty J., Weill M., and Durieux, B. (2013) *L'apport de la culture à l'économie de la France.* Rapport de l'Inspection générale des Affaires culturelles et de l'Inspection générale des Finances, Paris: Ministère de la Culture.

Magaudda, P., and Solaroli, M. (2011) I festivali artistici e la cultura pubblica europea, in *Il Mulino* **60**(5), 897-903.

Maughan, C., and Bianchini, F. (2004), *The Economic and Social Impact of Cultural Festivals in the East Midlands of England,* East Midlands Development Agency-Arts Council England.

Négrier, E., and Vidal, M. (2009) L'impact économique de la culture: Réels défis et fausses pistes, in *Economia della cultura,* no.4, 487-498.

Négrier, E., Djakouane, A., and Jourda, M. (2010) *Les publics des festivals,* Paris: Michel de Maule.

Négrier, E., Djakouane, A., and Collin, J. D. (2012) Un territoire de rock. Le public des Eurockéennes de Belfort, Paris: L'Harmattan, coll. *Logiques sociales.*

Négrier, E., Bonet, L., and Guérin, M. (2013) *Music Festival: A changing world,* Paris: Michel de Maule.

Négrier, E. (2015) Festivalisation: patterns and limits, in C. Newbold, C. Maughan, J. Jordan, and F. Bianchini, (eds.), *Festivals in Focus: Contemporary European case studies and perspectives*, Oxford: Goodfellow, 18-27.

Newbold, C., Maughan, C., Jordan, J. and Bianchini, F. (eds.) (2015) *Festivals in Focus: Contemporary European case studies and perspectives*, Oxford: Goodfellow.

Quinn, B. (2005) Arts Festivals and the city, in *Urban Studies*, **42**(5-6), 927-943

Robertson, R. (1995) Glocalisation: Time-Space and Homogeneity-Heterogeneity, in M. Featherstone, S. Lash, and R. Robertson, (eds.) *Global Modernities*, London: Sage.

Rojek, C. (2013) *Event Power. How Global Events Manage and Manipulate*, London: Sage.

Van Aalst, I., and Van Melik, R. (2012) City festivals and urban development: Does place matter? in *European Urban and Regional Studies*, **19**(2), 196-206.

Waterman, S. (1998) Carnival for elites? The cultural politics of music festivals, in *Progress in Human Geography*, **22**(1), 54-74.

# 3 Norwegian Festivals and a Music Economy in Transition: The art of balancing ambitions, expectations and limitations[1]

Daniel Nordgård

## Introduction

Somewhere around 10.30 p.m., July 3rd, 2002, David Bowie enters the stage at Odderøya, Kristiansand to perform at the *Quart-Festival* as the headlining act of that year. The atmosphere was electric as 12,000 fans (sold out) welcome the biggest act yet to visit Norway's biggest music festival. Bowie himself, wearing a loosened bow tie and a black and white suit, walks calmly to the front of the stage, takes a bow at his audience and opens what is considered a legendary concert in Kristiansand with 'Life on Mars'. A long-time volunteer at the *Quart-Festival,* I was in that audience and, although not a devoted Bowie fan, I was deeply fascinated by his appearance. I remember his presence; the calm and the control Bowie exercised from when he entered the stage until he left. I remember the line of songs that I knew by heart – songs that have been canonised years ago. I also remember noticing the difference in appearance from Bowie and the number of 'soon-to-be-stars' and 'could-have-been-stars', struggling to attain momentum and attention on stage. Here was a star – a true legend.

Both prior to, but mostly after David Bowie's concert at the *Quart-Festival* in 2002, there was a vivid discussion among Norwegian festival managers and journalists on whether it was at all sustainable for festivals to give artist fees as big as that rumoured to be the case with David Bowie. There were concerns on whether a sacred line had been broken with regards to the size of his fee, as well as claims that Mr Bowie was considered a 'stadium-artist' and hence whether such artists were at all economically sustainable to present in Norwegian festival programmes. There was a concern to whether at all Norwegian festivals had the capacity to present artists on this level.

Remarkably absent in the discussions of 2002, were any concerns related to 'the other artists', the names underneath the headlining acts; new audience behaviour;

or a potentially changing role of the festival. In 2015, however, these issues are more apparent and in the following I will attempt to discuss them in relation to a set of interviews I did with three Norwegian festival managers in the spring of 2011. I will attempt to describe how the festivals have been affected by significant change taking place within the music industries and, in particular, seek to explore to what extent these changes have affected the role of the festival, and most important, to what extent such change is at all recognised by the festivals.

## Background: music industry in transition

Popular music and the music industry are tightly tied together – the coexistence of creative as well as economic motivations are so congruent and complementary that it's difficult to tell where one ends and the other begins. This symbiosis of music creation and the music industry is thoroughly described by scholars such as Peter Wicke (1990), Keith Negus (1998) and Simon Frith (2001), when they describe the interactions between audiences, artists and the music industry. Wicke looks at rock music and how tightly the genre is connected to the music industry in communicating to its audience. He argues that the spontaneous or coincidental meeting between the artist and the audience builds on a myth. Rather, it's a product of the expectations artist and the music industry have of their audience and, conversely, the audience's expectations of the music industry and the artists themselves. You find much of the same reasoning in Negus' elaborations in *Music Genres and Corporate Cultures* (1999) – the music industry builds on a constant dialogue between industry, artists and audiences and such dialogue is by no means linear or hierarchical. The point I want to make here is that popular music builds on constant negotiations between artists, industry and audiences along both creative and economic motivations, a point that is important if we aspire to understand how current changes affect the music festival.

The live music industry is thriving. Ticket sales, audience numbers, festivals and concerts – all indicators are pointing upwards (Norsk Kulturråd, 2015, TONO, 2015). Live music add up to what has become the lion's share of the overall music economy in Norway (Norsk Kulturråd, 2015) and Norwegian festivals seems to be in rude health (Kunnskapsverket, 2015). While recorded music has seen a significant decline over the last 10-15 years (Nordgård, 2013, 2014), live music has grown tremendously and any study of the developments in music festivals need to take these events into consideration. In order to understand this surge in the live music economy, explanations can perhaps be found outside the music industry – in a general economic rise, people's spending power increases, or even perhaps there is an increased awareness of festivals as a generator of local identity and local economy (Hjemdahl, et al. 2007; Hjemdahl, 2013). However, these progressions need to be considered against developments in the overall music industry, in particular the recorded music industry. The music industry has indeed experienced dramatic changes over the last 10-15 years, mostly due to a significant drop in recorded music revenues in the wake of a digitalisation process, in many ways spurred by illegal file-sharing from the turn of the millennium (Wikström, 2009; Hesmondhalgh, 2013). Despite current developments that show a potential revival of the recorded music economy due to subscription-based streaming (Nordgård, 2013, 2014; Tchmuck, 2015), the turmoil in the wake of Napster has nonetheless had an impact on the recorded music industry in particular and the music industries more generally – also the live sector. Effects stemming from the digital turmoil are perhaps particularly evident in two cases, namely the skewed distribution in revenues – booking fees (Kreuger, 2005; Frith, 2007; King, 2009; Elberse, 2013), as well as audience behaviour – and the superstar/blockbuster effect (Schwartz, 2004, Frith, 2001; Kreguer, 2005; Elberse, 2013).

Already in 2005, Alan B. Kreuger raised concerns about the distribution of revenues in the live sector, arguing that there's an increasingly skewed distribution of revenues towards the top. Kreuger demonstrated that although the live sector is experiencing an economic surge, much of this relies on major, established acts who are able to dictate ever-higher ticket prices. As Kreuger demonstrates, in 1981, the top 1% of artists took in 26%, while in 2003, the top 1% added up to 56%. The current rise in the live sector seems to mainly accrue to what Kreuger refers to as superstars (2005). Kreuger's findings correlates well with Anita Elberse' findings in *Blockbuster: Hit-making, Risk-taking, and the Big Business of Entertainment* (2013), where she demonstrates a superstar effect highly amplified by the internet and to a large extent reserved for already established acts. There are a couple of important points to be made here, both echoing the work of both Kreuger and Elberse, which is that current successful acts seems to build on investments made in prior times by a risk-willing industry (record companies) and also that digital developments seems to amplify any superstar/blockbuster effect.

Perhaps the most explicit link between developments in the recorded industry and the live sector can be found in what is commonly referred to as Bowie theory (Kreuger, 2005:26). The theory builds on David Bowie's statement from 2002 that in the future, recorded music will become like running water – it will become ubiquitous – and the only unique thing left for artists is to tour. It's hard not to agree with Bowie's prophecy and it is worth noting that his statement came the same year Bowie appeared on stage during the *Quart-Festival*, allegedly receiving record-breaking artist fees and sparking a debate about the economic sustainability of Norwegian festivals. In other words, while Bowie expressed a rationale leading to what has later become the Bowie theory, it also represents a change in festivals' economic conditions, and more importantly, the distribution of live music revenues (Kreuger, 2005; Frith, 2007; Elberse, 2013). And although unknowingly at the time, the effects of Bowie theory was vividly discussed in Norway in 2002 in the wake of David Bowie's concert at the *Quart-Festival*.

## Three Norwegian festivals

In 2011, I interviewed the managers of three Norwegian festivals on how their festivals were impacted by changes in the music industry. The interviews were originally part of a project seeking to investigate the changes in artist fees and the economic sustainability in the live market. However, the interviews expanded this focus by introducing aspects relating to the festivals' changing role in presenting and creating new artist careers and the ever-changing dynamic with audiences and audiences' expectations. The three festival managers were Robert Dyrnes of *Bukta Festival* in Tromsø, Jan Ole Ottnæs of *Molde International Jazz Festival* in Molde and Claes Olsen of *Øya Festival* in Oslo. All three festivals represent the upper division of Norwegian festivals and *Molde* and Øya are considered cornerstone festivals by the Norwegian Government (which also include Government funding) in their respective genres (jazz and pop/rock) and both draw international media and coverage. Even though none of the festivals surpass 20,000 tickets per day, they are considered among the biggest festivals in Norway – both with regards to the economy, as well as capacity and programming. Unlike neighbouring countries such as Denmark, Norway does not have any festivals with the capacities such as *Roskilde Festival* or *Northside Festivals*. However, there are numerous festivals operating with 10-15,000 tickets sold per day, which is a factor that might have an impact on the internal competition among Norwegian festivals and I'll return to this below. Based on the interviews there are three distinct features I'd like to elaborate on and that I believe represent general characteristics of change in the Norwegian festival scene and, importantly, that represent change that could be traced back to the developments in the international music industry. In the following I will present them as three concepts labelled as the *competition*, the *artists* and the *audience*.

### The competition

There are changes in competition among festivals and other actors involved in the business of presenting live concerts to an audience – there's stiffer competition for both artists and audiences. Based on the interviews, there seems to be at least two developments incorporated in this concept of competition, namely an increasing scarcity of superstar artists that can easily sell out tickets and the amplifying effect of more festivals that compete for these artists and hence push prices even further up.

> A new trend I've seen recent years in relations to increasing booking fees is that more and more agents tries to sell their artists to a flat fee throughout Europa. They start with those they think can pay the most, and try to adopt this fee to the other festivals. It's like: we will do a concert in Norway and will have 100,000 euros, otherwise we'll drop Norway. They have plenty of festivals and countries to choose from. Before there was greater differentiation in relation to the size of the festivals, album-sales

> in that specific country, etc... Now, perhaps the artist set aside one week in Europe, and can choose the festivals with the best returns. This also applies to smaller artists who try to make themselves exclusive. What I want to say here is that this makes smaller festivals vulnerable. There are big differences in capacities on Norwegian and German festivals. This pushes prices upwards. (Claes Olsen, Øya)

> Things have changed in the last five to six years. [..] I think the world was a little more naive and a bit easier. It was perhaps a hierarchy in the booking world that was easier to deal with five, six, seven years ago. [...] It's about such things as festival positions, for example. I mean, at that time we had one big festival and that was the *Quart-Festival* and it was a bit like there was an unwritten law that if the *Quart-Festival* booked a band, they didn't play any other Norwegian festivals. (Robert Dyrnes, *Bukta*)

> But at the same time, there are too many festivals. There are too many who are willing to risk too much. And where there is not a festival, there are either organisations or sports clubs that are willing to take that risk. (Jan Ole Otnæs, *Moldejazz*)

There's a concern among the festival managers that there are too many actors involved in the market, many of whom are not even part of the live industry, but that nevertheless have great impact on competition and pricing. As Otnæs from *Molde* states: there are too many players who are willing to take too much of a risk. Interestingly, this may also relate to a break with former structures, in which there are new entrants in the market – entrants who may not know the business, but who nevertheless involve themselves in booking and promoting live events. There used to be more of a hierarchy among the festivals, with the *Quart-Festival* as the reigning actor, however, this has now changed with an increasing number of 'equal' festivals and an additional set of 'outsiders'. In principal, it should represent a positive development that you no longer have one actor with exclusive rights on the biggest touring acts. However, it may also represent a more complex and disorganised market in which competition among festivals leaves the agents to dictate price. In the past, if an artist was setting up a European tour and Norway was considered a valuable market, but with only one or two festivals that could book and host such an act, then considerations had to be made on this festival's capacity and audience – and hence pricing would be more dynamic. Today, however, with the significant competition among festivals and others, such considerations are redundant and flat fees are demanded regardless of capacities and markets.

As mentioned above, there's a second dimension related to the concept of competition, namely a concentration around a smaller segment of exclusive superstar artists. This particular issue became central during my dialogues with the festival managers. I'm presenting the concept of the artist as an extension of competition, as I believe the festival manager's increased awareness of artist development stems from the increasing competition.

## The artists

Closely linked to the first concept of competition is that artists previously considered stadium artists, also tour festivals. It seems plausible that this is linked to Bowie theory – that artists need to tour because that's the only unique thing left (Kreuger, 2005) – and that this again is very much linked to the developments in the recorded industry and hence an effect of digitalisation. The interviewees expand on this by addressing another issue, namely the vacuum below the headlining artists and the need for artists in the mid-range that can sell tickets. However, this also involves a segmenting of the market and, as Robert Dyrnes from *Bukta* elaborates, his own festival seems to have lost ground and is having to choose from lower levels of headlining artists, despite the fact that the festival is growing in size and economy.

> I believe *Bukta* has acknowledged that we're a rather small festival and that we have to choose artists from [...] well, when we started, I guess we could choose from 'the third level of artists', now we're choosing from a 'fourth level' and it just keeps going lower, you know. As long as the world is the way it is, with so many festivals and with so much money circulating in Norway [...] and the music industry being the way it is [...]. Our position has pretty much become that we are reliant on being very good at selecting the right smaller acts because we have to create the future headlining acts. We have to take part in creating the next Kaizer's Orchestra, the next Dum Dum Boys (Norwegian headlining acts). There's been a vacuum in ten years! [...] I think it's going to be hard because the world has changed and audiences have changed their behaviours and preferences very much, both with regards to concerts and recordings (Robert Dyrnes *Bukta*).

This last consideration from Mr Dyrnes seems important as he describes a business where the festivals have to take part in creating the next headliners of tomorrow. As such, Dyrnes addresses two issues, namely that the traditional music industry, with the record companies central in the processes, seems to be less capable of building up new artists' careers and hence that more responsibility lies on the festivals themselves. Also, there's a strategic consideration among the festivals that they build relationships with artists. Dyrnes elaborates on this by emphasising an aspiration to contribute to artists' 'rise to fame'. The rationale is that if the festivals take risks in booking and programming an artist in an earlier stage of their development, these artists may repay this risk by returning if they become big enough to headline.

This, however, may pose difficulties with regards to the audience, as their behaviours and expectations to programming have also developed and changed parallel with the changes in the music industry and the festival market.

## The audience

A very explicit concern among all three festival managers was the difficulties in balancing audiences' expectations with both the festival's own artistic ambitions and economic realities. Part of these concerns may relate to rather basic challenges of communicating properly with your audience and creating a mutual understanding of ambitions and visions. And although such a mutual understanding may have been properly established, the festival's audience is influenced by the increasing number of competitors' programming, as well as the festival's own programming.

> We have spoiled our audience. We saw that last year when we didn't have any 'mega-headliners'. It's too early to say whether it was a reaction on our programming or whether it was an effect of a disastrous weather. Last year (2010) we had Herbie Hancock, Jeff Beck and Missy Elliot as some of the international headliners and our experience was that people were more or less indifferent to it – kind of like, if you don't have a Leonard Cohen or a Sting, people seem to not care much. So even if it was the first time Missy Elliot performed in Norway, people were like... 'sure, it's big, but still...'. The problem is that when you have spoiled your audience over the years, there's an expectation that only the biggest stars will top our programme. And people don't understand that when booking a festival – a jazz festival – there needs to be some sort of relevance. For us it would be unheard of to book Elton John, however, for the audience in Molde, he's a big artist – a headliner. In other words, there's a huge challenge to communicate to our audience that there actually is a plan behind our programming beyond booking the biggest names. So, to find that balance between the big artists and what we consider to be our core mission – and to have people understand it – is really quite difficult (Jan Ole Otnæs, *Moldejazz*).

> When we started up in 2004, we had only Norwegian names on the programme. There hadn't been any festival in Tromsø for many years and we noticed that people were excited to see Norwegian bands such as Big Bang, Madrugada, Span and Sondre Lerche. [...] But then, on year three, we did a scoop and managed to book Mötorhead to headline, together with lots of great Norwegian bands [...]. From that year we have struggled with the monster called audiences' expectations. You see, people don't really know the difference. They believe that when we had Mötorhead that year, the only reasonable thing would be to have Metallica the next year and Iron Maiden the year after that. They don't understand differences in pricing and status among festivals and artists. (Robert Dyrnes, *Bukta*)

Audience behaviour and their expectations seems to be central to all three managers as it ties together the two other concepts; *competition* and *artists* by limiting the space in which festivals can manoeuver. The audience's expectations very much influence the pressure on festivals in relation to headlining artists and, hence limit the festival's possibilities of programming and booking. It relates to the festivals as something more than just an escalating list of artists – that music festivals also communicate something more, like an artistic ambition or ambitions to take part in the developments of artistic careers. But it also refers to the difficulties of balancing these ambitions towards audiences that have ever more demanding expectations of what sort of artists they should expect to see on their local festival. Part of this problem may stem from spectacular bookings from the respective festival, as with the case of *Bukta's* Motorhead booking, that spawn expectations for other spectacular bookings. It may also stem from an increasing number of superstar artists touring more extensively (Kreuger, 2005) and hence growing expectations to see the biggest names perform your local festival. An effect of the Bowie theory may be inflation in superstar tours, which may be traced back to audience's expectations.

## Balancing ambitions, expectations and limitations

Times have changed, with increasing prices for the greatest artists and fierce competition with other festivals – and as already stated, Norway has a vast number of festivals and no major festival with capacities similar to that of festivals like *Roskilde* and *Northside* in neighbouring Denmark. In other words there's an increasing competition among festivals considered equal in economic terms – which may represent a local phenomenon amplifying a global development. The interviews clearly suggest that there have been changes, although none of them suggest any direct link between the changes in the international music industry and their own leeway. However, they clearly demonstrate that prices for the greatest artists have increased significantly and that these are less accessible due to increased competition with several players, both among traditional festivals and others. Much of this can be explained by Bowie theory, suggesting that the changes in the live sector stems from changes in the recorded music industry. Adding to this, Simon Frith (2007) suggests that the change in artist fees is due to the loss of subsidies from record companies. His argument suggests that previous models built on live tours and concerts as part of an effective marketing tool for selling recorded music. Hence, record companies had an interest in minimising the costs for artists to tour and thus promote their new album. It was for the same reason that record labels tour support and especially so for less established acts. Frith's argument is that part of what is happening in the live industry is an effect of the demise of the record industry's subsidies for live tours. Tellingly, the dissapearance of tour support from the record labels was also something that was emphasised by the festival managers as an important reason for why it had become more expensive and difficult to book smaller and mid-range artists.

Both Dyrnes and Otnæs believe that the festival has a role in and a responsibility to introduce new artists to new audiences and hence help build new artists' careers. Jan Ole Otnæs from *Molde International Jazz Festival* gives jazz festivals in Norway much credit for the strong Norwegian jazz scene, with outstanding jazz artists headlining Norwegian festivals, as well as international ones. The festivals have helped expose artists to growing audiences and some of the festivals have had very explicit agendas of presenting a next generation of Norwegian jazz headliners. Arguably, this is not solely an effect of the digital shift, or the crisis in the recorded music industry. However, what has changed is the record industry and the record companies' risk-willingness and dwindling ability to promote and establish new talents to bigger audiences. Consquently, the festivals gain importance as a facilitator for connecting artists and audiences and hence the role of festivals has changed. If nothing else, at least for artists.

What then is the problem? The festival managers I interviewed are surprisingly coherent when it comes to the importance of their audiences and their expectations and behaviours, and it seems to be particularly within this dimension that part of the challenge lies. Based on the interviews there seems to be a discongruity between what the general public expect to see on Norwegian festivals and the financial and practical realities that the festival managers operate within. It's difficult – and even impossible – to accommodate parts of the demands. It may also be in direct conflict with what the festivals themselves consider to be their artistic ambitions and misions – it's simply not within their goal or vision to provide these artists. However, the festivals are not passive players and have themeselves plenty of oportunity to communicate to their audiences what they should expect to see on their festival's programme – and perhaps more importantly, what they should not expect to find. The most obvious measure to curb expectations would be to consistently refrain from booking superstar artists – even the extraordinary possibilities that would appear every now and then – and thus avoid expectations of even greater artists in future programmes. Still, this would degrade the festival as an arena for the unexpected – the extraordinary and the legendary – like that July evening in 2002 when David Bowie walked out to the front of the stage in Kristiansand, Norway, with a loosened bow tie and a bow. The key probably lies in the communication and a continuous negotiation between the festivals and their audiences as briefly described above with reference to Wicke (1990), Negus (1999) and Frith (2001).

Simon Frith (2001: 45) specifically refers to the music festivals as dependent on negotiations with audiences, having a set of expectations ranging from who will perform, where they will perform (and when), in combination with what other artists, as well as expectations on aesthetics, physical designs and accessibility. There are expectations with regards to security and safety, as well as some minimum requirements to toilet facilities and sewage. However, the festival also represents expectations of seeing and experiencing the unexpected – discovering new bands and artists, hearing a brand new sound, finding a partner, and for many it also represents a free zone for testing limits with alcohol and drugs (Tjora, 2013). The festival hence represents a paradoxical set of established expectations, bordering what we could call rituals, as well as the expectations for the unexpected. And perhaps the most evident example of such a paradox in expectations is related to bookings and programming. On the one hand there are hopes to discover something new, but at the same time there are very clear anticipations of seeing specific artists perform on a specific festival, often related to announced touring plans, the festival's position in the market or previous bookings.

The fine art of balancing and manoeuvring in this landscape is by no means an easy task, not least given the disruptions in the market, partly due to the digitalisation process – the effects of the Bowie theory. The festivals seem to have an expanded role in developing artists and building up audiences. On the other hand, all three festival managers that I interviewed, seems well aware of these changes and their own role.

## Bibliography


Elberse, A. (2013) *Blockbusters: Hit-making, Risk-taking, and the Big Business of Entertainment.* New York: Henry Holt and Company.

Frith, S. (2001) *The Cambridge Companion to Pop and Rock,* Cambridge: Cambridge University Press

Frith, S. (2007) Live Music Matters, *Scottish Music Review, Volume 1: Indeterminacy and Technology.*

Hesmondhalgh, D. (2013) *The Cultural Industries.* London: Sage.

Hjemdahl, K., Hauge, E., and Lind, E. (2007) *Festivaler på Sørlandet: Kultur I Kraftformat* FoU-rapport nr 4/2007

Hjemdahl, K. (2013) Festival som Utviklingsaktør? in A. Tjora. (ed.) *Festival! Mellom Rølp, Kultur og* Næring Cappelen Damm Akademiske, 87-108

IFPI, (2011), *Recording Industry in Numbers.*

Johansson, D., Larsson, M., (2008) *The Swedish Music Industry in Numbers: Economic Development Report 2000-2008.*

King, Ian, (2009) *Live Issues,* The Times UK, 21.07.09.

Kunnskapsverket (2015) *Nasjonal Festivalstatistikk 2014* Kunnskapsverket: Nasjonalt senter for kulturelle næringer. Rettrieved from http://www.konsertarrangor.no/media/1595901/20150811_festivalstatistikk_endelig.pdf

Krueger, A. (2005) The economics of real superstars: The market for rock concerts in the material world, in *Journal of Labor Economics,* **23**(1), 1-30.

Mortimer, J.H., Nosko, C. and Sorensen, A. (2012) Supply responses to digital distribution: Recorded music and live performances, in *Information Economics and Policy,* **24**(1).

Negus, K. (1998) Cultural production and the corporation: musikal genres and the strategic management of creativity in the US recording industry, in *Media, Culture and Society,* **20**(3), London: Sage Publications

Negus, K. (1999) *Music Genres and Corporate Cultures*, New York: Routledge.

Nordgård, D. (2013) *Rapport fra Nordgård-utvalget.* The Norwegian Ministry of Culture. Retrieved from: http://www.regjeringen.no/en/dep/kud/documents/reports-and-plans/reports/2013/rapport-fra-nordgard-utvalget.html?id=734716

Nordgård, D. (2014) *Rapport fra Musikernes fellesorganisasjons utvalg på strømming.* Musikernes fellesorganisasjon. Retrieved from: http://www.musikerorg.no/text.cfm/0_1915/rapport-fra-mfos-strxmmeutvalg

Norsk Kulturråd (2015) 'Norsk Musikk I Tall 2013' Norsk Kulturråd, retrieved; http://www.kulturradet.no/documents/10157/5d1e78ae-3dbd-43a5-a88a-c2d1e48c9222

Schwartz, B. (2004). *The Paradox of Choice: Why More is Less.* New York: Harper Collins Publishers

Tschmuck, P. (2015) Music Streaming Revisited: The Problem of Income Distribution Retrieved on July 28 2015 from Music Business Research, https://musicbusinessresearch.wordpress.com/2015/07/18/music-streaming-revisited-the-problem-of-income-distribution/

Tjora, A. (2013) Festivalfellesskapsfornemmelser in Aksel Tjora (ed) *Festival! Mellom Rølp, Kultur og* Næring Cappelen Damm Akademiske, 87-108.

TONO (2015) Årsrapport 2014 Retrieved from: http://www.tono.no/wp-content/uploads/2014/04/TONO-%C3%85rsrapport-2015_org_nett.pdf

Wicke, P. (1990) *Rock Music: Culture, Aesthetics and Sociology*, Cambridge: Cambridge University Press.

Wikström, P. (2009). *The Music Industry – Music in the Cloud.* Cambridge: Polity Press.

## Notes

[1] This article is an edited, updated and translated version of my contribution *Norske festivaler og en musikkbransje i omveltning: Kunsten å balansere ønsker, forventninger og behov* in the anthology edited by Prof. Axel Tjora; *Festival! Mellom rølp, kultur og næring* (2013).

# 4 Visual Arts Festivals and Globalisation: The rise of biennials[1]

Monica Sassatelli

Biennials or *biennales* are periodic, independent and international art exhibitions surveying trends in contemporary art; since the 1990s they have proliferated across the globe. Biennials are much more than curated displays, they constitute 'festival-exhibitions' working as "a public model and a shifting backdrop against which the meanings of contemporary art are constructed, maintained and sometimes irrevocably altered" (Ferguson et al., 2005: 48). Whilst most contemporary post-traditional festivals (Giorgi and Sassatelli, 2011) have ancient roots, it is only in recent years that they have become an almost ubiquitous fixture of cultural calendars in cities around the world. This current proliferation is even more striking for art biennials. They arguably originate from the *Venice Biennale,* held for the first time in 1895, but have long exceeded their European, Western origin to establish a global format. Up to the 1980s they were only reproduced in a handful of examples; today biennials and derivates (triennials and others) have become key institutional nodes linking production, consumption and distribution of contemporary art. With now over 150 biennials around the world, we are increasingly likely to encounter contemporary art through their mediation, directly as visitors or more indirectly via the nebula of critical discourse and more generally the media coverage they generate. The phenomenon attracting attention has become not just the biennials but more specifically the *biennalisation* of the art world.

The term *biennalisation* is used within the art world itself as shorthand to refer to the proliferation and standardisation of biennial exhibitions under a common (if rather loose) format. Sociologically, biennalisation can thematise the shifting set of cultural classifications, practices and values that differentiate the contemporary art world, affecting both its content (now sometimes referred to as *biennial art*) and the type of rationale and experience it crystallises. As phenomena that increasingly represent themself "on a global scale" (Vogel 2010), biennials offer a unique vantage point to access what is often termed 'global culture'. However, they remain rarely empirically studied in clearly defined contexts, especially beyond affirmation or negations of their measurable impact (Buchholz and Wuggenig, 2005). Reprising within the art world unsolved dilemmas in the analysis of cultural globalisation, alleged optimists see in biennials the "embracing of a democratic redistribution of cultural power" (De Duve 2009: 45); whilst pessimists point rather to the "recognition of a new form of cultural hegemony and re-colonization" (2009: 45). This chapter traces the rise of the biennial, across time and space, providing contextualisation and interpretation for what are now often hyperbolic accounts of "hundreds of biennials" (Seijdel 2009: 4) across the globe.

## From the 'super-salon' to festivalism: a view from Venice

At a cursory look, one of the first features to stand out in an analysis of contemporary biennalisation is the diversity of events that go under the name of biennial, *biennale* or similar. To understand biennalisation as a phenomenon and the biennale as a genre means first of all to prise out commonalities and family resemblances. Interestingly, and irrespective of how little some of the more recent biennials share with it, the lineage with the first biennial, founded in 1895 in Venice as a biennial exhibition of international art, soon to be known as the *Biennale,* is never forgotten and rarely challenged.[2] Festivals, including contemporary, professional festivals, tend to have founding myths (Giorgi and Sassatelli 2011). In the world of biennales, Venice is the origin myth for all of them, either to establish a continuum or to assume a more antagonistic relationship. It is thus worth looking at Venice, and at its own lineage, in some detail.

The *Venice Biennale* coined the concept and format of the periodical large exhibition surveying current trends and developments in one or more contemporary art forms, usually independent from previously existing institutions (museum or gallery) and their permanent directorship and curatorial choices. It did so combining aspects from previous models of art and trade exhibitions. Since the Parisian *salons* of the 19th century, independent art exhibitions had become a successful genre in themselves (Altshuler 2013). Similarly, the universal exhibitions or *expo,* following the great success of the first London expo in 1851 (*The Great Exhibition*), had become a recurrent, itinerant feature spreading throughout the world (Roche 2000). For curatorial aspects such as artists' selection and the role and composition of the selection committee the *Venice Biennale* took inspiration from other successful art exhibitions of the time, the *Secession* in Munich in particular (see Di Martino 2013). However the framework lending meaning and clout to the enterprise was borrowed from expos and their organising principle of individual exhibitions commissioned, managed and financed by participating nations.

Clearly smaller in scale, at least to begin with, the *Venice Biennale* shared the expos' ambitious, agenda-setting rationale and the framework of national competition. The *Biennale* sought to put Venice and newly unified Italy on the map of contemporary art, by creating that very map in the microcosm of the exhibition park, as an allegedly representative, state-of-the-art survey. Historians of the early *Biennale* always note how Italian and Venetian artists were clearly over-represented (West 1995). However, more than the questionable empirical achievement of universal representation, it is the aspiration to it that is relevant to understand how these art exhibitions were framed at the time, and how they evolved. Indeed, even in new biennales, regardless of being actually organised around national pavilions (a pattern that few tend to reproduce today, probably as much as for economic and organisational reasons as for the conceptual qualms), national (or regional) competition and gate-keeping remain underlying features.

Both expos and the *Biennale* by the early 20th century had progressively expanded from a central exhibition palace to a park composed of several national *pavilions*, thus providing a miniaturised world tour, under the expert guidance of curators. Whilst it may be pointed out that world fairs themselves developed from the model of the old city fair, the profound difference in the shift to world fair is in the coupling with modernity's rationalisation and instrumental reason, the ambition of the world fair to be an exhaustive, representative, 'universal' exposition of 'progress', and its embeddedness in national, bourgeois cultures already enwrapped in emergent, globalising phenomena. Like in the expos, the *Biennale* aspired to illustrate progress, providing legitimation and order.

By the late 1960s, reviewing the state of contemporary art ceased to be considered sufficient or acceptable as an explicit rationale. As well as questionable, it appeared redundant (Altshuler 2013). Combined with the effect of a much wider circulation of art publications and reproductions, novelty was not anymore a reason to travel to Venice. Turning to a thematic approach for a unifying concept, a 'curatorial turn' has gradually become more prominent in the history of art exhibitions (O'Neill 2007), with biennials often leading the way. Swiss curator Harald Szeeman's *Documenta 5*, the 1972 edition of the quinqhiennial exhibition held in Kassel, is often taken as starting point of the thematic exhibition away from national representation, held together by the vision of a curator-author instead. Other Venice rivals looking for a new *raison d'être* also started to emerge based on this premise; *Sydney Biennial* notably adopted a thematic approach since its inception in 1973.

The shift from territorial review to thematic interpretation, which Venice itself partially incorporated, further supported the consolidation and diffusion of this flexible format. As the art world became, or perceived itself as, increasingly complex, making sense of it and establishing criteria of validation (rather than simply (re)presenting a sample of an undisputed canon) became increasingly critical. As we shall see, by the time they started to grow exponentially in the 1990s, it had become clear that biennials were not just *exhibiting* the art world, but acted as one of its constituent parts. Every new edition, every new biennale inevitably augments the complexity it tries to reduce, biennalisation becoming a self-propagating phenomenon.

## Biennials and cultural globalisation

For several decades, Venice was the only biennale. Some histories include other large recurrent shows that emerged shortly after, such as the Canergie Institute's *Pittsburgh International* established in 1896, or the *Whitney Biennial* in New York established in 1932, or even the smaller *Corcoran Bienni*al in Washington in 1907. These tended to focus on American art only (Corcoran and Whitney exclusively) and were integral to the private museums that initiated them. More widely recognised as second biennial is *São Paulo*'s in Brazil, founded in 1951 and which fully adopted Venice's original model. Others started to follow: *Tokyo Biennial* (1952); *Alexandria Biennial* (1955), *Documenta* in Kassel (1955), *Paris Biennial* (1959). The proliferation meant an expanding and increasingly elastic concept. Variation concerns temporality (*Documenta* happens every five years, but especially in the early decades inconsistencies abound everywhere), coverage (*Alexandria* is devoted to artists from the Mediterranean) and approach (only *São Paulo* fully adopted a national representation model), as well as dimensions. Success and relevance are also not constant, as variation in longevity suggests (many end up lasting just one or two shows, famously in recent years the much acclaimed *Johannesburg Biennale*).

Until the last decade or so of the 20th century, even as the landscape was already becoming more complex, a mainstream view of a fairly clear and limited panorama was still possible: "In the early sixties… there were two biennials: the *Venice Biennale* and the *Bienal de São Paulo* – and every five years there was *Documenta*" (Block 2013: 104), writes influential curator René Block. He closes the passage however describing a completely different scenario: "Since then, not even forty years have passed and today we are confronted with so many so-called biennials, triennials, and quadrennials that it's almost impossible to get an overall perspective on them" (2013: 104).

At a close look, one sees that until the 1980s the development had been slow, with just a handful of influential biennials and at most about 30, in inclusive lists counting also minor arts biennials and short-lived attempts (Vogel 2010). It is with the 1990s that the growth becomes exponential, can no longer be ignored and starts being a matter for reflection. If smaller biennials were happily overlooked before, now hyperbolic metaphors on the "hundreds of biennials active all over the world" (Seijdel 2009: 4) have become the norm in the self-representation of the art world, where the proliferation of art biennials is seen as an expression of its own globalisation (De Duve 2009). Since 2009, a Biennial Foundation (BF), and since 2014 an International Biennial Association (IBA) strive to monitor them and organise their networking, further signs of institutionalisation and worldwide reach. Taking the BF estimate as the most authoritative, there are over 150 biennials, of which 44 per cent in Europe, 32 per cent in Asia, 21 per cent in the Americas, 9 per cent in Africa and 3 per cent in Oceania.[3] Even at a glance, the distribution is far from equal, but with biennials in over 50 countries across all the continents, claims of a 'global' status are confidently held (Vogel 2010); the IBA aims at equal representation across all continents by statute. That biennials constitute a cultural correlate of globalisation in the contemporary art world has itself become a trope, with biennials addressing globalisation and its corollaries (cultural exchange, hybridisation, cosmopolitanism, neoliberal capitalism and so on) in their themes and selections, as well illustrated by the proceedings of the first World Biennials Forum organised by the BF in collaboration with *Gwanju Biennial* (Bauer and Hanru 2013).

The *Venice Bienniale* remains a point of reference even for the most distant replicas, even if, especially for recent ones, as a counter-model: the forerunner of this is the *Havana Biennial*, founded in 1983 and explicitly claiming for itself the role of alternative, deliberately anti-western and representative of another modernity (Esche 2011; Papastergiadis and Martin 2011). The genealogy out of Venice certainly contains a degree of simplification – as an example among many, it has been noted with reference to the *Dak'Art Biennial* that a:

> biennale's sense of its own history is characterised by a strange trio of forces: continuity, amnesia and disruption. In Dakar frequent references to the first World festival of Black Arts (1966)... introduce another variable to the mix [...] As contrived as this claim of kinship may be, it at least allows *Dak'Art* to reflect on itself outside of the *Venice Biennale*, which scholarship on the subject takes to be the basis of all biennales (Vincent 2014: 5).

This is however precisely what makes the selective storyline significant as a genealogy that creates a shared imaginary of the biennial. Increasingly, recognising the strength of a diffuse model, biennials compete with each other but most of all they connect. After several partial and short-lived attempts, self-defined biennials are now connected worldwide, joining networks and sharing debates, as well as more implicitly being connected by the recurrence of the same curators and artists in biennials at opposite corners of the world. Sometimes common marketing tools are devised, such as the 'Grand Tour' promoted by *Venice, Documenta* and *Sculpture Projects Münster* as well as *Art Fair Basel* (Tang, 2007). In Central Asia and the Middle East similar forms of collaboration are underway, overall promoting a "host of new regional imaginations" (Rogoff, 2009: 115). These sometimes explicitly aim at creating regional centres away from Western hegemony which, given the European lineage of the format if not of contemporary art altogether, remains a major point of contention.

The proliferation of biennales and their connection to the host cities is an indication that place continues to matter. It is a useful rejoinder to some assumptions of early globalisation theories, which still haunt the art world – the disappearance of place or place relevance, the interchangeability of locales and the assumption of standardisation as dominant if not sole effect. As is the case with festivals and events more generally, having 'been there' is part of belonging to an art world and playing its game: "being there – not only in Venice, Basle, and Madrid but now in São Paolo, Dakar and Shanghai – has become another way to confirm social distinction on the viewer (as only slight exposure to art-world chatter, so often fluttering about the latest exotic jamboree, will confirm)" (Stallabrass, 2004: 26-7). New biennales fulfil the role of providing new possibilities of acquiring such badges of distinction for artists, audiences and cities alike.

This is where the critical tide starts to turn: the growth has been so obvious and the format so hegemonic that even within the art world biennalisation is becoming a source of concern. The stakes are well summarised at the start of the *Biennial Reader*:

> For some skeptics the word biennial has come to signify nothing more than an overblown symptom of spectacular event culture ... For others, the biennial is a critical site of experimentation in exhibition-making (Filipovic et al. 2010: 13).

On the one hand, there are positive views which see in the very fact of the reproduction of biennales a liberating process that displaces the long established cultural hegemony of the centre. Exemplary of this position is Arthur Danto's famous hyperbole on the Biennale as "a glimpse of a transnational utopia" (quoted in Tang 2011: 79). Viewed from the other extreme, biennales have become sites of an empty festivalism driven by entertainment and spectacularisation (Schjeldalh 1999). Diametrically opposed, the critical view sees biennials as an instance of cultural imperialism, dominated by mobile elites operating from a few, largely unchanged, locales.

Even those at the core of the art world struggle to interpret its biennalisation:

> Many of these events are simply not designed to be seen in their totality... Without a frame of reference to validate it, the kind of specific operation carried out by these shows in the field of art and culture, is barely, if at all, perceptible through the opinions of a host of commentators' (Basualdo 2003: 126).

From an external point of view, the unsolvable dichotomies of that debate can become critical measures to understand how concerns around issues of hierarchy and (cultural) capital are entangled within the production of novel forms of art, their attending discourses and aesthetic dispositions. From this angle, biennials provide a privileged viewpoint on the struggles and growing pains of new rationales providing acceptable and shared meaning for the contemporary art world. They are illustrations of the cultural logics of globalisation beyond the blueprint of national cultures and their strategies of representation.

## Art festivals and the expediency of culture

To interpret the growing and protean phenomenon of biennials, typologies may be useful and some have been outlined, classifying biennials on the basis of their curatorial approach, type of organisation, or contextual significance. Most take the heterogeneity of biennials for granted but see homogenisation as a risk of their overall trend from its Western origin as a "capitalist-philantropic entreprise", through to post-Second World War 'bloc-politic' intervention, to "flexible production- and event-oriented variety of the 1990s and 2000s" (Bydler, 2004: 388). More or less implicitly these typologies include a periodisation which describes a rather linear 'rise and fall' narrative for biennials, where the biennial is eventually destroyed under its own gigantism, having lost its original function and become prey of neoliberal capitalism and its imperative of instrumentalisation of culture. Finding a "synecdoche between the globalization of the marketplace and the biennalization of the art world" (Papastergiadis and Martin, 2011: 49), this is then taken as a thorough explanation of the biennial phenomenon. Biennalisation becomes an expression of what has been termed the "expediency of culture paradigm" (Yudice, 2003): what once had artistic and political finalities is, under globalisation and after the end of the Cold War, reduced to an encompassing economic rationality. It is in particular with regards to biennials' content and context – the art they display and the cities that host them – that the effects of its biennalisation within the expediency of culture can be usefully discussed in a little more detail, problematising such linear narratives.

Biennalisation is perceived to be such a dominant process that it comes to overshadow the art which it is supposed to showcase, sometimes now dubbed 'biennial art'. It is not just that being exhibited in one or more biennales adds provenance and thus value to contemporary art, fulfilling a function museums and art history fulfilled in earlier periods. More substantially the spread of biennials generates art suitable to its format and logic creating, as by-product if not intentionally, ad-hoc art, which by the same token is dismissed as more uniform, less challenging art (Stallabrass, 2004: Ch. 2 and 4). Perhaps not surprisingly, this is framed as corrupting and degenerative within the art world. For a sociology of art this is instead a constitutive process of a world or field based on shared conventions and rules. Yet, the contradiction between a contemporary art system based on a rationale of originality and singularity and material conditions promoting standardisation, already observed by Heinich (2005), assumes here another incarnation. The expression *biennial art* emerged in the late 1990s with the mushrooming of biennales as a derogatory term, as art of "bombastic proportions and hollow premises" (Filipovic 2005: 326). The expression itself suggests its dismissive judgement, as art that can be easily framed and classified, notably as "tokenistic representations of cultural diversity" (Verwoert 2010: 187). One point these critiques omit, however, is that all art, considered from the point of view of its institutional settings, is prey to these constraints, and biennial art may not ultimately be more unequivocally affected by this than church art or gallery art. What is true for biennials was, and is, true also for museums, galleries and so on: they are under pressure to conform to accepted aesthetic standards (Becker 1982). Understanding these constraints may help recognising biennial art as a phenomenon without the attending negative connotation as ways to work within and make sense of the constraints are outlined but not deterministically foreclosed by this institutional analysis. This should first of all open up new ways of looking at biennials and biennial art, rather than provide another totalising interpretation: looked in any detail, the art found in biennials is hardly easily understood as conveying a single message speaking within a single domain.

*Biennial cities* raise similar issues, whilst more clearly pointing to the macro or structural factors within which biennalisation occurs, foregrounding the expediency debate. Biennials are almost always named after the host city, for which such an event is often a recognised key step in what has been called a *worlding* process, as a "practice of centering, of generating and harnessing global regimes of value" (Roy and Ong 2011: 312). No matter how far from the Western progenitor, the urban nature of biennials connects them even more clearly with the artistic temporality of the current global avant-garde, excluding genres and artists belonging to local artistic fields less connected to this world-wide professional sphere. Like other mega-events and festivals, biennials now form part of strategies of place promotion, and as such the paradox of producing standardisation whilst promoting specificity has long been observed. The biennials' diffusion in the 1990s has coincided, more or less, with a shift from national to city promotion in cultural policies more generally, as part of a shift to entrepreneurialism in urban governance.

One issue here is that these concerns seem to be pitched against a nostalgic vision of traditional festivals premised on purer, more authentic rationales. What this degeneration tale tends to omit is that biennials always were about what today in cultural policy circles is called "culture-led regeneration". Take *Venice*, the revered progenitor. The *Biennale* was from the very beginning also an operation to rescue a dying star in the European cultural firmament. The founders did declare they meant to pursue art as a way to promote "fraternal association of all peoples" (Cit. in Vogel 2010: 14), however *Biennale's* historians from very early on saw that it was also geared towards tourism and prestige (Alloway 1968). This came to the fore when the Cinema section of the *Biennale* was established in the 1930s to prolong and salvage the seaside holiday season of the Venice Lido. True, in recently established *Biennales* the rhetoric is more explicit and specific, such as is the case for instance of *Liverpool Biennial*, created in 1998 invoking regeneration as its legitimising rationale (Papastergiadis and Martin, 2011: 45-6). Expediency however, economic *and* political, was never absent. Intrinsic, or cultural rationales always had to share ground with more instrumental or extrinsic ones, in never-settled equilibriums. In this too, new biennals follow and specify the original model, rather than simply transform or distort it – and in that they open much more interesting windows on contemporary culture.

## Bibliography


Alloway, L. (1969) *The Venice Biennale: 1895-1968, From Salon to Goldfish Bowl*, Greenwich: New York Graphic Society.

Altshuler, B. J. (2013) *Biennials and Beyond. Exhibitions That Made Art History: 1962-2002*, London: Phaidon.

Basualdo, C. (2010 [2003]) The unstable institution, reprinted in E. Filipovic, M. Van Hal and S. Ovstebo (eds.), *The Biennial Reader*, Bergen: Bergen Kunsthall, 124 - 135.

Bauer, U. M., and Hanru, H. (eds.) (2013) *Shifting Gravity (World Biennial Fofum N. 1)*, Ostfildern: Hatje Cantz.

Becker, H. S. (1982) *Art Worlds*. Berkeley: University of California.

Block, R. (2013) We hop on, we hop off: The ever-faster spinning carousel of biennials, in Bauer and Hanru (eds.), *Shifting Gravity (World Biennial Fofum N. 1)*, Ostfildern: Hatje Cantz, 104 – 109.

Buchholz, L. and Wuggenig, U. (2005) Cultural globalisation between myth and reality: The case of the contemporary visual arts, *ART-E-FACT*, issue no.4, available artefact.mi2.hr/_a04/lang_en/theory_buchholz_en.htm (last accessed July 2014).

Bydler, C. (2010 [2004]) The global art world, inc. on the globalisation of contemporary art, abridged and reprinted in E. Filipovic, M. Van Hal and S. Ovstebo (eds.), *The Biennial Reader*, Bergen: Bergen Kunsthall, 378 - 405.

De Duve, T. (2009) The glocal and the singuversal, in *Open*, issue *The Art Biennial as a Global Phenomenon*, **16**, 44 - 53.

Di Martino, E. (2013) *Storia della Biennale di Venezia 1895- 2013*, Enna: Papiro Arte.

Esche, C. (2011) Making art global, in R. Weiss (ed.) *Making Art Global (Part 1): The Third Havana Biennial 1989*, London: Afterall Books.

Ferguson, B. W., Greenberg, R., and Nairne, S. (2005) Mapping international exhibitions, in B Vanderlinden, and E. Filipovic, (eds.) *The Manifesta Decade: Essays on Changing Europe, Exhibitions, and Biennale Culture*. Cambridge: The MIT Press, 47 - 56.

Filipovic, E. (2010 [2005]) The global white cube, reprinted in E. Filipovic, M. Van Hal and S. Ovstebo (eds.), *The Biennial Reader*, Bergen: Bergen Kunsthall, 322 - 345.

Filipovic, E., Van Hal, M. and Ovstebo, S. (eds) (2010) *The Biennial Reader*, Bergen: Bergen Kunsthall.

Giorgi, L. and Sassatelli, M. (2011) Introduction, in L. Giorgi, M. Sassatelli and G. Delanty (eds) *Festivals and the Cultural Public Sphere*, London: Routledge, 1 -1 1.

Heinich, N. (2005) *L'Elite artiste. Excellence et singularité en regime démocratique*. Paris: Gallimard.

O'Neill, P. (2007), The curatorial turn: from practice to discourse, in J. Rugg, M. Sedgwick (eds.), *Issues in Curating Contemporary Art and Performance*, Bristol: Intellect Books.

Papastergiadis, N. and Martin, M. (2011) Art biennales and cities as platforms for global dialogue, in L. Giorgi, M. Sassatelli and G. Delanty (eds.) *Festivals and the Cultural Public Sphere*, London: Routledge, 45 - 62.

Roche, M. (2000) *Mega-Events and Modernity: Olympics and Expos in the Growth of Global Culture*, London: Routledge.

Rogoff, I. (2009) Geo-cultures circuits of arts and globalizations, *Open*, issue *The Art Biennial as a Global Phenomenon*, 16: 106 - 115.

Roy, A. and Ong, A. (eds.) (2011) *Worlding Cities: Asian Experiments and the Art of Being Global*, Chichester: Wiley-Blackwell.

Sassatelli, M. (2016) The biennalization of art worlds: The culture of cultural events, in L. Hanquinet and M. Savage (eds.) *Routledge Innternational Handbook of the Sociology of Art and Culture*, Abingdon: Routledge

Schjeldalh, P. (1999) Festivalism: Oceans of fun at the Venice Biennale, *The NewYorker*, July 5. 85 – 86.

Seijdel, J. (2009) Editorial, *Open*, issue *The Art Biennial as a Global Phenomenon*, **16,** 4 - 5.

Stallabrass, J. (2004) *Art Incorporated: The story of contemporary art*, Oxford: Oxford University Press

Tang, J. (2007) Of biennals and biennalists: Venice, Documenta, Munster, *Theory, Culture and Society*, **24**(7-8), 247 - 260.

Tang, J. (2011) Biennalization and its discontents, in B. Moeran and J.S. Pedersen (eds) *Negotiating Values in the Creative Industries. Fairs, Festivals and Competitive Events*, Cambridge: Cambridge University Press.

Verwoert, J. (2010) The curious case of biennial art, in E. Filipovic, M. Van Hal and S. Ovstebo (eds.), *The Biennial Reader*, Bergen: Bergen Kunsthall, 184-197.

Vincent, C. (2014) A non-linear history of Dak'Art, *C&.Platform for international art from African perspectives*, online (contemporaryand.com), special print edition Dak'Art 14, 4 - 5.

Vogel, S. (2010) *Biennials, Art on a Global Scale*, Vienna: Springer.

West, S. (1995) National desires and regional realities in the Venice Biennale, 1895-1914, *Art History*, **18**(3): 404 - 434.

Yudice, G. (2003) *The Expediency of Culture: Uses of Culture in the Global Era*, Durham: Duke University Press.

## Notes

1 This chapter is an abridged and edited version of Sassatelli (2016).

2 In this chapter I follow the common usage of interchangeably referring to biennial or *biennale* (from the original Italian) to indicate a type of event and institution; I use the term Biennale, with a capital B, as a short form for the Venice Biennale. Venice's lineage is not unchallenged (see Niemojewski 2010); however even alternative histories tend to fuel a discursive context in which Venice continues to wield the strongest gravitational pull and remains the origin myth, to emulate or criticise, for perennial festival-exhibitions more broadly.

3 www.biennialfoundation.org, last accessed July 2014, my calculation based on their A-Z list. Another authoritative source, the voluminous recent reader of *Biennial Studies* advances a vaguer estimate: "Over the years, the term has been used to refer to a vast landscape of different exhibition projects, with no source agreeing on their total number (currently thought to be somewhere between one hundred and two hundred around the world)" (Filipovic et al. 2010: 13).

# 5 Animating Places: A new festival phenomenon?

Maurice Maguire

## Introduction

From lighting town centres to ephemeral one-off events, from nights of cultural activity to small festivals, from year-long programmes to biennials and triennials, artists are engaging in a wide variety of activities that support the idea of place-making. Emerging from the practices of interventionist art, community engagement and installation, through the processes and debates of public artists we are now experiencing new models of artistic intervention in the public realm. They are, quite literally, animating places.

Alongside larger profile-building activities such as the *European Cities/Capitals of Culture*, the past 20 years has seen a significant growth in place-based festivals and events, one-off large scale events and city-specific commissions that aim, in one way or another, to animate public spaces and strive towards the idea of place-making.

Artists are leading on initialising street festivals; intervening with politically motivated 'guerrilla' tactics to enliven places, in opposition to stasis in public engagement, and in promoting and building festival activities – some overt others more covert. For some the focus is on social and cultural change, for others the intentions are more community orientated and celebratory. All contribute to a sense of place and engagement.

This chapter considers the emergent patterns of major events and festivals alongside the need to market places in competition with each other; the phenomena of culturally-focused and culturally-led events that bring places alive; the issues affecting both the artists as producers and the commissioning bodies; and the impacts and engagement of audiences. Within this exploration this chapter will address the question of whether there are principles that can be applied to the area of animation. Building on the idea that the relationship between people and place is given particular poignancy through festival and cultural engagements, a triad of place, people and purpose is emerging as a prism through which to see artists engaging in public spaces and, by doing so, contributing to place-making. The chapter will explore specific models of working that embrace three core ideas over and above this triad – the notion of making places, questions of identity, and ownership and celebration.

## *Wirksworth Festival*

The first two weekends of September in the English county of Derbyshire offer the intrepid and the curious some interesting adventures. As a visitor you can step into the homes of arts supporters, architect-designed living spaces and gardens and revel in community halls and churches to see the work of invited or commissioned visual artists and craft makers. As a result of which you engage in the shaping of place identity through the arts festival in the town of Wirksworth.

This rambling town with its steep vennels and alleyways, hidden nooks and crannies is host to the annual *Wirksworth Festival* which has, for some 20 years, promoted its artists and their work. A centrepiece 'art and architecture trail' fills the first weekend of the festival. Works of art can be seen in convivial domestic settings or in the bustling hall of crafts market, or alongside the significant architecture of the town's central church, St Marys. Here, the annual celebration known as Church Clypping, the historic root of the annual festival, creates a ring of humanity around the perimeter of the church to celebrate its existence.

Since 2008 the festival organisers have commissioned works in open competitions inviting artists to reveal and respond to the palimpsest of historical, social and cultural significance of the area, engaging local interests as well as those of the visitor in understanding more of this place, its heritages, its people (present and past) and its futures – all within a programme that takes as its centrepiece the architecture and surrounding landscape as starting points. While the two-week festival may be seen as simply offering a traditional fare of concerts, events and public engagements, the commissioned works, public performances and community events have taken a more purposeful stance by seeking to make more sense of this place. It is a town animated by its art and fortunate to be managed with and by local artists. Place here is defined by the historic town; memorised, replayed and re-envisioned, and the modern town; active and in the present day.

This was already fertile ground in 2009-11 when the ***re:place*** programme of site-specific contemporary art in Derbyshire was enacted. David Gilbert, the first art programmer for the festival and freelance curator based in the area, delivered the countywide ***re:place*** programme. The introduction to the programme notes:

> The title of the ***re:place*** project is deliberately ambiguous; on the one hand it is an art project about *place* – responses to places in Derbyshire, or the place that Derbyshire is – and on the other it is about *re:placing* the simplistic and selective perception of Derbyshire as a bucolic wilderness, a romantic landscape, and responding to the complexity, creativity and richness of the place (Gilbert, 2009).

Responding to this call, *Wirksworth* hosted two major commissions in the 2010 festival with works by Alec Finlay, a 'word-map' using sound, renga poetry and print available in-situ and on the web, 'White Peak; Dark Peak'; and Kate Genever, creating a multi-media archive of site-responsive work based on materials collected from a farm on the National Trust Longshaw Estate. These were shown alongside works by the region's recent fine and decorative arts graduates in the festival.

In the *Wirksworth Festival,* then, the initiative to welcome in people – both artists and audiences – for contemporary art is in parallel with the festival activities that allow for all the arts to be seen and engaged with. Wirksworth as a *genius loci* is an important dimension to the setting for works, and becomes part of the rationale to see these places anew, or at least to refresh our own ideas of what they are and mean.

Can the art produced and the process of production be seen as a catalytic force in place-making – shaping identity anew? The range of works in the festival offers audiences and residents opportunities to engage in the civic cultural life of the town and its environs celebrating the distinctiveness of place, in a geographic sense, how they are shaped through human interventions, and engaging in a new understanding of what it means to belong, as well as challenging our understanding of place and our place there.

## Place

Place itself is a much contested term, arriving on the landscape of cultural thinking in response to urban design processes and changes championed by Jane Jacobs in New York in the late 1960s and 1970s. It arrives in the vocabulary of artists at around the same time, but more specifically in relation to site rather than to place. Place emerges later as providing a rationale for the art that begins to appear in the public realm.

Humanistic geographers in the 1970s emphasised the concepts of space and place. Place is best understood as a locus of meaning. Tuan suggests in his introduction that in lived experience "the meaning of space often merges with that of place" (1977: 4). Conceptually we need to distinguish between the two, however:

> The ideas 'space' and 'place' require each other for definition. From the security and stability of place we are aware of the openness, freedom and threat of space, and vice versa. Furthermore if we think of space as that which allows movement, then place is pause; each pause in movement makes it possible for location to be transformed into place (Tuan, 1977: 4).

He later notes "when space feels thoroughly familiar to us, it has become place" (73). This is an important foundation in the idea of place-making which in itself suggests process. But is it possible to make places? Cresswell identifies places as being always "in process" and "more often the product of everyday practices. Places are never finished but produced through the reiteration of practices – the repetition of seemingly mundane activities on a daily basis" (2004: 82).

The development of the space/place argument is emphasised by Kelley in his discussion on the nature of public art and the role or potential of the artist as "an artist of place" adopting perhaps unfamiliar guises to make spaces into places with cultural significance and meaning:

> The condition of a place is the condition of an art of place. A place is a particular condition. Siah Armajani sees a place as an extension of the activity it contains and which, in turn, defines it as a place. He sees sets of tools used to generate a set of conditions that constitute a place. Those conditions are transitive and relational. They involve a web of human activities that give meaning to the place, that animate the tools. This is a place's practical dimension. In it, we recognise the theatre of place passing through tools, locations and sites (1993: 4).

Places can be both permeable and bounded, and can change (Massey, 1994) echoing the challenges that have affected some of our understandings of place-specific art works that have developed over the past 40 years.

The *Wirksworth Festival* is achieving some of the ideas of place-making, by drawing from the historic, cultural and social significance of sites, and from known qualities (and quantities) of place and using these through programming and the deliberate commissions to encourage new ways of seeing, celebrating and revitalising them. They are working within a cultural framework that encourages artists to interpret, examine and respond to place, and at the same time engage disparate audiences too, in those same places – perhaps with new meaning and understanding. The place is revitalised, animated by the art, and the purpose of the work is clearly focused on celebrating, exposing, exploring and exploiting place, with people. The cultural aspect of festivals begins to give meaning to the idea of place and our place within that.

## Animation

The question of revitalisation is central to the notion of place animation, providing a coming together of a number of core values and aims: to enliven; to change perceptions; to make greater than its parts; to completely alter our viewpoint and understanding; to give sites new meanings and thus enhance their attractiveness for local inhabitants and visitors; to give something life or *soul*.

The shaping of our cultural heritage is an ongoing business, we are today creating the heritage of tomorrow, and the important role of the artist in contribution to the meaning of places and shaping our cultural lives cannot be dismissed. From the heyday of student revolt in the 1960s the desire to engage with audiences outside the walls of academe and the cultural institutions of the post-war period was an emergent Western art ideal. Henry Moore saw the need to offer space to his work in the fields adjacent to his studio and successions of artists have changed their practices to engage not just with a new space and the notion of 'site-specific' art, but also to respond to and in some cases engage directly with audiences as both consumers and makers in streets and public spaces, or in the vastness of landscapes uninhabited. The way in was often through local festival activities, celebrations and events.

In the early years of the *Avignon Festival*, the fringe events that it spawned allowed for a new kind of engagement with audiences, and artists sought to animate these experiences – by literally animating the people with whom they wanted to work. When the theme 'New Forms of Cultural Action' was explored in 1973, it raised the question of the value of individual as against collective self-expression as a way of engaging ordinary lives in the cultural environment of its time, and to an extent the places where people live and work (Gaudibert, 1977).

Jean Hurstel amongst others was at the forefront of this pluralist movement of *culturele animateurs*, akin to the French and Italian socio-cultural animation movements of community activists and educators, but where the arts are a vehicle to express the needs, values, concerns, issues, desires of – and by – a community at a local level, thus being place specific. For the *Avignon Festival* experience it meant that the *Fringe* became a showcase for new ways of seeing people's engagement with their own cultures – a new democratisation of the arts was afoot and socio-cultural animation took hold, at least as an idea in the European region.

While the term *animateur* was applied in the UK experience, it tended to relate to the work of dance practitioners in the 1980s. The notion of animation and, in particular, place animation was only maintained in a small selection of what became know as the community arts movement. Earlier town and area based community arts projects, such as Telford Community Arts and the mainly Scottish New Towns Commission 'Town Artist' schemes, promoted place-specific work with an emphasis on the nature of place itself. These schemes also sought to engage the new and older inhabitants of these 'new towns' in building a shared sense of place. Glenrothes in Fife, a new town created in the late 1940s to house miners, was one of the first Scottish towns to experience street theatre in the 1970s (Harding, 2005).

The significance of place-making is a more recent phenomenon, emphasised in the development of public art commissioning as artists move away from the ideas associated with art in public spaces, and site-specific commissions and more towards the particular issues of people and place and how to combine these – not always a simple task, and sometimes controversial and contentious.

## Models of thinking

What is significant in the 1990s is the rise of the cultural planning approach with its realisation that the resources of a place may be used in the pursuit of an ideal – in strategic policy thinking about and for the place and its inhabitants or users/visitors. Bianchini and Parkinson (1993) describe the use of cultural resources as a tool in the regeneration agendas of urban conurbations from the late 1980s to the present day – addressing and reshaping the urban experience/landscape through creative processes so that all citizens may engage more fully in civic and cultural life, bringing together the industrial, social, cultural, civic, heritage and leisure interests of all to find creative solutions to city living.

The holistic view of cultural planning is not dissimilar to the 'synoptic' (Aristotelian) overview suggested in the early part of the 20th century by Sir Patrick Geddes in his analysis of the needs of communities in relation to the Old Town of Edinburgh and in the ways that his camera obscura and Outlook Tower takes one on a journey from overview of community as local/place to community in global/place (Geddes in Welter, 2001).

Geddes is noted for his vision and ocular viewpoint, and his ability to shape his understanding of the world we inhabit through his word-based 'thinking machines' – seeing the whole together as one evolving form. His initially rudimentary mappings of linked ideas form the basis of his most famous triad, a reworking of the ecological planning triad that French sociologist le Play, used as a framework to identify, establish and survey a region. For Geddes, the framework Folk-Work-Place forms a stimulating starting point to consider the type of social and cultural structures we may strive towards and, in turn, how these shape societies, civic and private. The triad works on the basis of the interrelationships between the three factors in each part of the triad thus: place-Work, place-Folk, work-Place, work-Folk, folk-Place, and folk-Work – on his 'chord of simple, practical life', forming one part of the more complex three dimensional map of city evolution and change in the diagram 'Notation of Life' (Figure 5.1).

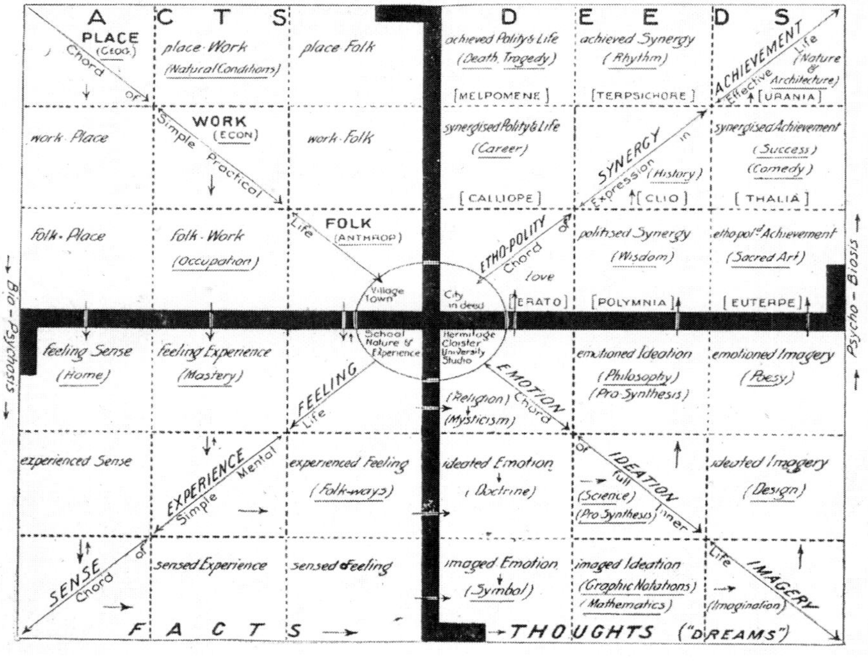


**Figure 5.1:** Geddes, P. (1927) Notation of Life, in Geddes *Cities in Evolution* (1949).

In a post-industrial world where places distinguish themselves by expressions of economic power, Geddessian thinking may seem alien, however it is worth considering the triad as a critical tool in place-making and place animation. The significance of place, place marketing, and place distinction in the globally competitive world of large cities is a major contribution to the growth of the event and the idea of the eventful city (Richards and Palmer, 2010). This is largely driven by a need to secure economic power, selling and marketing the city through its events and openness to festival activities ranging from the short specific arts event to the global and mega Olympian-scale sporting and cultural festivals.

What then of the people who are a part of a place? The scale of large cities precludes wholehearted engagement, however if the intention is firstly to animate the city, and to engage people in that process then the content must be meaningful to them, as well as to potential visitors. There are of course dangers that the arts event or festival is only established to act as a magnet, to entice in the curious who are then prey to other more 'mammon-led' activities. Artists of all disciplines then might consider if there is a role for an animation process that has a pre-determined outcome. Is a process that engages people to shape and engage with the content, and the place and perhaps encourages a critical reading of place with an intent to change perceptions, hearts and minds compatible with economically driven regeneration?

Taking the basic triad from Geddes this chapter proposes a working model using the title of 'place animation' that reshapes his original working model of the triad to People-Place-Purpose. A three legged stool with a seat of art at the core. Place animation establishes a convivial relationship between these three as symbiotic partners. The triad acts as a prism through which we may examine contemporary practices as well as engage in retrospective analysis. It is not, however, as Geddes would also note, a blueprint nor a formula; it is a lens, something to look through and explore the given situation. The contention is that artists and commissioners are, by virtue of their engagements, enacting place-animation in intent, if not in name.

In *Wirksworth* the works commissioned in 2011 used the title 'Situation Critical' as a starting point for artists to respond to as the basis for suggesting interventions in and for this place.

> We are interested in work that critically interrogates the situation that is Wirksworth: 'situation', a set of conditions in time and place – a convergence of site, non-site, place, non-place, locality, public space, context and time (Gilbert, 2011).

So this process of animation is not simply about the visitor experience, spectators following the Art and Architecture Trail. Animation draws from the fabric, the people and situations that they make, over time, sometimes mischievously, allowing for a more critically aware understanding of places and the factors that have shaped and continue to shape them.

Geddes notes; "We need to give everyone the outlook of the artist who begins with the art of seeing" (1949: 227). As with his holistic approach to planning, and the 'outlook' towers he recommended for all towns, we may see the evolution of places through a general survey, a seeing together of the whole may be a useful framework for place animation too.

## Animation in practice

There are many recent examples of place-making and shaping that have placed artists at the centre of processes of change – of image, perception and understanding. Some, such as the *Lumiere* project developed for Durham (City and County) by the producers Artichoke have literally transformed the way that this city is seen and enjoyed by visitors and residents. *Lumiere* has illuminated the city during three biennial events since November 2009. Building on existing interest in the city's projection of itself, the festival is commissioning new works within communities of the city, with international and local artists opening up the event to a growing audience and a growing number of active participants – as artists, volunteers, collaborators and guests. It is a transformative experience. Artichoke, on its website notes simply, "Artichoke is a creative company that works with artists to invade our public spaces and put on extraordinary and ambitious events that live in the memory forever." (Artichoke, 2015) *Lumiere* transforms place and people's perception of this city, not just as spectacle, but as an entity.

## *Setouchi Trienniale*

The final example to explore is that of the *Setouchi Trienniale* in Japan, a festival that has evolved over some 30 years, but which started out as a place-making programme to transform the destiny of the small islands of the Inland Setouchi Sea. In the period since 1995 a significant body of artists' work has accumulated, populated, changed and, as a result, animated these otherwise dying islands in Japan.

Described as an 'art destination' (Dempsey, 2006), the Benesse House is now the centerpiece of a host of commissioned and purchased artworks and architecture that has helped to transform the islands here, and the works continue to reshape not only the landscape but the perceptions of this place. The projects have assisted in building roles for the local communities in helping to shape change for themselves and their communities. Residents act as guides, hosts, cultural ambassadors and collaborators. 2014 saw the second triennial arts festival on twelve of the islands making up this unique situation. The project had humble but adventurous beginnings. Founded in 1986 by the publisher Tetsuhiko Fukutake (originally Fukutake and now Benesse Publishing), in association with the mayor of Naoshima island, its original intent was to establish a camp for children and a place of cultural education in a pristine setting on the island.

Building upon an already existing collection of art works purchased by the company, they opened Benesse House, a museum/hotel complex that displays a unique collection of contemporary art housed in contemporary architecture by Tadao Ando. Benesse, the company name, is taken from the Latin *bene esse* meaning 'to live well' and as part of its ethos it sees the need for responsible use of income alongside the needs of community and site. Visitors are encouraged to reflect on the meaning of 'well-being' while on the islands. Since its opening in 1992 a number of site-specific works in and around the house have been commissioned and more of the island's resources, including working with local residents, have been developed to support the enhancement of other places in the Art House Project that takes formerly abandoned houses and transforms them into works of art (Richard, 2010).

The project is now in the hands of the founder's son, the billionaire businessman Soichiro Fukutake. He explained in an interview in the *Financial Times*, "I want to revitalise each region with the good use of contemporary art, and I want this art activity to last forever. It's a message of how the world should be after capitalism" (Ellwood, 2010).

The history of the islands was an important factor – depopulation due to limited employment potential, a set of unfavourable environmental situations leaving a number of the islands polluted and with useless or redundant industrial infrastructures, all meant that the region of the Setouchi Sea needed to have some investment, but not just in the form of site specific art works – it is also about employment, local community cultural habits, the employment on cultural crafts local to the region and to an extent an animation process that has a strong philosophical, moral and cultural basis as well as an economic one.

In 2004 the company established the Naoshima Fukutake Art Museum Foundation coinciding with the opening of the Chichu Museum, once again using the skills of Ando in its unique architecture that incorporates commissioned works by James Turrell and Walter De Maria, as well as housing five of Claude Monet's Water Lilies paintings. By 2010 the activities of the foundation have increased to instigate the first of the *Setouchi International Art Festivals*, the second was in 2013. The first was staged over seven islands and the Takamatsu Port Area in the Seto Inland Sea. The foundation also opened four art installations: the Lee Ufan Museum on Naoshima, the Teshima Museum and Les Archives de Coeur on Teshima, and Inujima Art House Project on Inujima (Benesse, 2010).

The company has established a foundation for the promotion of regional culture, which in 2010 supported 35 groups to use contemporary art to build communities through creative and cultural activities. A third foundation aims "to help create communities where children and the elderly can live vibrant lives from both educational and cultural perspectives by supporting them in learning, living, creating and communicating" (Benesse, 2010). In 2010 this contributed to the localised activities in the Okayama Prefecture as the contact point for the *Setouchi International Art Festival*.

This in itself is a remarkable record of engagement. Taken alongside the cultural and employment activities across the islands, the intention has been to build communities, encourage cultural engagement and to develop or re-develop a stronger economic but clear cultural base to the islands and their inhabitants. Do the figures and outcomes stack up? In 2013 the number of islands included in the now named *Setouchi Triennale Festival* has increased from 7 to 12 plus the ports of Takamatsu and Uno. The number of artworks and commissioned works has increased from 75 to 200 including works now permanently sited, and visitor numbers have increased from 0.94 million to 1.07 million. So this is a project of some scale. It has increased in its overall impact with each exhibition, grown in influence in terms of its capacity to engage its resident Japanese community to volunteer, act as guides, open up their own houses, and to share the experiences of what appears to many on the Tokyo mainland to be a very different lifestyle, a haven of tranquillity that is unique to this place, and now no longer endangered.

In 2013 the festival extended over 108 days, and it offered a new experience to many who would not consider themselves to be lovers of contemporary art. As Cathy Hirano notes in her blog entry on the Triennale:

> A substantial number of local volunteer organizations and companies became enthusiastically involved. The artists also found many ways to involve the local people. The artists' interpretations of island life, history and nature helped residents see their islands anew, while interaction with many appreciative visitors gave them a glimpse of their area's potential and hope for the future (2014).

In this case, the substantive investment in securing new uses for redundant buildings and sites of industry, taken together with the commissioning of unique artworks and architecture to house these, and the encouragement and direct engagement with the communities on the (increasing) number of islands suggests that this place animation work is building a new vision for the Inland Sea, and the Okayama Prefecture. At the same time it is offering to each visitor a unique experience that allows for an intimate engagement with place, and the art that this place holds or encourages in its small inhabited spaces and larger uninhabited places.

## Conclusions

Place is a difficult and complex and multi-faceted concept that brings together understandings of the physical world, meaning production, processes and practices of power that mark relations between groups. It is central to the way we understand our position in society and is a central concept for enquiry and understanding humanity.

Geddes integrated an art school into the immediate vicinity of the Outlook Tower as part of his vision of the new Edinburgh which looked for new ways of seeing. His approach was rooted in community as collaborators not subjects and, thus, the conjunction of Place-People-Purpose as a starting point to examine place-animation as process offers a prism for enquiry.

Artists, with collaborators or alone, offer insights through cultural interventions in and of place. They broaden our engagement with and understanding of places, (re)shaping and revitalising our sense of belonging and being. We engage in festival activity on a one-to-one basis and, thus, the intimate moments of calm found in Japan will be echoed in similar experiences in Durham or Wirksworth.

The *process* of place, alongside the process of animation, suggests the core purpose of place animation is change, both in short-term impacts and in longer-term outcomes and that participation is an integral aspect. The outcomes and changes may be perceptional, emotional, cultural or physical, but all add to our understanding of place and our place there. Other outcomes may be shaped by political or power relations and relate in more pragmatic terms to economic, social and cultural demands and expectations, however, these are secondary to the process of experiencing place and learning through the animation work.

Small and large scale festivals offer valuable vehicles to consider and understand place both at the intimate levels suggested, but also as entities changing over time. Festivals act as an umbrella for exploration, celebration, investigation and display, and as a means of showing the process of animation and place together. Festivals are a platform for new ways of seeing, surveying and observing, and in setting and testing different ways of working. Crucially place specificity needs to be considered and revealed carefully, otherwise we slip into place simply as event experience and market.

## Bibliography

Art Setouchi (2015) http://setouchi-artfest.jp/en/about, accessed on 1/7/15.

Artichoke (2015) Home page, http://www.artichoke.uk.com/, accessed 10/12/2015

Benesse Holdings, Inc (2010) http://www.benesse-hd.co.jp/en/csr/feature/2010_3/foundation.html (accessed on 1/7/15).

Bianchini, F. and Parkinson, M. (1993) *Cultural Policy and Urban Regeneration*, Manchester: Manchester University Press.

Cresswell, T. (2004) *Place a Short Introduction*, Oxford: Blackwell.

Dean, T., and Millar, J. (2005) *Place*, London: Thames and Hudson.

Dempsey, A. (2006) *Destination Art*, London: Thames and Hudson.

Doherty, C. (2009) *Situation*, London: Whitechapel Gallery

Ellwood, M. (2010) The Art of Splendid Isolation, in *Financial Times* 08/042010 http://howtospendit.ft.com/art/1498-the-art-of-splendid-isolation, accessed 16/07/2015.

Gaudibert, P. (2002) Cultural action – integration and/or subversion, in J. Aherne, *French Cultural Policy Debates: A reader,* London: Routledge.

Geddes, P. (1949) *Cities in Evolution,* London: Williams and Northgate.

Gilbert, D. (2009) Re:place, http://re-place.co.uk, accessed on 30/6/2015.

Gilbert, D. (2011) *Wirksworth Festival – Situation Critical: A call for proposals for our curated* programme *and film and video salon,* Wirksworth: Wirksworth Festival.

Harding, D (2005) *Memories and Vagaries,* from website www.davidharding.net/article05/index.php (accessed on 1/7/2015).

Hirano, C. (2014) Setouchi Triennale Recap, http://www.art-takamatsu.com/blog/2013/12/setouchi-triennale-recap.html, accessed on 14/7/15.

Kelley, J. (1993) *Public Art - The New Agenda,* Keynote Address,University of Westminster, London

Massey, D. (1994) *Space, Place and Gender,* Cambridge: Polity Press.

Richard, S. (2010). *Arcadia in Japan,* Apollo, 172, 63-67. Retrieved from http://search.proquest.com/docview/894255622?accountid=10472.

Richards, G. and Palmer, R. (2010) *Eventful Cities: Cultural Management and Urban Revitalisation,* Oxford: Butterworth-Heinemann.

REVIEW: The island of inspiration. (2010). *Creative Review,* 52. Retrieved from http://search.proquest.com/docview/761280591?accountid=10472, accessed on 30/6/2015.

Smith, M. K. (1999, 2009) Animateurs, animation and fostering learning and change, in *The encylopaedia of informal education.* [www.infed.org/mobi/animateurs-animation-learning-andchange], accessed on 30/6/2015.

Tuan, Y, (1977) *Space and Place, the Perspective of Experience,* London: Arnold.

Welter, V. M. (2001) *Post–war CIAM, Team X, and the Influence of Patrick Geddes – Five Annotations,* http://www.team10online.org/research/papers/delft1/welter.pdf, accessed on 14/7/2015.

# 6 Republic of the Imagination: *Burning Man* and the culture of radical self-expression

Rachel Bowditch

*Burning Man*, it could be argued, is the best party on the planet and one of the most elaborate and complexly engineered. Where else could you have a dance party on a large duck where everyone is dressed as their fantasy avatars; or sit on an art car called 'The Bleachers' designed like stadium seating to watch and be watched, complete with referees in the standard black and white attire directing playa traffic; or mount a double-decker bus that resembles an underground rave in Eastern Europe; or dangle from cables as you smash your opponent to hard core punk rock at the *Thunderdome*; or find yourself at a large open-aired dance party with over 5000 people dancing to the world's most famous DJs and electronic music acts such as Bassnectar and Beats Antique? *Burning Man* has elevated the art of partying to epic proportions from mobile niche environments to large-scale international acts drawing crowds of thousands. At *Burning Man*, you can create your own experience and any desire you might have can be found and fulfilled on the playa. It is as if everyone's fantasy is being played out simultaneously and it is in the collision of these fantasies that meaningful encounters occur.

**Figure 6.1:** Aerial View of Black Rock City. 2012 (Photograph: Scott London)

However, to confine and reduce analysis of *Burning Man* to 'the world's best party' would be to overlook the intricate complexity and layers that constitute this epic annual desert event. The evolution and history of the event has been well documented from a variety of perspectives (See Doherty, Bowditch, Chen, Gilmore, and others) so I will not repeat those histories here. The first official book to chart the history of the event was Brian Doherty's *This is Burning Man: The Rise of a New American Underground* (2006) mapping the early formative years of the event from its inception in 1986 on Baker Beach in San Francisco, the impact of the Cacophony Society on the development of the *Burning Man* ethos, to the transfer of the event to the Black Rock Desert in Nevada in 1990.

Since 1986, *Burning Man* has evolved from founder Larry Harvey's personal healing ritual into a contemporary cultural phenomenon where ritual, religion, visual art, and performance collide on an epic scale. During the week before Labor Day (the first Monday in September), approximately 68,000 people gravitate towards the ancient lakebed of Lake Lahontan in the Black Rock Desert, Nevada to build 'Black Rock City.' Black Rock City is a temporary simulation of a real city – one on the cusp of perpetual disappearance – replete with street signs, roads, theme camps, villages, hundreds of huge interactive art installations, a temple, hundreds of 'art cars', a post office, an airport and hundreds of planned and spontaneous performances. A 40-foot wooden effigy of a man stands on an altar at the center of Black Rock City as the axis mundi of the *Burning Man* community, around which art, performance, and community revolve. The Man stands at the end of a monumental avenue lined with wooden spires, like a Neolithic temple complex, its linear streets evenly dividing the semicircular array of civic architecture, arranged from 2 o'clock to 10 o'clock around the figure, replicating the shape of an enormous clock face. The entire event culminates on Saturday night in the ritual burning of the 40-foot wooden effigy of a Man, followed on Sunday night by the burning of a wooden temple.[1]

Just as abruptly as it appears, with a lifespan of one very intense week, Black Rock City vanishes. An important coda to the festival is the total cleaning and restoration of the desert, erasing all evidence of the City's evanescent presence. Black Rock City remains only as a trace in photographs, videos, writings, oral histories and memories. During the months of Black Rock City's nonexistence, the *Burning Man* community continues to exist across the US and the world via an elaborate network called the '*Burning Man* Regional Network'. However, the event is becoming too popular, a syndrome that compromises the festival's very existence.

The transition from Baker Beach in San Francisco to the Black Rock Desert in Nevada signified a radical shift in the event from a casual gathering of friends on a beach to a 'zone trip,' a Cacophony term inspired by Andrei Tarkovsky's 1979 film *Stalker*.[2] *Zone trip #4* is where the relationship between Cacophony and *Burning Man* begins, forever changing the history of both. From the start, the concept of 'leave no trace' was one of the core principles. Cacophonists would go into a space and be very careful not to destroy anything, and that idea preceded the desert event. The Society always cleaned up after itself and that same philosophy was taken to the desert. In Cacophony tradition and style, as the Man went up in flames, the group was instructed to wear party finery.[3] As Louis Brill recalls, "women in elegant gowns, men in tuxedos, others in bizarre costumes. Drinks were hoisted, people were toasted; there was joy in the air" (2006). These participants brought with them the ethos of the San Francisco underground Bohemian culture that was to shape the culture of Black Rock City. From this first 'zone trip' to the desert, two important seeds were planted: invented ritual practices and Dadaesque performance. This fusion with Cacophony shaped the unique artistic and carnivalesque world informing the ethos and aesthetic of *Burning Man* culture over the next two decades.

## Immersive environmental theatre

From the very beginning, total immersion in the experience became a central tenet of *Burning Man*. In fact, a cardinal rule governing Black Rock City is the mandate to participate – bold letters on the admission ticket spell out, 'PARTICIPATE!' *Burning Man* is a temporary republic, where art and creativity govern the community. Black Rock City is an opportunity for artists and activists to create an ideal world, one where art and creativity hold central importance. It is the epic scale of the playa that makes movement across it inherently theatrical. *Burning Man* creates an environment in which participants have a stake in the event and are responsible for its existence. They are willing to dedicate time, energy and resources towards building a world in which each person has the responsibility of its creation. This investment in time and energy creates a fertile space for creativity and play – an environment where everyone is involved and each participant is a player.

Anyone who enters the 5-mile boundary of the City is in essence a performer, and any action, movement or gesture within this arena becomes a performance. As Stuart Mangrum stated in the *Burning Man Summer Newsletter* (1998):

> Unlike a rave or a concert, *Burning Man* is not a spectacle/commodity that can be experienced passively. That's the real meaning behind the 'No Spectators' tag: not to draw lines of exclusion, but to remind us of our mutual agreement to entertain each other. There is no official bandstand, just the vast empty stage of the desert, with no proscenium to separate the audience from the players. You are the show (Mangrum, 1998).

Travelling through Black Rock City, one notices the conspicuous absence of a 'main stage' – something that is the main focus of any other major festival. The only exception is on the night of the Burn and the Temple burn, when all attention focuses around the Man and the temple.

Blurring the distinction between art and everyday life is a basic tenet of *Burning Man* opening up possibilities for interaction, participation and transformation. Kaprow's definition of 'happenings' as "unrehearsed and performed by nonprofessionals, once only" (2003: 63) offers a way to understand the chance encounters of Black Rock City as a kind of happening. Many of the performances on the playa eliminate actors, plots and rehearsals, yet maintain a basic structure and score. Concepts and costumes are often constructed and planned in advance but the element of chance plays an enormous role in the actual performance. While many of the performances on the playa are not as structured or scored as the happenings of the 1960s, they evoke a similar quality of an encounter, with the juxtaposition of chance elements and the blurring of participant and spectator relationships. As in many of the performances at *Burning Man*, happenings involved nonprofessionals who performed functionary roles and carried out mundane tasks, leaving to the audience the job of putting together their own associations (Kirby 1994: 7).

While immersive theatre has become a recent theatrical trend as evidenced by groups such as Punch Drunk, Third Rail and Gale Gates among others, *Burning Man* takes immersive performance to a new level of 'total engagement.' All of the spaces within Black Rock City constitute a single, charged performance environment where 'anything' can happen. *Burning Man*, with its myriad installations and performances, camps and venues, creates what Kirby called a 'total' experience; no spectator-participant can see all of the performances at once (1965). Not only does *Burning Man* transform the desert into a city and a performance space, it is also constantly negotiating the harsh conditions of the desert from drastic temperature changes and strong winds to dust storms and heat waves affecting the citizens and performances within those boundaries. The layers of *Burning Man's* environmental theatrical landscape come alive, charged with possibility and potential by engaging in a complex system of transformation where entirely new relationships are possible. As the week in the desert progresses, citizens not only move through the bounded space but also wear the desert on their bodies, feel it on their skin. The thin, opaque white dust of the playa clings to every pore, every piece of clothing and every object, so that, by the end of the week, the participants, the desert and the environment have synthesized and merged into one.

While Black Rock City is full of performances of the everyday, planned and unplanned happenings and elaborate spectacles, it has also evolved into a society based on play. Like the formalized play of carnival, it is a break from everyday life, what Falassi calls 'time out of time' (1987: 11). Crossing the threshold into Black Rock City, the metaphoric line drawn in the sand, one enters a modern-day incarnation of Rabelais' world of sixteenth-century carnival as theorized by Bakhtin — a multidimensional world that temporarily transforms and inverts the normative social world, suspending business, commerce and motorized traffic, opening the streets to pedestrians (1984). It is a festive time during which Burners enter a temporary utopian realm of community, freedom, equality and abundance (ibid.: 11); for the duration of *Burning Man*, there is no other life outside it allowing participants to negotiate and redefine their freedoms and to act upon their wildest fantasies by reinventing themselves and designing new personas (ibid.: 255).

Black Rock City is an enormous playground – a hermetically sealed universe bound by rules determined in advance, rules that define a temporary world of play. *Burning Man* is a finite game with a definitive beginning, middle and end – with finite spatial and temporal boundaries – while *Burning Man* culture is an infinite game that is recreated each year, opening up possibilities of endless variations within the very finite world of Black Rock City. At this level, *Burning Man* is a paradox: an infinite game contained within a finite one; *Burning Man* happens inside Black Rock City and yet extends – conceptually and in terms of the play world created – beyond its limits. Once the rules and boundaries of Black Rock City are accepted, there is room for infinite artistic freedom and experiences; if these rules are transgressed, the whole play world collapses. As Johan Huizinga notes, "the play-community generally tends to become permanent, continuing even after the game is over" (1970: 12). Distinguishing between work and play helps to clarify why so many people spend their vacation days from 'real work' engaging in the 'play work' of building Black Rock City. As a volunteer, the 'work' is fulfilling and enjoyable because it is self-selected and intrinsically motivated, therefore fitting into the category of play (see Katherine Chen).

Caillois determined two principles of play: *paidia*, play that is free and spontaneous, the epitome of anti-structure manifesting a kind of uncontrolled fantasy; and *ludus*, play that is calculated, regulated, hierarchical, and rule-bound (1961: 28). Most of the playing experienced at *Burning Man* appears to be *paidia*. However, even a little digging reveals that a lot of what is going on is *ludus*. Behind every moment of seemingly free play is both a lot of planning by the players and close oversight by the organizers and the authorities. In *Man, Play, and Games* (1961), Caillois divides play into four types: *alea*, *mimicry*, *agon* and *ilinx*. *Alea* is Latin for the game of dice and covers all games of chance. The state lottery, Russian roulette, slot machines, and raffles all fall into this category. *Agon*istic games include all competitive sports and board games. *Ilinx*, associated with vertigo, applies to a wide range of activities from rollercoasters to illicit sexual relationships: anything that undulates and disorients (ibid.: 23–8). One can find all of these modes of play in Black Rock City but *alea* serves as *Burning Man's* connective tissue. Chance encounters and spontaneous activities make any journey through Black Rock City an unpredictable, exciting and surprising experience. Chance as a technique of artistic creation was used in the twentieth century by the Dadaists. And more than 80 years later, concepts of chance and indeterminacy are one of the chief governing forces of Black Rock City. Surrealists Tristan Tzara and André Breton would be in seventh heaven if they could wander through the City and see their ideas and theories so effectively realized.

## Personal transformations: Reimagining yourself

All of this playing often results in personal transformations. People come to the playa to play; they try out new selves by means of mimicry and other modes of play. Sometimes, these new selves and names stick. The playful world of Black Rock City provides an inviting place to be whoever you want to be. In a way, *Burning Man* realizes an ideal American freedom: self-invention. Burners enjoy their annual opportunity to recreate themselves, adopt new identities and take on 'playa names' which are either given or self-selected and which often stick upon re-entry into the 'default' world. A new identity usually requires a new look, a total costume that masks the old self of the default world. *Burning Man board* member Michael Mikel marvels at how the idea of costuming from the Cacophony Society was taken to extremes at *Burning Man*: *Burning Man* gives you the opportunity to 'recreate your identity.' While every imaginable costume can be found on the playa, the *Mad Max* aesthetic is pervasive—a dusty post-apocalyptic punk rock look mixed with sexy neo-burlesque and Steam Punk—leather, fur, goggles, knee-high boots, hot pants, and corsets.

While costuming is an important aspect of carnival, so are parades and processions, which thrive in Black Rock City. Every day, there is at least one parade, often more, hosted by the various theme camps from the Pink Parade (all participants in hot pink); the French Maid Brigade Parade; the Burning Marching Band; and the Orange Parade to name a few. Traditionally, Friday is the day for the annual Critical Tits Bike ride—a segregated gender-specific event that can have over a thousand participants biking topless through the streets. The parades of Black Rock City are open to anyone and for the most part are a source of laughter and merriment both for those participating and those spectating. The parades give the various camps a chance to display themselves to the rest of the community, participating in what Schechner would call 'direct theatre' (1993: 83).

## *Burning Man* is sold out

For the first time, *Burning Man* sold out in 2011, marking a significant transition in the history of the event—the demand far exceeds the supply. A contested 2014 article in the *New York Times* by Nick Bilton, 'A Line Is Drawn in the Desert: At Burning Man, the Tech Elite One-Up One Another,' focuses on how *Burning Man* has become an attraction for internet billionaires from Facebook founder Mark Zuckerberg, Amazon CEO Jeff Bezos, and Google mastermind Sergey Brin changing the face and nature of *Burning Man*; however as early as 1996, *Burning Man* has had an intimate relationship with the Silicon Valley innovators and multi-millionaires. Bruce Sterling's article featured in a 1996 issue of *Wired Magazine* entitled 'Greetings from *Burning Man!* The New American Holiday', drew even more attention from the budding tech industry. With the advent of the Internet, *Burning Man* started attracting participants worldwide. The Silicon Valley's dot-com millionaires had discovered *Burning Man*, and they poured money and resources into building elaborate theme camps and innovative art installations, often incorporating new technology such as lasers and Tesla coils, pushing the work to a new level of ambition and scale. In fact, this relationship has had a large impact on the shaping and evolution of the desert event.

What is a more recent phenomenon is mega-celebrities like P Diddy flying in for the day, making a splash and leaving, and the 'ready-made' millionaire camps. As one participant who camps with Silicon Valley entrepreneurs said, "We used to have RVs and precooked meals. [...] Now, we have the craziest chefs in the world and people who build yurts for us that have beds and air-conditioning in the middle of the desert!" (Bilton, 2014). While most theme camps have dues ranging from $50 to $600, his camp fees were $25,000 a person—collectively the entire camp costing over $2 million. While opulence has always been a characteristic of *Burning Man* from the first desert burn in 1990, where participants wore their finest ball gowns and tuxedos for the burn, in recent years, the level of flash has reached new heights. What has evolved is the complexity and scale of the villages and theme camps, increasing exponentially each year.

As Brian Doherty has noted, "Anyone who has been going to *Burning Man* for the last five years is now seeing things on a level of expense or flash that didn't exist before. [...] It does have this feeling that, 'Oh, look, the rich people have moved into my neighborhood.' It's gentrifying" (Bilton 2014). Some of these camps come with 'sherpas' or paid help to run and manage the camps, which is a significant departure from the 'radical self-reliance' tenet of *Burning Man's* ten organizing principles.

Long-time Burner Daniel Pinchbeck, author of *2012: The Return of Quetzalcoatl*, believes *Burning Man* represents:

> a new fusion of financial and corporate culture with the psychedelic counterculture. This is a new phenomenon – it means or how it will develop in the immediate future. [...] I think this helps put into context the ongoing invasion of the super wealthy into the scene: in actual fact, they have no place else to go. The mainstream paradigm is derelict, corrupt, and vacant. [...] However, the negative potential, the danger, is that the deeper liberational impulses of the counterculture are dropped in favor of a new form of hedonistic / narcissistic spectacle that suits the international jet set, with art cars replacing yachts and designer psychedelics replacing champagne and wine. (Pinchbeck, 2014)

A Burner, Chris Pruitt, who was the artistic coordinator at *Playa School*, an upscale camp that has been criticized for being a 'plug 'n' play' camp argues:

> People want to find ways to complain about it but I want to look at the positive. The artists are the ones benefiting from this. Someone wants an art car but doesn't have the technical skills. There are artists who have the

> skill set to build them. A rich patron will pay an artist to have their dream art car built. Both parties win. People are able to follow their passion. To me, it also creates a community of people over shared passions and new communities are coming out of it. What is wrong with that? (Pruitt, 2015)

This represents a shift from the patron/artist model transaction that typically occurs within a gallery context with the gallery getting 50% of the commission. Here, it takes out the middleman – the transaction is direct – from patron to artist. The artists win in the end.

As the ultra-wealthy are only a tiny minority within the population of Black Rock City placing the blame on them for this shift is perhaps unfair and overstated. As *Burning Man* photographer Scott London suggests:

> There is nothing inherently wrong with big crowds and increasing popularity. And fabulous events always attract rich people. What is at stake is the fragile nature of self-expression and spontaneous creativity. As *Burning Man* becomes bigger and more tightly managed each year, there is something stifling that happens to the creative impulse. There is also the problem of acculturating all these newbies – many of whom come to party and dance all night, not to engage in performance art or street theater (London).

What is a stake is the fragile eco-system of creativity and radical self-expression as these values get diluted from year to year with increased crowds of newcomers who do not understand the creative culture of *Burning Man*.

The tension between commodities, commerce and the 'gift economy' has always been present within the culture of *Burning Man*. Apart from the purchase of a ticket for $380, nothing is for sale on the playa except coffee and ice—representing a commerce-free environment. In 2005, Robert Kozinets, a professor at the Kellogg School of Management, and John F. Sherry, an anthropology professor in the Mendoza College, University of Notre Dame, decided to conduct a study on whether temporary communities such as *Burning Man* could exist outside the marketplace (Kozinets and Sherry 2005: 87). They thought *Burning Man* would be a perfect place to study life outside the market but when they first arrived in Black Rock city they observed:

> How amazingly ironic it was, then, to walk through *Burning Man* for the first time, to walk through the vast neon-tubed, electroluminescentwired, uber-strip mall of the place, the signs competing for attention, the touristic cameras, the elevated RVs on prime real estate, the lowly K-Mart tent shanty-towns. [. . .] We found a sign that mocked capitalism while also celebrating it—the familiar sign of the Hard Rock Café, that read, 'Welcome to the Black Rock Café.' [. . .] We had gone a long way to penetrate the anti-marketing zone, only to be once again confronted by popular brands and commodities for sale. (ibid.: 88)

**Figure 6.2:** The Man burning, 2006 (Photograph Scott London)

Kozinets and Sherry read *Burning Man* as a demonstration of the powerful lengths to which consumers feel they must go in order to decommodify products, services, even their own identities (ibid.: 101). Products are 'purified' through the acts of decommodification, which include customizing, masking or transforming brand names; burning branded objects and turning commoditized products into gifts (ibid.: 20). Still, brand names are ubiquitous. Upon entering Black Rock City, one sees a vista of Budget and U-Haul rental trucks, RVs and cars, creatively transformed to become a temporary shelter for a week, some disguised but many still boldly displaying the corporate logos. The irony behind covering a logo, on a Pepsi can for example, is that you are still drinking a Pepsi and you still bought the product at the supermarket before you entered the desert. As Kozinets and Sherry's research demonstrates, this anti-brand event also uses the language of brands to parody and invert images from the market. Kozinets and Sherry's guiding question—whether consumers can actually get outside the grips of the market—has led to the realization that one cannot. They found that *Burning Man* is a 'theatre of consumption' (Firat and Dholakia 1998: 13), a temporary enclave that represents a lively, expressive and creative model for consumption. Theatres of consumption, as theorized by Firat and Dholakia, emerge as alternative models of commerce within the dominant market economy. As Kozinets and Sherry point out, *Burning Man*, in its festive celebration of abundance and excess, holds much in common with the mood and tenor of ancient marketplaces (2005: 101). What they call 'indulgent consumption' is demonstrated by the amount each individual spends before arriving in Black Rock city. Their research indicates the average amount spent per person was between $500 and $750, with a considerable percentage spending thousands of dollars (ibid.: 99).

## Limits to Black Rock City

The future of *Burning Man* is intimately linked to the organization's with the Bureau of Land Management (BLM). It pays over $4 million dollars a year to host the event on public land constituting the largest event held on public land in the United States. The population jumped from 30,586 in 2003 to 69,613 in 2013 –an increase of 39,027 in ten years. For the first time the Bureau of Land Management issued a four-year Special Recreation Permit until 2016 capping the population at 70,000 participants as well as well as fine tuning "public access, traffic control, resource management, dust abatement, fire management, event security and public safety, event setup and signage, runway and aircraft, sanitary facilities, and event take down and clean-up" (Chase 2013).

In 2005, when I asked one of the six founding members Harley K. Dubois about the future of the event, she candidly replied: "Only a certain kind of person is going to come out here. It isn't growing that rapidly anymore, only a few thousand [more] each year. [...] The questions we continually ask ourselves are: How much space do we have? How many more people can you fit onto this playa? How can you get people into the city safely and how can you get them out? Those are the limiting factors" (2005). According to founding board member Crimson Rose, the government still remains the biggest threat because it has the power to shut down the event at any time. She jokes, "They wish we would go away but they like the money we bring in" (2008).

*Burning Man* founding board member Michael Mikel sees a significant transformation taking place:

> In a sense, *Burning Man* really grew up. Things are much different. We are a real operation and a real business that fits in the world. We are no longer the underground that we once were. Three years ago, *Burning Man* was listed in the travel guide that appears in every hotel room in Northern Nevada and Tahoe. And I thought, this is significant. We went from the bad rebellious group to a part of the tourist attraction for Nevada. *Burning Man* is starting to become a strong part of the economic culture. Now we are being courted by Nevada's tourist bureau as a main attraction. (2008)

*Burning Man* has refined and capitalized on terms such as 'transformational experience', 'participation', 'community' and 'radical self-expression' – that have market value in the 'experience economy'. Everyone wants to have a transformational experience, find community and feel included – and that is its strongest selling point. People will pay untold amounts of money to find those things and *Burning Man* fills that niche market – the product is affective and ephemeral rather than a tangible commodity. While the event began as counter-cultural and marginal, with its sky-rocketing mainstream popularity it has had to adapt and evolve to the pressures of supply and demand for this type of 'experience economy' (Gilmore and Pine 1999). *Burning Man* offers a commodified ritual experience in 'participatory culture', mutating and transforming from community to community, yet also remaining recognizable as *Burning Man*—a brand as distinct as any other.

*Burning Man* continues to grow and evolve organically and exponentially as a social phenomenon and cultural movement, having had a profound impact – sometimes positive, sometimes not – on hundreds of thousands of lives as many people are transformed and discover a community that exists beyond Black Rock City – both temporally and geographically. Their experiences are communicated through word of mouth, the most powerful form of viral marketing in existence. For Pinchbeck, *Burning Man* is not only an art movement but also a transformational and cultural shift towards a higher consciousness and a revitalized mode of being in the world (2014). The desert is where the seeds for redefining community are planted, taking root in the consciousness and behavior of those who have made the pilgrimage. Once people return to their home communities they manifest *Burning Man* ideals in their everyday lives, inspiring real life changes in themselves and in those they are in contact with. While *Burning Man* culture teeters on the edge between the counterculture and the mainstream, the vibrations from Black Rock City, while ephemeral, physically resonate throughout many levels of U.S. culture, both consciously and unconsciously, creating new paradigms of performance, installation art, community, and ritual – reawakening a revitalized spirit in the twenty-first century.

## Bibliography

Bakhtin, M. M. (1984) *Rabelais and His World*. Bloomington: Indiana University Press.

Bilton, N. (2014) A Line Is Drawn in the Desert: At Burning Man, the Tech Elite One-Up One Another, in *New York Times*, August 20. http://www.nytimes.com/2014/08/21/fashion/at-burning-man-the-tech-elite-one-up-one-another.html

Bowditch, R. (2010) *On the Edge of Utopia: Performance and Ritual at Burning Man*. London: Seagull Books.

Brill, L. (2006) *The first Year in the desert*. Available at: www.burningman.com/whatisburningman/1986_1996/firstyears.html (accessed 28 April).

Caillois, R. (1961) *Man, Play, and Games*. Glencoe, Illinois: Free Press.

Chase, W. (2013) Black Rock City LLC Awarded 4-Year Event Permit, Voices of Burning Man, June 24. Accessed June 17, 2015. http://blog.burningman.com/2013/07/news/black-rock-city-llc-awarded-4-year-event-permit/

Chen, K. (2009) *Enabling Creative Chaos: The Organization Behind the Burning Man Event.* Chicago: University of Chicago Press.

Doherty, B. (2004) *This is Burning Man: The Rise of a New American Underground.* New York: Little Brown.

Dubois, H. K. (2005) Interview with author. San Francisco. 10 March.

Falassi, A. (1987) *Time Out of Time: Essays on the Festival.* Albuquerque: University of New Mexico Press.

Firat, A. F., and Dholakia, N. (1998) *Consuming People: From Political Economy to Theaters of Consumption*. London: Routledge.

Gilmore, J. H., and Pine B. J. (1999) *The Experience Economy: Work is Theatre and Every Business a Stage*. Boston: Harvard Business School Press.

Gilmore, L. (2010) *Theatre in a Crowded Fire: Ritual and Spirituality at Burning Man*. Berkeley: University of California Press.

Huizinga, J. (1970) *Homo Ludens: A Study of the Play Element in Culture*. London: Paladin.

Kaprow, A. (2003) [1966] *Essays on the Blurring of Art and Life*. Berkeley, CA: University of California Press.

Kirby, M. (1994) [1965] Happenings: An introduction, in M. R. Sandford (ed.), *Happenings and Other Acts*. London: Routledge, 1–38.

Kozinets, R. V. (2002) Can consumers escape the market? Emancipatory illuminations from Burning Man, in *Journal of Consumer Research*, **29**, June 2002.

Kozinets, R. V. and Sherry, J.F.. (2005) Welcome to the Black Rock Café, in L. Gilmore and M. van Proyen (eds.), *After Burn: Reflections on Burning Man*. Albuquerque: University of New Mexico Press.

London, S. (2015) Email correspondence with author. June 22.

Mikel, M. (2008) Interview with author. Burning Man Headquarters, San Francisco. 12 March.

Mangrum, S. (1998) What is burning man? in *Burning Man Summer Newsletter*.

Pinchbeck, D. (2007) *2012: The Return of Quetzalcoatl*. New York: Jeremy Tarcher/Penguin.

Pinchbeck, D. (2014) Facebook post. September 10. Pruitt, C. (2015) Interview with author. June 18, Phoenix, Arizona.

Rose, C. (2008) Interview with author. Burning Man Headquarters, San Francisco. 11 March.

Schechner, R. (1973) [2000] *Environmental Theater*. New York: Applause Theatre.

Sterling, B. (1996) Greetings from Burning Man! The New American Holiday. *Wired* **4**(11): 196

# Notes

1 See Bowditch 2010.

2 A 'zone trip' was entering a "post-apocalyptic world where things change when you are not looking at them. At the center of this zone is a little room where all your dreams become real. There is this quest that people go through to get there" (ibid.). Some 'zone trips' were held in abandoned houses, warehouses or in an unusual neighborhood.

3 The first order of business was to raise the Man—the entire entourage had to use thick rope and their combined body weight to hoist him to an upright position. A circle of tents was formed to create what is now considered the first village, and a central tent made from a pole and a single parachute became a communal hang-out area, the prototype of what is now called 'Center Camp'. There was no formal organization of tents and nor were there any porta-potties. They had no permits from the BLM and the authorities were unaware of the event—the location of the camp was deep in the desert and not visible from the main road.

# FOCUS ON WORLD FESTIVALS

## SECTION 2
## MANAGING FESTIVALS: POLICY, IMPACT and PEOPLE

# Introduction

## Jennie Jordan

The management of festivals is a topic that could cover a whole book, so it is notable that the contributors to this section, who include festival managers, cultural policy officers and academic researchers, are largely outwardly facing – interested in markets and funding, audiences and communities, new ideas and growth. Such an outward focus is not an indication of lack of concern about staff and volunteers, Autissier's (2015) research into volunteer management practices and Puchkova and Elkanova's chapter in this section both illustrate that festivals think very hard about organising and motivating volunteers, for example. Does the importance placed on impact studies, sponsorship and ticket sales imply that there are more pressing issues facing festival producers, specifically the sourcing of public sector grants or maximisation of other income streams? The complexity of festival finances and stakeholder interests means that leaders are constantly trying to understand the relationships between their festivals and audiences, residents, sponsors, tourists and local and national governments (Hewison and Holden, 2011). From research in *Focus on Festivals* (Jordan, 2015) it is clear that developing new audiences vies with artistic quality in festival leaders' priorities, not least because new audiences are both a source of revenue in themselves, and help to validate public sector subsidy. In an era of new public management and evidence based policy (Belfiore, 2004), assessments covering economic, social, political and environmental impact are not only useful for strategic planning, they are essential tools for convincing funders of the festival's value.

Simon Brown (Chapter 7) and Alison Shin-Yi Huang (Chapter 8) both explore the policy potential of festivals, and highlight some of the choices and difficulties faced by municipal authorities and national governments when working with festivals. Festivals are often put forward as essential parts of a city's brand and place marketing to attract tourists, but this raises interesting managerial issues. How much direct governmental control is appropriate at local or national level? Do festivals themselves have the skills to manage large scale, tourist-focused events? What responsibilities should governments have for helping to develop these skills and to co-ordinate the festival sector's development? Are festivals the best way to achieve policy objectives such as economic and community development or environmental improvements?

Partnership with a governmental agency is a key factor identified in Chapter 9. Here Silvia Guglielmini considers the internationalisation of *Galway Arts Festival*, asking what the driving forces were behind the name change, and what differences it has made to the festival's management practices. She identifies the importance of responding to globalisation and economic pressures with an entrepreneurial eye to new sources of income. The case study is a good example of what Morey et al.'s (2014) call the extended festival experience and where Velt et al. (2015) have researched audiences' responses to watching a festival on TV, Guglielmini emphasises the festival's strategic use of digital media to broaden its reach, develop new types of interactivity with audiences and artists and to secure its future. She also discusses the importance of genuine, long-term partnerships in enabling *GAIF* to retain its cultural specificity whilst building a recognisable, international tourist brand.

*Rock In Rio* (Chapter 10) offers a contrasting model of internationalisation. Vanessa Martin's chapter traces the growth of the festival over thirty years and four countries. The case study outlines the festival's strategic focus on sponsorship and the customer experience. Festival director Medina's consistent and early understanding that audiences are as an essential part of a festival's atmosphere and appeal as the artists on stage is similar to that of the *Burning Man* organisers (see Chapter 6), yet it has led him to create a very different type of event. *Rock in Rio* is perhaps the ultimate example of a commercial music festival. It makes full use of experiential marketing techniques to produce memorable experiences for audiences (Pine and Gilmore, 1998), and to provide the perfect forum for brands to activate relationships with festival-goers (Anderton, 2015), ensuring it has an important and on-going income stream through sponsorship, brand licensing and merchandising. It is sponsors' brands that co-create *Rock in Rio* alongside the participants and the staff team.

Medina refers to the festival's employees as the *Rock in Rio* family, and places a high value on staff commitment and low turnover. Puchkova and Elkanova (Chapter 11) are also interested in issues of staff management in their research into how festivals use team management practices to encourage loyalty, motivate workers and volunteers and ensure good communications in three festivals in St. Petersburg, Russia. Their research raises interesting differences between festivals and the larger companies that are usually the focus of these kind of studies and which use teams and team building techniques in an attempt to improve efficiency and motivation. Motivation, loyalty and communication do not appear to be major concerns for those interviewed, raising the question as to what these festivals might teach other sectors about successful staff management.

The question of how to manage large scale music festivals efficiently and cost effectively in order to ensure that they are financially resilient in the face of turbulent economic times is at the heart of János Szabó's research (Chapter 12). Using business and data analysis tools not often applied to festivals, Szabó has analysed trends in audience figures and budgets of five festivals with audiences of over 100,000 over a number of years as they grow, develop and mature. Comparison of the festivals' product life cycles indicates the need for continuous innovation if they aren't to lose market share to each other, or to new entrants, but this doesn't come without risks. Unless festivals keep a weather eye on their expenditure, on new ideas and the quality of the experience, they will see costs rise beyond what be covered by ticket price increases, leading to downturns in attendance.

As Poulsson and Kale (2001) discuss, the specific experience ingredients that customers value and are willing to pay more for are not often addressed in research. Yet the rise of customer relationship management software running behind most ticket outlets means that many festivals have the data to undertake analyses of actions they have taken. Analysing existing data with the management tools discussed by Szabó or with others, could help festivals to make better, evidence-based strategic decisions.

Internal financial and sales data are important sources of information, but they cannot answer all of the questions festival managers need to be able to answer in order to thrive in complex environments, with different stakeholders looking for a variety of social, economic and artistic outcomes. Brown's research in Chapter 7 into the decision-making process behind Leicester City Council's Festivals' Review, underlines the importance of festivals having a, usually quantitative, evidence base, that is accepted by policy-makers (Belfiore 2004). Those with research that appeared to prove that the festival was bringing more money in to the city than it was costing were rewarded with increased subsidies.

Whilst acknowledging the significance of economic impact for acquiring resources, Mathilda van Niekerk (Chapter 13) and Jen Snowball (Chapter 14) address different aspects of 'impact' and data collection in their research into two South African festivals.

UNESCO's report into the collection of statistics about festivals argues that "despite the multidimensional character of festivals, assessments often follow a one-dimensional, economic approach. Rarer examples of assessments have been presented which measure social and environmental impacts. None of these can be said to yet have found complete acceptance such that one would describe them as forming part of any standardised international methodology" (2015: 49). Focusing on South Africa's *National Arts Festival*, Snowball reviews a variety of impact studies that have attempted to measure economic, socio-cultural and environmental impacts. She identifies several socio-cultural measures that festivals routinely collect for marketing and management planning, but rarely include in impact reports, such as a audience demographics and responses to attitudinal questions.

In her chapter about the *Innibos National Arts Festival*, Mathilda van Niekerk draws our attention to the event's impact on local communities' quality of life. Using research undertaken over six years, she explores residents' perceptions of the positive and negative effects the festival has on the town, both during the festival period and throughout the year. The study is interested in social, environmental, economic and political impacts. Whilst community members are concerned about damage to the city's built and natural environments as a result of the crowds attracted during the festival, they are believe that *INAF* is good for its image, profile and the local economy.

Roberta Comunian, Lydia Fraser-Ward and Silvie Jacobi's study (Chapter 15) tests the potential of the extra sociability found at festivals to support urban regeneration through animating high streets. It sees urban festivals as sites in which research can be undertaken into the economic, social and cultural dynamics that are played out on the high street; how communities use specific public and social spaces; and for testing interventions that might then be incorporated into city plans (see Dooghe 2015 for another example of this approach in action in Rotterdam).

Maughan and Radošević (Chapter 16) take a longer term view as they explore the integrational roles that festivals can play in their cities and regions. The *International Festival of Comics* (*FIDB*) in Angoulême in France showcases comic books and graphic novels, a genre that, along with stand-up comedy and more recently video games, has had to fight hard to be recognised as a legitimate art form. When the festival launched in 1974 it very quickly came to be seen as a part of the debate about the cultural value of the form. It has worked with educational providers, the publishing industry, libraries and employers to establish Angoulême as 'City of the Image', the centre of an industry cluster that has diversified from printing and paper-making, into animation, illustration and graphic arts. The festival's central role in raising the arts form's profile and working to develop college courses is identified as an important factor in the cluster's development.

It appears that, whilst economic impact is likely to remain a weighty factor in political decision-making, particularly where festivals are part of a creative industry cluster, there are indications that social and cultural factors might be growing in influence. Residents' quality of life and sense of wellbeing will influence local voters, and festivals that receive municipal subsidy need to understand if communities feel they are a positive or negative addition to city life. Surveys of festival-goers and residents, ideally repeated over a number of editions, can do more than simply provide marketing data; they can explore attitudes and perceptions of social, cultural, environmental and economic impact. Bakhshi et al. explain that approaches such as contingent valuation or willingness to pay, in which the public as asked to place a monetary value on a product, service, experience or landscape can be applied to culture and the arts, even if individuals don't participate themselves. The concept of value can, they argue "include benefits to the whole community. The concepts of 'existence', 'option' and 'heritage' benefits have been developed precisely in order to capture the valuation that the public places on such wider community benefits" (2009: 10). Measuring the value of culture in order to justify public subsidy is a complex issue, and increasingly important in South African, Australian and European cultural policies, meaning that festival producers will have to continue finding ways to measure their impact.

Commercialisation and entrepreneurial paradigms are also in play though and it is clear that sponsorship, sales, merchandising and individual giving are growing income streams for commercial and not-for-profit festivals. These stakeholders' interest in festivals may be different to those of the public sector. Sponsors want to promote positive experiences they can be associated with, while philanthropists want events that have a positive impact on a beneficiary community. The research methods provided in this section are a useful starting point for a festival researcher or manager seeking to undertake their own social impact research or attempting to make decisions about investments in products and experiences that are likely to be valued by potential festival-goers.

## Bibliography


Anderton, C. (2015) Branding, sponsorship and the music festival, in G. McKay, (ed.) *The Pop Festival: History, Music, Media, Culture*. London: Bloomsbury, 199-212.

Autissier, A. (2015) Volunteering for festivals: why and how? In C. Newbold, C. Maughan, J. Jordan and F. Bianchini, (eds.) *Focus on Festivals: contemporary European case studies and perspectives*, Oxford: Goodfellow, 138-146.

Bakhshi, H., Freeman, A. and Hitchen, G. (2009) *Measuring Intrinsic Value: How to Stop Worrying and Love Economics*, London: Mission Models Money.

Belfiore, E. (2004) Auditing culture: the subsidised cultural sector and the New Public Management, in *International Journal of Cultural Policy*, **10**(2), 183-202.

Dooghe, D. (2015) Festival City – Rotterdam, in C. Newbold, C. Maughan, J. Jordan and F. Bianchini, (eds.) *Focus on Festivals: contemporary European case studies and perspectives*, Oxford: Goodfellow, 147-158.

Hewison, R. and Holden, J. (2011) *The Cultural Leadership Handbook: How to Run a Creative Organisation*, Farnham: Gower Publishing.

Jordan, J. (2015) Festival leadership in turbulent times, in C. Newbold, C. Maughan, J. Jordan and F. Bianchini, (eds.) *Focus on Festivals: contemporary European case studies and perspectives*, Oxford: Goodfellow, 107-117.

Morey, Y., Bengry-Howell, A., Griffin, C., Szmigin, I. and Riley, S. (2014) Festivals 2.0: consuming, producing and participating in the extended festival experience, in A. Bennett, J. Taylor and I. Woodward, (eds.) *The Festivalization of Culture*, Farnham: Ashgate, 251-268.

Pine, J. and Gilmore, J. H. (1998) Welcome to the experience economy, in *Harvard Business Review*, July-August, 97-105.

Poulsson, S. H. G. and Kale, S. H. (2001) The experience economy and commercial experiences, in *Marketing Review*, **4**(3), 267-277.

Velt, R., Benford, S., Reeves, S., Evans, M., Glancy, M, and Stenton, P. (2015) Towards an extended festival viewing experience, *ACM International Conference on Interactive Experiences for TV and Online Video*, 3-5 June 2015, ACM.

# 7 Leicester: 'Festival City,' or a City with Festivals?

Simon Brown

## Introduction

This chapter examines the notion of 'festival city' in relation to festivals and events in the City of Leicester, and considers whether a coordinated approach to festivals is appropriate for the city. Through in-depth interviews it examines to what extent the drawing together of festivals and events is important to a selection of the city's key stakeholders, including the festival organisers and the policy makers, and the potential roles for the local authority. It looks at whether there are place identity and economic benefits of drawing the festivals together, and the value of a promoting a title such as 'Festival City'. In contrast, a city with festivals may be defined as a city where, although many festivals happen, there is no, or very little, coordination, and no shared strategy, particularly in relation to the role of local government. This is also distinct from a 'festival city' in that festivals are seen as separate and promoted as such, with no clear overall purpose, though recognised as positive for a city and actively encouraged. Crucially this chapter asks if leadership in developing a focused, coordinated approach to festivals may be better positioned outside the municipal council. Although the role of the local authority would remain important in providing funding and access to resources, we ask if it could potentially achieve more through developing delivery partnerships.

For the purposes of this chapter a 'festival city' has been defined as a city where there is coordination of festivals for the purpose of creating a brand to promote tourism and support place marketing. It may also have benefits in raising the profile of smaller events, widening audiences, and increasing potential for raising sponsorship or accessing funding. As we shall see, other UK cities such as York, Bath and Cheltenham have all used this coordinated approach with their festival programmes. This chapter will focus on the City of Leicester where, even within an environment of huge cuts to public spending, there is a commitment to culture, and in particular festivals, as seen in its investment in festivals and the 2013 bid for UK City of Culture, for which it was shortlisted. Leicester has a large number of festivals and its culturally and ethnically diverse population is reflected in its strong mix of arts, cultural and religious festivals.

In a major study of festivals in Leicester Vernon Davis observes:

> Fifty years ago it would have been relatively straightforward to describe and explain the festivals celebrated in Leicester. Virtually all of them were at least nominally Christian. Since the end of World War II Leicester has emerged as one of the major multi-cultural cities of present day Britain, with a richness of traditions and customs (1996: 5).

Leicester is now recognized as a culturally diverse city with a population of 329,839 of which 45.1% are white British, compared to the national figure of 79.8% (Leicester City Council, 2013). Leicester is a post-industrial city that has undergone a considerable amount of physical regeneration in recent years and has used culture as a significant part of that strategy.

## Use of festivals and events

The role of culture has been well recognised in supporting the ambitions of cities and in particular in changing their image, as highlighted by Bianchini and Landry:

> The presence of artists and other cultural producers ...helps restore vitality, develop a positive image, create additional employment and break cycles of decline (1995: 13).

There is an increasing recognition of the importance of a city's or a region's image and of place marketing in order to compete for tourists and investment and to attract skilled knowledge workers (Clifton, 2011). This is also particularly important for the many post-industrial UK cities such as Liverpool, Glasgow and Bristol that are seeking to re-invent themselves. For writers like Wood the role of events in post-industrial areas can be seen:

> to transform cities from places of daily routine into places of play and entertainment and although this transformation is temporary (for the duration of the event), the affect on those experiencing it may be longer lasting in terms of attitude change. In Blackburn Local Authority the events are seen as "a tremendous opportunity to bring large numbers of our citizens together in a 'feel good' environment for two way communication with ourselves helping to develop closer relationships with them" (2002: 791).

Though this study focuses on festivals and events, there is a recognition that this may detract from other aspects of a wider cultural offer in the city. Festivals can be used as a short-term solution by politicians wanting quick, highly visible benefits (Landry, 1995), which could lead to them being supported at the expense of alternative cultural offers. The risk of a short-term solution is that it may not be sustainable and therefore consideration needs to be given to the long term and how the development of festivals can also benefit the wider cultural sector within the city. In a recent study of local cultural policy in Norway, an increase in support to culture has been identified, however there has been a structural change in the sector with a shift from institutions to events (Henningsen et al., 2015). Henningsen et al observes:

> As local governments downscale their obligations as direct producers of cultural activities through cultural institutions, such as public libraries and culture schools, they increasingly take on a role as facilitators of an emergent 'event culture', as signaled by growing expenditure on cultural festivals and culture houses (2015: 2).

The study suggests that the allocation of resources by local authorities in Norway to these areas is "a way of enhancing their future room for economic manoeuvre, as it is relatively easy to reduce these costs in times of economic strain" (2015: 16). However Henningsen et al. feel that:

> organisations' flexibility equals economic vulnerability. As public funding is transferred from traditional local cultural institutions to festivals and other transient organisations, a sharp decline of funding for the local cultural sector as a whole is more likely in the event of a downturn in the overall economy (2015: 18).

Within this context the study focuses on the role of festivals and how these are used as part of the overall cultural strategy:

> In the context of urban development, from the early 1980s there has been a process that can be characterised as 'festivalisation', which has been linked to the economic restructuring of cities, inter-city competitiveness, and the drive to develop cities as large-scale platforms for the creation and consumption of 'cultural experience' (AEA Consulting, 2006: 16).

Cities are increasingly looking to use festivals as a tool to brand the city, in some cases using the title of 'festival city', with a highly successful example being Edinburgh, which has achieved a coordination of key festivals for marketing purposes but also in combining resources and in strategic direction. However, although Edinburgh is a great example it is limited as a comparator for this study. It is *the* festival city in the UK if not the world, and has a long track record of very well established festivals of quality and scale, that existed long before they were grouped together and branded as 'Edinburgh Festivals'. However, it is useful in as much as a benchmark of a 'festival city' and, therefore, in questioning this or similar terms.

Other examples include York 'City of Festivals' (2011), which is a title promoted by *Visit York*, and involves a series of festivals and events spread over the year and used as a marketing tool. Belfast has created a *Festival Forum*, a voluntary collective of festival organisers and agencies working together to build on their existing strengths. The forum is developing a coordinated approach to the planning, programming, promotion and management of festivals across Belfast by sharing and presenting ideas, skills training, marketing incentives and grants, and coordinating a festival events calendar (Belfast City Council, 2014). Beyond the UK other cities are using festivals, such as Montreal *Festimania*, which groups together more than eleven festivals during the summer to affirm it as a 'city of festivals' (Tourisme-Montreal 2013). Ottawa has developed a coordinated approach:

> in response to festival organisers, politicians, and the tourism industry recognising the need for Ottawa's events to be carefully scheduled, properly planned, and effectively promoted (Richards and Palmer, 2010: 145).

These examples show different approaches, where cities have sought to use the coordination of festivals as a form of place marketing, and in others have attempted to coordinate festivals to create a more professional approach and support the sectors development.

## Marketing, economic impact, programming, and local authority leadership

Through using interviews carried out with a selection of stakeholders from Leicester City Council and local festival organisations ,this section considers if Leicester could be classed as a 'festival city' – one where the festivals are a central part of its place identity. It explores whether there is an existing or potential for co-ordination, what the benefits might be and, specifically, what role the local authority mighty play. The key themes that emerge can be structured into four main headings: branding and place identity; the economic impact through tourism marketing; programming and curation; and issues of leadership and funding with the local authority.

### Branding and place identity

Richards and Palmer (2010) argue that "events are increasingly recognised as a potential tool for image change by cities" (p.374). Previous research has shown the value of festivals in making, "a significant contribution to promoting the place where they happen with 64.4% of the audiences of festivals in one regional study feeling more positive about the place where they had taken place" (Maughan and Bianchini 2003). With this in mind, festivals might be used to help create an identity for Leicester.

It is important that a city considers what makes it authentically unique in order to compete in the tourism market. Bowdin argues cities need to "strive for authenticity and the expression of the unique characteristics of their communities" (2011: 127). There needs to be a strong message that can then be used as PR for the city, and used to increase tourism and inward investment.

An important factor in place identity (in particular where a city is looking to change its image or focus on a particular attribute) is the way in which a city markets itself, which can include the use of slogans. "Good slogans lay out a city's vision, reflect its spirit, and create enthusiasm and momentum" (Avraham, 2004). Though a slogan such as 'festival city' can show vision and momentum it should still be used carefully and should accurately represent the place, the usage of slogans though must also be at least somewhat 'congruent with reality' (Kotler et al., 1993). However, as Geoff Rowe (CEO Big Difference Company) warns, "there is a risk of misrepresenting a place, and the phrase should be used with caution, in Leicester it may be a misleading slogan" (Rowe interview 2014).

One of the ways the group representing arts festivals in the city, Leicester Arts Festivals (LAF), is making a difference is to have a joined up approach, with logos on each other's websites and joint adverts. David Hill (Director of Art-Reach) suggests that, "LAF may be better placed [than Leicester City Council] for quality control of marketing for festivals, due to a clear focus on arts festivals and having more freedom in terms of design and use of new digital methods" (interview 2014). The local authority provides access to marketing opportunities for festival organisers such as poster and banner sites, and web presence (Rowe interview 2014) but Pravin Mistry (Director of the *Leicester Belgrave Mela*) argues that, "the local authority should take more of a lead on the marketing function, in particular to be able to assist smaller festivals that may not have a budget for marketing" (interview 2014). The difference in opinion here may be due to capacity issues within the different festivals, some of which rely more heavily on volunteers than others.

There needs to be a connection between festivals and the place they are based, "The events should, however, be consistent with the destinations overall image and cultural heritage" (Pugh and Wood, 2004: 65). Richards and Palmer highlight the importance of:

> a strong symbiotic relationship with the locations they are staged in: the event should strengthen the sense of place of that location and the location should help distinguish the event. (2010: 418).

It could be argued that the use of festivals as a brand is also more established in other cities that are 'ahead of the game'. David Hill cites Birmingham as a city which has developed a strategy that is very clearly looking to "use festivals to profile as an 'international' city" (interview 2014). Geoff Rowe considers that, "it would be false of Leicester to promote itself as 'festival city' as this would mis-represent itself and create an expectation of being similar to Edinburgh, which it is not, and is an unfair benchmark" (interview 2014). Indeed, Edinburgh now promotes itself as the "world's leading festival city" in recognition of its prominence amongst the increasing number of cities using the term.

It is important to note that the extent to which festivals are established in a city is significant. David Hill comments that, "it takes a considerable amount of time to develop the idea and brand of a 'festival city' and for that to change perceptions of a place" (interview 2014). This is a key point in distinguishing between

Leicester, which has relatively few established events that are over 10 years old and other cities with far more established festivals, "for an event to have a good chance of successfully branding a destination, it needed to be tied to the same destination for 5 – 10 years" (Jago et al., 2002). Additionally, Richards and Palmer (2010) argue that evidence from *European City of Culture* research shows that this may be more like 15 to 25 years.

Another major part of Leicester's identity is the diversity of communities living there, something which is heavily reflected in the large number of cultural and religious festivals in the city. Indeed "in Leicester the profile (of festivals) is high because of religious and cultural festivals rather than arts festivals" (Rowe interview 2014). However, there is some suggestion that the terminology used in publicity about the city and the diversity message needs to change.

It may be more useful to talk in terms of an international city, as highlighted in the Cultural Ambition Statement, produced by Leicester's Culture Partnership Board, where it urged to build 'on our international connections' (Culture Ambition Leicester, 2012). Harrison comments that:

> In Leicester not enough information is given on what the festivals are about, in particular the religious and cultural ones. There is perhaps an opportunity for the city to use festivals and, in particular, focus on religious and cultural festivals, to support a wider message about the international nature of Leicester and its role in being a blueprint for European cities whose populations are increasingly made up of many different cultures (interview 2014).

## Economic impact

In a city such as Leicester, which is not an established tourist destination, festivals might play an important role in increasing visitors and the economic impact that brings. Pravin Mistry considers that in order to promote the city using festivals, the city has to have an infrastructure to support tourism. This would include city centre signage, maps, clearly marked routes to cultural venues and outdoor performance spaces and enhancement of 'gateways' such as the railway station. In addition it needs a more joined up approach between festivals and permanent visitor attractions to provide a wider offer.

A cautious approach needs to be taken when considering creating festivals with the main aim of attracting visitors for an economic reason. Festivals need to be authentic and connected to place, growing organically, Maughan and Bianchini (2003) consider that festivals should have grassroots-based character and should not be artificial manufactured by tourism or place marketing authorities. Mistry suggests that festivals are started because of a particular need and explains that the *Leicester Belgrave Mela* started "because of a need from the community for a platform to perform and for people to come together" (interview 2014). Once it was running and established it was recognised that there was an economic benefit, in particular with its move to the city centre. However the economic impact is secondary and Hill considers it to be one of the least important factors for festivals to focus on as, "it should be incorporated in all the other benefits such as social and around place identity" (interview 2014). It could be argued that events where the focus is on the community are actually better placed to attract tourists rather than those specifically set up with that purpose.

> If the primary objective of the event is community involvement, entertainment and 'fun for fun's sake' then an additional positive outcome is likely to be increased economic activity and tourism. This focus on social benefits for local people may in fact be more successful in the long term than events designed to attract tourists which often have negative impacts on local communities (Wood, 2002: 793).

As well as the direct impact of consumer spending in the city, there is also the recognition that festivals can help to change the perception of the city and help in attracting businesses and bringing investment. "Businesses have confidence in confident cities with a vibrant cultural offer" (Blyth interview 2014).

Businesses may recognise that there is a wider benefit from events in creating a positive city image, which helps in changing perceptions of those that live here, and for those outside. Harrison explains that on the day of the Kasabian 'homecoming' gig at Victoria Park in Leicester in 2014, with an attendance of 50,000, many shops recorded a fall in sales. However, they were still positive about it and felt it was good for the 'cool brand' of the city, helping to show Leicester as an exciting place to live, work, and visit (interview 2014).

Festivals can lead to economic benefit through attracting visitors and businesses to the city however, in Leicester, there needs to be more development of a wider tourism offer and improved infrastructure. For festivals the economic benefit to a city is a byproduct; if the festival offer is of a high enough scale and quality it will attract visitors and create an economic boost. This will only happen if the festival's programme is attractive.

## Programming

Programming is highlighted in this study as this is a key factor in determining the festival offer that the city can promote and the image it creates. This can be seen in cities' responses to *European Capital of Culture* or *UK City of Culture* titles, where the idea that the city or region itself becomes, as Richards and Palmer (2010) would describe, 'a stage' to be curated. It would need to be a coordinated approach to give coherence and distinctiveness to an overall year of programming, to make it sustainable and to fully engage the key stakeholders. Both Liverpool and Derry are examples of cities that have gone through this process of using the cities themselves as stages to create year-long programmes.

In marketing festivals in a city, some have adopted the approach of promoting a large number of festivals that provide a year round programme. For example York promotes over 30 festivals as part of its 'York City of Festivals' brand. These include food, music, arts, and sports events, from the *York Chocolate Festival* to the *Early Music Festival* (York Festivals, 2011). Other cities however have focused on the promotion of particular festivals, for example Cheltenham concentrate on four key well-established festivals. These are spread over different months, with the *Jazz Festival* in May, the *Science Festival* in June, the *Music Festival* in July and the *Literature Festival* in October (Cheltenham Festivals, 2014). Though there are other cultural festivals and events in the city these are the key events with national and international profile, and of high quality programming. There is also potential benefit in the sharing of resources, for example *Cheltenham Festivals* has a central administration including press office and box office. Though these examples show different approaches to programming there is a question over the extent to which either could be considered a festival city. The interviews suggested that quality of programme was an important factor, Hill considered that a festival city:

> has a long track record of substantial festivals that have an international reputation that have an element of a joined up and connected approach. (interview 2014)

Clearly it is important that the festivals are of a certain standard and all of those interviewed agreed that Leicester did not have a sufficient number of festivals at a sufficient level of quality, scale and national or international profile. There appears to be an issue around quality of programming in Leicester with some of those interviewed commenting that there was little or no quality control for many of the events.

As in Cheltenham, there is potential to pick key events that offer more opportunity for promotion. However this may be a more complex decision where the local authority plays a role in the development of festivals, as Hill comments, "the local authority is required to be inclusive and cannot be too narrow in its support and promotion of festivals" (interview 2014). Hill suggests an external group such as Leicester Arts Festivals (LAF) may be better placed to offer quality control in particular in the coordination of programming and marketing. A narrower approach in developing a group of festivals around a theme such as artistic content may be more useful in developing a clear festival brand. Also in bringing together the festivals in a group such as LAF there is a positive sharing of ideas and also a sense of organisers becoming "more aware of the competition" encouraging them to "up their game" (Hill interview 2014). It was commented that there is a tendency for organisers to do what they have always done if there is no one to show them a different way, and that, "collaboration can raise the bar of artistic content through support and challenge" (Blyth interview 2014). The local authority may have a role in helping to raise the bar through commissioning of new work. For example, Durham County Council has commissioned artists in creating 27 light installations across the city for the *Lumiere Festival* (ACE, 2013). In partnership with the Arts Council and arts organisation Artichoke, this investment introduced external ideas that helped raise the creative and professional bar, and led to the festival attracting 175,000 visitors in only its third year.

In developing a festival city there is some recognition that there should be more than just a short intense period of activity but rather a wider programme throughout the year helping to extend the tourist season (Getz 1997). However the interviews showed that it is not necessarily important to have a year round programme, but that it is more important to have key events that fit a purpose (Hill interview 2014). In Manchester they have recognised key 'pillar events' that contribute hugely to visitors coming to the city and to the profile of Manchester. The local authority focuses resources on these giving guaranteed support over a long period. In Leicester it is suggested that there does need to be a more strategic view on the overall festival programme in order to ensure that, !the festivals are still relevant and that as a city we nurture the festivals we want to see established" (Rowe interview 2014).

Staging lots of festivals in a city such as Leicester can be useful in helping communities feel connected and creating the perception that there is a lot going on, but a more focused approach on a few festivals may help to raise the quality and scale of programming. However, taking a more selective approach raises issues of who might be best placed to lead on making these decisions and what the role of the local authority might be.

## The role of the local authority

It is clear from this study that the local authority has a key role in developing the festival offer in a city in terms of financial support and leadership. Those outside the council who were interviewed see the council as not just providing funding for festivals but "playing an important role in helping festivals to find their own funding, and laying the foundation where it is necessary for festivals to grow" (Mistry interview 2014). This is particularly the case with the local authority having links to businesses that individual festival organisers may not have. An example was given of work being carried out by an arts organisation on behalf of Barking and Dagenham Council. They are running an event where opportunities for financially supporting different events in 2015 will be presented to businesses on behalf of the Council. The businesses are specifically those that have long-term contracts with Barking and Dagenham. The Council invests a considerable amount in these companies so this is an opportunity for them to show support to the local area (Hill interview 2014).

In some cities the private sector has been given a sense of ownership by the creation of an external advisory board that may include the local authority but only as a member. In achieving private sector investment the local authority can help in facilitating, but needs to step back from too much involvement, "there is still the idea that the council is a big monolith, and puts off business from getting involved" (Hill interview 2014). It seems that councils can create a perception that they have all the resources and power. However there are many others who have ability and ideas. In Leicester, "leadership ground is there for the taking", it was recognised that there are things the Council does well and is better placed to deliver, however there are other functions where it is better for the council to "enable and not deliver" (Blyth interview 2014).

A good example of this would be the *City Festival* in Leicester which started in 2013, where, though the Council does take a lead in the overall organisation of a 10 day programme of events, many of the events themselves are directly managed by external organisations. The Council may be able to provide support around licensing, security and facilitating the use of public spaces, but the content is managed by others who have links and connections that the City Council may not have. It appears that the way in which the Council works is changing from its traditional function in leading delivery of service, "the role of the council is changing, City Centre Management has changed from being operational to now working in partnership, which is really positive" (Harrison interview 2014).

This idea is supported by Hill who suggests that the Leicester Arts Festivals (LAF) group could take a leadership role in developing a strategy for festivals. There is an expectation that the local authority has to be inclusive and may have historical or political reasons for supporting a festival, whilst LAF could hold a more objective view. Others in more community based organisations argue that the local authority does still have a leadership role in developing festivals as a brand for the city, in supporting festivals around event management and also in how funding is distributed. Pravin Mistry, who represents an organisation that he says is very much rooted in the community, considers local authorities to have the most neutral viewpoint.

Some local authorities in the UK are seeking to reduce involvement in services they have previously supplied and in particular in non-statutory functions such as sports and the arts. Despite this, local authorities still have a key role to play in supporting festivals: in funding, having access to resources, and in ensuring that communities are included. It may be that the local authority's role becomes more about enabling a coordinated focused group of festivals to develop a strong festival brand under the leadership of external organisers who are not under the same political restrictions.

## Conclusions

These findings show that with the associations that the phrase brings, the use of the term 'festival city' in Leicester is not appropriate and not helpful in being used as a brand or slogan for the city. Other cities and in particular Edinburgh are far more established and have a more unique claim. In general, the present position for festivals in Leicester links far more to the description of a city of festivals defined by a loose coordination and strategic direction.

However the idea of creating a brand around a select programme of festivals with a common theme, which could be promoted nationally is one that the findings showed might have potential. It would require focusing resources on the few key festivals, and packaging them to be a strong offer. As one of Leicester's key unique elements is the international nature of its residents and consequently the cosmopolitan nature of its festivals, one possible approach may be to focus on a few established festivals that are linked to different cultures and to develop the scale and quality of those. For example the *Diwali* events in Leicester are well established, represent something of the uniqueness Leicester has in terms of the different cultures in the city and have the potential to have an even stronger reputation by developing the scale and quality of the offer to visitors.

In investing in key festivals and increasing their quality and scale in order to be promoted nationally, there is a risk of alienating the local community. Any investment should take this in to consideration and should look to engage local people in order for festivals to increase a sense of residents of the city connecting with that place.

With a major economic benefit to the city of festivals being tourism there needs to be a better tourist infrastructure in place to support the festivals. Also there needs to be a better link between festivals and businesses in the city, with a coordinated approach bringing festivals together to create links with retailers and leisure businesses to find out what might benefit them.

Though this study has shown that the title of 'festival city' may not be appropriate, it may still be useful to create a message that Leicester is a city with an environment where festivals can be delivered and developed. The findings highlighted that the local authority has an important role in funding, facilitating, and promoting festivals and making the city a great place to set up a festival or to bring an established festival. However a more arms-length approach was desired, to enable through partnerships rather than to simply organize, fund and deliver.

## Bibliography


AEA Consulting. (2006) *Thundering Hooves – Maintaining the global competitive edge of Edinburgh's Festivals*, London: AEA Consulting.

Arts and Business (2012) *Private Investment in culture 2010/11 – Less Public. More Private? Arts Funding in a Cold Climate*, London: Arts and Business.

Arts Council England (ACE). (2013) *Visitors gather in Durham for Lumiere Festival* Available from http://www.artscouncil.org.uk/news/arts-council-news/visitors-gather-durham-lumiere-festival/, accessed 05/12/14.

Avraham, E. (2004) Media strategies for improving an unfavorable city image, in *Cities*, **21**(6), 471-479.

Beflast City Council (2014) –Festivals, Available from http://www.belfastcity.gov.uk/tourism-venues/culture/festivals.aspx, accessed 24/05/13.

Bianchini, F. and Landry, C. (1995) *The Creative City*, Demos:London

Bradford City Council, (2013), *Bradford a leading cultural city*, Available from www.bradford.gov.uk/.../0/BradfordCulturalPlandraftJanuary2014.pdf, accessed 15/11/14.

Bowdin, G. (2011) *Events Management, (*3rd edition), Oxford: Butterworth-Heinemann.

Cheltenham Festivals. (2014) Available from www.cheltenhamfestivals.com.

City of Edinburgh. (2007) *Inspiring Events Strategy*, Available from http://eventsedinburgh.org.uk/files/documents/inspiring-events-strategy.pdf, accessed 08/10/14.

Clifton, N. (2011) Regional Culture in the Market Place: Place Branding and Product Branding as Cultural Exchange, in *European Planning Studies*, **19**(11), 1973-1994.

Cultural Ambition Leicester. (2012) Available from www.culturalambitionleicester.co.uk, acessed 14/09/13.

Davis, V. (1996) *Leicester Celebrates: Festivals in Leicester Past and Present*, Leicester City Council: Living History Unit.

Getz, D. (1997) *Event Management and Event Tourism* New York: Cognizant Communications

Henningsen, E., Håkonsen, L., and Løyland K., (2015) From institutions to events - structural change in Norwegian local cultural policy, in *International Journal of Cultural Policy, Taylor and Francis Online 01 July 2015.*

Jago, L., Chalip, L., Brown, H., Mules, T. and Ali, S. (2002) The role of events in helping to brand a destination, in *Events and Place Making* conference proceedings, Sydney: Australian Centre for Event Management.

Kotler, P., Haider, D. H., and Rein, I. (1993) *Marketing Places*, New York: Free Press.

Landry, C. (1995) The Creative City, London: Demos

Leicester City Council. (2013) Census 2011, Available from: http://www.leicester.gov.uk/your-council-services/council-and-democracy/city-statistics/census2011/key-statistics/who-we-are/ethnic-group/, accessed 24/05/13.

Leicester City of Culture. (2013) Available from: http://www.leicestercityofculture2017.co.uk/cityofculture.aspx, accessed 04/10/13.

Maughan, C., and Bianchini, F. (2003) *Festivals and the Creative Region* Arts Council England: London.

McGuigan, J, (2005) The Cultural Public Sphere, in *European Journal of Cultural Studies*, **8**(4), November 2005, 427-443.

Mooney, G. (2004) Cultural policy as urban transformation? Critical reflections on Glasgow, European City of Culture 1990, in *Local Economy*, **19**(4), 327-340.

Pugh, C., and Wood, E. (2004) The strategic use of events within Local Government: A study of London Borough Councils, in *Event Management*, **9**, 61-71.

Richards. G., and Palmer, R. (2010) *Eventful Cities – Cultural Management and Urban Revitalisation*, Oxford: Butterworth-Heinemann.

Tourisme-Montreal. (2013) Available from http://www.tourisme-montreal.org/What-To-Do/Events/festimania-montreal, accessed 16/05/13

Wood, E. (2002) Events, civic pride and attitude change in a post-industrial town: Evaluating the effect of local authority events on residents' attitudes to the Blackburn Region, in *Events and Place Making*, conference proceedings, Sydney: Australian Centre for Event Management.

York Festivals. (2011) Available from http://www.yorkfestivals.com, accessed 23/05/13.

# 8 Perspective of *Taiwan Lantern Festival*

Alison Shin-Yi Huang

## Introduction

In 2000, the Tourism Bureau (Taiwan) announced a set of new policies to develop the tourism industry in Taiwan. The main purpose of these new policies was to meet the challenge of globalisation in the twenty-first century. The policies revealed the strategy of adopting a localised approach to festivals and to promote them to the international tourism market. This would encourage local government, cultural workers and event companies to get involved and to increase the development of the festivals industry in Taiwan. Since then festivals have sprung up like mushrooms, with events such as commercial activities or agriculture products being wrapped up into festival modes (Chiu, 2012).The policies encouraged the rapid growth of festivals in Taiwan and this has led to debates such as: lack of sustainable planning, community involvement, or a long term business strategy and the consequential unstable quality, wasted budgets and high homogeneity. All these issues are discussed here.

Following on from the tourism policies, the Tourism Bureau (Taiwan) selected twelve major events which correspond to the annual twelve month calendar, and created a brand for the project that provided tourists with different choices of activities to organise during their visit. In the first stage the twelve major events were distributed in different cities and mainly focused on traditional and religious activities (Li, 2007). Today the project has been rebranded and expanded to *Time to Celebrate - Taiwan Tourism Events*, in which the number of recommended events has risen to thirty-four and comprises a variety of different types of events (Tourism Bureau Taiwan, 2015).

In the recommend events, *Taiwan Lantern Festival* is the largest in scale and has the biggest budget of those listed by the Tourism Bureau and local government. The festival has been held for 26 years since 1990. Over that time, the scale and the costs of the festival have significantly changed, for example, between 1990 and 2015 the number of festival visitors has increased from 1.2 to 13.7 million.

The festival is held on January 15 (Lunar calendar). As well as the *Taiwan Lantern Festival* other lantern festivals such as *Pingxi Sky Lantern Festival, Taipei, Taichung* and *Kaohsiung Lantern Festivals* are held at the same time. The form and style of the *Taiwan Lantern Festival* and *Taipei, Taichung* and *Kaohsiung Lantern Festivals* are similar. The vast number of lantern festivals now in existence raises questions about the necessity of holding the national *Taiwan Lantern Festival*, which we shall discuss later in the chapter.

## The history of the lantern festivals

Two thousand years ago during the Han dynasty on the 15 day of the first lunar month, monks used to light lanterns in the temples to demonstrate their respect to Buddha. The emperor Hanmingdi, a pious Buddhist, commanded all the national buildings including temples and royal palaces to light lanterns on the day to pray for blessings. As time passed by, the custom became one of the five most important festivals in Chinese society, and also has significant meaning to people as part of ceremony to welcome the New Year. Today, the red oval shaped lanterns have become the symbol of Chinese activities, especially being used to celebrate Chinese festivals or to create an atmosphere in Chinatowns around the world.

According to China's various folk customs, people get together on the night of the *Lantern Festival* to celebrate with different activities. *Lantern Festival* customs and activities vary regionally, including lighting and enjoying (floating, fixed, held and flying) lanterns, appreciating the bright full moon, setting off fireworks, guessing riddles written on lanterns, eating tangyuan (sticky rice balls), lion dances, dragon dances and walking on stilts (China Highlights, 2015).

In 1989, the former Minister of Transportation and Communications, Clement C. P. Chang decided to hold a lantern event which assembled all the lanterns from the temples in Taipei, therefore people could enjoy the *Lantern Festival* in one place to avoid transportation difficulties. This was the origin of *Taiwan Lantern Festival* (Tourist Bureau, Taiwan, 2009).

## *Taiwan Lantern Festival*

The first lantern festival was held at the main plaza of the Chiang Kai-shek Memorial Hall in 1990 and attracted 1.2 million visitors. In the 1990s, because of Taiwan's economic rise, people started to seek more leisure activities, hence the *Lantern Festival* became a popular choice for people to spend their New Year vacation. The market demand led to the content and subject of the festival providing more variety and entertainment. Over the next 9 years, the festival became the most popular event in Taiwan. In 2001, in order to balance north and south Taiwan, the central government decided to move the festival from Taipei to Kaohsiung which attracted 5 million visitors. After 2 years in Kaohsiung, the festival transformed into a touring festival to improve the local economy and the reputation of local government and was named the *Taiwan Lantern Festival*. At the same time, the local governments of Taipei and Kaohsiung noticed the market demand and benefit of holding a *Lantern Festival*, and with encouragement from the nation's tourism policies, the lantern festival developed into the *Taiwan, Taipei and Kaohsiung Lantern Festival*.

When the Tourism Bureau received the mission of holding the lantern festival from central government they decided to develop a festival which would compare with other international events such as *Oktoberfest* – Munich's beer festival in Germany and *Sapporo Snow Festival* in Japan. Taiwan is not the only country to hold lantern festivals, which can also be found in China, South Korea and Singapore. The question of how to maintain the traditional elements yet to stand out next to those festivals was a significant one for the project leaders and so the Tourism Bureau invited experts, professors from the history, humanities and folk culture fields to help position the festival and provided suggestions.

'Folk culture roots, tradition and internationalisation' were the guiding principles decided by the lantern festival committee. These changed the structure of the festival. For example, rules were developed governing the various subjects of lanterns. In order to maintain the craft of lantern making, competitions were held to help nurture the next generation of lantern artists. The rules also emphasised the installation and ceremonies surrounding the event in order to create the New Year atmosphere. In 2001, the festival started to involve local government, which brought the local community, industry and citizens together. Moreover foreign cities such as Hong Kong, Macau, Tottori and Kagawa, Nanjing and Sichuan were invited to demonstrate their lantern craft at the festival. The success of the festival brought it to the attention of the international media. In 2008 the American Discovery Channel TV programme 'The Fantastic Festivals of the World' highlighted the *Taiwan Lantern Festival* and ranked it as one of the best in the world. In 2015, the international media praised that *Taiwan Lantern Festival* in Taichung as being like 'Disneyland without roller coasters'.

The touring festival, as it had become, added local elements which changed the components of the festival. Guaranteeing the quality of the festival and the benefit to the host city was the major concern for the Tourism Bureau. According to Regulations for Evaluation of 2016 *Taiwan Lantern Festival* (2016) the principle guidelines for choosing the host city are: convenient transport, attractiveness, usable ground and sufficient finances. The participating city would have to complete a proposal to prove their ability to run the festival. The Tourism Bureau convenes an evaluation committee, examines the various venues that have applied, deliberates on the proposals then decides on the winning city. Besides this, the central government also considers the development potential when choosing a city, and how this will help promote the city by holding this mega event. During the festival, central government controls the main lantern area which includes the main theme lanterns, the traditional lantern area, the joyous lantern area, the exchange lantern area and the competition lantern area. The lantern competition area exhibits lanterns made by students from elementary schools, high schools, universities and other adults. Each year, eight months before the festival, the Department of Education received a subsidy from central government to organise a lantern camp for local students, teachers and their families. The lantern artists teach the participants the know-how of making lanterns. The finished products then participate in the competition and are displayed at the *Taiwan Lantern Festival* with more than 1,000 other pieces. The competitions are at national level and accept lantern products from all over Taiwan, among them are works from inmates of the prison, which always perform at a very high standard and win the most awards. It can be said that the lantern camp and competition nurture the lantern artists of the future and teach the lantern craft to children, passing on their folk culture. The purpose of designing lanterns covering different topics is to maintain, pass on and exalt traditional lantern craft. Compared with central government areas, local government has multifarious lantern displays, the majority of topics refer to administrative departments of the city. For example, the industry technology lantern area, from the Department of Urban Development, the low-carbon sustainable lantern area from Department of Environmental Protection. The *Taiwan Lantern Festival* is also the promotion platform for particular city government departments; for example in 2015 *Taiwan Lantern Festival* in Taichung, the Department of Agriculture, Taichung designed a Flora Expo Lantern area to promote the *2018 Flora Expo* in Taichung.

In addition to lantern displays, the most momentous task for city government is the integration of the 20 task forces. The 20 task forces comprise all the necessary administrative departments of the city government involved from initiation to the closure phase of the *Taiwan Lantern Festival*. This involves the Department of Cultural Affairs curating the performances, the Department of Transportation managing the significant transportation planning, and the Department of the Construction in charge of land grading, asphalt concrete pavement, water and electrical engineering etc. The lead task force is the Comprehensive Planning Team which performs the integration, coordination, communication and time management role within the Department of Tourism. Moreover, the Department of Tourism liaises with Tourism Bureau (Taiwan). The comprehensive planning team arranges regular conferences and delivers updated information to ensure integration between central and city government.

## Advantages of cooperation

The first 10 years of *Taiwan Lantern Festival* established the foundation of the festival, that includes the know-how, structure and reputation. It also has transformed the lantern industry. The policy of rotating the *Taiwan Lantern Festival* between Taiwanese cities has injected new elements to the festival each year. This gives the media a variety of new material to report on, and also means that people visit the festival not just once, but each Lunar New Year, no matter if they were from Taiwan or abroad, to experience each different cities' approaches to the festival. The majority of the cities holding the festival are far from the capital hence visitors might plan a one to two day trip which generates economic benefits from transportation and communication, to restaurants, souvenir shops, hotels and other tourist attractions. From 2011 to 2015 the economic output of the festival has increased from 5.6 billion (170 million US$) to 12.6 billion (384 million US$). The investment budget has also expanded, from 300 million (9 million US$) to 430 million (13 million US$) (2016 *Taiwan Lantern Festival* consultant proposal, 2015). According to the Hsinchu County Government (2014) the 2013 *Taiwan Lantern Festival* in Hsinchu invested 736 million (22million US$), the highest on record. The 2015 *Taiwan Lantern Festival* in Taichung used 35 hectares of ground, across 4 districts to exhibit lanterns, programmes and events, and accommodated 13.7 million visitors from Taiwan and overseas.

The *Taiwan Lantern Festival* is one of the main projects of the Tourism Bureau, and also the largest annual event for the Ministry of Transportation and Communication in Taiwan. One of the benefits for the Tourism Bureau of organising the *Taiwan Lantern Festival* is that it is able to assist local Departments of Tourism to develop local tourism. Moreover, local government then benefits as it is able to mobilise all of its departments involved in the festival and broaden the benefits of holding the festival in their area. To organise a mega event like *Taiwan Lantern Festival*, all departments have to be involved in planning. Each department has to collect material, study references and discuss with each other in order to complete the proposal. This requirement changes the environment of local government, as the *Taiwan Lantern Festival* is a complicated, long term and large scale event. For example, the Department of Transportation needs the details of the site to be used from the Department of Tourism in order to plan the transportation scheme, and the Department of Construction requires the transportation scheme so that it can arrange the land grading schedule and budget, the departments who are in charge of the lantern areas cannot undertake the construction until the Department of Construction finishes the project etc. All the processes are closely linked to each other, so if one department delays, this will have a knock-on effect on the whole event. Holding the *Taiwan Lantern Festival* encourages connections between departments, and demonstrates the ability of a city government to organise the mega event. What's more, *Taiwan Lantern Festival* provides a stage for local industry to exhibit new products and brands; business participates in the festival by designing for the brand lantern exhibition, and they also donate staff and volunteers; universities support the festival by providing tour staff from the relevant subject; community groups, schools and associations across the city participate. These abundant resources working together show the vitality and prosperity of the city.

The benefits of cooperation also brings cultural exchanges as the organising cities invite sister cities to exhibit their own representative lanterns and join in the performance programme, helping to meet the goal of city promotion. Invitations also go to international cities, especially those in Asia who are renowned for their own lantern craft or hold lantern festivals of their own; these are all invited to display their lanterns at the*Taiwan Lantern Festival*. Besides, the Tourism Bureau attends lantern festivals around the world to demonstrate the craft of lanterns from Taiwan. The strategy imperceptibly boosts the *Taiwan Lantern Festival* as the world's most elaborate lantern craft and largest scale lantern festival. The *Taiwan Lantern Festival* also raises the international profile of the cultural attractions of Taiwan. The *Taiwan Lantern Festival* not only attracts Taiwanese tourists but also international tourists which provide local government with a great opportunity to promote the city brand awareness outside Taiwan. To the tourism department, the lantern festival provides a platform to demonstrate their governance plan and policy, moreover to communicate with its citizens and involve them at every level with the running and celebrating of the lantern festival.

## The problems facing the *Taiwan Lantern Festival*

To its opponents, the festival wastes huge amounts of tax revenue, building the temporary facilities; making disposable lanterns and creating environmental pollution etc. The opponents of the *Taiwan Lantern Festival* feel that there should be a discreet public discussion about its retention or abolition.

For many years, the key debate has been about 14 day festival's budget (430 million in 2015, 13 million US$). On the basis of budget distribution pie chart of *Taiwan Lantern Festival* (2016 *Taiwan Lantern Festival* consultant proposal, 2015), nearly 60% of the budget is spent on the 20 task forces, the remaining 40% goes to the lantern area plan and to lantern production. In the 60% of the 20 task forces' budget, the Transportation and Site/Facilities team capture nearly 35% . Most of the budget of the Transportation Team is used to hire the shuttle buses, drivers and manage staff in bus stations and parking lots, to encourage visitors to take shuttle buses to the venue instead of driving their car; and nearly 20% of budget is expended on preparing the festival grounds to make it suitable by introducing concrete pavements, water and electricity and other facilities. In the preparation not all the venues require the same facilities, as this depends on the planner's configuration and the lantern area design. Moreover the restoration requirements of landlords after the event are one of the factors needing to be solved.

The material required for making a lantern varies, such as bamboo, wood or steel wire for the frame; paper or silk for the shade. Generally speaking, a lantern's life is about 3 months to 6 months in outdoor conditions and most of the lanterns, especially the lanterns from competition camp would be abandoned after the festival. This is part of the dispute over the festival being a waste of money and a cause of environmental pollution. Furthermore, in order to economise, most of ground cover involves Portland cement concrete pavements, which cause the serious problem of dust pollution.

Beside the debate on the budget, the core curation of the festival is an issue that has been widely discussed. At the beginning when the festival was formed, 'the folk culture root, tradition and internationalisation' were set as the principles of guidance for the *Taiwan Lantern Festival*. In the Regulations for Evaluation of 2016 *Taiwan Lantern Festival* it states that in order to celebrate Tourism Festival and promote folk culture internationalisation, the festival must be held in cooperation with city government and other non-government resources. No doubt, central government has clear curating goals and aims regarding the content and maintenance of the traditional lantern craft. However, advances in science and technology have made the use of LED lights and projection simpler. Festivals such as *Festival of Lights* (Lyon, France), *I Light Marina Bay* (Singapore) and *Signal – Prague Light Festival* (Czech Republic) are famous for the use of light and projection. The difference between light and a lantern is clear to central government; even so, most of the officials in local government do not understand the core concept of a lantern. The comprehensive planning team being asked to design light shadow shows instead of lanterns is commonly seen in the planning stage of the lantern area, which affect the curation of the festival. The lantern festival could be modern, using light projection and hi-tech source material, nevertheless, the lantern craft is the protagonist, any creation and innovation should be developed based on the lantern craft; that is the root of the festival.

Another issue is that of unsophisticated lanterns in the festival, as officers from local government may not be skilled in distinguishing the quality of lanterns; they may have no experience in designing a proper lantern display area, and also the procurement law limits the choice of lantern supplier / artists. Some of exhibited lanterns cannot compare even with the competition lantern from inmates of the prison, which may influence people's aesthetic and understanding of lantern craft and display, developing a wrong idea of the quality of lanterns. For visitors that may reduce their intention to revisit the festival in the future. This should be confronted and responded to with a strategy to prevent the situation from continuing to deteriorate.

## Further development

*Taiwan Lantern Festival* has been organised for 25 years within the Tourism Bureau, and the festival operating system is passed on and continually improved. However, most local government administrations lack the experience to integrate and plan this kind of mega event, hence a consultant company will play a significant role in the project. In other words, the ability of the consultant company will greatly affect the success or failure of the festival.

The debate on the role of central government to record and provide know-how for such things as the *Taiwan Lantern Festival* operations bible has been discussed. In the process of implementing the festival, questions such as how many volunteers do we need; how much budget should we invest in transportation and lantern making; how did the last city government plan portable toilets in the 32 hectare area and procedures on opening ceremony, satellite news gathering arrangement etc. are all questions asked by the local government. It would be more efficient if central government were to record essential statistics from different years of the festival for the host city. In a similar way, analysing data transfer of information would provide references for the organisers at the time of decision making, strategy planning and curation. Moreover, the information provided would support the evaluation system. The evaluation system is supposed to help once a festival is awarded to a city; information provided includes visitors numbers (by their nationality and place of departure); economic output (the income from different industries), floor area utilised etc., this enables cross-reference in order to help with making the right decisions.

At the same time as the *Taiwan Lantern Festival*, Taipei and Kaohsiung have local lantern festivals as well. *Pingsi Sky Lantern Festival* in New Taipei city, *Yenshui Fireworks Festival* in Tainan, *Bombing of Master Han Dan* in Taitung are all famous events that celebrate lantern festivals, however Taiwan is a small country with 23 million people, and to avoid the competition between each of the festivals, there is a need to integrate and plan a lantern tour package. This is an issue needing to be solved.

In 2013, the *Taichung Lantern Festival* was the first to be Taiwanese ISO 20121-certified (Event Sustainability Management System) by Taiwan's MICE Promotion Programme, and the world's first lantern festival to achieve this international standard. *Taiwan Lantern Festival* is the flagship mega event in Taiwan, and it should implement better environmental protection policies and procedures to improve its sustainability stature. In the ISO 20121 Guideline, sustainability issues cover environment, economy and society. These three factors highlight the need to reduce the festival's carbon footprint; create more stages for lantern craft artist to deliver work; and to cultivate the aesthetics of lantern art in order for the festival to endure.

## Conclusions

The *Taiwan Lantern Festival* has built up a reputation in Taiwan and the rest of the world. To be able to compete with the fast progress of technology and globalisation is the next challenge for the organisers. The advice provided here is that Taiwan local government should learn lessons from previous festivals hosted in different cities. They should analyses statistics and design a proper scheme, for example the number of visitors, the floor area utilised, the services (free shuttle bus, free gifts) and fireworks show etc., instead of wasting money on pursuing higher and higher visitor numbers. Although the Tourism Bureau had indicated the appropriate floor area for lantern exhibition is around 6-10 hectares (Regulations for Evaluation of 2016 *Taiwan Lantern Festival*, 2016), it is the convention that every year will surpass last year's event, and the numbers will naturally increase. Even those areas that are not essential elements of the festival, such as the fireworks, central government requires that fireworks are included in the opening and closing ceremonies. In the 2013 *Taiwan Lantern Festival* in Hsinchu they planned fireworks twice to three times a day which cost a large amount and caused much environmental pollution. The ever-expanding scale does encourage economic activity, however appropriate limitations on spending might encourage local government to spend its budget money wisely and efficiently.

As time goes by, the unique New Year atmosphere might not be familiar to younger generations, therefore to design novel and interesting events as part of the festival are the major goals to attract young people and nurture them to become loyal audiences of the lantern festival. Moreover, placing interactive activities between the lantern areas are recommended to keep pace with the times and requirements of audiences, particularly younger ones. Finally, the key event of the lantern competition could be extended and upgraded to become part of the curriculum in art classes of elementary schools, which would help promote the lantern festival and make lanterns available to all children throughout Taiwan not just in the festival-organising city.

Lighting lanterns symbolises a smooth future and good luck to people and their families. *Taiwan Lantern Festival* represents folk culture and is part of the Lunar New Year celebrations which has raised the international profile of the cultural attractions of Taiwan and has profound implications for the Taiwanese people. A successful future transformation of the *Festival* is expected by its audiences, and it is important that festival organisers meet their expectations.

## Bibliography

Chang, Y. C. (2008) Research of festival planning strategy of local government, *National Kaohsiung University of Hospitality and Tourism*. Available from: http://etds.nkuht.edu.tw/etdservice/view_metadata?etdun=U0018-1211200714562404, accessed July 16, 2015.

China Highlights (2015) *Chinese Lanterns*. Available from: www.chinahighlights.com/travelguide/culture/lanterns, accessed July 17, 2015.

Chiu, K. L. (2012)*The Ins and Outs and Actual Situation of Modern Art Festivals in Taiwan.* School of Theatre Arts, Taipei National University of the Arts. *Taipei Theatre Journal* **15**: 49-78.

Hsinchu County Government (2014) *Taiwan Lantern Festival.* 24 November. Available from: http://www.hsinchu.gov.tw/zh-tw/Event/NewsDetail/48102, accessed: 17 July, 2012.

Lin, K. C. (2007) *Taiwan Folk culture and Festival*

Meet Taiwan. (2013) Taiwanese MICE Industry to Adopt ISO 20121 Available from: http://www.meettaiwan.com/en_US/greenexhibition/menu/M0000729/Overview%20of%20MICE%20Sector%20Compliance%20Progr...html, accessed 25 July 2015.

Tourism Bureau (Taiwan) (2009) Reviewing 20th anniversary of the Taiwan Lantern Festival, Taipei: Tourism Bureau, Republic of China (Taiwan).

Tourism Bureau (Taiwan) (2015) *Regulations for Evaluation Taiwan Lantern Festival.* Taipei: Tourism Bureau, Republic of China (Taiwan).

Tourism Bureau (Taiwan) (2015) *Time for Celebration – Taiwan Tourism Events.* Available from: http://eventaiwan.tw/en/news/detail_8126_2601, accessed July 5, 2015.

# 9 *Galway International Arts Festival*: What's behind the internationalisation of a name?

Silvia Guglielmini

## Introduction

*Galway International Arts Festival* (*GIAF*) takes place in July in the West of Ireland and combines different art-forms including theatre, music and the visual arts. It comprises comedy and street spectacle, as well as a discursive strand centred on creativity called *First Thought Talks*. The festival was established in 1978 as an outlet for professional artists living in the area and a stage to showcase national and international artwork. It was originally called *Galway Arts Festival* and added the term 'international' to its title in 2014.

This name change could be interpreted as a strategic marketing move to position *GIAF* in a broader circuit of international events, but is also an interesting starting point to discuss *GIAF*'s transformation as informed by globalisation. Globalisation is a complex interplay of economic and cultural dynamics shaping the sense of the world as a smaller place, where 'new global elements coexist alongside existing and established local or national cultural forms' (Robins, 1997: 19). Globalisation goes hand-in-hand with technological progress and the information economy, which is based "on the capacity to create new knowledge and to apply it rapidly, via information processing and telecommunications, to a wide range of human activities in ever-broadening space and time" (Carnoy *et al.*, 1993: 6). As the world becomes interconnected, there is increasing competition to gain financial resources and hold a share of people's attention. This emerged quite clearly in an interview held with John Crumlish, who has been *GIAF*'s Chief Executive since 2002:

> [As a festival, you have to] be interesting and engaging, which ... creates a massive challenge because so many people have much bigger budgets and are attempting exactly the same thing. You are no longer competing with festivals; you are competing with Google and whoever else wants somebody's attention.

While globalisation pushes towards homogenisation, it does not erase specificity. Specificity survives in tradition, in hybridity – the crossover of cultures or 'glocal' models – and also in tensions and frictions (Robins: 18). This chapter contends that, while organisations may tend towards standardisation, their interacting stakeholders orientate organisational performances towards specificity. As Bianchini and Maughan noted in *Focus on Festivals*, "no festival is an island, cut off from the needs and aspirations of its stakeholders" (2015: 241). Grappling with the question of how *GIAF* is negotiating its internationalisation, this chapter will focus on one stakeholder in particular: Fáilte Ireland, which is Ireland's tourism authority. It will be argued that tourism is an important realm for festival development – one in relation to which entrepreneurial festival leaders negotiate specificity in times of globalisation.

## Internationalisation, tourism and globalisation: the balance between specific and universal festival features

It is not uncommon for festivals to change their names. For example, corporate sponsors negotiate the association of their names to prestigious events in order to strengthen their brands and provide their employees with quality entertainment and non-monetary benefits (Finkel, 2010). As sponsors withdraw their support, festival leaders find new commercial partners, and this can lead to renaming. The addition of 'international' does not necessarily stem from a commercial agreement; festival leaders can plan it as 'conversation changer'. Like a logo, the name is a material marker of a festival's brand. Brands are however complete only when "ideas about the product accumulate and fill the brand markers with meaning" (Holt, 2004: 3). Indeed, every aspect of a festival's brand reveals a story and should 'talk' to the consumer instantly and effectively (Norton, 2015: 134).

The notion of 'international' conveys complex dynamics affecting the programme and the network of stakeholders involved in the festival. Writing about international arts festivals in small countries, Regev identifies an organisational isomorphism to which artists and audiences contribute. Both stakeholders typically are 'cosmopolitan omnivores', whose sense of taste embraces hybridity and divergent cultural experiences as informed by globalisation (2011: 136-137). The programmes consequently push the boundaries associated with the festivals' geographical locations, and the festivals' structure accounts for typical units: great variety of events to showcase "the wide horizons of the organisers and potential audiences"; packages of tickets at reduced prices; exclusive events; 'consecrated' artists juxtaposed to other artists "to construct an aura of artistic equivalence between the peripheral and the metropolitan"; competitions and awards to augment the festivals' authority in the artistic field (2011: 146-150). Klaić et al. have analogously observed that international arts festivals embrace similar organisational practices, including the production of new artistic capital, which affirms the festivals' value and purpose (2004: 33).

In the context of tourism management, in which festivals constitute a distinct kind of product "for which the drivers of consumption are linked to the hedonic rather than the utilitarian aspects of life" (Ferdinand and Williams, 2013: 203), the dynamics described above are approached as a combination of inward and outward activities. Inward activities imply that "resources are brought from foreign markets", or are performed "by foreign providers in the home country". Outward activities entail the reverse (2013: 204). Given this multiplicity of activities, it is appropriate to speak of multiple processes of internationatialisation"o ccurring truly pragmatically, with companies seizing opportunities to operate in an international market where they arise" (Pillmayer and Scherle, 2014: 337).

## Tourism and technology

One can put these processes in the context of globalisation. Tourism is based on the "endless production of difference" (Jaworski and Thurlow, 2010). But globalisation, as the product of many converging factors including "technology, transnational corporations, new methods of communication and distribution systems as well as new vistas of competition", constitutes the background to "an economy conceived of as mainly the same in all its parts" (Wahab and Cooper, 2001: 4). The stakeholders of the tourism industry operate in an increasingly standardised way. Amongst these stakeholders, there are those running enterprises aimed at producing travel and tourist products, tourist attractions including cultural facilities and institutions, and "the ordering institutions and bodies set up to regulate commercial behaviour and social externalities associated with such production" (Britton [1991] in Cornelissen 2005: 677). Many stakeholders focus on competition and the diversification of services, and take into account changing values and lifestyles including people's predisposition to experience by discovering personal capacities and developing them (Poon, 1993; Vanhove, 2001). Tourism stakeholders also value technology. Technology not only supports tourist experiences, it also recruits tourists as participants in a process of co-creation, which entails "the joint creation of value by the company and the customer" (Neuhofer et al., 2014: 341). It can also empower the experience because it "needs to exist for the experience to happen" (2014: 347).

Festivals may embrace these practices, especially when they involve commercial partners and have leaders whose actions reflect effective models provided by other festivals and comply with the standard operating procedures and normative pressures entrenched in professionalism (Finkel, 2009).

Focusing on technology, many professionally run festivals use social media for festival promotion (Klaić [2007] in Silvanto, 2015: 89). The use of digital technology can also support the cultural relevance of festivals in terms of the democratisation of culture (Gordziejko, 2015). It has the potential to empower or strengthen the role of festivals as depositaries of values, since it allows them to be manifestly present in both public and private spaces (Gielen, 2010). Digital technology, it seems clear, can support internationalisation as a means for promotion in the strict sense of putting a festival's name 'out there'. It is less obvious, however, how this happens when festivals try to balance the co-presence of specific and universal features, which in turn makes them interesting (and competitive) tourist products.

The academic discourse centred on how tourism stakeholders pursue internationalisation 'is still in its infancy' (Pillmayer and Scherle, 2014: 321). Certainly, however, one must be careful to establish too strong a connection between tourism and festivals through the lens of internationalisation. Internationalisation could be approached as "a constitutive moment in the entrepreneurial identity of a company" (2014: 329) and in the lifecycle of an arts organisation. It can be an initiative driven by new leadership and a way of expanding the activities of a mature organisation (Paris and Leroy, 2014). Tourism is, however, an important globalised context that is dominated by the conception of culture as a resource (Yúdice, 2003). It is an exemplary 'realm of performance' – a network of performers and institutions to which festivals belong, and in which they negotiate production with other stakeholders.

## Performing difference

Globalisation effectively broadens the geographical basis for homogenisation that, from an organisational point of view, is achieved through direct imposition, modelling and professionalisation (Di Maggio and Powell, 1983). Globalisation can also be seen as the background for communal 'solutions' to issues such as the 2008 financial crisis and the consequent economic recession, which has made the case for public subsidy of festivals difficult in many countries (Jordan, 2015). Much academic literature on arts management and leadership refers to entrepreneurship as a necessary aspect of leadership in uncertain times (i.e. a standard). Entrepreneurship in fact implies the ability to turn to alternative income sources and "constantly elaborate new ideas and to be innovative ... to be different to the others and maintain ... uniqueness on an ongoing basis" (Verbanova, 2013: 15).

Entrepreneurship can be seen as a form of managerial performance or, borrowing from Yúdice, a managerial 'constitutive force' (2003: 12). Festival leaders perform in a competitive environment, characterised by diversity. Diversity is indeed a resource in a contemporary world where everything from the economy to political and social practices has become cultural (2003: 251). In this context, internationalisation is not a question of mere entrepreneurship, but depends on the interplay between entrepreneurial festival leaders and other stakeholders, who themselves perceive diversity as a resource. The relationship between *GIAF* and Fáilte Ireland will be explored in this light.

## A brief history of *Galway International Arts Festival*

Different discourses lie behind the festival's establishment in 1978. The founders' shared a common motivation, namely their passion for the arts (Quinn, 2003). The festival also embodied the discourses of democratisation and access to the arts, which emerged in Ireland in the second half of the 1970s (Clancy, 2004). During the 1980s, the invited artists were showcased in small venues to an audience mainly comprising local people. The festival conducted its first audience survey in 1994 and, although by then it had started to grow and change, the survey found that 60% of the audience came from the city of Galway. A good portion (25.1%) was classified as 'Irish visitors', but 9.25% of these visitors came from County Galway (Envision, 1994: 5-6).

During the 1990s the festival grew in terms of size and cost, most of which was programme-related. Comedy became a section of the festival, while a children's section including workshops, readings, plays and film screenings was established in 1991. A multi-act concert known as *The Big Day Out* was organised on the periphery of Galway city and showcased Irish and international artists. The *Big Top*, a circus tent became a venue for international theatre companies, concerts and family events (*Galway Arts Festival*, 1989-99a). The festival's cost rose from about IR£380,000 (about €482,500) in 1989 to IR£871,844 (€1,107,014) in 1999. The greatest portion of *GIAF*'s budget was the result of successful ticket sales, fundraising and commercial sponsorship (*Galway Arts Festival*, 1989-99b). In these years, *GIAF*'s programme internationalised, although the participation of Galway-based artists was maintained (Quinn: 73).

The Arts Council nominated *GIAF* as a Regularly Funded Organisation in 2008, when the title was established, and continues to be the most important source of public funding for *GIAF*, contributing over 38% of the festival's income in 2010 (The Arts Council, email, 2013). Although *GIAF* was not instituted with tourism goals in mind, it grew to be a successful tourist attraction for domestic and overseas visitors alike. In 2010, 'overseas visitors' composed 27.3% of the festival's attendees. This estimate largely exceeds the average of 17.1%, which characterised 190 festivals and events applying for Fáilte Ireland's financial support in 2010 (Fitzpatrick Associates, 2011). Being assigned €200,000 in 2015 mostly for marketing purposes, *GIAF* was in receipt of the second-highest grant from Fáilte Ireland to a festival or an event (Fáilte Ireland, 2015).

## The pragmatic side of *GIAF*'s internationalisation

In *GIAF*'s financial statement for 2010, the board of directors expressed concern for the 'greatest risk and uncertainty' linked to both public and private income sources (*Galway Arts Festival*, 2010). While reacting to this predicament through creative relationships with the corporate sector, *GIAF* also became a pilot organisation for a fundraising capacity-building programme called *RAISE the Business of Arts Fundraising*, which was launched by the Arts Council in 2012. At the same time, *GIAF* engaged in a process of renovation by first reframing the organisation's objectives. According to the financial statements, these objectives had remained unvaried since the early 1990s and included the improvement of the festival programme, the enhancement of its promotional campaigns and the consolidation of its financial viability through public and private sponsorship (*Galway Arts Festival*, 1992-08). In 2010 the objectives conveyed ambition in terms of internationalisation and a sense of awareness with regard to the dynamics shaping the organisation:

1. **Excellence**: to be one of the best festivals in the world presenting a dynamic, exciting and innovative programme of the highest international standards
2. **Access**: to present the best possible arts experience to as many people as possible
3. **Leadership**: to act as an artistic leader in the presentation and origination of work
4. **Artists**: to encourage, support and facilitate artists with the development of their work
5. **Policy**: to drive the arts agenda locally and nationally and be positively influential internationally
6. **Resources**: to identify and consolidate the resources necessary to achieve our vision.

(*Galway Arts Festival*: 4).

Noticeably, the audience for whom the festival should represent a vehicle to access the arts is not geographically defined. A stronger tourist remit and the digitalisation of the festival experience are useful perspectives to explain this change.

## The production and co-production of new ideas

*GIAF*'s name change was preceded by the emergence of specific activities, whose common denominator is the production of *GIAF*-branded content for international dissemination. In 2013, *GIAF*'s *First Thought Talks* was inaugurated, embodying the hope to inspire "new ideas and new ways of looking at our world" (*Galway Arts Festival*, 2013). To an extent, *GIAF* had long been engaged with what Delanty calls 'the discursive model' of arts festivals, which often accompanies 'the showcasing model' in international events (2011: 217). The presence of post-performance talks with artists and directors has characterised the festival since the 1990s, but the new section covers a variety of themes from economics to politics and common places in literature. It is inquisitive rather than informative, as it is hoped to stimulate questions and states of mind. Hence, it has the potential to be particularly central to *GIAF*'s objective of being positively influential, where this ambition is interpreted as its ability to host 'communities of practice' (Comunian, 2015) that involve and affect audiences, artists and institutions alike.

According to Crumlish, *GIAF*-branded artwork meets organisational goals such as supporting artists' careers, but also increases "the uniqueness of the festival" and makes it "a more interesting cultural tourism product" (interview). *GIAF*-branded work is particularly produced in the realm of theatre. In the 2000s, the festival co-produced several new plays including Mark Doherty's *Trad* (2004) and Christian O'Reilly's *Chapatti* (2014). It also produced an extensively re-written version of *Misterman* (2011) by Enda Walsh. These plays have starred internationally well-known actors and have been showcased internationally, especially in the UK and the USA. The co-production partners include international companies such as the US-based *Northlight Theatre of Skokie*, which worked on *Chapatti*. British and American audiences are an English-speaking public but also represent two core tourist markets, whose experiences traditionally revolve around the consumption of Ireland's culture in the form of literature, theatre, ancestry and imagined way of life (Cronin, 2003; Bennett, 2004; Wright, 2008; Bolger, 2012). It makes sense to reach out to the USA and the UK, because these markets are already loyal to the specificity of Ireland's cultural brand, which *GIAF* nurtures by providing new insights into Ireland's cultural life. However, it cannot be argued that tourism-related objectives drive production. *GIAF*-branded work has in fact been showcased in other countries, which are arguably not as significant in terms of tourism. For example, Helena Jonsdottir's dance-based project called *Open Source* (2004) has been showcased in the Netherlands, and has then continued to develop in Iceland. In this light, it is possible that *GIAF* could contribute to strengthening the presence of Ireland's brand in these countries, and positively impact cultural tourism figures.

The ability to attract tourists is at the basis of a win-win relationship with Fáilte Ireland, which is in turn central to *GIAF*'s internationalisation. Since the 1990s, *GIAF*'s leaders had been targeting tourists as a means of generating more income to feed a growing festival with many international acts (Quinn 2003: 73). However, steady and substantial support from the tourism authority arrived only in the early 2000s. In 2005, following the spectacular growth of cultural tourism (Furlong, 2009: 217) and a heavier government investment in festivals through the establishment of Fáilte Ireland's programme called *Festivals and Cultural Events Initiative* (renamed as *Festivals and Participative Events Programme* in 2011), *GIAF* became a cornerstone in a €1m marketing campaign aimed at re-launching the West of Ireland as a tourist destination. While facilitating *GIAF*'s publicity activities in the USA and the UK, Fáilte Ireland has also increased its grant-in-aid to the festival. In 2010, for example, the grant constituted 10% of the festival's overall income (Crumlish, email, 2013). This contribution is significant considering that, on the basis of the data provided by the festival to the author, Fáilte Ireland's grant constituted 0.7% of the festival's income in 2002.

## The digital journey: the case of GAFTV

Fáilte Ireland is involved in the funding of another internationalising activity: the construction of a digital experience. *GIAF* developed a multi-lingual website in 2007 and, as of 2015, the website is available in Spanish, French, German and Gaelic. *GIAF* is present on interactive platforms such as Facebook, Twitter, Google+ and Instagram, and has developed GAFTV, which broadcasts via website and online video platforms including YouTube. GAFTV was conceived in 2009 and it has since evolved into a vehicle for the global dissemination of an image that the festival controls. The author has carried out content analysis of promotional videos produced in 2011 by Galway Arts Festival TeleVision (GAFTV) focusing on GAFTV videos as platforms for GIAF's internationalisation. Overall, six sub-themes emerge in the research within the thematic framework of internationalisation:

1 The presence of international artists.
2 The presence of an international audience.
3 The involvement of consecrated artists.
4 Internationally touring artists.
5 Exclusive events.
6 Cosmopolitan flair.

GAFTV's productions represent *GIAF* as in constant flux between the international and the local, passing through the national. They circulate meanings that put *GIAF* in the same realm as other international festivals, but also mark the attachment of the festival to the infrastructure of the city. They even hint at *GIAF* as a space for cosmopolitan experiences. Far from empowering the festival experience, digital technology contributes to both making 'a bit of festival' available anytime and anywhere and creating a frame of reference for people who are not familiar with *GIAF*. As John Urry's theory of the 'tourist gaze' suggests ([1990] 2002), tourists are attracted by this sense of familiarity combined with the aspiration of living the extra-ordinary (in the case of festivals, the non-ordinary is rooted in their 'one-off' nature). Through GAFTV – Crumlish argues – *GIAF* aims to facilitate people's 'journeys through the festival', and also hopes to attract 'people who have never been to Galway slowly deepening their relationship so someday they will come' (interview).

## Conclusions

Focusing on the process of internationalisation, this chapter highlighted three strategic realms in which arts festivals can simultaneously act as consumable brands and cultural institutions: the discursive model, new productions, and the digital space. It is perhaps premature to claim that *GIAF*'s internationalisation activities have proven effective. For example, noting *GIAF*'s presence in a crowded digital space is not sufficient to argue that *GIAF*'s digitisation has been a successful step in terms of audience and tourism development. It is however clear that *GIAF* has not simply adapted to the economic rationalities embedded in recession. It has actively shaped its profile according to hybridity, as GAFTV's productions reveal. It has entrepreneurially renovated the dynamics of the organisation by focusing on content production and instituting a win-win relationship with Fáilte Ireland. In doing so, *GIAF*'s manager has aligned the festival's growth ambitions with Fáilte Ireland's goal of growing a competitive culture-centred brand. A content-based strategy seems a valid choice, since new content can expand audiences and be a source of royalties; it can also appeal to corporate sponsors seeking to establish a connection with their audiences.

It is evident that tourism is a realm for an internationalising performance directed by *GIAF*'s leaders and grounded in the tendency "to be the same but different", as Tom Inglis puts it (2009). This understanding can be useful for the purpose of a nuanced analysis aimed at examining the contribution of contemporary festivals to public culture, which is an underdeveloped theme (Sassatelli, 2015: 32). Tourism was found to play a role in how *GIAF*'s leaders construct the festival as a content generator and cultural institution, but this does not mean that *GIAF* is merely dominated by a commercial logic; it rather performs to fit a dominating commercial logic. So, further research should investigate how this logic enables *GIAF* and other similar festivals to be influential arenas for the participation of different social groups in 'society-making', and how tourism in particular facilitates, disrupts or even prevents this process.

Technological platforms can indeed be useful to extend participation, but are also depositaries of memories in times of globalisation. Memories are a cornerstone of any experience (Ellis and Rossmann, 2008; Ralston *et al.*, 2007). They nourish co-creation, which does not confine tourists to the role of mere consumers of culture, but makes them participants in cultural production. Memories are also important for festivals' competitive profiles, positioning them on the map of a global marketplace for experience-makers. To better understand the connection between festivals, technologies and the generation of memories, audience-based research is necessary. This should investigate whether festival technologies serve the purpose of memory banks affecting those who have already attended the festival, which would in turn affects festival production; or if they can be envisioned as an effective prospective strategy to generate new visitors. As discussed, the case of GIAFTV simply suggests that these purposes can co-exist, making the boundaries between tourism and festivals' cultural relevance even more blurred. Technological platforms can finally be useful filters to study festivals' interaction with society, as well as their internationalisation.

Because reaching out to as many people as possible is a condition for contemporary arts festivals to survive in turbulent times, internationalisation can be seen as an inherent dimension of technologies. This implies that there is not necessarily a deliberate approach to the use of technologies, but there is a conscious approach to the involvement of specific stakeholders in festivals' internationalising processes. GIAF's internationalisation is embedded with its legitimisation as a 'worldy' arts festival, since Irish and international artists were found to voice GIAF's international and even cosmopolitan flavour. This adds a strictly performative dimension to the study of how peripheral festivals internationalise, which builds an important bridge between the socio-cultural and the managerial approaches to festival studies.

## Bibliography

Andersson, T. and Getz, D. (2008) Stakeholder management strategies of festivals, *Journal of Convention and Event Tourism*, **9** (3), 199-220.

Bennett, S. (2004) Performing ireland: Tourism and the Abbey Theatre, *Canadian Journal of Irish Studies*, **30** (2), 30-37.

Bianchini, F. and Maughan C. (2015) Introduction: Section 4: the Future of Festivals, in C. Newbold, C. Maughan, J. Jordan and F. Bianchini (eds.), *Focus on Festivals – Contemporary European case studies and perspectives*, Oxford: Goodfellow, 240-244.

Bolger, M. A. (2012) Buttering up the British: Irish exports and the tourist gaze, *In/Print*, **1**, 87-96.

Business to Arts (2010) Shining the light on successful sponsorship – an assessment of Ulster Bank's festival sponsorship. Available at http://www.businesstoarts.ie/pdfs/Shining_the_light_on_successful_sponsorships.pdf, accessed July 2 2015.

Business to Arts (n. d.) Case studies. Available at http://www.businesstoarts.ie/case-studies/sponsorship-case-studies/ulster-bank-galway-international-arts-festival/, accessed 1 July 2015.

Carnoy, M. Castells, M. Cohen, S. and Cardoso F. H. (1993) Introduction, in M. Carnoy, M. Castells, S. Cohen, and F. H. Cardoso (eds.), *The New Global Economy in the Information Age. Reflections on Our Changing World*, Univeristy Park, PA: Pennsylvania State University, 6-14.

Comunian, R. (2015) Festivals as communities of practice: Learning by doing and knowledge networks amongst artists, in C. Newbold, C. Maughan, J. Jordan and F. Bianchini (eds.), *Focus on Festivals – Contemporary European case studies and perspectives*, Oxford: Goodfellow, 53-65.

Clancy, M. (2009) *Brand New Ireland?*, Farnham: Ashgate Publishing.

Clancy, P. (2004) Rhetoric and reality. A review of the position of community arts in state cultural policy in the Irish Republic, in S. Fitzgerald (ed.), *An Outburst of Frankness. Community Arts in Ireland – A Reader*, Dublin: tasc at New Island, 83-114.

Cornelissen, S. (2005) Producing and imaging 'place' and 'people': The political economy of South African international tourist representation, *Review of International Political Economy*, **12** (4), 674-699.

Cronin, M. (2003) Next to being there: Ireland of the Welcomes and Tourism of the World, in M. Cronin and B. O'Connor (eds.), *Irish Tourism: Image, Culture, Identity*, Clevedon: Channel View, 179-195.

Delanty, G. (2011) On the cultural significance of arts festivals , in L. Giorgi, M. Sassatelli and G. Delanty (eds.), *Festivals and the Cultural Public Sphere*, Oxon: Routledge, 217-226. Google Play edition.

Di Maggio, P. J. and Powell. W. W. (1983) The iron cage revisited: Institutional isomorphism and collective rationality in organizational fields, *American Sociological Review*, **48** (2), 147-160.

Ellis, G. D. and Rossman, R. J. (2008) Creating value for participants through experience staging: parks, recreation, and tourism in the experience industry, *Journal of Park and Recreation Administration*, **26** (4), 1-20.

Envision Marketing Consultants (1994) *Galway Arts Festival Final Report*, Galway: Envision.

Fáilte Ireland (2015) Donohoe announces €320,000 in second phase of funding for major festivals and events in 2015, released on 8 December 2014. Available at http://www.failteireland.ie/Utility/News-Features/News-Library/Donohoe-announces-%E2%82%AC320,000-in-second-phase-of-fund.aspx, accessed 10 December 2014.

Fáilte Ireland (2012) *Cultural Insights Initiative Drives Cultural Tourism*, released on 29 February. Available at http://www.failteireland.ie/Utility/News-Features/News-Library/Cultural-Insights-Initiative-Drives-Cultural-Touri.aspx, accessed on 2 June 2015.

Ferdinand, N. and Williams, N. L. (2013) International festivals as experience production systems, *Tourism Management*, **34**, 202-210.

Finkel, R. (2010) Re-imaging arts festivals through a corporate lens: A case study of business sponsorship at the Henley Festival, *Managing Leisure*, **15** (4), 237-250.

Finkel, R. (2009) A picture of the contemporary combined arts festival landscape, *Cultural Trends*, **18** (1), 3-21.

Fitzpatrick Associates (2011) *Overall Economic Contribution of Festivals and Events 2010*. Dublin: Fáilte Ireland, 2011.

Furlong, I. (2009) *Irish Tourism 1880-1980*, Dublin: Irish Academic Press.

GAFTV (2011) *YouTube Archive*. Available at https://www.youtube.com/user/gaftv/videos, accessed 3 July 2015.

Galway Arts Festival (1989-99a) *Official programmes*.

Galway Arts Festival (1989-99b) *Directors' report and audited financial statements*. Available at http://www.solocheck.ie/, accessed between 2013 and 2014.

Galway Arts Festival (2010) *Directors' report and audited financial statements for the year ended in December 31st 2009*. Available at http://www.solocheck.ie/, accessed November 13, 2013.

Galway Arts Festival (2013) *First Thought e-zine special*, newsletter received 12 July 2013.

Gielen, P. (2010) The arts institution in the globalised world, *Journal of Arts Management, Law and Society*, **40**, 279–296.

Gordziejko T. (2015) Belonging and unbelonging: The cultural purpose of festivals, in C. Newbold, C. Maughan, J. Jordan and F. Bianchini (eds.), *Focus on Festivals – Contemporary European case studies and perspectives*, Oxford: Goodfellow, 265-275.

Holt, D. B. (2004) *How Brands Become Icons: The Principles of Cultural Branding*, Boston: Harvard Business School Press.

Inglis, T. (2009) *Global Ireland: Same Difference*, London: Routledge.

Jaworski, A. and Thurlow C. (2010) Language and the globalizing habitus of tourism: Toward a sociolinguistics of fleeting relationships, in N. Coupland (ed.), *The Handbook of Language and Globalization*, Hoboken, NJ: Wiley-Blackwell, 255-286.

Jordan, J. (2015), Festival leadership in turbulent times, in C. Newbold, C. Maughan, J. Jordan and F. Bianchini (eds.), *Focus on Festivals. Contemporary – European case studies and perspectives*, Oxford: Goodfellow, 107-117.

Klaić, D., Hansen, K., Bacchella, U., Bollo, A. and Di Stefano E. (2004) *Festivals: challenges of growth, distinction, support base and internationalisation*. Available at http://www.fitzcarraldo.it/ricerca/pdf/ricerca_festival_tartu.pdf, accessed 20 November 2014.

Meade, R. (2011) Brand Ireland: Culture in the crisis, *Concept*, **2** (3), 1-7. Available at http://concept.lib.ed.ac.uk/index.php/Concept/article/view/131 accessed 28 June 2015.

Neuhofer, D., Buhalis, D. and Ladkin, A. (2014) A typology of technology-enhanced tourism experiences *International Journal of Tourism Research*, **16**, 340-350.

Norton, J. (2015) The Diggers' Festival: Organising a community festival with political connotations, in C. Newbold, C. Maughan, J. Jordan and F. Bianchini (eds.), *Focus on Festivals – Contemporary European case studies and perspectives*, Oxford: Goodfellow, 127-137.

Paris, T. and Leroy F. (2014) Managing transition in an artistic company with entrepreneurial management: a case study of group Bernard Loiseau *International Journal of Arts Management*, **16** (2), 42-54.

Pillmayer, M. and Scherle N. (2014) The tourism industry and the process of internationalization in the Middle East: The example of Jordan, *International Journal of Tourism Research*, **16**, 329-39.

Poon, A. (1993) *Tourism, Techologies and Competitive Strategies*, Wallingford: CAB International.

Quinn, B. (2003) Shaping tourism places; agency and interconnections in festival settings, in M. Cronin and B. O'Connor (eds.), *Irish Tourism: Image, Culture, Identity*, Clevedon: Channel View, 61-79.

Ralston, L. S. Ellis, G. D. Compton, D. M. and Lee, J. (2007) Staging memorable events and festivals: an integrated model of service and experience factors, *International Journal of Event Management Research*, **3** (2), 24-38.

Regev, M. (2011) International festivals in a small country: rites of recognition and cosmopolitanism, in L. Giorgi, M. Sassatelli and G. Delanty (eds.), *Festivals and the Cultural Public Sphere*, Oxon: Routledge, 2011, 132-149. Google Play edition.

Robins, K. (1997) What in the world's going on?, in P. du Gay (ed.), *Production of Culture/ Cultures of Production*, London: Sage, 12-47.

Sassatelli, M. (2015) Festivals, urbanity and the public sphere: reflections on European festivals, in C. Newbold, C. Maughan, J. Jordan and F. Bianchini (eds.), *Focus on Festivals – Contemporary European case studies and perspectives*, Oxford: Goodfellow, 28-39.

Silvanto, S. (2015) How to Flow in C. Newbold, C. Maughan, J. Jordan and F. Bianchini (eds.), *Focus on Festivals – Contemporary European case studies and perspectives*, Oxford: Goodfellow, 89-97.

The Arts Council (2014) *Irish arts sector private investment report*. Available at http://www.artscouncil.ie/uploadedFiles/wwwartscouncilie/Content/Publications/Research_reports/Private-Investment-Report-March-2014.pdf, 2 July 2015.

Urry, J. (2002) *The Tourist Gaze*, 2nd edn, London: Sage.

Vanhove, N. (2001) Globalisation of tourism demand, global distribution systems and marketing, in S. Wahab and C. Cooper, *Tourism in the Age of Globalization*, London: Routledge, 123-156.

Verbanova, L. (2013) *Strategic Management in the Arts*, New York: Routledge.

Yúdice, G. (2003) *The Expediency of Culture - Uses of Culture in the Global Era*, Durham: Duke University Press.

Wahab, S. and C. Cooper (2001) Tourism, globalization and the competitive advantage of nations, in S. Wahab and C. Cooper, *Tourism in the Age of Globalization*, London: Routledge, 3-21.

Wright, A. (2008) Managing the American tourist experience in Ireland: An Emotional Context, *International Journal of Business and Management*, **3** (8), 85-92.

# 10 *Rock in Rio*: The Festival

Vanessa Martin

## Introduction

With its first edition in 1985, *Rock in Rio* transformed the cultural and art scene in Brazil. Before it, the country was not well regarded by artists and their international managers. Thirty years later, *Rock in Rio* is one of the largest festivals in the world with successful editions being held in several countries.

Since its creation, Roberto Medina has understood the importance of the public in ensuring the success of the event. For him, "the stage was the heart, but the audience was the head, legs and arms... It was all part of the *Rock in Rio* body and every organ should receive equal treatment" (Carneiro, 2011: 42).

The success of the festival can also be explained by the professionalism, determination and efficiency of its implementation throughout its history. This chapter shows how *Rock in Rio* has become one of the largest festivals in the world and details the strategy behind the actions that have helped the festival achieve this.

## How it all started

*Rock in Rio* is a significant milestone for several generations of fans and also for Brazilian show business, placing Brazil in the spotlight on the global entertainment scene. In commemorating its 30th anniversary in 2015, *Rock in Rio* has many other reasons to celebrate, namely being one of the most valuable brands in the world of entertainment, playing a critical role in the professionalization of the major events in the country, and having opened the country to international artists.

Sixteen other editions have been held: in Rio de Janeiro, Lisbon, Madrid and Las Vegas (2015). Taking into account all Brazilian, Portuguese, Spanish, and American editions, more than 7.7 million people have attended the event which has been broadcast to 1 billion viewers worldwide (by TV and internet). Over 1,359 musical acts have performed on the event stages, totaling 1,200 hours of music. In the 2013 edition 185 countries received the festival, and it was covered by 500 journalists (Teresa-Levin,2015a).

The first edition of the festival began on 11 January 1985. The difficulties were monumental and impressive. Nonetheless, its statistics are quite magnificent. The place chosen for the construction of the first City of Rock was an area that needed 77,000 trucks with earth to level the marshland and tons of manure to fertilize the grass. 400 bathrooms, two shopping malls and two mini hospitals were built, a wall measuring three meters high and two kilometers long was constructed, and 450 coconut trees and 85 palm trees were planted. About 1.38 million people were present during the 10 days of shows.

At that time, hiring artists was another challenge of epic proportions, as they charged astronomical rates to play in Brazil or refused invitations to travel to South America. The demands and requirements for the dressing rooms and support infrastructure were also exaggerated.

The structure of the stage measured 5,600 square meters (eighty meters wide and twenty meters high) and was 3.3 meters off the ground. It had a triple platform that ran on rails, which enabled a band to play, while another stage could be prepared for the next attraction. In order to meet so many attractions a day there were 12 dressing rooms and two green rooms, a large lounge for 120 people and a 24-hour restaurant.

The lighting consumed 2 million watts just for the audience. Only 20% was directed to the stage. For that edition, the entire sound system was imported, hired from the US, as there was no such equipment available in Brazil, with 70,000 watt capacity for 250 speakers, spread across 4 tables of 32 channels each. Altogether, there were 100 tons of equipment and much of the staff responsible for handling that consisted of technicians from other countries. Sixteen years later, the construction of the City of Rock was made solely by Brazilians.

In the edition of 2013, there was a total of 105 hours of music for 595,000 people. The staff was made up of 1,200 people.

## The successful tripod of *Rock in Rio*

In order to better understand the *Rock in Rio* phenomenon, one should take a look at the profile and the ideas of its CEO. Charismatic, visionary, very intelligent, humble, kind, and polite, Roberto Medina has had a key role in creating the event and in its business strategy.

He structured the event on an unbeatable tripod: a strong and essential focus on the consumer, on the *Rock in Rio* family (as he calls his team) and on the exceptional relationship with sponsors' brands ensuring they gain exceptional value from the festival.

The participant is the essence of the festival. According to the definition of Medina:

> It is a set of actions where the public is the big star. It is about the people who are there. And that is very clear to me. We have a gesture, on each day that opens the festival, which is the whole team going to the door when people come in and we applaud them. It is because it is them we have to applaud, not the artist. We have to applaud them, those who are giving

> the possibility for us to be there. Without the warm audience, this star is worthless. I think I give such attention to the public that no other festival in the world does, because that is the origin, the DNA of Rock in Rio (Medina interview 06/08/15).

The *Rock in Rio* family consists of all company employees. When it comes to hiring, they look for people with a strong, friendly and sensitive human side. They have already let talent people go from the technical side who did not have the desired profile. And Medina is generous enough to listen to the opinion of the team prior to decision-making:

> I have always wanted to make a family. Many of the people have been here from the very beginning. And I think everyone is touched by *Rock in Rio*. I am a good administrator of souls, well, dreams ... That's what I know how to move (Medina interview 06/08/15).

Thus, by feeling valued and respected, employees perform their duties with renewed vigor. This position has generated conditions and fostered team building which has resulted in low staff turnover and a group of people very committed to the company. Consequently, the quality of services provided by staff, suppliers and partners are now chosen with the same frame of reference, thus initiating a virtuous cycle.

However, also very relevant to the success of the festival is its transformation into a smart and efficient business platform, where sponsors' brands communicate creatively and profitably with active and potential consumers. Since the first edition of the event, the relationship with sponsors has been influenced and benefited from its creator's understanding of advertising.

> When *Rock in Rio* came up, I had no brands, because I had no show business experience. Then I borrowed a little bit of my knowledge as communicator and advertiser to try to create a solution through brands. Brands would never come to a music event. And I had been arguing for some time about 360° communication. Well, then I had to create a story that did not end between the 1st and the last day of the festival. It had to be much more before that. I have to make a communication project out of it in order to be able to bring brands. I have to sophisticate here because brands have to feel comfortable and make a communication project. Ok, there you had the first festival framework (Medina interview 06/08/15).
>
> In the first design, Brahma alone invested US$ 20 million. 30 years ago. Today it would be like US$ 200 million. It was something extraordinary, not based on the festival. I never sold the festival. The festival was the end of a great advertising party. Nobody hires sponsorship of *Rock in Rio* to speak to 700,000 people – otherwise they would be throwing money away. That is a minor part. What they buy is the *Rock in Rio* brand to talk for a whole year on the air. And I try to create a new permanent information machine

> in order to make the brand energized in order to be worthwhile. I produce non-stop information (Medina interview 06/08/15).

The combination of those three ingredients is the basis of the recipe for success of *Rock in Rio* throughout 15 events during its 30 years of existence.

## Participants have a voice at the event, interacting with one another and with brands

As explained previously, the participant's appreciation as the mainstay of the event, is the main driver of decisions and actions of the event organizers. The quality and comfort of the public are sacred mantras for the organization of the festival, as well as the restriction of the maximum number of public every day, which is always below the maximum capacity of the City of Rock. In the inaugural edition, for the first time in the country, the audience was lit in order to highlight its importance to the event.

The main theme of the event is to create consumers' emotional ties with the *Rock in Rio* brand and with the sponsors' brands. Therefore, the organization listens extremely closely to the audience. A representative example is a few weddings a year that take place during the event, they are pre-selected by the organization. The reason? In 2011 a letter from a Red Hot Chilli Peppers fan touched the CEO:

> I brought in the Red Hot on her wedding day. And her friends are also fans and were coming to see (the event). I called her and asked, 'Don't you want to make your wedding at *Rock in Rio*?' Then she freaked out. She came to the event. She got married at *Rock in Rio*. And so it was, it was no initiative of mine. It was to answer a letter that moved me. I blew the wedding unintentionally. I had to provide a solution. And she got happy: she got married there, with all her friends. And it was very nice (Medina interview 06/08/15).

Back in 1985, the City of Rock offered "two installed malls, each with a square and trees and 15 stores of 42m² with pinball, jeans, sneakers, records, videos, instruments, buttons, stickers, ice cream, sporting goods, camping accessories, film developers, natural food, books, posters, chocolates, sweets, pizzas, cakes, drug stores, and café." (Carneiro, 2011: 122 – 123). From the start, the design of the festival was to be an event for the family, where more than one generation could talk about it. This was the reason for the inclusion of James Taylor in the line-up of the 1985 edition (White, 2005) and it is a theme that has guided the selection of artists ever since. For the CEO, the festival's success is the result of simultaneous actions, interrelated and focused on details:

> I think the biggest challenge is not one, but rather a set of actions. The biggest challenge is for you not to miss details. The city has to be very beautiful. The flowers have to be pretty. I change the flowers the day before. I

> have already argued because of flower color. I do not miss details, even the small ones. And that is in everything. The note I send, it has to have a care in the delivery. I guess that is what resulted in the history, in the success of *Rock in Rio*. I do not see things as single things (Medina interview 06/08/15).

All this care is valued by the public: a survey conducted in 2015 in five major Brazilian cities, pointed out that *Rock in Rio* is the most popular event in Rio de Janeiro, with 73.3% of respondents having already been to it or wanting to go (Teresa-Levin, 2015b).

## Marketing and branding: consolidating success

The essence of experiential marketing is to create meaningful and extraordinary experiences around the brand or product. And events are among the best ways to provide these experiences to consumers (Anderton 2015, Pine and Gilmore 1999).

*Rock in Rio* has always been a great communication platform for brands. The secret, according to Medina:

> "is an advertising project. I made the project so that, if I was at the other end as vice president of marketing, I would approve of it" (Medina interview 06/08/15)

Among other actions designed to extend the residual value of the event, the organizers hold several events throughout the year that generate continuous content and buzz about the festival, such as, press conferences to launch the line-up, presentations of sponsors announcing sponsorships. Or presenting to potential sponsors, interviews with artists, etc.

Since the first edition, *Rock in Rio* has invested in brand licensing, sales areas and merchandising (T-shirts, buttons, visors, sunglasses, stickers, etc.). Nearly 2 million T-shirts of the event (Neves, 2006: 122) have been sold. As an inspirational brand and one which has great impact on the final consumer, *Rock in Rio* offers great revenue potential and has a history of success of licensing to partner companies. There is a growing commitment of music companies to strengthen the relationship with the younger audience.

In previous Brazilian editions, some of the main sponsors promoted contests that gave away tickets to fans by associating the brand of *Rock in Rio* to their products, such as in the promotions 'I am going to *Rock in Rio* with Globo.com', 'You + 4 Fox friends at *Rock in Rio*' and 'Heineken and you at *Rock in Rio*', offering tickets, access to VIP areas and activations of brand experience, exclusive and differentiated products during the festival. The approach Itaú Bank came up with for the 2013 festival was fun and amusing: it awarded a pair of tickets to the festival to the person who showed the greatest kindness to a busking guitarist playing on the streets of Rio de Janeiro, in the days before the event. A recording of the action of the winner was made by hidden cameras and the video was posted on YouTube, which in a few days hit 2.2 million views (Rocha, 2013a).

For the 2001 edition, based in Rio de Janeiro, the festival licensed 70 products that totaled R$ 800,000 in royalties and revenues of R$ 10 million to suppliers and retailers. 60,000 caps, 15,000 mugs, 20,000 cups, 450,000 shirts, 3,000 glasses, 21,000 towels, and 25,000 notebooks were sold.

Mondelez obtained excellent results during the 2011 edition: the festival brought 2.5% share increase of Trident gum, and spontaneous media coverage of the event was worth three times the value of the sponsorship. Between the 2011 and 2013 editions, the brand's market share rose by 5.5 points to 58%, consolidating it as the country's leading brand. Those achievements caused the company to double its sponsorship to include the Club Social Crackers as well as Trident gum as both brands target young people. From investing 40% of the brand's marketing budget, the company's sponsorship spend rose to 60% of the budgets of each brand. They occupied 260 square meters of floor area with two floors: the press and VIPs at the upper level, and multiple attractions for the public on the lower level, including an augmented reality stage to record 40-second performances, posted on Facebook page of the company and on the performance's own page (Trident). The gum brand also offered 'Turbo Drop', a green elevator with a drop of 37 meters (in the previous edition it was 11 meters), for up to 700 people/hour. Club Social Crackers has invested in cosmetics (six make-up artists did makeup and hair for the public and photos showing before and after were available), they also provided an 'on stage for a minute' performance recording, designed for LED panel and shown on the outside of the stand (Rocha, 2013b).

Among the promotions developed by Volkswagen in 2015, was a limited edition production of Golf and Fox cars in honor of the *Rock in Rio*. They had unique visual details, such as adhesive strips on the sides of the body with musical instruments; event name on the front fenders, pedals with aluminum cover, etc (Mundo Do Marketing (2015a).

The 2015 edition at Rock City in Rio de Janeiro, despite the unfavorable economic environment in Brazil, achieved an absolute record in the 30 years of its existence: 42 companies associated their brands with the event and there were 640 licensed products. The expectation of the organizers is that the economic impact from the sale of official products, divided into 76 categories, surpassed R$ 2 billion (about US$ 600 million). Among the brands that have licensed products are Volkswagen, Chilli Beans, Colgate, Paco Rabanne, Pepsi, Taco, Wöllner and Bacardi.

The organizers have estimated the economic value of media space and sponsorship related to the festival in almost R$ 1 billion (about US$ 300 million) of communication throughout the year. Investments in the *Rock in Rio* brand have reached US$ 530 million. The 2015 edition had master sponsorship from Banco Itaú, in addition to Ipiranga, Volkswagen, Heineken, Pepsi, and Oi.

## Engagement and close connections between participants, sponsors and organizer

Edition after edition, the festival presents novelties and promotes the integration of the event with participants in an interactive and engaging way. The 2015 edition saw the festival reach 11 million followers on social networks. In the previous edition, two years earlier, the event's official website had 4.5 million visits and reached 34.2 million people on social networks. YouTube had 341,329 hours of viewing (Rock in Rio, 2013).

For the 2015 Rio de Janeiro edition, the event developed an app that offered various experiences to users. With a simple map to help them get to the City of Rock with the attractions, transportation tips for the event, etc. and interaction on the official social networks. With the tool 'My schedule and line-up' it can create a custom schedule of shows. The 'What's hot' resource displays the main artists of the event. At *Rock in Rio* Hunt, by filling out a card with photographic challenges, users can share it with friends (Mundo Do Marketing,2015b).

On the event website, fans can access the '*Rock in Rio* Forever', an interactive map that brings together events that marked the 30 years of the festival, in addition to becoming a protagonist of the event, creating their own avatar and telling their stories. Among the defining moments is Freddie Mercury's performance of *Love of My Life* at the first festival in 1985.

The business platform created by *Rock in Rio* enables and encourages brands to create and deploy numerous interesting ways to talk to their active or potential consumers using the event as the main theme. Through the 'Caçada Oi' app, OI, the Brazilian mobile phone company and one of the sponsors of the event encourages users to win prizes as they seek QR Codes spread around the festival.

Sky, in its third consecutive participation, produced unique content and pre-event actions on the event theme in their official channels and on its social networks, enhancing its participation in the festival. The #SKYrocks platform shows the history of the bands with graphics and songs of the line-up artists, as well as videos specially produced about the history of the iconic rock guitars. Its booth at the festival has the shape of a guitar and has coverage on Instagram and Facebook, with the participation of the movers and shakers.

In 2013, Banco Itaú promoted multiple activities, such as the Ferris wheel and the public video recording with groups of friends imitating a band, playing to an audience who shouted their names. It was shared on social networks through biometric registration. These impacted more than 5 million people, generated more than 8,600 shares, 110,000 likes and 65,000 comments (Teresa-Levin, 2013).

In that edition, the event's official website had 4.5 million visits and official social media registered for more than 10 million fans. The festival's official app has been downloaded 156,000 times and YouTube videos viewed 341,329 hours.

## Sustainability

Each and every action is grounded and driven by corporate strategy, which in turn is defined by the guidelines and references from their directors. At *Rock in Rio*, social and environmental responsibility is a serious matter and it is conducted with great passion and commitment by staff. The directors of the festival consider it as payback for everything they have received. This parameter is used in all editions, in and out of Brazil. And they want to expand more and more activities.

The economic impact of the 2013 edition of Rio de Janeiro, published by Riotur, Rio's tourism agency, was R$ 1 billion (about US$ 300 million) and the average occupancy rate of hotels was 90%. It generated more than 140,000 jobs. So far, *Rock in Rio* indicates that more than US$ 23.2 million have been invested in social and environmental projects.

The social and environmental project 'For a Better World' was created in 2001 in order to encourage people to reflect on a better world and to be an instrument of mobilization and sensitization. Over the years it became the parent project in various social and environmental initiatives. That year (2001), the festival donated 5% of the funds for social projects, 70% of them dedicated to assist 30 poor communities in Rio de Janeiro, on the education of young people between 17 and 29 years old, from low-income families. The rest was donated to UNESCO (United Nations Educational, Scientific and Cultural Organization). According to the organizer, with an investment of US$ 16,520 million from the festival and partners, this project promoted a number of initiatives, such as:

- Mobilization of more than 450,000 students, 53,000 teachers and 1,060 schools on sustainability.
- Installation of 14 sensory rooms in NGOs for mentally and visually impaired children.
- Over 119,000 trees have been planted since 2006.
- Compensation of 100% of the event's CO2 emissions (audited by Deloitte) and investment in an emission-reduction plan, as well as a manual of good practice for sponsors and suppliers.
- Installation and equipping of 10 music rooms in municipal schools in peaceful areas of Rio de Janeiro.
- Professional training courses in the repair and maintenance of musical instruments and donation of instruments, through a partnership with 145 post offices in the state of Rio de Janeiro.
- Construction of a Health Center in Maranhão.
- 2,200 musical instruments donated to more than 150 NGOs from all over Brazil who work with education and social inclusion through music.

- Training of 3,200 young people in elementary school in Rio de Janeiro.
- Creation of 70 classrooms in poor communities
- Construction of a school in Tanzania (Ribeiro, 2011).

## Conclusions

The history of *Rock in Rio* is very rich in learning about many aspects, such as the operational, structural, management, and in corporate strategy and generosity, illustrated by the 'For a better world' project.

The distinguished trajectory of *Rock in Rio* can be explained by several factors, but they are all grounded by the tripod 'Focus on the consumer – Rock in Rio Family – relationship with brands.' The center of the *Rock in Rio* universe is the audience, to which extreme care with comfort and safety of people and the beauty of the grand space is directed. The layout and content of these actions to the audience are created and executed with care and dedication by the *Rock in Rio* Family staff. The final completion comes from the excellent return of sales and visibility that the brands of the sponsors receive from the complete communication project the festival provides to partner companies. And all this, basted by social and environmental actions and operated in creative and differentiated projects, carried out since its creation, in all editions and countries.

## Bibliography

Alexandre, R. (1977) *Dias de luta: o rock e o Brasil nos anos 80*. São Paulo: DBA, 2002.

Alzer, L., and Claudino, M. (2004) *Almanaque dos Anos80: Lembranças e curiosidade de uma década bem divertida*. Rio de Janeiro: Ediouro.

Anderton, C. (2015), Branding, sponsorship and the music festival, in G. McKay (ed.), *The Pop Festival: history, music, media, culture*. London: Bloomsbury, 199-212.

Calderia, J. (1997) *Uma viagem pela história do Brasil*. São Paulo: Companhia das Letras, 1997.

Carneiro, L. (2011) *Rock in Rio: a história do maior festival de música do mundo*. São Paulo: Globo.

Mundo Do Marketing (2015a) Volkswagen produz carros do Rock in Rio, http://www.mundodomarketing.com.br/ultimas-noticias/33534/volkswagen-produz-carros-do-rock-in-rio.html, accessed 12 May 2015.

Mundo Do Marketing (2015b) Rock in Rio desenvolve aplicativo para celular em parceria com a Oi, http://www.mundodomarketing.com.br/ultimas-noticias/34127/rock-in-rio-desenvolve-aplicativo-para-celular-em-parceria-com-a-oi.html, accessed 7 August 2015.

Neves, M. E. (2006) *Vendedor de sonhos: a vida e obra de Roberto Medina*. São Paulo: Melhoramentos.

Pine, J.B. and Gilmore, J.H. (1999) *The Experience Economy*, Boston, MA: Harvard Business School Press.

Ribeiro, E. (2011) Rock in Rio lança projeto social, www.meioemensagem.com.br/home/marketing/noticias/2011/06/08/Rock-in-Rio-lan-a-projeto-social.html#ixzz3kAKWsENj, accessed 28 August 2015

Rocha, R. (2013a) Itaú: sucesso digital vai para off-line, http://www.meioemensagem.com.br/home/marketing/noticias/2013/09/19/Itau-sucesso-digital-vai-para-off-line.html#ixzz3kAFHA6Iy, accessed 20 August 2015.

Rocha, R. (2013b) Mondelez dobra investimento no Rock in Rio, http://www.meioemensagem.com.br/home/marketing/noticias/2013/08/21/Mondelez-dobra-investimento-no-Rock-in-Rio.html#ixzz3k9x1zhzq, accessed 25 August 2015

Rock in Rio (2013) Se Perca Nos Numaros Estratosféricos Que Fizeram Do: Rock in Rio 2013 O Maior Festival Do Planeta!, http://www.rockinrio.com/infografico2013/, accessed 17 August 2015

Teresa-Levin (2013) O brilho do Itaú no Rock in Rio, http://www.meioemensagem.com.br/home/marketing/noticias/2013/09/26/O-brilho-do-Itau-no-Rock-in-Rio.html#ixzz3kA8tC1uy

Teresa-Levin (2015a), Rock in Rio: recorde no licenciamento, http://www.meioemensagem.com.br/home/marketing/noticias/2015/06/17/Rock-in-Rio--recorde-no-licenciamento.html#ixzz3jrIsSLuJ, accessed 25 August 2015

Teresa-Levin (2015b) Rock in Rio: popular com paulistas e baianos, http://www.meioemensagem.com.br/home/marketing/noticias/2015/04/01/Rock-in-Rio-popular-com-paulistas-e-baianos.html#ixzz3jrSWe4RM, 24 August 2015

Ursini, N. (2013) Marcas se exibem no Rock in Rio http://www.meioemensagem.com.br/home/comunicacao/noticias/2013/09/13/Marcas-se-exibem-no-Rock-in-Rio.html#ixzz3k9vkh3Ju, 25 August 2015

White, T. (2005) *James Taylor: Long ago and far away – his life and music*. London: Omnibus Press.

# 11 Building the Festival Team: A case study of Saint Petersburg art festivals

Svetlana Puchkova and Elena Elkanova

## Introduction

In working to understand contemporary festivals, one of the most significant debates is how to manage a festival effectively in the face of increasing competition. In this sense, effective team management is crucial. However, there has been little discussion on the teambuilding phenomenon at festivals. Such features as fluctuations in the number of employees, different categories of employees and involvement of various stakeholders make festivals stand out from other business projects. So, commonly accepted teambuilding practices cannot be simply copied and applied to arts festivals. The purpose of the chapter is to explore particular features of team management at arts festivals in Saint Petersburg. The city, being the main cultural centre of Russia, presents an appropriate field of study. The number of festivals held in the city is increasing each year, as a result of city administration policies (St. Petersburg Committee of Culture Statistics, 2015). There are, however, a limited number of surveys that examine Saint Petersburg events, and it is difficult for researchers to get open access to reports of festival organisations. The authors attempt to fill the gap by presenting major aspects and common team management problems that festival organisations come across.

This chapter provides an overview on a variety of team management processes in three specific festivals. Festivals' team structures, recruitment practices, training and motivation strategies were researched. The authors focus on staff retention and issues relating to the status of different workers that influence team management practices such as decision-making processes, organisational culture, participant interdependence, communication and team size in particular. Research is based on interviews with the festival director, one permanent and one temporary employee for each event, analysis of social media, official websites, articles, and observational method. The chapter presents a part of survey that was carried out in 2014 by the authors. In 6 months, 30 expert interviews were conducted. This chapter deals with three brief cases which were designed as a result of interviews with nine respondents and observation method (the authors took part as visitors in *Open Library* festival and were involved in the process of organizing *International Conservatoire Week Festival* as volunteers).

## Festivals teambuilding

Research amongst Fortune 500 companies in the USA has shown that building teams is a popular method used for staff development and training (Loevingsson, 2005). Sometimes the term 'team' is used to define an approach to structure work. In some cases, organisational culture is implied (e.g. "We are all members of one team"). The most widely accepted definition of a team is: "a small number of people with complementary skills who are committed to a common purpose, performance goals, and approach for which they are mutually accountable" (Katzenbach and Smith, 1992). Often this definition is supplemented by discussion of roles being distributed between team members and of their joint work being for a limited period (Salas et al. 1992). Most of the teams are made up of five people to carry out a project and their joint work lasts on average for 1-2 years. Team leaders name lack of motivation among team members and work coordination as the main challenges of teamwork (Thompson, 2006).

The basic papers on group and team formation were written in 1960-1980s (Bales, 1965; Gersick, 1988; Tuckman and Jensen, 1977; Tuckman, 1965, etc.). Thus, the fundamental principles of teambuilding have existed for many years. However, the topic is still widely discussed (Topchik, 2007; West, 2012; Garfield and Dennis, 2013; Dyer and Dyer, 2013). Russian authors study teamwork mainly in organisational behaviour and human resource management frameworks (Latfullin and Gromova, 2004). The main problem of the scientific literature on teamwork is a lack of practical orientation in the research (e.g. approaches to the development of effective teams). It should be emphasised that there cannot be unified practices of teambuilding that are applicable for any organisation; methods should be adapted to the industry and the company, its organisational structure and culture.

There are a limited number of surveys that examine specific features of festivals' team management. In the festival management context, one cannot claim that the term 'team' is widely used by festival experts, although it appears in some papers (Wagen, 2007; Hanlon, 2002). Festivals provide various services that are intangible, inconsistent and short-term 'products'. Therefore, coordinated work by the whole team plays an important role. Moreover, aspects such as the involvement of different stakeholders (e.g. local community, authorities, media, partners, artists, sponsors and audience) and project structure are reflected in the work scope and volume, and necessity of attracting temporary staff. However, except for major events, the presence of an HR department or HR manager is not common in festival structures.

## Team management at the Saint Petersburg arts festivals

At present Saint Petersburg remains the most popular tourist destination in Russia, attracting both foreign and Russian tourists. In terms of classical culture, Saint Petersburg has the reputation as the cultural capital of Russia, including classical music, opera and ballet theatres, museums, exhibitions, great variety of shows (Gordin and Matetskaya 2012).

Festivals contribute to Saint Petersburg's image formation, however nowadays festivals in the city are targeted at local citizens. Study of festival practices in Saint Petersburg over the last few years showed that most widely spread common event types were musical, multi-genre, theatre and film festivals. This is obviously due to the high level of music and artistic culture in the city (Gordin and Matetskaya 2010).

The city administration supports a significant number of events by means of direct funding via committees of the city administration or allocating resources via cultural institutions under the control of the Committee on Culture. Festivals regardless of format, genre, scale, or the legal status of the organiser can apply for this support. There are a great number of small and middle-size festivals, local events, holidays and different public activities that have great importance for local people of the region. Many Saint Petersburg festivals are organised by non-governmental institutions, organisations and performers' teams (Gordin and Dedova 2015). In this chapter, three cases of such festivals will be discussed.

### *Cultural Capital Contest*

The *Cultural Capital Contest* was held for the first time in 2010. It lasts for 2 days and takes place each year. The contest includes performances from professionals and amateur artists in various genres (classical and modern) and an award ceremony. The contest has the following nominations: vocal, choreography, instrumental performance, theatre. The main requirement for all performances is to be connected with Saint Petersburg. The goals of the event are to support talented performers and to introduce theatre and music to citizens.

The event is organised by Creative Association Cultural Capital, which is a corporate and entertainment event agency and is mainly funded by the agency's revenues. The Creative Association's current business activities allow it to organise this non-profit event. The festival is held with the informational support of the Committee of Culture and Committee on Youth Policy and Relations with the NGOs of Saint Petersburg. Some support is provided by the local government, the Saint Petersburg House of Cooperation with UNESCO and the creative unions of St. Petersburg. The agency also works closely with non-profit organisations such as the Foundation for the Development of Science, Culture and Media (NIKA) and other charity funds.

Permanent staff consists of five persons, but the organisers understand the need of extending the team: "Hence, as the company develops, an experienced professional fundraiser will be needed." Search for sponsors is difficult mostly due to time constraints. The financial issue is critical for the *Cultural Capital* project as it is a socially oriented project and entrance to the shows is free. Sometimes tickets are distributed, indicating a numbered seat to increase the feeling of obligation of the potential audience member.

Organisers communicate closely with the participants and partners in advance. Participants apply and pay a registration fee. Transport, accommodation and meals are at the expense of the agency and are provided by subcontractors. Among the partners of the *Cultural Capital* are small business companies (e.g. photo studios, chain stores of musical instruments). Festival organisers carefully select the contractors, trying to keep in touch with those they are comfortable to work with and who matches their requirements.

Creative Association outsources non-core areas of activity, including accounting and design, and deals exclusively with the creative programme. Volunteers are not involved because "they need to be supervised" and there are no extra people in the team to do it, but temporary staff are employed (administrators and concertmasters). Creative Association *Cultural Capital* consists of young, creative people. They are educated in the arts field and the team appreciates their involvement in the arts and the creative process. They try to find people who share the same vision and values, but it is very difficult to find a designer, for example, and the results have been unsatisfying, with a lack of understanding of what the team is trying to achieve.

The employees of the festival *Cultural Capital* have no clear duty regulations and, although the responsibilities and functions are distributed among the employees, frequently they overlap with each other. Mutual help, decentralisation and cooperative decision-making are principles of the festival organisation. Relationships in the team are informal and friendly. The Art Director says that there are no conflicts, just creative disputes. According to the organisers, teambuilding attempts are not required, because everyone knows each other and is united by one idea. As for training, the staff attend all programmes they are invited to (e.g. educational programmes of the Institute of Cultural Programmes), because they realise that sometimes they do not have enough knowledge and experience in management, particularly in promotion and fundraising. There is no need for joint activities and visits, as everyone travels together on all corporate parties and events. Employees meet each other during the day, doing current work. As for the concept of teamwork, the Festival Director believes that it makes more sense to talk about team building in the context of major international festivals (e.g. festival *Roskilde* that draws volunteers to work there).

## *International Conservatory Week Festival*

The *International Conservatoire Week Festival* (*ICWF*) was established in 2001 and since that time has been held annually at the Saint Petersburg State Conservatoire named after composer Rimsky-Korsakov. The project is non-profit making. The festival is supported by Ministry of Culture of the Russian Federation and the Committee for External Relations of Saint Petersburg.

Partners from the Higher Music Schools from different countries are invited, Conservatoire students and staff also participate in the festival. The festival aims to show the relevance of music in Russia and abroad, and to promote young talent. In addition to concerts the festival has an educational function: well known bands and artists organise conferences and educational seminars, public lectures, rehearsals and master classes, and presentations of musical instruments.

The initiative to hold such an event came from Lydia Volchek, who is head of department at the Conservatoire and, now, director of the festival. She organised the festival with the help of supporters and co-thinkers. There was some resistance and negative attention from the administration of the Conservatoire, and the organiser faced many difficulties before the event was recognised. During the festival students and teachers should be busier than during the ordinary educational process; the administration did not want to contribute, some teachers also felt kind of jealousy and did not provide spare rooms. Besides as the festival was new, it had big problems with financing. Organisers had to invest their own resources and find some sponsors. These problems are in the past. The festival has been held for many years, and is now recognised and respected.

The board of trustees consists of general consulates of the USA, the Netherlands, Israel, the Republic of Armenia, the British Council in Russia, the Polish Institute, the Italian Institute of Culture and the Russian-Turkish Cultural Center. They cover all the expenses on travel or accommodation of artists. Funds of the general consulates and foreign partners (foundations and high schools) are the main source of financing.

Nowadays the organising committee consists of deans of faculties and heads of departments of the Saint Petersburg Conservatoire. The group of people directly working on the project organisers team is called the administrative group. The group includes the director of the festival and another nine people: the financial specialist, press secretary, three music editors and four coordinators.The team is not particularly stable; employees leave for a variety of reasons, for example when leaving the Conservatoire. New people recruited to work on the festival automatically join the team of festival organisers.Employees from the technical support, curation and administrative departments; some experts and volunteers also participate.

The search for volunteers is carried out in advance of the festival. Organisers provide instruction for them to get ready for the festival. Volunteers are usually Conservatoire students or other universities students mostly students philologists and economists. Thus, economic students conduct surveys of visitors, analysing the festival's promotion, doing informational support; journalism students undertake interviews and shoot videos. Volunteers in these areas are important since organisers are not able to carry out these functions because of lack of time.

The musical editor believes that fluctuations in the number of employees of the festival and the temporary workforce is not a problem, but a necessity, dictated by the specifics of such activities. For example, the organisers do not need to meet guests at the airport because volunteers can do this.The help of volunteers is often needed to accompany the bands performing at the festival. Support also includes organising meals and leisure time, translation functions and guided tours. Volunteers accompany their allotted performers everywhere. The volunteers operate independently and are not in contact with each other. Sometimes volunteers receive some bonuses for their role, but they mention that not many students are interested in organising the festival, preferring to participate in the festival as a performer.

Organisers exploit the Conservatoire's reputation; they have a list of contacts which is growing each year. The Conservatoire, in addition to education, is engaged in promoting concerts, which simplifies the festival's search for groups and performers. The programme is planned in advance, but sometimes it has to change as it can be hard to negotiate with well-known musicians with tight schedules. The timings of the festival can also change, so sometimes there is a need to replace a conductor or other musical ensemble. The organisers try to invite different artists every year, but for the closing and opening ceremonies they usually invite famous musicians or conductors, who take the lead.

Some functions are outsourced, including design (printing activities), website administration, photography and translating services. As a rule, they cooperate with reliable companies and specialists. The Committee on Foreign Relations often contributes in issues associated with foreign performers, providing interpreters, for example.

Each staff member has their own responsibilities, but everybody is in contact with each other and shares information. Relationships in the team are rather formal. In respondents' opinions, techniques of teambuilding are not required, as all they are working in one department of the Conservatoire and see each other every day, have a common goal and interest in the festival. Some difficulties arise with partners, e.g. consulates often fail to submit documents on time.

## *Open Library Day Festival*

*Open Library Day Festival (OLD)* is a social project. The main goal of the project is to reorganise public libraries in the city. The festival has been held twice: on July 2013 in New Holland (the creative area in Saint Petersburg) and on October 2014 in the Mayakovsky Library. The festival is a non-profit event with free entrance for the visitors. The event lasts for one day. The programme consists of creative meetings, speeches, presentations, lectures, master classes, round tables, debates, concerts and public poetry readings. Famous writers, publishers, journalists, musicians, politicians and other famous people invited as guests. Library employees are central to the festivals organisation, they are ready to help, communicate and interact.

*Open Library Day Festival* is a good opportunity to organise events, presentations, social discussions, or a series of activities, using the festival as a platform. Visitors often offer their assistance in event organisation, some of them provide specific help, support, printing activities or just good ideas. Social networks offer the best possibility to find people who can help to organize a festival and participate in this event. *OLD* is an interactive festival, and engages its visitors in a large field of discussions.

Volunteers are recruited through the VKontakte community (VK is the most popular Russian social network), where they can find information about the festival and how to apply.Volunteers are usually divided by zones and each of them has their own tasks.After the festival ends, the same official community in VKontakte provides information about the best volunteers, about their contribution to the festival, expresses gratitude to the volunteers with photos of the best participants and pictures of the most important events during the festival.The volunteers are mainly young women. Many of them take part in the festivals organisation repeatedly.

One of the organisers stated: "It can be very difficult to manage volunteers, some of them have no responsibility as they have no salary. I have paid some volunteers, in this case they have more responsibilities and there is a guarantee that they will not let you down. Staff should either have salaries to have a commitment, or they should have strong motivation." The motivations of volunteers are different, too. Some volunteers are students of the North-West Printing Institute and are interested in collecting data for research papers. Several volunteers are people who were engaged in Saint Petersburg Book Salon organisation, book fairs or somehow connected with the Lenizdat publishing house. Some are interested only in communication with musicians ('to hang out with them'). Others want to feel the atmosphere of the festival. Some of the volunteers have event organisation experience (e.g. one of the volunteers was the organiser of concerts in the creative space) and they want to enhance their experience of dealing with larger venues. Volunteers admit that if not involved in organisation they would have definitely attended the event as a visitor. It should be noted that volunteers are always involved in the promotion and information distribution about the festival, and always repost news from the community.

There are informal relationships among the organisers of the project: all participants are friends. The team of organisers is somewhat removed from the temporary employees. The organising team is a sort of closed system. They always welcome new ideas and interact with volunteers, but temporary staff are kept at a distance. It is difficult to know if this is a problem or not. On the one hand, many people who participate in the process from time to time (not on permanent basis), like volunteers, already have jobs with salaries and do not want official employment. On the other hand, students of some universities or people simply interested in the cultural sphere would welcome their cooperation with *OLD* transferring into full-time employment.

As for volunteers, they often interact with each other; they know each other and some of them are good friends. Sometimes performing joint tasks, replacing each other, gives the opportunity to relax. During the events volunteers have to communicate with all the other members: they are given orders, assignments, report necessary information, etc. Organisers strongly encourage and assist the volunteers, never leave them alone and let them have time to rest. Volunteers are coordinated by organisers. They recruit them, supervise them, solve all the problems they can't cope with. The second *OLD* festival had a lot of volunteers and they all had clear tasks. According to volunteers, they liked the atmosphere of the festival and were glad to work in the project. However, much of the overall volunteers' impression depends upon personal contacts with organisers and participants.

Conflicts may happen, but they are mostly connected with participants and guests, as many debates are very emotional. Sometimes it is rather difficult to communicate with the visitors. "Sometimes you really can't predict what to expect. There can be tricky questions, visitors can lose their temper. Fortunately, this happens very rarely", admits one of the volunteers. Guests may be unpredictable, too. For example, at the last festival one of the invited guests became angry when one of the visitors gave a critical comment against his speech. But this is an exceptional case; most of the invited guests are well-known, intelligent people, with good communication skills.

Organisers always take responsibility and manage crises. The volunteers' coordinators give advice to volunteers and staff in case of such situations, but the organisers themselves usually come to the rescue and resolve conflicts.They don't leave volunteers and the library staff alone in case of conflicts.

Volunteers help only during the event. They are not involved in the development of the festival events and decision-making process. If any of the volunteers wants to share ideas, they can write down this information individually, because usually there is no general meeting and results discussion after the festival.

## Findings and conclusions

Festival teams tend to be small, but also need to be able to scale up for the duration of the event itself. Each of the festivals researched manages this process in a distinct way, although there are some similarities. The term 'team' is used in relation to the team of organizers (the administrative group). One can speak about teams of temporary employees only in the case of a high degree of interaction between them, but, as a rule, a volunteer is assigned to a certain area and does not have contact with other volunteers.

Roles and responsibilities are distributed between teammates, but all members are dependent on each other. Organizers do not involve recruited personnel or other stakeholders (partners, premises representatives, contractors) in decision-making processes. Moreover, the festival team is a closed independent system, and it is hard for an 'outsider' to become an equal part of it.

The use of volunteers or freelance staff is common to all of the festivals surveyed. Volunteers tend to be used for tasks such as stewarding and meeting and greeting artists. Freelancers are recruited for their skills in a particular area that the core staff team cannot cover, either because they do not have the time, or do not have the expertise to do so. Festival organizers are wary of giving volunteers too much responsibility, both because they do not know if they will be reliable and because they do not want to exploit them. The problem of staff mobility is largely dictated by the specificity of the festival organization. To manage such fluctuations in the number of employees, it is necessary to provide a source of qualified staff. As the survey showed, teams tend to hire the same seasonal workers and volunteers, collaborate with the same trusted contractors or attract employees using recommendations of colleagues and personal contacts. Usually an event team is engaged in diversified activities (e.g. education, concerts organization), which is why the professional networks are highly used, especially if responsible tasks are concerned, like guides or accompanying musical bands.

There are festival organizations which do not attract volunteers. It is note-worthy that these festivals are not designed for a mass audience, and instead of inexperienced volunteers, the organizers prefer to hire professional managers. Some have already established contacts with universities, and it is not always due to personal relationships, but also specifically established contacts between organizations. There are diametrically opposed attitudes towards volunteers. Some organizers tend to attract professionals for reward and to have volunteers to be at their beck and call. On the contrary some managers stimulate temporary workers. They use encouragement, support and assistance, gratitude in public social media messages, give the possibility of gaining experience or credits for students as methods of reward. With regard to the volunteers, many of them being students, have a desire to be included in the team of permanent employees. The motivation of volunteers vary: some of them state that if they had not been involved in organizing process, they would have definitely participated as visitors; others were only interested in being involved as performers.

Moreover, the conditions in which the emergence and rapid development of the festival movement took place should be taken into account, especially the lack of training for event specialists. Universities and institutions in Saint Petersburg do not have a music management department. There is no ground for event managers growing. Event managers start at the age of 20 as beginners in narrow areas (accompanying, volunteer, assistant). For 2-3 years they have to work for a small salary and gain experience, and what is more important connections. This experience allows you to see the whole process from beginning to end. Any working experience can be then integrated into its current activity: one of the respondents worked in hotel, at the consulate, at a translation bureau, and as a bartender before becoming a festival manager.

Teambuilding is not an issue that any of the festivals researched felt was important for the permanent staff as the small core groups were already functioning as effective teams, in their opinion. Communication was good and organizers were aware of the each other's workloads and tasks, so could offer support when needed. None of the festivals suffered from high levels of staff turnover that could be attributed to poor team relationships. The level of teambuilding amongst volunteers varies, however, and may explain why some festivals are more successful at recruiting and retaining volunteers than others. The authors of the chapter would like to stress the fact that usage of such practices as teambuilding, staff training, and meetings can be explained by the subjective attitude of the festival director towards these techniques. Moreover, 'building teams' can be built into the current activities of the organization and can be used unconsciously, as the authors imply, designing teams, setting communication channels, role distribution, conflict management, etc. by 'building teams'.

As a rule, the organizers pay attention to the process of selection and recruitment, and rarely focus on the procedure of entering a new employee in the team – adaptation. The study showed that the organizers are also paying little attention to promoting both permanent and temporary staff. In the case of volunteers it is particularly important.

The authors would like to highlight the lack of communication between people involved (training sessions, feedback meetings) not only in the context of temporary staff, but also third party companies that are involved. The administrative group is highly dependent on other suppliers and partners. The festival requires an enormous number of agreements. Some security companies offer help to collect documents for the police, government, emergency and ambulance services. The venue's administration team can provide some services, such as electricity, and some of the security and advertising, but mainly they are not involved in the running of the actual festival. It is necessary to begin negotiation with the owners of a venue in advance, almost a year before the event, to make sure that the venue will be free for the dates required. Every aspect is discussed with a venue owner and all terms are listed in the lease contract (especially if it concerns UNESCO heritage sites). Furthermore, at the festival, there are different zones such as the food court and art market. Despite the fact that all of these zones should be prepared in advance, participants are often disorganised, providing information too late.

Though some organizers have admitted the crucial anti-crisis role played by the Committee on Culture this year (2015), they often complain about its policy and comment that the Committee does not provide enough money. However there are always lots of applicants for subsidies. Also it is important to say that when the heads of committees change, priorities also change. In addition, there is always strong competition in the event business. Festival administration cannot rely on the fact that the festival will be paid off only by ticket sales; the festival can never become profitable without governmental support or sponsors. A large-scale concert or festival is paid off by 60-70% of sponsorship funds. Searching for a qualified fundraiser specialist is an urgent issue. It cannot be claimed that the list of sponsors is always the same, as sponsors' policy and budgets change.

It is often necessary to obtain visas for performers, and in this case relations with embassies and consulates play crucial role. Established relationships make it easier to get along with, but unfortunately employees constantly change or areas of responsibility shift (there is a two year limit on diplomatic service). The organization is also a matter of cooperation with performers, and setting or deepening relationships with visitors. Artists' behaviour and decency play a very important role (avoidance of illegal actions or banned substances transportation), otherwise there is a high risk that they will be stopped at the border. The issue has become particularly important after *Bloodhound Gang* had their Russian visas revoked because the authorities objected to the bass player's on-stage treatment of the national flag. To gain the loyalty of the audience and to make it feel involved and implicated in the event, the organizer should give an opportunity for the audience to express ideas, give feedback and somehow influence decisions (e.g. some Saint-Petersburg event organizers conduct social media surveys to identify which performers visitors would like to see). In other words, it is very important to take into account that the performance result depends greatly upon all the stakeholders involved, in this sense all of them form a team, and the human factor is an aspect that should not be neglected.

## Bibliography

Bales, R. F. (1965) The equilibrium problem in small groups, in A. P. Hare, E. F. Borgatta and R.F. Bales (eds.) *Small Groups: Studies in Social Interaction*, New York: Knopf.

Dyer, W.G. and Dyer, J.H. (2013) *Team Building: Proven Strategies for Improving Team Performance* (5th ed.). Jossey-Bass, Somerset.

Garfield, M. and Dennis, A. (winter 2012–13) Toward an integrated model of group development: Disruption of routines by technology-induced change, in *Journal of Management Information Systems*, **29**(3), 43–86.

Gersick, C. (1988) Time and transition in work teams toward a new model of group development. *Academy of Management Journal*, **31**(1), 9–42.

Gordin, V. and Dedova M. (2015) Social entrepreneurship in the informal economy: a case study of re-enactment festivals. *Journal of Enterprising Communities: People and Places in the Global Economy* **9**(1), 6-16 © Emerald Group Publishing Limited 1750-6204.

Gordin, V. E. and Matetskaya, M. V. (2010) *Saint Petersburg festivals: aspects of cultural policy and cultural tourism*. Paper presented at the Global Events Congress IV: Festivals and Events Research: State of the Art. Leeds Metropolitan University, 14-16 July 2010.

Gordin, V. and Matetskaya M. (2012) Creative tourism in Saint Petersburg: The state of the art.*Journal of Tourism Consumption and Practice*. **4**(2), 55-77.

Hanlon C. (2002) Managing the pulsating effect in major sport event organizations.PhD thesis.Victoria University of Technology, 576.

Katzenbach, J. and Smith, D. (1992) Why teams matter. *McKinsey Quarterly*, **3**(25).

Latfullin, G.R., and Gromova, O. N. (2004) *Organisational Behaviour*. St-Petersburg: Piter.

Loevingsson, K. B. F. (2005) *A to Z of Management Concepts and Models*. London: Thorogood Publishing.

Salas, E., Dickinson, T. L., Converse, S. and Tannenbaum, S. I. (1992), Toward an understanding of team performance and training, in R. W. Swezey and E. Salas (eds), *Teams: Their Training and Performance* (Norwood: Ablex), 3 – 29.

St-Petersburg Committee on Culture. Statistics (2015) URL: http://www.spbculture.ru/ru/statistics.html [Accessed 20.07.2015].

Tompson, L. (2006) *Teambuilding*. Moscow: Vershina.

Topchik, G.S. (2007) *First-Time Manager's Guide to Team Building*. AMACOM Books, New York.

Tuckman, B. (1965) Developmental sequence in small groups. *Psychological Bulletin*, **63**, 384-399.

Tuckman, B. and Jensen, M. (1977) Stages of small group development revisited.*Group and Organizational Studies*, **2**, 419- 427.

Wagen, L. (2007) *Human Resource Management for Events.Managing the event workforce*. Oxford: Butterworth Heinemann.

West, M. A. (2012) *Effective Teamwork: Practical Lessons from Organizational Research* (3rd ed.). New York: Wiley-Blackwell.

# 12 Large Festivals – Great Struggles

János Zoltán Szabó

## Introduction

Contemporary music festivals in late modern European culture have different histories, focuses, missions and geographical conditions. This chapter calls for deeper analysis of the development of festivals that is rooted in cultural anthropology, sociology and the sciences – a multidisciplinary approach. Without this, festivals will simply be known as recurring celebrations, thematic ritual events reflecting the basic values and the worldview shared by the participants that are the basis of their social identity. However, nowadays, the economic importance of festivals has become even more rigorously evaluated, whilst complicated ways to measure cultural impact are often left out, even from detailed reports.

Most studies emphasise the difference between Eastern and Western European festivals (Newbold et al. 2015), however, the life cycle of a festival is influenced by factors that are similar wherever they take place: marketing, promotions, sales, audience development and quality, improvement challenges etc. As the size of the festival market has grown, new questions are being asked about economic efficiency. In this study I will search for similarities in the development of five major Eastern and Western European festivals, namely *Glastonbury Festival* (United Kingdom), *Roskilde Festival* (Denmark), *Sziget Festival* (Hungary), *Exit Festival* (Serbia), and *Woodstock Festival Poland* (Poland). I will also analyse the *Sziget Festival's* life cycle in detail in order to go deeper into the issues and discuss ways to further research music festivals.

In analysing these festivals, the main selection criterion was what they have in common: they attract more than 100,000 visitors yearly, but readers might also recognise that all of them follow the message of the original *Woodstock Music and Art Fair* – commonly called *Woodstock Festival* and labelled as 'An Aquarian Exposition: 3 Days of Peace and Music', in Bethel, New York, 15 – 18 August, 1969. The primary reason for choosing this topic was not just intellectual interest, but also the fact that these festivals are competitors in the festival business market. Cultural managers usually try to avoid overlapping dates with their competitors, as these festivals do in most cases:

- *Glastonbury Festival* (GB): 24 – 28 June 2015
- *Roskilde Festival* (DK): 27 June – 4 July 2015

- *Exit Festival* (SR), 9-12 July 2015
- *Woodstock Festival Poland* (PL): 30 July – 1 August 2015
- *Sziget Festival* (HU), 10-17 August 2015

This is a nice competitor schedule; therefore they created the chance for those who want to spend almost the whole summer at festivals. In other words, it seems that for those visiting just one summer festival in a season the competition is absolutely open – headliners are international in all cases. Even for those who visit a festival in their own country and one festival in another country. Furthermore, these festivals can all be scheduled into a band's tour as well – critics often discommend festivals on a national level that put the same music groups and presenters on stage.

## Life of a festival

Two festivals were established in the 1970s (*Glastonbury* – 1970, *Roskilde* – 1971) however the Eastern European festivals were established after 1989; two in the 1990s (*Sziget* – 1993, *Woodstock Festival Poland* – 1995) and one in 2001 (*Exit*). By now all of them have been in the business for at least fifteen years.

Since the 1970s enormous societal changes have taken place in these five countries on both sides of the former Iron Curtain, and these cannot be analysed in a short chapter such as this, however, a special focus should be given to the societal context of festivals. The social change that fundamentally created the chance for festivals is strongly linked to two processes: that of a cultural paradigm shift and that of higher education expansion (in other words: changes in youth experience). These processes have had a profound effect not just on festivals but on the overall social change in countries in transition.

On the one hand, due to the expansion of higher education, a large percentage of young people have become a separate social group that could live relatively free from social expectations, both in cultural and financial senses, creating their own consumption habits. In 1900, there were some 500,000 students worldwide, while this number increased to 100 million by 2000 (Schofer and Meyer 2005: 898-900). This process accelerated exponentially in the 1960s in the West, in accordance with social needs and soft state control on education. In societies in transition, countries in Eastern Europe where the state had strongly controlled education, this exponential process began at least 20 to 30 years later because it had been prevented, slowed down and postponed by non-democratic socialist governments. What Western markets and societies developed in 40-50 years, Eastern European countries followed in 10-20 years. There is still a feeling of lagging behind and of running at double speed at the same time. Nevertheless the European Union's (EU) 2020 Strategy contains a target that at least 40% of 30 to 34 year-olds should have completed third level education. That is definitely a target for the Eastern European countries, but Western countries are already mostly around this level.

On the other hand, educational expansion was followed by a cultural paradigm shift. This is often described as youth culture, including every aspect of culture followed by young people (dress, music, life style etc.) and has become widely accepted by the whole society as mainstream. Although there are differences still, by the turn of the 21th century these two processes have reached similar social effects in countries of the European Union: there is no real question that youth culture is widely accepted as general mainstream culture.

In parallel to social change, business trends in the service sector, including festivals, have changed too. Opera festivals and city festivals in the past were all loss-making events; however, the festivals analysed here are all profit-making or break-even events. If turning to youth culture is a social trend, then the turn to a marketing approach is a business trend of late modernity. In the last 50 years the leading marketing trend turned the focus away from price and distribution to a general focus on meeting customers' needs and on the benefits received from a product or service (product/service as experience). This change in business approach created the chance to use marketing concepts for the general process of communication, exchange and events (Witzel 2003).

All the festivals analysed here had different types of difficulties in the beginning, however, there was only one festival that was not organised every year. *Glastonbury*, originally called *Pilton Festival*, has special stories about the interval between 1972 and 77, and the pauses in 1980, 1988, 1991, 1996, 2001, 2006 and 2012. Apart from the early years the main reason was that the festival was organised on a greenfield site. As this festival always followed the ethos of the hippie, counterculture, and 'free festival' movements, organisers respect the land where the event takes place, therefore ecological thinking is essential. Knowing this it is not surprising that organisers gave the land to the local population in the 'fallow years' and take a year break in every fifth year (the next fallow year will be 2017/18). Besides this 'fallow year', most festival organisations have a continuous operation with employees or freelancers paid continuously, having a product that is an event that take place every year, thus, their position can be evaluated by their lifecycle.

For this chapter I will use the expression 'lifecycle' to describe the marketing position of a festival on the basis of a model taken from product lifecycle management (PLM). PLM is commonly understood as a model to describe the position of a product continuously present on the market for a number of years. As summer events, festivals are seasonal products, but they count as market leaders in the summer events market. Competition is getting stronger and stronger, which means that the position of a festival frequently changes and this changing process is evaluated on the basis of the number of visitors. Plotting visitor numbers for each festival reveals a really different shape in the five cases (see Figure 12.1).

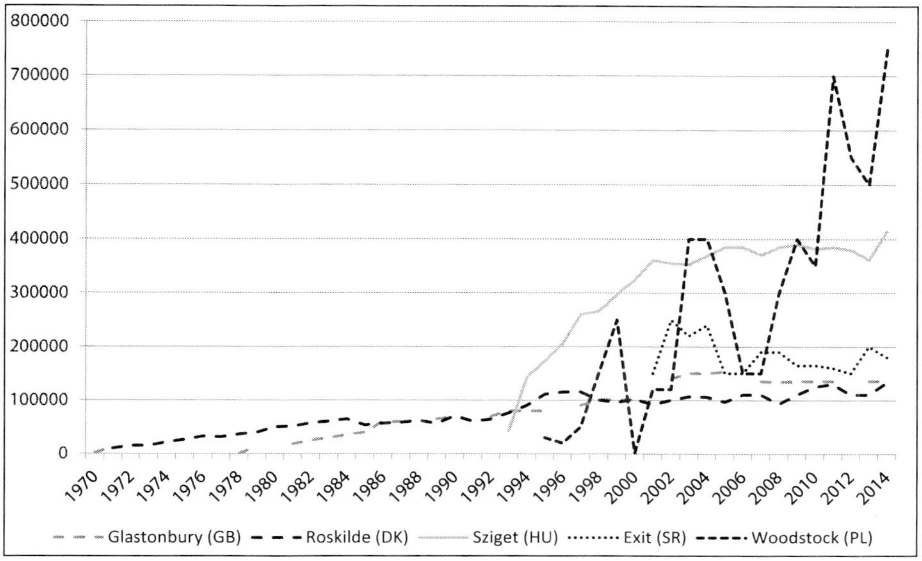


**Figure 12.1:** Number of visits at festivals analysed (1970-2014).

*Source:* www.glastonburyfestivals.co.uk, www.roskilde-festival.dk, www.sziget.hu, www.exitfest.org, www.woodstockfestival.pl

First of all, what may surprise many readers, the top three festivals in terms of the number of visitors are all in Eastern Europe. Second, the development process of attracting more and more visitors follows a different model in most cases. *Glastonbury* seems not to be fighting for more visitors any more, while *Roskilde* shows a modest, but continuous development over the years. *Woodstock Festival* (PL) seems to still be running a visitor growth programme. *Exit* started as a much larger festival than it is today, showing a shift in its marketing approach, while *Sziget* followed a 'small steps' strategy, after a significant growth in the1990s. Although these were small steps for the *Sziget*, on the other hand that would be huge steps for most small or medium size festivals.

PLM has four main steps; introduction, growth, maturity and decline, as described by Kotler (2002: 390-400). These steps cannot be easily analysed across the lifetime of the festivals analysed here, as renewal has happened several times in the lifespan of the events. Therefore it makes sense to reduce the time line to the last fifteen years. It also means that it is possible to have a closer look at the growth and decline phases, including the rare years of the maturity phase.

In this chart *Glastonbury* shows the most balanced maturity position, however, they had more visitors before 2005 than after. Maturity is reflected in the fact that they usually sell all the tickets in one single day (as in 2015). Organisers are probably aware of the fact that to keep the mature position is more important than fighting for new and more visitors – that role should be fulfilled by other festivals in the UK at least. The danger of this position is that new audiences have a relatively limited chance to get there with such a small window of opportunity to obtain tickets. This generates the necessary audience for the festival, although only visitors coming from the middle and upper middle class can afford this event and those who seek the prestige of 'being there'. Indeed, organisers limit the number of visitors, rather than growing to meet market demand for the festival.

The other well balanced festival is *Roskilde*, but some small changes can be identified in Figure 12.1. Organisers have made efforts to increase the number of visitors by 30% in the last 15 years. There were 102,000 estimated visits in the year 2000; however, there were three years when this number fell under 100,000: 2001, 2005 and 2008. All the three points could have been the first step of a decline period, but each time organisers made efforts to increase the number of visitors. Stronger and stronger efforts were made as is displayed in the chart, and when the numbers started to fall again in 2012 and 2013 the basis was high enough to stop falling at 110,000. Generally the financial crisis (2006-2013) appears to have been a difficult period for festivals around these years. Just as *Sziget* and *Woodstock* (PL) had financial setbacks and saw a drop in visitor numbers in this period of time, whilst *Exit* suffered from financial and visitor problems from 2009 up to 2012. Nevertheless *Roskilde* showed four examples of renewal; the fifth is still developing, since they hit a record 133,000 visits in 2014. These measures of renewal and growth probably pulled *Roskilde* back into the maturity phase of the lifecycle, at least audiences growing from 110,000 to 130,000 might be considered as a stable position. Organisers cannot be satisfied and confident in the future, they have to find a way to keep the number of visitors above 100,000 and keep the festival atmosphere and infrastructure in that state which can be expected or required by returning audiences. It is understandable that newcomer visitors will be welcomed; they will ensure the preservation of the festival. The festival longs to find new audience segments in order to offer protection in tough times, which will probably not be rare in the future in a market the size of Denmark.

Eastern and Central European festivals had to fight a bit more to maintain their ship on the right PLM course. *Exit Festival* started as a challenge to the *Sziget Festival* and there might be a kind of visitor's suction effect because in the period of 2002-2004, 2007 and 2013-2014 the two festivals' attendance numbers moved in opposite directions. The organisers invested a lot into the renewal of *Exit Festival* three times and reached better results, while the organisers of the *Sziget Festival* invested in quality improvement in other years, particularly in 2005-2006 and in 2009-2011 and successfully overcame the decline phase and stayed in a mature position – despite financial losses. The last renewal experiment in 2014 enabled the *Sziget Festival* to reach a new record of visits with 415,000 guests and the process continued because this number reached another peak with 441,000 visits in 2015. It seems that *Exit* also found its own way because about 180,000-200,000 visitors can make a good festival, but the next renewal might be expected soon. In accordance with the trends neither *Exit* nor *Sziget* can create large-scale change in number of visits, however, both festivals have a sensitive position in the mature phase of the product lifecycle management process. In a market the size of Serbia or Hungary, large scale festivals are necessarily international and that can have serious security conditions. In 2015 immigrants from the Middle East started to follow the path that leads throughout Novi Sad and Budapest and this might raise questions about festivals in 2016.

The situation is completely different in the case of *Woodstock Festival* (PL), where this non-commercial event is obviously in the growth stage. After the introductory years (2000-2002) there was a hectic development process that ended up with it being the largest festival in East-Central Europe. This hectic change included years when the audience more than doubled from one year to another (2002-2003 and 2010-2011) meaning an approximate 300,000 increase each time – this is what could cause real problems for festivals like *Exit, Roskilde* or *Sziget*. A trend line could show that *Woodstock* will reach the level of 1 million visitors in 3-5 years and then new problems will arise in the mature phase of PLM.

To sum up the analysis of the lifecycle management process, the data has showed that four of the five festivals are balancing to keep their prominent position in PLM. However, it is still true that in the case of East-Central European festivals larger deviations can be observed in the development process in comparison with the Western-European festivals analysed. Surprisingly Eastern and Central European festivals attract 2-8 times more visitors at least, which has a double message: on the one hand *Roskilde* and *Glastonbury* have self-control that makes them sustainable in the long term, while *Exit* and the *Sziget* recently experienced record numbers, not to mention that *Woodstock* is likely to achieve the one million visitor record. When growth records are not as important as they are today, organisers will have to make more effort to keep their festivals in the developed state by starting a kind of renewal process every 2-4 years and start to focus on sustainability.

## Efficiency of a festival – example of the *Sziget Festival*

The new youth era is characterised by the pop-rock festival as a symbolic form of cultural mediation created by counterculture, which then became popular and widely accepted by youngsters and former youngsters. Counterculture has totally reformed musical life, dress codes, fashion and cultural conformity over the last 50 years and festivals played an important role in this process. Beside its uniqueness as a social phenomenon, new business solutions have been introduced to the festivals market as well: this group of festivals has strong market orientation that is interesting to study. Readers should be reminded that traditionally festivals have not been about making profit and, in most cases, are rather a strain on the city budget. All the historical arts festivals (including Wagner's *Bayreuther Festspiele, 1876* or *Verona Opera Festival/ Ente Lirico Arena di Verona* ), international film festivals and city festivals have to cope with tight budgets, and invest enormous energy to insure that they cover all their expenses. This raises the question, what are the new 'conformist festivals' doing more efficiently than those that require subsidy?[1]

The economic impacts of these festivals should not be evaluated solely by the number of visits, but on the basis of the size of their balance sheets, too. From this point of view, the festivals analysed above all have the capacity and opportunity to count the number of visitors (tickets sold) but financial data are more limited. The *Sziget Festival*, established in 1993, was mentioned among the five festivals and having the financial data makes it possible to analyse the changes (breaks and shifts) in the budget and the audience over these 21 years. For analysing efficiency I have used an indicator called Cost per Thousand (CPT) that helps to count and visualise the financial trends and predict possible future outcomes.

In 2014, *Sziget Festival* had a record budget of 3.65 billion HUF (equivalent of 12 million EUR) and reached another record in the number of visitors with 415,000 visits in eight days. This data shows the result of efforts made to reposition the festival in the last few years. The following multi-scale chart (Figure 12.2) displays two indicators: one is the annual total budget and the other is the number of visitors. It is clear how different dynamics were realised in the number of visits and the budgets over the years. The 1990s were the golden years in financial terms, since the audience became larger at cost of a relatively modest increase in the budgets. It can be clearly seen that the number of visitors was balanced between 350-390 thousand over the twelve years since 2001, while expenses dramatically increased, especially between 2001 and 2008. The increase in expenses was more pronounced before and after, so the increase of visits could not produce the same dynamism that caused problems in a financial sense. Two to three years with negative balances can make shareholders worried about the future of the company (at that time it was quoted on the stock exchange) responsible for the *Sziget*. Indeed, organisers spent more money in this period of time and the event moved one step forward to higher quality of services, and the festival finally has become a reinvented brand. On the one hand organisers invested more and more money into the event in order to reach a developed state in quality, on the other hand there was high inflation that undermined these efforts.

Indeed the management of the *Sziget* felt the pain of crisis in 2011 when they decided to invest more in the festival, not in the quality in general, but in the programme. First results were disappointing: only a small percentage increase in the number of visits were recorded. In 2012 they invested a little bit less into the festival and fewer numbers of visits were recorded as well. By 2013 – also because of other reasons – the festival's worst financial result, a large loss, was calculated. Then in 2014 they took the financial difficulties seriously, which did not mean smaller budget, but rather spending more and creating more and new areas and attractions. This time financial results and recorded visits confirmed all the efforts that made *Sziget* what it is today: 'Island of freedom' (as its slogan suggests).

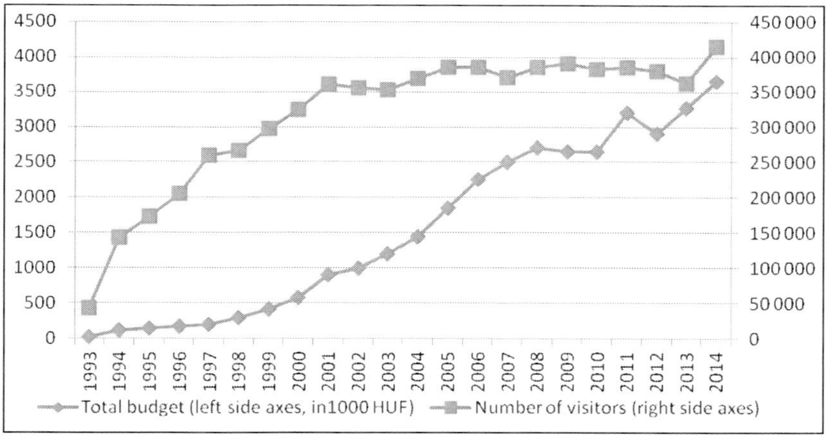


**Figure 12.2:** Budget of *Sziget Festival* and number of visitors (1993-2014). *Source: Sziget Festival*

Beyond the number of visits and budgets, it makes sense to analyse the amount of money that is spent for every visitor, in other words, how much money was needed to entertain a visitor for a day? This is what the cost per thousand (CPT) indicator tells us. In 2014, the *Sziget Festival* entertained every single visitor for daily cost of 8,795 HUF (equivalent of 29 EUR), that is not the highest rate among Eastern European festivals, although the daily entrance fee was about 16,000 HUF (equivalent of 53 EUR). Weekly and advance tickets were sold at a lower daily price, of course. To conclude, this is what one visitor day costs, but it does not say anything about efficiency and predicted futures. For that purpose another comparison is needed alongside CPT and the number of visitors, this is to be found in the next chart (Figure 12.3).

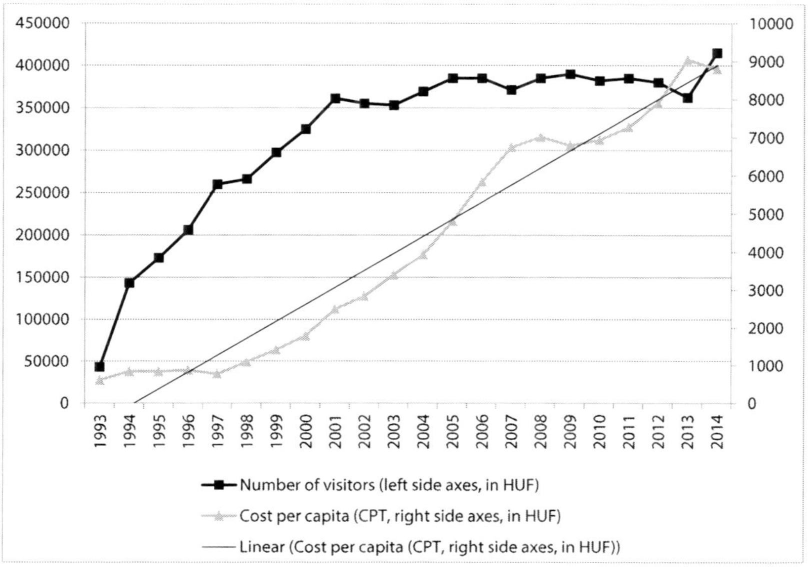


**Figure 12.3:** Visits to *Sziget* and cost per visit (CPT). Source: *Sziget Festival*

In this time scale the CPT indicator proves that a strong investment was made by the organisers into the festival's quality between 2006 and 2008. The CPT indicator line shows that costs increased ahead of sales in this period of time, but before and afterwards the CPT followed the trend line (black line) until 2013, when the index reached the psychologically decisive amount of 9,000 HUF per visitor. It was also signalled by the losses made by the festival. The two difficult periods reflect additional expenditure on quality improvements in 2006/2008 and 2013, this was the primary reason of the increased budget, but the market did not tolerate it. Better services are generally welcomed, of course, but only up to a certain level and cost. Price-increasing factors were reasonably tolerated until 2005 but not between 2006/2008 or in 2013. In other words, extended services went beyond the needs that visitors were willing to pay for.

2014 was a real turning point, because the average daily cost of visitors returned below 9,000 HUF. The organisers kept expenses as low as possible and made efforts to accommodate more visitors (more space was needed). They invested in the physical infrastructure in order to increase the number of visitors, earn higher income and profit, thus the investment was paid off finally. One question remains: what future awaits for the *Sziget Festival*? The organisers have chosen an expansion strategy; more visitors mean more income. However, this large number of visits can only be stabilised by more and more rationalisation and expansion efforts that are not easy on a real island on the Danube. As far as I can see the Eastern European festival market has matured, therefore the same market position cannot be kept for another twelve years (as happened between 2001-2013) without changes.

Visitors simply get bored with festivals organised in an unaltered way. The lesson for 'conform' festivals is: it's time to get interesting again! Those who follow the festivals sector might have noticed that 'new conform' festivals have already started to renew their festival form, not in the sense of artistic genre, but in the sense of new attractions like young architects' concepts made of wood, or unusual giant animal installations made of natural materials, or a big wheel (Sziget Eye). I should not forget about a VIP section that is one of the most profitable sections of festivals recently – although this might be against the ethos of equality.

The economic activity analysed in this chapter, especially the CPT indicator, suggest that the *Sziget Festival* has followed the same trend since 1997. The trend line also suggests that the CPT indicator should be kept under the trend line as much of the time as possible – until major changes happen in the concept.

## Data envelopment analysis of festivals

Efficiency can obviously be evaluated in a timeline of a specific festival on the basis of budgets and number of visits, but how can the efficiency of different festivals be compared? In this final section I will make an attempt to introduce the Data Envelopment Analysis (DEA) method that was developed to evaluate organisations engaged in the same or similar activities. This analysis is usually used for the identification of effective and ineffective units in an organisation. In the case of festivals, different festivals operate in different conditions, but their activities are in general similar, therefore the information about effectiveness might be useful for organisers and researchers too. DEA is based on input and output data that can be in different units, a balance sheet can be used as input, while the number of visits can be an output (Cooper et al. 2006).

In the case of the festivals analysed here, one can find that *Woodstock* (PL) entertained visitors for the least financial investment as shown by CPT (20 EUR/capita/day), eleven times less than *Glastonbury Festival* (222.22 EUR/capita/day). This might be the consequence of the fact that *Woodstock* (PL) is a dedicated non-commercial event with free entrance, while *Glastonbury* collects money to donate; nearly 3 million EUR is donated on an annual basis to not-for-profit organisations and projects like Greenpeace, Oxfam, Water Aid and other humanitarian causes which enhance the fabric of our society. On the other hand, strong competition can be observed in the case of the other three festivals: the *Sziget* (28.92 EUR/capita/day), *Exit* (32.22 EUR/capita/day) and *Roskilde* (39.85 EUR/capita/day) works with relatively close CPT data.

| 2014 | Estimated budget in EUR* | Number of visits | CPT (EUR) | X=100/ CPT | Relative effectiveness (DEA) |
|---|---|---|---|---|---|
| Woodstock (PL) | 15,000,000 | 750,000 | 20.00 | 5.00 | 100% |
| Sziget (HU) | 12,000,000 | 415,000 | 28.92 | 3.46 | 69.2% |
| Exit (SR) | 5,800,000 | 180,000 | 32.22 | 3.10 | 62.1% |
| Roskilde (DK) | 5,300,000 | 133,000 | 39.85 | 2.51 | 50.2% |
| Glastonbury (UK) | 30,000,000 | 135,000 | 222.22 | 0.45 | 9.0% |

**Figure 12.4:** Relative effectiveness of the festivals analysed

| 2014 | Estimated budget in EUR* | Number of visits | CPT (EUR) | X=100/ CPT | Relative effectiveness (DEA) |
|---|---|---|---|---|---|
| Sziget (HU) | 12,000,000 | 415,000 | 28.92 | 3.46 | **100%** |
| Exit (SR) | 5,800,000 | 180,000 | 32.22 | 3.10 | **89.6%** |
| Roskilde (DK) | 5,300,000 | 133,000 | 39.85 | 2.51 | **72.5%** |

**Figure 12.5:** Festival efficiency with standard commercial policy

*Own estimations on the basis of former years' budgets

Using the data the DEA method recommends counting the most efficient festival as a 100% benchmark in order to provide precise results. To do so I converted data into a comparable format by using x=100/CPT equation. In this ranking *Woodstock* is the most efficient benchmark at 100%, therefore all of the other festivals are on lower percentages. Two festivals with absolutely different policies (for profit vs. non-commercial) resulted in unbalanced DEA relative effectiveness percentages.

Apart from the two festivals with non-commercial policies, three festivals are left. The efficiency of the *Sziget* and the *Exit* are similar to one another, the difference is about 10% that might be accounted for by specific local conditions and purchasing power. On the other hand *Roskilde* is on a relatively lower level, but one should not forget about the difference of price level between Eastern/Central and Western countries.

Obviously there are limits of this method, though if the model/procedure is applied in a proper way, it could provide great help for organisers wanting to ascertain their desired position in terms of efficiency. In accordance with the DEA relative efficiency model mentioned above, DEA can be used with various output data, e.g. separating home country or foreigner visits that provides the opportunity to visualise the effectiveness by a so called 'efficiency border'. DEA together with product lifecycle management are efficacy tests that do not reject the market and provide information for decision-making, saving time and money that might be wasted experimenting with pricing and would be a great help for festivals organised by publicly financed organisations.

## Conclusions

In the 1970s and 1980s, festival markets developed slowly but continuously in Western Europe, however, Eastern European countries were opened only in the early 1990s after the end of the Cold War: official culture and security policy had controlled those events which attracted large audiences until the end of 1980s. Although social change began in the 1990s, Eastern/Central European festivals were created as bottom up initiatives and organisational teams lacked experience and knowledge in large scale event organisation and marketing. Expansion of higher education, a cultural paradigm shift and mainstreaming of youth culture were postponed until the turn of the century in these countries. The festival scene nevertheless had a great role in adjusting and influencing cultural conformity in this process.

The festival market has now become well developed in both Eastern and Western Europe. It means that the main players are established; newcomers have to face financial, technical and marketing difficulties and the calendar as well. A mature market requires a strong market presence from old players, which includes a continuous struggle for renewal. Organisers need information not just on customers' needs, but on economic efficiency and the lifecycle position of the festival as well. In this chapter I analysed the application of three models on festivals; namely CPT, PLM and DEA models. In the examples introduced I found that CPT might be useful in discovering trends in a festival's efficiency, while PLM gives advice for organisers about the need for renewal and, last but not least, DEA helps to produce a picture of relative efficiency.

Future research can dig deeper into festival efficiency in a number of ways; for example the CPT trend line could be compared across different festivals, which might lead to it being able to forecast future winners. As another option, future analysis of PLM could be used for more precise identification of market position and also give opportunities for identifying the start of the decline phase. Finally, DEA relative efficiency rankings could help identify and discover competitors on one hand, or be used for the analysis of the efficiency of festival units (within a festival organisation) on the other. All in all, festival efficiency is a more and more complex question and festival organisations are increasingly becoming serious players in the extensively growing European and also worldwide leisure market.

# Bibliography

Cooper, W. W., Seiford, L. M., and Tone, K. (2006) *Introduction to Data Envelopment Analysis and Its Uses.* New York: Springer.

Getz, D. (1993) Corporate culture in not-for-profit festival organisations, concepts and potential applications, in *Festival Management and Event Tourism,* **1** 11-17.

Kotler, P. (2002) *Marketing Menedzsment* (Marketing Management) Budapest: KJK-Kerszöv.

Newbold, C., Maughan, C., Jordan, J., and Bianchini F. (eds.) (2015) *Focus On Festivals, Contemporary European Case Studies and Perspectives.* Oxford: Goodfellow.

Schofer, E., and Meyer, J. W. (2005) The Worldwide Expansion of Higher Education in the Twentieth Century, in *American Sociological Review.* **70**(6), (Dec. 2005), 898-920.

Szabó, J. Z. (2015) Festivals, Conformity and Socialisation, in C Newbold, C. Maughan, J. Jordan, and F. Bianchini, (eds.) *Focus On Festivals, Contemporary European Case Studies and Perspectives.* Oxford: Goodfellow.

Turner, V. (2002): *A rituális folyamat* (The Ritual Process). Budapest: Osisis

Witzel, M. (2003). First among marketers, in *Financial Times.* August 6th 2003.

## Notes

1 The term 'new conformist festivals' is used here to mean those that programme music identified with music from the 1970s countercultural movements and which have an audience which is aging alongside the music. For a wider discussion of festivals and conformity see Szabó in Newbold et al. 2015: 40-52.

# 13 Community Perceptions on the Impacts of Art Festivals on Overall Quality of Life: A case study of the *Innibos National Arts Festival*, South Africa

Mathilda van Niekerk

## Introduction

Art festivals have witnessed a boom in the past few years; with new festivals proliferating that cater to every taste and region, in what has become a vital source of revenue and publicity for cities and artists (Eventbrite, 2014; Relaxnews, 2015). The ideal arts festival represents a carefully crafted mixture of artists, a variety in its programming, being visually spectacular, and also meeting its social objectives (The Guardian, 2015). Art festivals in general are important for many reasons, some of which are to grow the regional and local economies, to promote the specific destination, to contribute to the livelihood of the artists and the local community, displaying different forms of art and to create specific images of the destinations. An art festival should therefore not only exist or take place; it should make some form of contribution to its stakeholders (Getz and Andersson 2010). When art festivals are, therefore, hosted in a specific area the lives of the local community become affected by it either in a positive or in a negative way.

Art festivals have various impacts (socio-cultural, environmental, political and economic) on stakeholders, and on one of the most important stakeholders, that is, the local community. For years festival impact studies have mainly focused on the economic, environmental and socio-cultural impact of festivals on the local community, but a limited number of researchers have conducted studies to measure the impact of art festivals on the overall quality of life of the community members and the community as a whole. In order to do this, it is important to look at which socio-demographic variables influence the quality of life of the community and its members. Quality of life research studies aim to understand how these various impacts of art festivals are internalized by the local community and how they influence an individual's overall life satisfaction (Andereck et al. 2007). This chapter therefore attempts to answer the following questions:

1 How are impacts of art festivals (socio-cultural, environmental, political and economic) perceived by community residents?

2 Do these perceptions of art festival impacts influence their sense of well-being and overall quality of life?

3 Which socio-demographic variables influence the quality of life of the community and its individual members?

The chapter therefore captures the perception of festival impacts on the community and relates these impacts to the measures of overall quality of life, both personally and as a community, as well as determines which socio-demographic variables influence quality of life.

# Background: review of research and literature

## Socio-cultural, environmental, political and economic impacts of art festivals

Literature reveals that festival impacts can be analysed from different perspectives: socio-cultural, environmentally, politically and economic. Firstly, the socio-cultural impacts of festivals have been viewed as either being positive or negative. With respect to the positive socio-cultural impacts of festivals, evidence suggest that festivals help with creating new forms of entertainment; build national pride; provide the community with the opportunity to meet new people; offer chances for interaction between the community and festivalgoers; and increase good norms and values. It also allows the community to form part of the organisation of the festival, promote culture locally. On the negative side the festival will cause unruly behaviour; stimulate an increase in criminal activities; cause a decrease in facilities and social moral values; as well as stress and discomfort on the lives of the local community (Delamere et al., 2001; Fredline et al., 2003; Karlsen and Brändström 2008; Kim et al. 2008; Moscardo 2007; Nunkoo and Ramkissoon 2011; Reid 2007, Rollins and Delamere 2007; Rooney-Browne 2008; Small 2007; Hede et al. 2003).

Secondly, there is the environmental perspective of festival impacts, positive and negative. Focusing on the negative impacts of festivals, studies have shown that communities will have difficulty finding parking during the festival; noise levels and waste will increase; the natural and the built environment will be damaged; traffic congestion will increase; there will be too many people in the local community; and it will be very difficult for the local community to find a quiet location within the city. Positively the festival will assist with the maintenance and improvement of the facilities in and around the festival terrain and public transportation during the festival will increase (Delamere et al. 2001; Nunkoo and Ramkissoon, 2011; Shirley et al. 2006, Sherwood 2007).

Thirdly, there is the political perspective of festival impacts, both positive and negative. Positively, the image of the city will increase; the economic status of the area will be improved, and the local community will take ownership of the festival. On the negative side it is seen that public funding is misused and can be better used for other more important and life benefiting activities (Delamere et al., 2001; Tomljenovic and Faulkner, 1992; Mossberg and Getz 2006; Nunkoo and Ramkissoon 2011; Reid 2006)

Lastly, the economic perspective of festival impacts both positively and negatively (Crompton and Mckay 1994). With respect to the positive economic impact of festivals, evidence suggest that festivals help improve the standard of living, increase job opportunities, increase the value of properties in the community, assist local businesses to increase their revenue, stimulate business opportunities and ensure that the tourists stay longer in the area after the festival. On the negative side the festival might cause and increase in prices for certain services and goods and increase living costs; benefit only an elite group of people; or increase the leakage of money out of the area due to external suppliers that are used during the festival ((Delamere et al. 2001; Nunkoo and Ramkissoon, 2011; Tomljenovic and Faulkner, 1992; Crompton and Mckay, 1994))

Festival organisers would need information that demonstrates how the festival is doing not only from a quantitative perspective, but also from the qualitative perspective that would incorporate how the community perceives the factors that contribute to the quality of life (Andereck and Nyaupane, 2010). To this end, it is therefore important to determine the perception of the community in relation to how they experience the festival, in other words, how the community feels the festival influences the aspects of community life that they deem as valuable and contributing to their life satisfaction.

## Quality of life

While scholars do not yet agree on a precise definition for quality of life, (Kruger et al., 2013; Massam, 2002; Dissart and Deller; 2000; Smith and Puczkó, 2009;) and quality of life is a difficult and a vague concept, in its simplest form it can be seen as a person's satisfaction/dissatisfaction with their life. It therefore ranges from positive to negative. Quality of life also usually means the same as well-being, the person's sense of happiness or unhappiness, satisfaction or dissatisfaction (Kim et al., 2013). Quality of life can be measured from a non-material or a multiple material dimension that shapes the human experience (Easterlin and Angelescu, 2012; Stiglitz et al., 2010). This multifaceted concept involves more measures, indicators and issues. The consensus of researchers is that the concept of quality of life can be defined by two fundamental sets of processes and components. The first relates to internal, psychological mechanism producing satisfaction with life (Kruger et al., 2013), secondly the external condition that trigger the internal mechanism.

Quality of life is captured by both objective and subjective indicators. Objective indicators measure the circumstances of people's lives, such as income and education attainment. Subjective indicators capture self-reporting accounts of individuals' happiness or satisfaction with a list of functions, needs or capabilities (Stiglitz et al., 2009) or the satisfaction with various aspects of life (Andereck and Nyaupane, 2010). Many quality of life measures such as the Human Development Index (HDI), the Gross Domestic Product (GDP), as well as other measures, only measure one of the two basic dimensions of community-related quality of life. Components of the objective dimension include economic factors such as employment, income, or job security. Environmental factors include measures such such as crowding, litter, traffic congestion, noise and air or water pollution. Social factors considered might be family structure, cultural integrity, and job security. However, when the community evaluates the quality of life, they will incorporate a subjective dimension into the measure. They will incorporate personal perceptions and feelings about their environment (Dissart and Deller, 2000). The subjective dimension is emotional and value laden, covering factors such as feelings of well-being, life satisfaction, happiness and beliefs about standard of living (Davidson and Cotter, 1991; Diener and Suh, 1998; Dissart and Deller, 2000; Grayson and Young, 1994). Quality of life in a community therefore consists of the sum of all the individual community members' feelings consequently, and the perception of the objective condition within the community for example economic activities, socio-cultural institution and environmental conditions.

Other socio-demographic variables that have been identified in literature as influencing quality of live include age, education, income, occupation, gender, years in the community and neighborhood noise (Andereck and Nyaupane, 2010; Andrews and Withey, 2012; Eckersley, 1999; Henderson, 1990; Lloyd and Auld, 2002).

One can argue that festivals affect many stakeholders. One of the most important stakeholder groups is the local community. Much research is therefore needed to better understand how festival impacts affect the community residents' overall sense of well-being or quality of life. This study is designed to capture the perception of arts festival impacts on the community and relate these variables to the measures of quality of life, as well as identifying the socio-demographic variables that influences quality of life.

## Overview of the *Innibos National Art Festival*, South Africa

Arts festivals have become important in South African society because of a growing need among the broader public for various forms of art. According to Hauptfleisch (2007) and Coetser (2002), Afrikaans arts festivals started in the 1990s in South Africa. They were actually developed when the Afrikaans speaking population, about 7 million of the 51 million people currently living in South Africa began to fear the extinction of their language and culture. This fear arose under the new South African dispensation, which expressed preference for English as the lingua franca of the new South Africa after the 1994 democratic elections.

Hauptfleisch (2007) confirms this fear and states that the original impetus of many of these Afrikaans arts festivals was: 'the need to celebrate, re-establish, empower and maintain the cultural heritage of Afrikaans speaking South African in the face of the language diminished official status from co-national language of English to one of 11 official national languages'. As a result arts festival like the *Klein Karoo National Arts Festival* [*KKNK*] opened its doors in 1995. The main aim of the festival was to promote Afrikaans, preserve the Afrikaans arts and culture, and encourage people to perform in Afrikaans again. The *Aardklop National Arts Festival* followed in 1998 and the *Gariep Arts Festival* in 1999, various other Afrikaans festivals followed soon after. All of these festivals have managed to stimulate the creation of Afrikaans play writing and in themselves constitute events whose name is now to celebrate the Afrikaner culture and all of its diversity.

The *Innibos National Arts Festival* is one of these festivals that opened its doors in 2003 in Nelspruit, Mpumalanga, South Africa. Currently in its twelfth year of existence, this four day family orientated festival, has managed to draw more than 100,000 people each year. The festival brings together more than 200 top Afrikaans performing musicians, actors and artists from all over South Africa to show case their talents. The festival hosts theatre, music, cabaret, literature, visual arts and children's theatre. Besides the production and theatre taking place all over Nelspruit, festivalgoers can also enjoy more than 200 craft and art and food stalls, beer gardens, restaurants and children's entertainment area (Innibos, 2015; Mpumalanga Gaming Board, 2015).

## Methodology

In order to determine the socio-cultural, environmental, political and economic impact of the *Innibos National Arts Festival* on the community, longitudinal research has been conducted over six-years with the local community. More than 900 questionnaires were completed over a six-year period, determining the socio-cultural, environmental, political and economic impacts of the *Innibos National Arts Festival* on the local community. The last two years the questionnaire also measured the impacts of the festival on the overall quality of life of the community and the residents (n=473). The questionnaire's scales consisted of five broad categories: demographic information, socio-economic information, visiting patterns, socio-cultural, environmental, political and economic impacts and the impact on the overall quality of life of the festival on the community. Every year during the festival 30-40 qualified and trained field researchers asked the community in and around the festival terrain, local restaurants and shopping malls to complete the questionnaires. The questionnaire was also online available on the official website and the community could access it up to two weeks after the festival.

# Findings

## Demographic information

Demographic data revealed that on average the sample contained more females (60%) than males (40%). Figure 1 indicates that there has not been much of a change in the age distribution of festival attendees over the six years of the study, with more than 70% of the festival attendees falling into the 26 - 45 year old category.

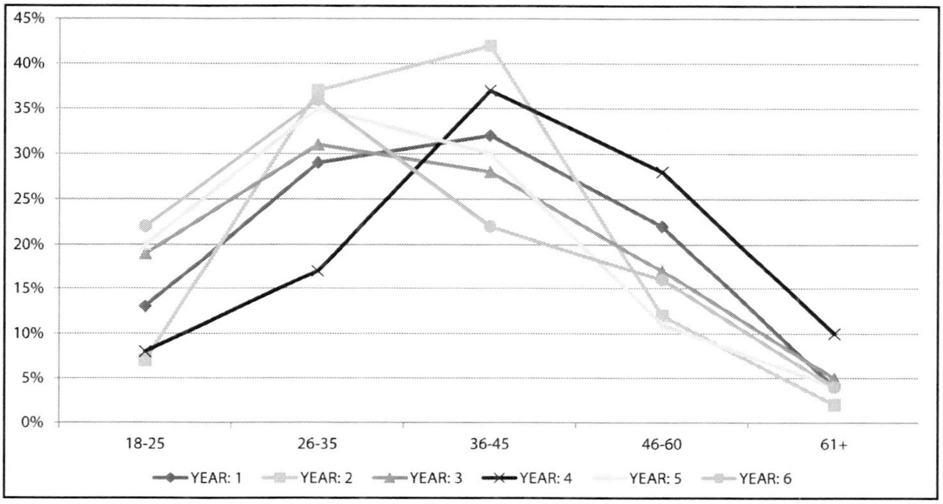


**Figure 13.1:** Demographic information

## Socio-economic information

When analysing the socio-economic information of the community, it was found that 4% had no school qualification, 32% had grade 12 qualification (finished high school), 32% had a three year diploma, 21% a degree and 11% a post graduate qualification. 64% of the local community earns less than R10,000 (R12.80=$1) gross income per month, while 39% earned more than R10,000 per month. This is much higher than the local average over a wider area, whereonly 5% earn more than R10,000 per month. Over a six-year period, 64% of the community indicated that they spend more money during the festival than what they usually do. While 13% showed that they earned more money during the festival than what they would normally earn. The extra income for the local community was generated through providing accommodation, selling products, overtime, and part-time work.

## Visiting patterns

More than 98% of the local community members indicated that they have attended the festival over the six years, while 95% indicated that they would attend the festival the following year. When asked if they will leave Nelspruit during the festival, less than 15% on average indicated that they would. Although the festival has positive and negative impacts on the local community, the high attendance figure as well as the high returning figures indicates that the local community are overall very supportive of the festival. This will also ensure that the festival is sustainable in years to come.

## Socio-cultural, environmental, political and economic impacts

The community perceives the socio-cultural impacts of the festival both positively and negatively (Figure 13.2). From a positive perspective the festival creates opportunities for the community to do interesting activities (88%), engage in new forms of entertainment (84%), makes them feel proud to live in the city (84%), meet (84%) and interact (74%) with new people and promotes culture locally (78%). Although the festival also creates negative socio-cultural impacts on average less than 40% of the community feels that the festival causes stress for the local community, decreases accessibility to facilities, decrease moral values and an increase in criminal activities.

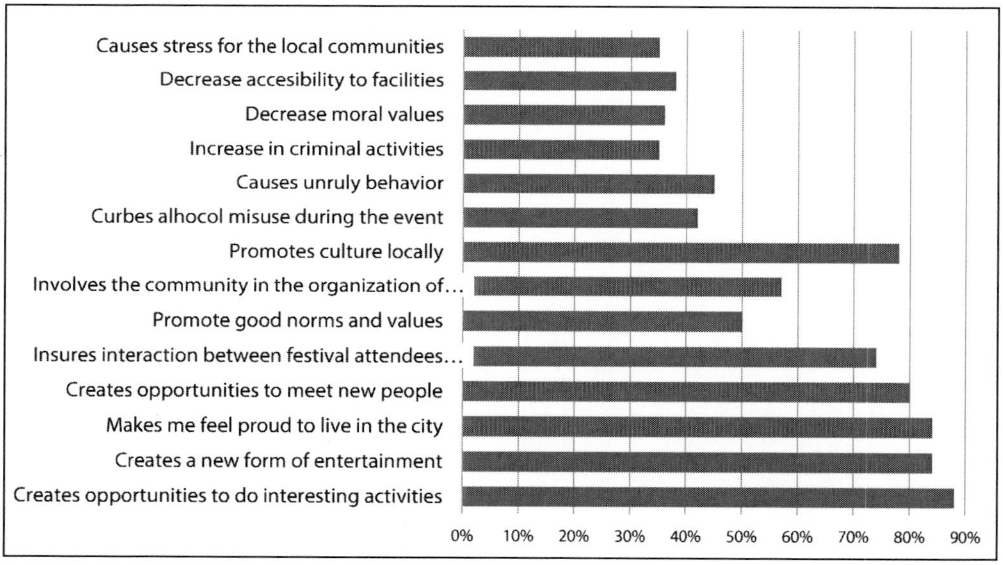


**Figure 13.2:** Socio-cultural impacts

The community also perceives the environmental impacts of the festival both positively and negatively (Figure 13.3). The community is in agreement that traffic congestion, waste, noise levels, maintenance of facilities and public transportation increase during the festival. According to them there are too many people in the city during the festival and it becomes very difficult to find quiet space during the festival. They are also of the opinion that both the built and natural environment gets damage during the festival.

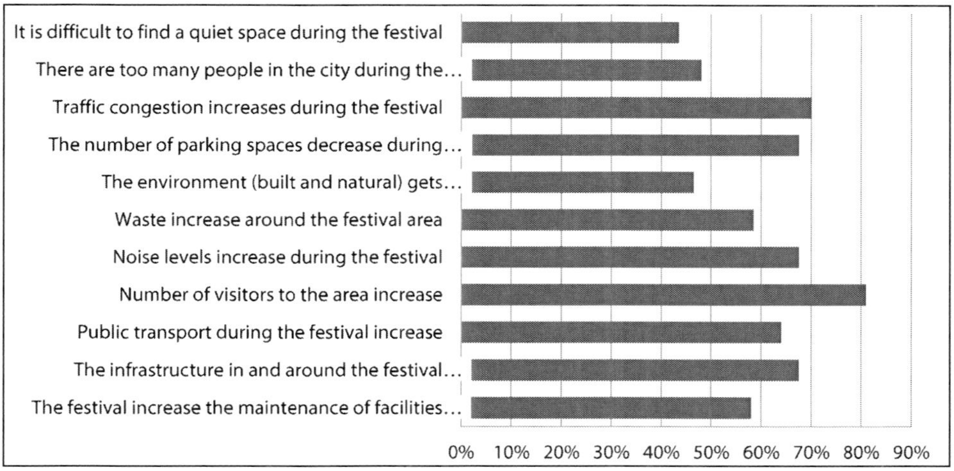


**Figure 13.3:** Environmental impacts

Figure 13.4, indicates a positive and negative political impacts of the festival on the community. Overall, the community perceives the festival to improve the image (78%) and economic status of the city (82%). The local community also takes ownership of the festival (60%), but there is no consensus as to whether public funding is being used wrongly. Fifty percent of the local community feels that public funding is used correctly by supporting the festival and 50% of the community feels that public funding should be prioritised for other more life sustaining activities like housing, water, electricity and job creation.

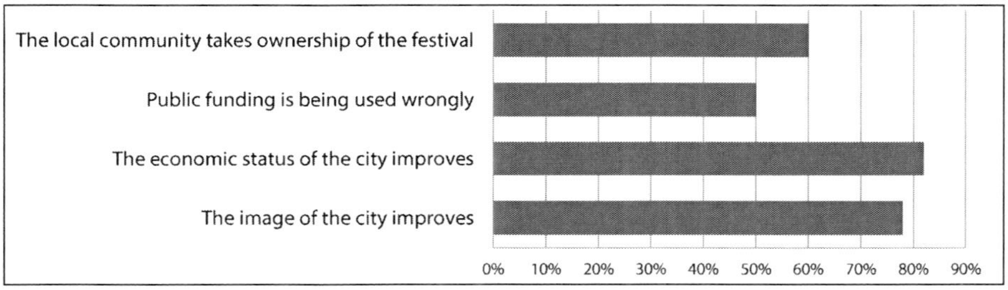


**Figure 13.4:** Political impacts

The positive and negative economic impacts of the festival were also measured. The community indicated that the positive economic impacts of the festival include: job opportunities that are created (82%), money spent by tourist stimulates the local economy (78%), opportunities are created for local businesses (72%), businesses have a higher turnover, marketing of the area stimulates investment interest, the quality of life improves because of the festival, tourist stay longer after the festival, the value of property increase, and people might even relocate to the city because of the festival. On the negative side prices increase and there are higher living costs during the festival, public money can be spent better elsewhere, money is leaking out of the economy and only rich people benefit from the festival.

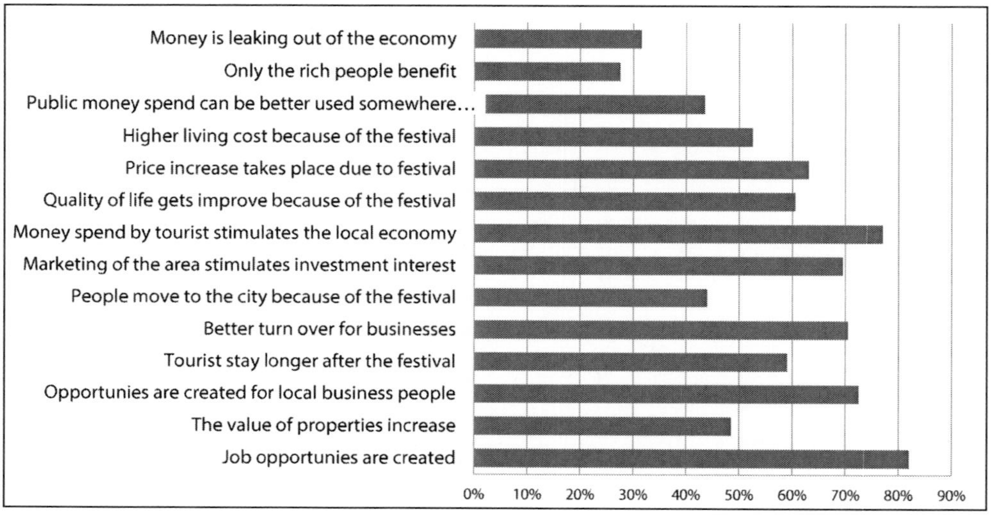


**Figure 13.5:** Economic impacts

## Impact on the overall quality of life

The local community indicated that the festival influences the quality of their personal life either very positively (29%) or positively (43%). 25% stated the festival has no influence on their personal life and only 3% said the festival negatively or very negatively influence the quality of their personal life. Similar results were obtained when asking about the influence of the festival on the overall quality of life of the community.

Although the festival created some inconvenience in traffic congestion (29%), parking (32%) and shopping (3%) the overall feelings of the local community were still positive. Over a six-year period an average 68% of the community indicated their feelings as predominantly positive, 25% as slightly positive, 5% indicated neutral feelings and 3% slightly negative. There were some differences in responses between different demographic groups within the community, with satisfaction levels varying dependent on gender, age and number of years in the community.

## Summary and recommendations

The number of arts festivals has increased remarkably in recent decades. Although various researchers have focused on the socio-cultural, environmental, political and economic impacts of these festivals, research identifying the impacts of the festival on overall quality of life of its local community is lacking. This chapter aimed to address this gap by determining how the socio-cultural, environmental and economic impacts of the art festival were perceived by community residents, how these impacts influence their overall quality of life and the socio-demographic variables that further influence quality of life.

The *Innibos* organisers have done exceptionally well to establish and maintain a very positive attitude from the community towards the festival. Although all positive and negative impacts (socio-cultural, environmental, political and economic) are recognised by the community they are overall very positive about the festival. This can be attributed to the fact that the organisers have involved the community in the planning and organisation of the festival. Results indicated that the overall quality of personal life is influence by education levels and age. Quality of life is less influenced amongst people with higher education levels than those individuals with lower levels of education. Elder people have also indicated that the festival has a higher influence on the quality of their lives than the younger generation. The quality of life of the community is influenced by gender, age and years in the community. Men's quality of life was more influenced by the festival than women. Older people identified a higher influence on their quality of life than younger and people who have lived in the community for more than eight years indicated that the festival does not have a real influence on their quality of life. People who have lived in the area for less than a year have indicated that the festival contributed to their quality of life more positively.

The findings are important for festival organisers in the host community. They need to develop not only short-term perspectives and goals for the festival, but also a long-term strategy of residents' and community overall quality of life and the sustainability of the festival.[1]

# Bibliography


Andereck, K. L., Valentine, K. M., Vogt, C. A., and Knopf, R. C. (2007) A cross-cultural analysis of tourism and quality of life perceptions, *Journal of Sustainable Tourism*, **15**(5), 483 – 502.

Andereck, K. L., and Nyaupane, G. P. (2010) Exploring the nature of tourism and quality of life perceptions among residents, *Journal of Travel Research*, **50**(3), 248-260.

Andrews, F. M., and Withey, S. B. (2012) *Social Indicators of Well-Being: Americans' perceptions of life quality*. Springer: Science and Business Media.

Coetser, J. (2002) *The South African War: Occasion and event in Afrikaans theatre*, presented at the conference; Once there was a war: the South African war in literature, presented by the Department of Information Science, 27-29 May, University of South Africa, Pretoria.

Crompton, J. and Mckay, S. (1994) Measuring the economic impact of festivals and events: some myths, missaplications and ethical dilemmas, *Festival Management and Event Tourism*, **2**, 33-43.

Davidson, W. B., and Cotter, P. R. (1991) The relationship between sense of community and subjective well-being: A first look, *Journal of Community Psychology*, **19**(3), 246-253.

Delamere, T. A., Wankel, L. M., and Hinch, T. D. (2001) Development of a scale to measure resident attitudes toward the social impacts of community festivals, Part I: Item generation and purification of the measure, *Event Management*, **7**(1), 11-24.

Diener, E., & Suh, M. E. (1998). Subjective well-being and age: An international analysis. In K.W. Schaie & M.P. Lawton (Eds.) *Annual Review of Gerontology and Geriatrics*: Vol. 17. Focus on emotion and adult development (pp. 304-324). New York: Springer.

Dissart, J. C., and Deller, S. C. (2000) Quality of life in the planning literature, *Journal of Planning Literature*, **15**(1),135-161.

Easterlin, R. A., and Angelescu, L. (2012) *Modern economic growth and quality of life: cross-Sectional and time series evidence*, Netherlands: Springer.

Eckersley, R. (1999) *Quality of Life in Australia*, Discussion paper, Canberra, Australia: The Australia Institute.

Eventbrite, (2015) *Top 2014 Music Festival Trends and Insights*, available from: www.eventbrite.com/acdemy/music-festivals-trends-2014/ Access 26 July 2015.

Fredline, L., Jago, L., and Deery, M. (2003) The development of a generic scale to measure the social impacts of events, *Event management*, **8(**1), 23-37.

Getz, D. and Andersson, T. (2010) Festival Stakeholders: Exploring Relationships and Dependency Through a Four-Country Comparison, *Journal of Hospitality and Tourism Research*, **34**(4), 531-556.

Grayson, L., and Young, K. (1994) *Quality of Life in Cities: An overview and guide to the literature*. Lawrence Erlbaum.

Hauptfleisch, T. (2007) Festivals as eventifying systems, *Festivalising*, 39-47.

Hede, A., Jago, L. and Deery, M. (2003) An agenda for special event research: Lessons from the past and directions for the future, in *Journal of Hospitality and Tourism Management*, **10**(3), 1-14.

Henderson, K. A. (1990) The meaning of leisure for women: An integrative review of the research, in, *Journal of Leisure Research*, **22**(3),228-243.

Innibos (2015) Available from: www.innibos.co.za, Access 26 July 2015.

Karlsen, S. and Brändström, S. (2008) Exploring the music festival as a music educational project, in *International Journal of Music Education*, **26**(4), 363-373.

Kim, Y., Kim, S. S. and Agrusa, J. (2008) An investigation into the procedures involved in creating the Hampyeong Butterfly Festival as an ecotourism resource, successful factors, and evaluation, in *Asia Pacific Journal of Tourism Research*, **13**(4), 357-377.

Kim, K., Uysal, M., and Sirgy, M. J. (2013), How does tourism in a community impact the quality of life of community residents? in, *Tourism Management*, **36**, 527-540.

Kruger, S., Rootenberg, C., and Ellis, S. (2013) Examining the influence of the wine festival experience on tourists' quality of life, in, *Social Indicators Research*, **111**(2), 435-452.

Lloyd, K. M., and Auld, C. J. (2002) The role of leisure in determining quality of life: Issues of content and measurement, in, *Social Indicators Research*, **57**(1), 43-71.

Massam, B. H. (2002) Quality of life: public planning and private living, in, *Progress in Planning*, **58**(3), 141-227.

Moscardo, G. (2007) Analyzing the role of festivals and events in regional development, in *Event Management*, **11**, 23-32.

Mossberg, L. and Getz, D. (2006) Stakeholder influences on the ownership and management of festival brands, in *Scandinavian Journal of Hospitality and Tourism,* **6**(4), 308-326.

Mpumalanga Gaming Board. (2015) Innibos Kunstefees. Available from: www.emnotweni.co.za. Access 26 July 2015.

Nunkoo, R. and Ramkissoon, H. (2011) Developing a community support model or tourism, in *Annals of Tourism Research,* **38**(3), 964-988.

Reid, G. (2007) Showcasing Scotland? A case study of the MTV Europe Music Awards Edinburgh 2003, in *Leisure Studies,* **28**(4), 479-494.

Reid, G. (2006) The politics of city imaging: A case study of the MTV Europe Music Awards Edinburgh 03, in *Event Management,* **10**(1), 35-46.

Relaxnews. (2015) With boom, music festivals become big business. Available from: www.news.yahoo.com/boom-music-festivals-become-big-business-192119635.html Accessed 26 July 2015.

Rollins, R. and Delamere, T. (2007) Measuring the social impact of festivals, in *Annals of Tourism Research,* **34**(3), 805-808.

Rooney-Browne, C. (2008) Changing the way we look at libraries?: An evaluation of East Renfrewshire's Look at Libraries festival, in *Library Review,* **57**(1), 50-66.

Sherwood, P. (2007) *A Triple Bottom Line Evaluation of the Impact of Special Events: The Development of Indicators.* Doctorate edn. Melbourne: Victoria University.

Shirley, M., Armitage, V., Barden, T., Gough, M., Lurz, P., Oatway, D., South, A. and Rushton, S. (2006) Assessing the impact of a music festival on the emergence behaviour of a breeding colony of Daubenton's bats (Myotis daubentonii), in *Journal of Zoology,* **254**(3), 367-373.

Small, K. (2007) Social dimensions of community festivals: an application of factor analysis in the development of the social impact perception (SIP) scale, in *Event Management,* **11**(1-2), 45-55.

Smith, M. K., and Puczkó, L. (2009) *Health and Wellness Tourism,* London: Routledge.

Stiglitz, J. E., Sen, A., and Fitoussi, J. P. (2010) Report by the commission on the measurement of economic performance and social progress, in, *Paris: Commission on the Measurement of Economic Performance and Social Progress.*

The Guardian. (2015) *Arts Festival experts share the tips for the perfect event.* Available from: www.the Guardian.com/culture- professionals- network/2015/my/27/arts-festival-expert-tips-for-perfect-event, Accessed 26 July 2015.

Tomljenovic, R., and Faulkner, B. (2000) Tourism and older residents in a sun-belt resort, in, *Annals of Tourism Research,* **27**(1), 93-114.

## Notes

[1] To read more about the festival, visit their website at: www.innibos.co.za

# 14 Valuing Arts Festivals: A case study of the South African *National Arts Festival*

Jen D. Snowball

## Introduction

The South African *National Arts Festival* (*NAF*) is in its 42nd year and has evolved to be one of the largest cultural festivals in Africa. The value of cultural festivals extends well beyond the financial (that is, economic) impact, including such things as building social cohesion, cultural capital and identity. Significant advances in measuring such values, using both qualitative and quantitative techniques, have been made in the past 30 years. Nevertheless, economic impact studies are still one of the most widely used valuation methods for cultural events, largely because they demonstrate to funders, government and artistic producers the monetary contribution of the events to the city or region in which they take place. Economic impact studies are thus a powerful tool for arts proponents in arguing for increased resources and demonstrating the impact of this sector of the cultural industries. Using research undertaken at the *National Arts Festival,* this chapter discusses the measurement of festival impacts, describing the method and results, and pointing out how festival organisers used the information. It also demonstrates how impact studies, if conducted in multiple years, can track changes in festival audience composition, which can be useful for event management and organisation.

## Cultural value: definition and measurement

The value of arts and culture, what are now referred to as the cultural and creative industries, has tended to be underestimated in both developed and developing countries alike. Towse (2011) argues that this is because the cultural or creative industries, at both national and international levels, have been poorly served in terms of the collection of data, which tends to be spread across a number of government departments and captured in different ways in each country, making rigorous international comparisons difficult. This is exacerbated by the unique feature of arts and culture compared to other sectors: that it gives rise to two separate, but related, forms of value: intrinsic value and instrumental value.

Intrinsic value refers to the unique cultural and social value that the event provides, and includes such things as inspiration, education, identify formation and pride in one's cultural heritage. It can also contribute to social cohesion and the formation of social and cultural capital. All these are non-market values, that is, they are not easily quantifiable in terms of a market price, mostly because they are not bought and sold. There are, however, ways of measuring these non-market values. For example, stated preference methods, such as willingness to pay (contingent valuation) or choice experiments (conjoint analysis), can be used to create a hypothetical market in order to quantify some of these more intangible values. They have been used widely in cultural economics to value everything from festivals to museums, galleries and heritage sites, and are able to add an important dimension to any valuation study (Snowball, 2008).

Instrumental values are those market impacts that are associated with the event and can be traced through the additional spending that takes place in the region. For example, visitor spending on accommodation, food, transport, tickets and so on, contributes to the economic development of the region. While instrumental values are an important part of the value of a cultural event, they are not unique to it. For example, a similar economic impact might be achieved through staging a sporting event or a conference. Nevertheless, the financial impact of an event can be an important component of its value, particularly if residents of the impact area make a financial contribution to staging the event (for example, through taxes used to finance extra services, or more directly, though public sponsorship). In this case, economic impact studies can be a useful tool to determine the returns from the event. So, despite the fact that arts proponents and event organisers know that economic impact studies capture only the instrumental values associated with a cultural event, this kind of information can be very useful in providing justification for new and ongoing financial support.

Reflecting the growing realisation of the importance of arts and culture, the South African Department of Arts and Culture (DAC) commissioned a Cultural Mapping Study (DAC, 2014). This was the first study in the country to locate all arts and culture firms and foundations (as defined by the UNESCO Framework for Cultural Statistics), and estimated their contributions to the economy, employment and skills development. Using an Input-Output analysis to track the backward and forward linkages, the Mapping study found that the cultural industries contributed 2.9% to South Africa's total Gross Domestic Product (GDP) in 2013/14, which is in line with results from other countries, like Australia and Chile (DAC, 2014). The contribution to employment (directly and indirectly) was 3.6%, a not inconsiderable amount given South Africa's ongoing unemployment rate of nearly 25% (SA Quarterly Labour Force Survey, 2014).

The danger of these sorts of studies, however, is that they may result in policy-makers and funders losing sight of the intrinsic values associated with arts and culture. In comparison to other sectors of the economy, the cultural industries make a small financial contribution, which could mean that they could face decreasing attention and funding. Valuation studies are starting to respond to this challenge in a number of ways, not least in pointing out the ways in which they can contribute to achieving some of the social and developmental goals of governments. For example, in South Africa, the Department of Arts and Culture is guided by the 1996 White Paper on Arts and Culture, "which sought to bring about the transformation of Arts, Culture and Heritage, and to redress the legacy of apartheid in the sector". The revised White Paper (2013) makes provision for the development of the creative economy in South Africa, with specific reference to its role in promoting social cohesion. Key goals of the revised White Paper on Arts and Culture are to:

- Firmly and unambiguously make definitive policy statements that recognise, support and facilitate the role and contribution of the Cultural and Creative Industries to building social cohesion, national unity and pride; and as a key economic growth sector.
- Increase sustainable provision of financial resources directed at the implementation of visible outcomes based on results oriented programmes and projects that can be monitored and evaluated for impact, reach and depth across the entire spectrum of South African society in general, and previously disadvantaged communities and individuals in particular.

Thus, while it is important to acknowledge the contributions of arts and culture to economic growth and employment, one should not lose sight of the sector's contribution to social goals as well. This is particularly the case in South Africa, where society is still divided by the long history of apartheid.

UNESCO (2015) produced a guide to the collection of data about cultural festivals as part of their Framework for Cultural Statistics, entitled *Festival Statistics: Key concepts and current practices*. The report identifies several challenges in the collection of festival statistics, such as the lack of a standard model or method, which make international (or even national) comparisons difficult, and that very few studies address the socio-cultural value of festivals, thus offering only a limited view of the value of these kinds of events. The UNESCO report identifies four broad types of impact studies: economic impact, environmental impact; socio-cultural impact; and tourism impact. Few studies measured all of these impacts, the most common method being the use of an Input-Output model to track the increase in economic activity as a result of increased visitor spending. However, they do report a growing number of studies in the other areas. An example of a festival impact study that used a combination of multiple valuation techniques is the *Operaestate Festival Veneto* (Carnelli, 2015). The study investigated the role of the festival in regional development over its 30 year life-span. Data was collected from multiple points of view, including from audiences, local residents, artists and other regional stakeholders, such as municipalities, to measure festival impact in a holistic way over time.

Other than multiplier analysis used in economic impact studies, one area in which some progress has been made in developing and testing a universal method is in measuring the social benefits and costs of hosting cultural festivals. For example, there has been considerable testing of the Festival Social Impact Attitude Scale, developed by Delamere et al. (2001). The purpose of the Scale is to measure the social impacts of hosting a cultural festival on local residents by asking a number of Likert Scale (strongly disagree; disagree; neutral; agree, strongly agree) questions, and then using principal component factor analysis to identify dimensions (clusters) of determinants of social value. The method has been tested at other festivals and events, for example, the study by Bagiran and Kurgun (2013) at the *Foca Rock Festival* in Turkey. Social benefits identified included the role of festival in building place identity ("it helps to show others why their community is unique and special"), building social cohesion ("it makes community groups work together to achieve common goals") and social capital ("it strengthens friendships"). Social costs included such things as an increase in traffic congestion, litter and environmental damage.

The UNESCO (2015) report on festival statistics suggests that festival impact studies have relied too heavily on methods developed in tourism studies and events management, and that methods more specific to festival studies need to be developed. The rest of this chapter discusses impact studies that have been conducted at the South African *National Arts Festival*, including economic impact, socio-cultural impact, and environmental impact.

## The economic impact method

Tourism events attract new money into the impact region and create direct and indirect impacts through re-spending of the initial injection. Economic impact studies attempt to answer the question: if the event had not taken place, what would the loss of revenue to the impact area have been? An economic impact study thus calculates all the additional economic activity that takes place in the region as a result of the event. This means that normal expenditure by local residents and expenditure that is likely to have taken place anyway, should not be included. The same applies to sponsorship from inside the impact area, since it is likely that, even if the event had not taken place, this money would still have been spent in the impact area (Crompton et al, 2001; Crompton, 2006; Snowball, 2008).

Economic impact starts with the first round, or direct impact, of spending by visitors and festival organisers, although some of this spending flows out of the system immediately in the form of profits and manufacturer margins. Indirect and induced expenditure is stimulated in the impact area as the initial injection is re-spent (known as the multiplier effect). Indirect impact results from the successive rounds of spending that take place as the new money within the region is re-spent. Induced impact refers to the next round of spending caused by the change in income and as a result of stimulated production. Total impact is the sum of direct, indirect and induced impact.

The size of the multiplier (which determines the size of the indirect and induced impacts) depends on the characteristics of the impact area. The smaller the area, the greater the amount of re-spending that takes place outside of it (referred to as 'leakages' from the system), and the smaller the multiplier size. The multiplier can be calculated using regional input-output tables that track the upstream and downstream linkages within a particular economy. For example, Saayman and Rossouw used input-output tables and a Social Accounting Matrix (SAM) to estimate provincial multipliers for the South African *National Arts Festival*. Their findings showed that the aggregate production multiplier for the Eastern Cape Province, in which the festival takes place, was 2.77 "Therefore, for each rand spent by festinos in the region, 177 cents are generated additionally in terms of indirect expenditure" (2011: 617).

Some excellent online economic impact calculators, specifically adapted for cultural events and institutions, also exist, such as the Economic Impact Calculator (EIC) developed for the Georgia Department of Economic Development in the US by Bruce Seaman. Something to keep in mind is that most economic impact studies measure only the short run impact of the additional spending in the region, not long run impacts. One of the recommendations of the UNESCO guidelines for festival statistics (2015) is the importance of developing good baseline statistics so that changes over time (longitudinal studies) can be tracked.

There are a number of common errors made when calculating economic impact. One of the most important is the over-estimation of the multiplier, defined as the "failure to adapt the multiplier to the specific region, including the failure to recognise that smaller less self-sufficient regions have smaller multipliers due to more extensive spending leakages" (Seaman, 2012). Baaijens and Nijkamp (2000) conducted a meta-analysis of eleven economic impact studies from different countries and developed a rough-set analysis model. Variables identified as significant determinants of the size of the income multiplier are population size, surface area, number of tourist arrivals, and tourist type. If the information required to estimate a multiplier for a specific impact area is not available, such information, combined with data on regional variables, can be used to estimate one, followed by some sensitivity analysis.

Other than providing an economic impact number, economic impact studies have great potential to provide other useful information. The best studies are based on a significant number of face-to-face interviews with a carefully selected sample of festinos (festival-goers), which provides a wonderful opportunity to collect data, not only on visitor spending, but also on their activities, their opinions and their ideas for future development and improvement.

# Impact studies at the *National Arts Festival*

The *National Arts Festival* (NAF) is an eleven-day winter festival that takes place in June/July each year in the small university town of Grahamstown. Started originally in 1974 as a celebration of English heritage and culture, it has developed into a multi-cultural mixed arts festival that includes theatre, music (contemporary and classical), dance, physical theatre, comedy, fine art, public art, public lectures (*WordFest* and *ThinkFest*), a craft market and much else. It is organised along similar lines to the *Edinburgh Festival*, with a carefully selected and highly sponsored *Main* programme, and an un-curated *Fringe* programme that is open to all producers who can cover their costs. In 2013, the *National Arts Festival* sold more than 155,000 tickets, and put on 2,500 performances on the *Main* and *Fringe*. In addition to ticketed shows, there are a number of free, public art events. Performances are mainly (but not always) in English and include South African, African and other international participants.

The following section presents a case study of impact studies conducted at the South African *National Arts Festival*, with a focus on Snowball and Antrobus' 2013 study, but also including brief examples of how socio-cultural impacts can be measured.

## Economic impact

The main aims of the 2013 research at the *National Arts Festival* were to update the demographic profile of attendees to the *NAF* in 2006 and to calculate the economic and socio-cultural impact of the festival on both the town in which the event took place (Grahamstown) and the Eastern Cape Province. The design of this study was based on a conceptual model used for determining the economic impact of the *Edinburgh Festival*. The study consisted of data from festinos (682 observations, based mostly on face-to-face interviews, but also including data from 80 self-completion questionnaires) and online surveys of artistic producers and media representatives.

Some commentators (Crompton et al 2001; Crompton, 2006) suggest that visitors who would have come to the region anyway (to visit family or friends or to do business), known as time-switchers and casuals, as well as the spending of local residents, should be excluded from the calculations. In previous studies (Snowball and Antrobus, 2004, 2006) 92% of respondents stated that their main or only reason for coming to Grahamstown was to attend the festival. Spending data collected for local Grahamstown residents also made it clear that "only spending in addition to your normal monthly expenses" should be reported. For the calculation of total economic impact on the Grahamstown region, the additional spending at the festival of local Grahamstown residents was thus included, since it is likely that, if the *NAF* had not taken place, the majority of this spending would have taken place outside of the impact area.

The multipliers for the 2013 *NAF* study were estimated using rough set analysis (Baaijens and Nijkamp, 2000), comparisons with other, similar studies and based on previous *NAF* studies. It is important to keep in mind that the impact area makes a great deal of difference to the multiplier size and thus the total economic impact. For example, the multiplier for the Grahamstown economy is estimated to be only 1.18 (meaning that for every R1 of direct impact, a further 18 cents is generated in indirect and induced impacts). Recall that, for the Eastern Cape Province, Saayman and Roussouw (2011) estimated that the multiplier was 2.77, indicating that, for every R1 of direct impact, a further R1.77 is generated in indirect and induced impact. In general, the larger the impact area, the greater will be the size of the multiplier.

The ticket sales method was used to estimate visitor numbers, that is, by dividing the number of tickets sold by the average number of ticketed events attended by respondents, it is possible to estimate how many people attended the festival, including local residents, who made up around 20% of festinos. A total of 155,421 tickets were sold on the *Main* and *Fringe* at the 2013 *NAF*. Local festinos reported attending an average of 6.2 ticketed shows at the 2013 festival, while visitors from outside Grahamstown attended an average of 8.2 shows. The average number of ticketed shows attended by both groups of festinos was 7.8.

Dividing the total number of tickets sold by the average number of tickets bought, thus gives a total number of festinos of around 20,000, around 16,000 of whom were visitors from outside the host city. However, it should be kept in mind that festinos spent an average of 6 days and 5 nights at the festival, giving a total of nearly 120,000 visitor days.

First round total spending by all groups was calculated to be nearly R110m (Figure 14.1). However, some of this spending is likely to leave the region immediately, thus having no real impact on the economy. For example, the vast majority of artists came from outside the impact area, so money spent on ticket sales is likely to flow out immediately. To avoid an over-estimation of the economic impact of the NAF, it was thus assumed (as in previous reports) that there is an immediate 30% outflow.

| Group | Expenditure |
|---|---|
| Visitors | R55,407,440 |
| Locals | R4,909,520 |
| Producers | R16,324,748 |
| Media | R1,283,132 |
| Sponsorship from outside the impact area | R31,869,663 |
| Gross Total Initial Impact | R109,794,503 |
| Net Initial Impact | R76,856,152 |
| Total Impact: Grahamstown | R90,690,259 |

**Figure 14.1:** Table of the impact of the *NAF* on the local economy. *Source*: Snowball and Antrobus, 2013.

It should also be borne in mind that the above calculation excludes certain costs and benefits that the festival generates. For example, benefits not included are the long term growth and development effects on the town, rather than only the short term yearly impact that the economic impact study measures; and the value of the positive spillovers that accrue to all Grahamstown residents as a result of the festival, like feelings of pride, educational opportunities, entertainment, etc. (See Snowball and Antrobus, 2001; and Snowball, 2008 for further information on how willingness to pay studies can be used to measure the value of such benefits). Increased costs to local businesses, via increased competition and a drop in regular customers, are also not included, nor are increased costs to the municipality (e.g. additional refuse removal) and to the state (e.g. extra policing).

Thus, while not capturing the total value of the festival, economic impact numbers can be very useful in demonstrating the economic importance of an event. For example, the 2013 *NAF* study was reported in a wide range of local media and quoted by government officials from the Department of Arts and Culture. All these reports emphasised the job creation and economic growth potential of the event. In an interview with the *Mail and Guardian* the Festival Director, Ismail Mohammed, also highlighted the benefits to the local economy: "In a city with an incredibly high level of unemployment the festival provides a large number of seasonal jobs and training for locals." At the 2014 festival, the Deputy Minister of the Department of Arts and Culture (DAC) hosted a breakfast meeting specifically to talk about the economic impact of the festival. In a press release, they stated that, "The Department of Arts and Culture (DAC) is proud to support the *National Arts Festival* as this is aligned with our Mzansi Golden Economy (MGE) strategy that is aimed at developing the arts through substantial investment in festivals. Festivals draw and develop audiences, create jobs and build markets for the arts." In a developing country context, where there are so many calls on the public purse, being able to demonstrate that public support of a cultural event has the ability to address concerns such as job creation, skills development and economic growth, can make a big difference to the ability to raise funds from both public and private sponsors.

## Socio-cultural values

In addition to the calculation of the economic impact number, impact studies can also provide useful opportunities for organisers and funders to track the progress and development of the event, as well as measuring at least some of the intrinsic, socio-cultural benefits that arts and culture provide. For example, economic impact studies routinely track festino demographics.

After the end of apartheid in 1994, one of the most important aims of institutions like the *NAF* was to encourage more diverse participation in terms of both audiences and performers. This was important from the point of view of both artistic quality and relevance, and in terms of continuing to access public funding. One way of tracking such transformation was to compare the percentage of English-speaking festinos over time – information captured routinely in a long line of economic impact studies (Figure 14.2).

| Year | % English speakers |
|---|---|
| 1987 | 85 |
| 1989 | 79 |
| 1996 | 70 |
| 1997 | 61 |
| 2001 | 75 |
| 2003 | 53 |
| 2004 | 54 |
| 2006 | 64 |
| 2013 | 61 |

**Figure 14.2:** Table of the percentage of English speakers at the *NAF*

The proportion of data collected by self-completion questionnaires and interviews differs between studies, possibly accounting for some of the variation across years (since questionnaires were presented in English, and those who read and write English easily are more likely to fill in an English language questionnaire). Nevertheless, it is quite clear that the audience profile of festinos has changed considerably over the time period in question.

The NAF Director has also pointed out that the festival is about more than just money:

> It is important that we measure the impact of the festival not only in monetary terms but also in the way that it contributes to nation-building. It is crucial to note how the festival positions South Africa internationally… At a local level, the festival continues to be a minefield with hidden cultural gems that are unearthed each year. When one considers that international icons such as Sibongile Khumalo, William Kentridge and Dada Masilo took their initial steps at the *National Arts Festival*, then we still need to measure the impact of this festival by the way in which it has allowed South Africa's cultural treasure chest to overflow (Ismail Mohammed in an interview with the *Mail and Guardian*, 2014).

Following on from methods used by the 2011 *Edinburgh Festival* study, questions to measure some of the socio-cultural intrinsic values that the *NAF* provides were included in the 2013 study. Festinos were asked to respond to a number of statements about the value of the *NAF* on a one to five Likert Scale, where 1 meant strongly disagree; and 5 was strongly agree.

One of the important roles of an arts festival is audience development and widening of the cultural experience, that is, in building what Throsby (2001) refers to as cultural capital. For example, festinos were asked to respond to the statement:

"When I am at the festival, I am more likely to take risks and go to shows and events that are new to me, and that I haven't experienced before." Seventy two percent of respondents agreed or strongly agreed with the statement, showing that the festival encourages festinos to experience new art forms. The average score (out of 5) was 3.9, slightly higher than for attendees at the *Edinburgh Festival* (where the average was 3.7). This sort of data can also be analysed for different segments of the audience. In the case of this question, an interesting finding was that more black people agreed with this statement (scoring an average of 4.1) than other groups, perhaps also an indication that the *NAF* is succeeding in its aim to attract and develop more diverse audencies.

Responses to the statement "The festival is an event where people from different cultures and backgrounds can meet and talk together" showed that nearly 40% of festinos strongly agreed with the statement, with a further 30% agreeing. The average score was 4 out of 5. This is an encouraging indication that the *NAF* offers important opportunities for interaction and conversation across race, class and cultural backgrounds and can play an important role in building social cohesion.

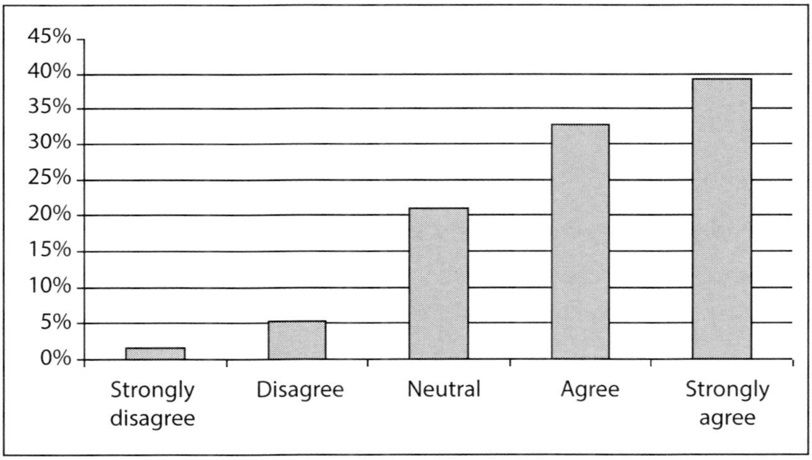


**Figure 14.3:** Responses to the statement: "The festival is an event where people from different cultures and backgrounds can meet and talk together"

Methods like this can also be used to measure the socio-economic impact of the event on local residents, but a better way of doing this would be to run a separate study. As in many South African towns, income and wealth are still divided along racial lines, with many black communities living some distance from the town centre and struggling more than their white counterparts to meet daily needs. Do they benefit from the festival? To answer this question, a contingent valuation study was conducted in 2003 with a stratified sample of local residents (Snowball, 2005). Results showed that, although households from lower income areas benefited less in terms of direct earnings, they acknowledged the non-market, socio-cultural benefits that the event provided. In some cases, attitudes towards the festival were more positive amongst lower income groups than in the higher income areas of the city. It was concluded that, although people from high income areas attend more ticketed shows and gain more in terms of festival earnings, positive values also accrue to lower income area residents, and that festival valuation studies need to take these non-market values into account as well.

## Conclusions

Measuring the impact of cultural festivals is a complex process, but can provide useful data to organisers and current and potential funders. While the majority of studies have focused on the economic (financial) impacts of events, there is also a need to develop standard methods to measure other kinds of socio-cultural impacts (UNESCO, 2015). Visitor surveys, often used to collect data for economic impact studies, can be adapted, relatively easily, to measure some of these other kinds of impacts.

## Bibliography

Arts and Culture Minister Nathi Mthethwa to address the *National Arts Festival* official opening. http://www.gov.za/arts-and-culture-minister-nathi-mthethwa-address-national-arts-festival-official-opening

Baaijens, S., and Nijkamp, P. (2000) Meta-analytic methods for comparative and exploratory policy research: An application to the assessment of regional tourism multipliers, in *Journal of Policy Modeling*, **22**(7), 821-858.

Bagiran, D. and Kugun, H. (2013) A research social impact of the *Foca Rock Festival*: The validity of the Festival Social Impact Attitude Scale, in *Current Issues in Tourism*. Available: http://dx.doi.org/10.1080/13683500.2013.800028

Carnelli, L. (2015) Operaestate Festival Veneto: A socio-cultural and economic analysis, in Newbold, C., Maughan, C., Jordan, J. and Bianchini, F (eds.) *Focus on Festivals: Contemporary European Case Studies and Perspectives*. Oxford: Goodfellow.

Crompton, J. (2006) Economic impact studies: Instruments for political shenanigans? in *Journal of Travel Research*, **45**, 67-82.

Crompton, J., Lee, S., and Schuster, T. (2001) A guide for undertaking economic impact studies: The Springfest example, in *Journal of Travel Research*, **40**, 79-87.

Delamere, T., Wankel, L. and Hinch, T. (2001) Development of a scale to measure resident attitudes towards the social impacts of community festivals, *Event Management*, **7**, 11-24.

Edinburgh Festivals Study (2005) Edinburgh's Year-round Festivals 2004-2005 Economic Impact Study. Available: http://www.efa-aef.eu/newpublic/upload/efadoc/11/festivals_exec_summary_final_%20edinburgh%2004-05.pdf Report by SQW Ltd., Edinburgh and TNS Travel and Tourism, Edinburgh.

Mail and Guardian (2014) National Arts Festival: Fab, 40 and on fire, Available: http://mg.co.za/article/2014-06-26-fab-40-and-on-fire-for-the-arts

Revised White Paper on Arts and Culture (2013) Department of Arts and Culture (DAC), South Africa. Available: https://www.dac.gov.za/sites/default/files/REVISEDWHITEPAPER04062013.pdf

Saayman, M. and Rossouw, R (2011) The significance of festivals to regional economies: Measuring the economic value of the Grahamstown *National Arts Festival* in South Africa, *Tourism Economics*. **17**(3) 603-624.

SA Quarterly Labour Force Survey (2014) *Quarterly Labour Force Survey* – Quarter 4 2014. Statistics South Africa. Available: http://www.statssa.gov.za/publications/P0211/P02114thQuarter2014.pdf

Seaman, B. (2012) *Economic Impact Calculator (EIC)*. Commissioned by the Georgia Department of Economic Development, USA.

Snowball, J. (2005) Art for the Masses? Justification for the public support of the arts in developing countries: Two arts festivals in South Africa, in *Journal of Cultural Economics*. **29**(2), 107-125.

Snowball, J. (2008) *Measuring the Value of Culture: Methods and Examples in Cultural Economics*, Germany: Springer-Verlag.

Snowball, J. (2011) Cultural Value, in R. Towse. (ed.) *A Handbook of Cultural Economics*, Second Edition. Cheltenham: Edward Elgar.

Snowball, J., and Antrobus, G. (2001) Measuring the value of the arts to society: The importance of externalities for lower income and education groups in South Africa. *South Africa Journal of Economics*, **69**(4), 752-766

Snowball, J., and Antrobus, G. (2004) *The National Arts Festival Festino Survey 2004* Commissioned by the *National Arts Festival*, Grahamstown, South Africa.

Snowball, J., and Antrobus, G. (2006) *The National Arts Festival Festino Survey 2006* Commissioned by the *National Arts Festival*, Grahamstown, South Africa.

Snowball, J., and Antrobus, G. (2013) *The National Arts Festival Festino Survey and Economic Impact Analysis 2013* Commissioned by the *National Arts Festival*, Grahamstown, South Africa.

South African Department of Arts and Culture (DAC) (2014) Arts and Culture Minister Nathi Mthethwa to address the National Arts Festival official opening. South African Government. Online: http://www.gov.za/arts-and-culture-minister-nathi-mthethwa-address-national-arts-festival-official-opening, accessed 9/12/2015.

Towse, R. (2011) Creative industries, in R. Towse (ed.) *A Handbook of Cultural Economics*, Second Edition, Cheltenham: Edward Elgar.

UNESCO (2015) Festival Statistics: Key concepts and current practices 2009, in, *UNESCO Framework for Cultural Statistics Handbook*, no. 3. Available at: http://www.uis.unesco.org/culture/Documents/fcs-handbook-3-festival-statistics.pdf

# 15 Festivals on the High Street: Revitalising business and communities in the UK

Roberta Comunian, Lydia Fraser-Ward and Silvie Jacobi

## Introduction

This chapter considers the tradition and impact of festivals taking place in high street settings. Using examples from the UK it reflects on recent issues that have affected the decline experienced by high streets in the UK and explores how arts festivals and public outdoor events have been used to revitalise business and community engagement. We will explore two case studies in London presenting current research on mapping community and business engagement in these settings.

Festivals have historically been highly embedded and integrated within the socio-economic life of societies, for example as celebrations and cultural activities embedded within fairs, markets and squares. However, while in recent years we have seen more and more festivals blooming in many communities, bringing new cultural and social life to our cities, we have also seen the decline of independent economic activities on high streets, with increasingly unsustainable rents pushing smaller traders out in favour of large chains and cheap imported goods often resulting in an increase of empty shops. This chapter questions whether there could be more integration and engagement between artistic activities embedded in festivals and local shops, through cultural intervention that is mutually beneficial.

The first part of the chapter brings together the literature on arts festivals and their impact in communities and places, with recent issues emerging in the UK about the decline of the high street and its viability, which has been highlighted in extensive academic and policy reports (Wrigley and Dolega, 2011; Portas, 2011). Here, we highlight the importance of considering culture as a key ingredient in the future development of high streets, raising awareness of festivals in bringing the right mix of social, cultural but also economic opportunities for local high streets and presenting two case studies which highlight these integrated dynamics. In the second part, we discuss the case studies and methodologies adopted. The case studies are recent arts-focused interventions that specifically use cultural activity to stimulate positive social engagement with the high street whilst directly supporting local economic investment and customer loyalty. The conclusions reflect on the limit of current methodologies and our current ability to map and capture the interconnection between social, cultural and economic impact of festivals and their potential future role in the regeneration of high streets.

# Festival and high streets: trajectories of engagement

## Festival and impact: background

Festivals have historically always had a strong connection with local communities and place, as they provided a platform through which place-specific traditions and communal creativity could be celebrated. This served as a way to express the distinct relationship between identity and place while also being a setting for social interaction, which in itself furthers 'local continuity' and knowledge production (Quinn, 2005). While certain aspects of these traditional notions and functions of festivals have been sustained until today, globalisation has blurred the boundary between local and global, leading to a diversification of festivals in terms of their functions, cultural dimension and audience reach. Along with globalisation, the trend of increasing urban entrepreneurialism and city competition between competing global cities (Sassen, 2001) fostered an environment in which festivals became prominent features of creative city strategies (Landry, 2008). They were often linked to improving a city's image or reputation while creating place distinctiveness to attract visitors and tourists, along the lines of festivals as destinations and city showcases (Van Aalst and van Melik, 2012). In this relation festivals have been recognised as drivers of economic development, by bringing temporary cultural functions to the local area, often hoped by local authorities to increase land and property values and attracting commercial interest as part of a larger-scale urban regeneration strategy (Ley, 2003).

While measuring economic impact has been an exercise of increasing importance to justify public funding during times of austerity, Arcodia and Whitford (2007) recognise that festival impact is multiplied beyond economic impact. They argue that it stretches across socio-cultural, political, and physical environmental impact; of which there are not just positive outcomes but also a wealth of negative factors to consider, such as the mismatch between local and global interests regarding the use of space and the possible impact of a festival on gentrification. While measuring economic impact can be studied on the basis of a quantitative analysis of direct and multiplied spending (Crompton and McKay, 1994), measuring long-term social and cultural impacts in the context of culture-led urban regeneration has been considered more of 'a mystery' (Bailey et al., 2004) due to the place-specific complexity that needs to be studied qualitatively.

A wealth of literature has more recently focused on urban festivals as social space, following Lefebvre's (1991) notion of space as a system of changing social relationships and interactions, which shape and continuously reproduce spatial aesthetics and cultural processes tied to that same space. Stevens and Shin's (2014) paper analyses festivals as social space by researching their capacity for fostering social interaction on the local scale despite prescribed meanings and political and economic instrumentalisation. On another social scale, festivals can also be considered as 'communities of practice' (Comunian, 2015), connecting people with similar cultural, professional or social backgrounds from different countries, cities and regions (comparable to academic conferences or business trade fairs). Hence the hub and networking aspect of festivals is an important element for the cultural economy, providing a platform for artistic and professional development and knowledge exchange between local, national and global.

## Contemporary struggles: revitalising the UK High Street

While acknowledging the impact of festivals for the regeneration of cities and communities, the highly politically debated future of British high streets serves as a relevant and timely case study field for testing connections between festivals, urban regeneration and cultural development. As the mind map below (Figure 15.1) suggests, festivals on the high street directly bridge economic impact with cultural dynamics and social capital. While economic impact aligns with the interest of local authorities wishing to bring back business to the high street as well as increasing retail activity and consumer spending, high streets are crucial public spaces where social capital and community connections are formed (Dobson, 2015). Most importantly, the cultural dynamics of festivals stimulate new momentum and focus for the high street as a distinct place and community hub beyond commercial activity through interaction between cultural practitioners and their engagement with local audiences and visitors.

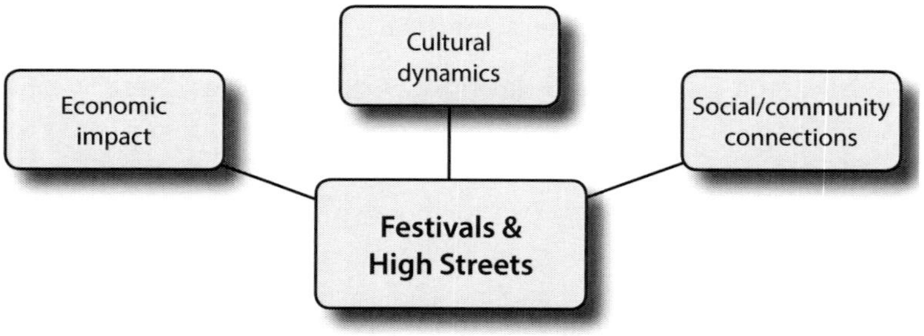


**Figure 15.1:** Festivals and High Streets (own elaboration)

With increasing shop vacancy rates (doubling between 2009 and 2011) and spending growing away from the high street in out-of-town shopping centres (now making up 50% of total retail spending), the 2010 coalition government commissioned retail specialist Mary Portas (2011) to assess the current situation of UK high streets and to think about its future role as retail and community destination. While providing practical recommendations for mostly short-term policy aimed at bridging governance scales and kick-starting structural change for efficient high street management, Portas stresses the importance of high streets and town centres as inherently cultural and social destinations catering for the needs of local communities. In response to this, festivals have the capacity to bring back community pride and provide a sense of place attachment and belonging (Quinn, 2005).

While the high street policy push has brought forward "diverse yet overlapping ideas designed to stimulate British high streets" (Hubbard, 2015: 1), there is a clear lack of empirical data on how high streets actually function (Arvizu Machado et al., 2013). This has to some extent led to unnecessary duplication of policy effort without forging local links, as well as funding often directed towards short-term goals. The wealth of simultaneously developed policies and initiatives (e.g. GLA, 2011; Gov.uk, 2013) appears to have been triggered by a strong surge to pour funding into this field of policy, such as in London through the Mayor's Outer London Fund and the 'Portas Pilots' across the country from 2011 onwards. This provided unique opportunities for cultural organisations to shape proposals towards high street regeneration, providing them with a new context for their work and securing finance to support new cultural production. Festivals, as showcased in the Greater London Authority (GLA)'s recent report *Culture on the High Street* (GLA, 2013), present a unique opportunity not just to animate communities and spaces through cultural production and consumption, but also to serve as instrument for participatory research integrated in the festival's experience and activities. This can, in a practical and creative way, nurture local understanding of how communities use high streets and help to find solutions for regeneration that are both inclusive and efficient along the lines of a 'Connected Communities' vision (Rowson et al., 2010). The GLA (2013) report showcases how cultural intervention has the capacity to trigger innovation and change, in the areas of economic development, inclusive place branding and raising quality in delivery of cultural events.

There have been many bottom-up developments that provide an alternative and often cost efficient approach to innovation on the high street. Whether this is in relation to incubating local trade through alternative currencies (Brixton Pound, 2015) or through initiatives around transferring empty property back into use (Thompson, 2010), alternative economies illustrate that change and resilience for high streets emerges through local need and existing socio-economic interaction. Bridging again to the role of festivals within this context, they sit at the intersection of all the fields addressed in many of the current debates around high street regeneration and as such could provide new purposeful incentive for mediating between local trade, cultural intervention, participatory research and policy making. One can problematise again that festivals only offer short-term visions, based often on a week or weekend of activities, yet it is hoped they have capacity for wider and more long-term impact that is yet to be researched within the context of high street regeneration.

# Case studies and methodology

The chapter builds on action-research practices developed through the partnership between researchers at King's College London and a community interest company established in 2013 called Fantasy High Street. The partnership allowed researchers to monitor and experiment with new modes of engagement between festival programming, local communities and high street businesses.

Fantasy High Street is a not-for-profit arts organisation that utilizes the imagination and creativity of performance and visual artists to demonstrate the unique characteristics of high street businesses and their products and services. It aims to celebrate the local high street as an essential community hub, creating interactive installations, performances and events which defy imagination, whilst exploring the values of public space. In addition, the company also works in a variety of other public spaces, from parks to museums to celebrate the importance of shared space within communities with an aim to question the future role of the British high street, and look beyond its economic value to its social value.

In the chapter we use as case studies two projects run by Fantasy High Street, one developed in July 2013 and one in June 2015, both based in London. The first intervention was supported by the business improvement district (BID) Waterloo Quarter and aimed to deliver a high street animation project in Lower Marsh, a small high street situated directly behind Waterloo Station in Zone 1 Central London. The second case study involved *Crystal Palace Overground Festival*, an annual free community festival spread across Westow Park and Crystal Palace Park. In both cases, we aimed to test new methodologies to measure the impact of the festival's activities on the local high street economy, whilst also creating interactive arts activities to heighten visitor enjoyment of both local resources.

In the first case study, the festival included arts activities both inside and outside shop spaces. These were evaluated with quantitative data collection on footfall, evidence of visitor behaviour through observation, qualitative interviews with business owners, visitors and artists, plus an interactive installation which collected written feedback and rating of experience. In the second case study, innovative RFID (Radio Frequency Identification) technology is used to measure how visitors interact with cultural content in the festival programme and local high street shops through a bespoke adventure trail.

## Lower Marsh Revitalisation - Waterloo, London (July 2013)

Although ideally located in the heart of the city, Lower Marsh is hidden from the immediate view of the thousands of passing commuters who use Waterloo Station every day; the street was renowned for lacking footfall, despite its excellent retail offer and broad range of independent shops and market traders. As the local BID, Waterloo Quarter was keen to support regeneration of this high street and increase its broader public appeal and awareness. They had successfully applied to the Portas Pilot programme for funding to deliver a range of projects including a property owners' forum, a market traders' training programme and a series of public engagement activities that would help raise the profile of the street. One such project was the commission of Fantasy High Street to deliver a 'Fantasy Cafe' as part of the annual food festival that took place in Lower Marsh each July.

As a not-for-profit arts organisation Fantasy High Street's raison d'être was to transform everyday shops into magical, interactive enterprises which defied imagination. The purpose of this newly formed partnership was to allow both the BID and the cultural organisation to trial something new, an ambitious combination of arts and business whereby an ordinary restaurant would be turned into a 'Fantasy Cafe' where customers would be invited to enjoy a meal in a wholly new way, with actors from a theatre company called Stamp Collective using games, storytelling and performance to encourage visitors to try foods they had never tasted before. In some cases food colouring was added to particular drinks to explore the limits of customers' usual taste sensations and associations with certain flavours. By exploring food with a sense of play and fun, the aim was for customers to have an unforgettable culinary experience which not only promoted the menu of the vendor but also offered a high quality arts experience at the same time. Two additional performers were placed on Emma Cons Gardens, a small public square on the opposite side of the street which had good visibility from pedestrians and passing traffic. As the street performers caught the attention of passers-by they invited visitors to play games, make chalk drawings on the pavement and solve mysterious clues about food before crossing them over the road towards the restaurant and Lower Marsh high street.

This project, a test 'fantasy shop' model, was part of a larger Soft Launch event for Fantasy High Street who used the financial commission from Waterloo Quarter to leverage further funding from Arts Council England's Grants for the Arts programme and Creativeworks London to trial a number of other cultural interventions in Lower Marsh alongside the Fantasy Cafe. These included: a) a community engagement project called 'The Loveliness of Lower Marsh' which aimed to used a combination of theatre-making and game playing to connect residents with their local high street in a positive way, b) an Ideas Exchange project called 'Fantasy Window Display' which directly partnered a visual artist with a shop owner to work together on a artistic window installation, c) an academic research project with King's College London to trial new methods to measure the economic and social impact of these cultural activities on local businesses and residents.

'The Loveliness of Lower Marsh' was an extension of an existing programme of work by theatre-makers Coney, who were commissioned by Fantasy High Street for this project. This community engagement event focused on testing how arts and cultural activity in the high street could directly support improved relations between residents and businesses as well as gather important information on local identity in relation to the street. Artists recruited local residents and business owners to become 'secret agents' of loveliness; each recruit was given training, a codename and specific missions to carry out anonymous acts of kindness for other people in their neighbourhood. All the missions culminated in an exhibition of photographs and messages documenting life in the street and some of the acts of loveliness that took place during this time, which were on display for a week in one of the high street's cafés. This was supported by an additional text message treasure hunt which led visitors to various shops, stalls and physical features of Lower Marsh, imparting anecdotal information about the people who lived and worked there whilst also encouraging participants to look beyond the initial surface appearance of the area. At its core was an objective to spark positive social change on a micro-geographic scale, locating and emphasising a common identity through the shared use of one street and the impact it had on people's daily lives.

The Ideas Exchange was a third strand of activity that aimed to identify various methods for artists and businesses to work together to share their knowledge and expertise, creating an artistic response to a practical business issue. Looking specifically at visual merchandising and the many similarities between curating visitor journeys around galleries and customer journeys around retail space, a small commission was offer to one artist/business partnership to co-create a window display. What The Butler Wore clothing shop worked with visual artist Carrin Robertson to create a temporary kaleidoscopic display which used patterns from various second-hand clothes within the shop as inspiration, attracting people to the shop window and drawing visitors inside for increased footfall.

The research partnership between King's College London and Fantasy High Street culminated in an evaluation matrix of methodologies put into practice as part of the Soft Launch event. Some were observation-based, measuring attendance and fluctuations in footfall to the area, surveys with high street users and businesses to assess changes in consumer behaviour. By observing footfall patterns in the weeks before and after the event as well as during the event days, we were able to make comparisons to assess the impact of the festival on high street usage.

In the week prior, footfall was fairly low throughout the morning with a peak during the lunch period which doubled figures, followed by a sharp decline in the afternoon. This lunch-time rush supported observational evidence that the majority of high street users were aged 25-64, local office workers and mostly white with some Asian and Black ethnic diversity. Data collected during the event dates demonstrated an evident rise in footfall, with numbers doubling in the morning from the previous week, being 38% higher during lunchtime and six times higher during the afternoon. This increase was not solely due to the work of Fantasy High Street and was aided by the presence of additional market stalls and activity on Emma Cons Gardens as part of the food festival launch, however participant figures for the combined arts strand activities showed over 600 people directly engaged with local shops as part of the activity, with participating shop owners noticing an increased interest in their businesses from passing footfall; the cafe hosting The Loveliness of Lower Marsh exhibition noticed customer numbers double during the event days and even opened up on the Saturday when it is usually closed due to low footfall, selling out of all of their food produce that day. Street performers helped to animate the area, handing out leaflets about the project, and the interactive market barrow frequently drew the attention of passers-by who were pulled out of their daily routine to explore new activity on the high street. The nature of the events drew media interest as well, securing coverage in prime time London radio channels and magazines, which the BID had often struggled to secure for the food festival events in previous years. The footfall data also showed a broader diversity in the attendees, with a marked increase in the presence of children, suggesting more families using the street than usual and more spread in ethnic diversity. Although a short-term activity lasting only a few days, the event demonstrated continued impact, with increased footfall observed in the week following, retaining the doubled figures for the morning and increased attendance during lunch hours.

## Carrier Crows Project - Crystal Palace, London (June 2015)

The 'Carrier Crows' project was a digital arts trail taking place as part of *Crystal Palace Overground Festival* using RFID sensors within silicon wristbands. It works by using a unique ID tag (i.e. a microchip) and a reader. Most new smartphones and tablets have the appropriate hardware installed to read RFID tags and simply require appropriate software to identify the tag and process the data. All that is required is physical contact. Based on this technology, Fantasy High Street created an interactive adventure trail with multiple stops around both the festival and the local high street. The purpose of this project was to trial how existing hardware and software technology solutions could gather information about audience spending habits across multiple sites. As a free community-led event, *Crystal Palace Overground Festival* was an ideal subject to test how effective a system of this nature could be within an unticketed event and where the potential gaps and limitations were, which if proved effective, could be useful for future product development. By creating stops on a trail throughout the local area, participants were encouraged to explore a variety of arts events as part of the festival as well as number of local shops and cultural resources in the area. Part festival pass, part local loyalty card, the Carrier Crow wristbands were trialled over two days with users able to touch in at as many or as few reader points as they wished. As a free activity participants were incentivised to follow clues and touch in at several stops to win a free prize at the end. Each stop also provided a special benefit, either a discount in a local shop, a free gift or a special behind-the-scenes interaction with artists in the festival including one-on-one drawing classes and children's craft workshops.

The participant data was kept anonymous and the wristbands only recorded when specific reader stations were tapped in at. The limitations of the existing technology did not allow for a direct communication between readers and shop payment till systems, however the readers provided an additional tap in option for when participants wished to redeem special offers, therefore the data gathered included not only how many stops people visited, and when, but also if they intended to spend money in the shop or redeem special arts activities, providing unequivocal data that the activity brought direct footfall to local businesses and an intention to spend money there.

## Key findings

For the purposes of this study, which only included a sample of 111 participants, some useful information was revealed as the organisation's first steps into RFID evaluation methods. For example, the analysed data revealed that twice as many women signed up for the project as men, with a high influence from those accompanying them (family, children, friends), meaning that people attending on their own were far less likely to try it. More than half of all the wristbands touched in at readers on the adventure trail chose to redeem the special arts activity or discount offer in the shop, with an almost equal spread across both economic and artistic incentives.

The geographic spread of the stops in this case study was fairly large due to the layout of the festival in relation to the local high street, and patterns in touch point timings demonstrated that participants chose to stick to adventure stops that were close together, even when clues were offered for activities further afield. Naturally some stops were more popular than others which could be due to their location on the trail, participant familiarity with the area or the visibility of signage at each location, but there is no doubt that the accompanying printed map enabled participants to choose the order of their adventure, presenting a certain dichotomy going forward as to the extent to which the trail should be curated for artistic and enjoyment purposes, and how much participants should be able to choose their own pathways at their convenience and interest. To some participants, the orienteering nature of the trail – following clues and moving in a predetermined route between stops – was the major driving factor for them to visit more of them and explore a larger amount of the area; for others this was a deterrent that required too much of their time or was too generalist for their interests, reducing the number of stops they visited, therefore further experimentation and study of the journey curation needs exploration in the future. However, the RFID wristband as a methodology proved particularly effective as a motivation factor, encouraging interest and involvement from participants and businesses alike far beyond more conventional means such as the post-event online survey which had a much lower response, and a great deal of data could be gathered from this initial sample group in terms of the geographic reach of the festival's impact.

## Conclusions

The two projects represent an evolution of our understanding of the relation between high street and arts festivals and how they can be measured and assessed. In both cases, the aim was to understand the impact of engagement activities that bridge the social, cultural and economic dynamics on the high street. The Lower Marsh project laid strong foundations for Fantasy High Street as an arts organisation moving forward. It aimed to capture – in an artistic and embedded way the artistic and cultural value of intervention that brought people to reflect around the value of shops and dynamics of consumption (such as enjoying a meal) with an understanding of the value it adds in bringing communities together and supporting local livelihoods. Working within the arts festival field it is easy to experience the need for developing creative research methodologies to assess the social and economic impact of arts and cultural activities on the high street. Much of the early work in the first case study had focused on building upon existing monitoring protocols: surveys, questionnaires, headcounts and interviews, but finding creative methods for their implementation that incorporated evaluation into the artistic process itself. For example the interactive fruit stall in Lower Marsh was both an interactive game and method for gathering important data.

Through the two years that followed the first case study, qualitative feedback continued to be gathered this way, with the audience invited to write postcards to fairies or leave messages in bottles in the river as part of themed events which could use communication with fictional characters from the events' performance and installations as a method for gathering participant feedback. However, collecting hard data which could provide insight beyond empirical evidence for the economic impact of Fantasy High Street's work was still proving a challenge. Many events, although short-term had seen a direct benefit to local businesses in terms of customer spending and loyalty, although the majority of this information was gathered through observation and interviews with shop owners and visitors. Even the most committed, energetic and excited high street shop partners proved reluctant to share specific details of financial takings during event dates, resulting in a lack of corroborative evidence to analyse for changes to local customer spending habits. Of those shops that would provide some indication of sales, it was difficult to ascertain how much income was a direct cause of the arts activity delivered, and how much could be due to existing footfall, changes in weather, disruptions to local transport or other events and activities in the area. Therefore Fantasy High Street was continuing to search for more efficient means to gather data relating to economic impact, which could directly compare arts activity with local customer spending and any positive or negative impact beyond observation alone.

Much of Fantasy High Street's artistic work from 2013-2015 included the use of trigger-sensor technology, such as infra-red, sonar and camera proximity sensors, which would be hidden within installations or live performances to cleverly engage audiences with lights, sounds and voices based on their movement around space. For example, the company would create light and sound installations where trees would light up or flowers would talk and sing when passers-by approached them. This built on the company's brand image as a creator of magical and imaginative interactive events in town centres, and therefore it seemed the most natural course of action to consider how this knowledge could be utilised to capture important information relating to the economic impact of these artistic interventions.

In terms of new avenues for further research, the findings from the Crystal Palace intervention have shown us that we need to be more adventurous in terms of how to map and measure engagement and make evaluation not an afterthought added at the end of an event but as a way to go about the event – engaging with the community and their cultural and consumption activities in a more reflexive way. It is hoped that this would empower audiences to feel part of the arts activities as well as give them a sense of the future possibilities within their community and economic activities taking place on their high streets.

## Bibliography

Arcodia, C. and Whitford, M. (2007) Festival attendance and the development of social capital, in *Journal of Convention and Event Tourism,* **8**(2), 1.

Arvizu Machado, C., Bielecki, J., Montero Jalil, D., and Walt, N. (2013) *High Street Magnifiers,* London: LSE Cities

Bailey, C., Miles, S., and Stark, P. (2004) Culture-led urban regeneration and the revitalisation of identities in Newcastle, Gateshead and the North East of England, in *International Journal of Cultural Policy,* **10**(1), 47-65.

Brixton Pound (2015) *The Brixton Pound - Money that sticks to Brixton - B£.* [online] Brixton Pound. Available at: https://brixtonpound.org/ [Accessed 28 Jul. 2015].

Comunian, R. (2015) Festivals as communities of practice: Learning by doing and knowledge networks among artists, in *Focus on Festivals: Contemporary European Case Studies and Perspectives,* (eds.) C. Newbold, C. Maughan, J. Jordan and F. Bianchini, Oxford: Goodfellow, 53-65.

Crompton, J. L., and McKay, S. L. (1994) Measuring the economic impact of festivals and events: Some myths, misapplications and ethical dilemmas, in *Festival Management and Event Tourism,* **2**(1), 33-43.

Dobson, J. (2015) *How to Save our Town Centres: A radical agenda for the future of high streets,* Bristol: Policy Press

GLA (2011) *High Street Network*. Available at: https://www.london.gov.uk/priorities/regeneration/high-streets/high-street-network [Accessed 26 May 2015].

Gov.uk (2013) *Future High Streets Forum - Groups - GOV.UK*. Available at: https://www.gov.uk/government/groups/future-high-streets-forum [Accessed 26 May 2015].

Hubbard, P. (2015) *Whose High Street? Class and disgust in visions of town centre regeneration*. Academia.edu. Available at: https://www.academia.edu/7799558/Whose_high_street_Class_and_disgust_in_visions_of_town_centre_regeneration [Accessed 26 May 2015].

Landry, C. (2008) *The Creative City: A toolkit for urban innovators*, (2nd edn.), London: Earthscan.

Lefebvre, H. (1991) *The Production of Space*, Oxford: Blackwell.

Ley, D. (2003) Artists, aestheticisation and the field of gentrification, in, *Urban Studies*, **40**(12), 2527-2544.

Portas, M. (2011) *The Portas Review: An Independent Review Into The Future Of Our High Streets*. London: Department of Business, Innovation and Skills.

Quinn, B. (2005) Arts festivals and the city, in, *Urban Studies*, **42**(5-6), 927-943.

Rowson, J., Broome, S., and Jones, A. (2010) *Connected Communities: How Social Networks power and sustain the Big Society*. London: RSA.

Sassen, S. (2001) *The Global City: New York, London, Tokyo*, Princetown: Princeton University Press.

Stevens, Q., and Shin, H. (2014) Urban festivals and local social space, in *Planning Practice and Research*, **29**(1) 1-20.

Thompson, D. (2010) *Empty Shops Toolkit*. Museums, Libraries & Archives.

van Aalst, I., and van Melik, R. (2012) City festivals and urban development: does place matter? In *European Urban and Regional Studies*, **19**(2), 195-206.

Wrigley, N, and Dolega, L. (2011) Resilience, fragility, and adaptation: new evidence on the performance of UK high streets during global economic crisis and its policy implications, in *Environment and Planning-Part A*, **43**(10), 2337.

## Notes

1 Fantasy High Street was able to work with King's College London and to conduct these research projects alongside its activities thanks to funding from Creativeworks London, an Arts and Humanities Research Council (AHRC) funded initiative to bring researchers, creative entrepreneurs and businesses together to explore the issues that impact on London's creative economy. We acknowledge the support of Creativeworks London in 2013 through a Creative Entrepreneur In Residence award and in 2015 through the BOOST Award programme.

# 16 Are You Having a Laugh? Comedy and Festivals in the 21st Century

Christopher Maughan and Ljiljana Radošević[1]

> Humour manages to span the actual and the virtual in its eclectic and paradoxical potential, as playing and festivals do. Like that of festivals its power is ambivalent and transgressive.
>
> (Crociani-Windland, 2011: 182)

Humour and comedy are emergent topics for academic researchers whose work is illuminating our understanding of the power and purpose of humour and comedy for people and society (Lockyer and Pickering, 2005; Jeffries, 2014). However, much of this output discusses the impact of humour and comedy itself and little has been written about it in the context of a festival. This chapter takes as its focus two established and successful festivals: the *International Festival of Comics* (*FIBD*) in Angoulême, France; and *Dave's Leicester Comedy Festival* (*DLCF*) in England.[2]

This choice reflects several factors. The first is that the authors have had personal experience of both, Radosevic with *FIBD*, and Maughan with *DLCF*. These personal insights have been aligned with selected theoretical perspectives to provide an analysis which seeks to draw out factors of relevance to those studying and/or working in a festival, in particular how a festival and its management culture need to change through time and with time (life cycle theory); the relationship of a festival to its artistic and cultural roots (liminal/liminoid effects); and the impact of commercial culture on both.

Comedy and the desire to laugh are universal. The cartoonist Robert Makoff discussed the distinction between humour and comedy in the following way: "all comedy has humour, but not all humour is comedy. Humour is the much broader category of anything that may make us laugh, such as a loud fart at a funeral, which is funny but not comedy. Comedy is a form of professional entertainment, consisting of jokes and sketches intended to make people laugh" (Mankoff, 2014). The works of Aristophanes, born in 446 B.C., are noted for their political satire and abundance of sexual innuendo, features that we easily recognise today in humour based comics and stand-up comedy. The history of contemporary comics is traced back to artists such as Hogarth and subsequently to satirical magazines of the nineteenth century. Comedy as a feature of performance has a special place in theatre, dance and music, and of course in the UK within the music hall tradition. However, whole festivals devoted to comics or performed comedy feature less prominently in the festival culture tradition.

One of the most important European comics festivals resulted from a personal passion for comics of three enthusiasts, Groux, Mardikian and Moliterni, who set up the *Angoulême Festival* with the goals of challenging the prejudice that comic books were merely reading material for children, and the censorship that they saw as restricting the art form. In 1972 the first team organised an exhibition about comics titled '*Dix millions d'images*' which lasted for fifteen days and generated a collective buzz in the city. The team then set up an association, *Salon international de la bande dessinée*, which they kept going until 1996 when it assumed its present name *Festival International de la Bande Dessinée* (*FIBD*, 2015). From its humble beginnings in 1974, the festival now takes place over four days at the end of January and currently attracts over 200,000 visitors every year to a town of just 42,000 inhabitants. The festival has brought considerable attention to Angoulême itself whose 13th century city centre and walls provide a striking setting within which the festival has been nurtured.

Their initiative did not take place in a vacuum as in the 1960s several important developments occurred that contributed towards better understanding and appreciation of comics in France. The Centre for the Studies of Graphic Literature, a club for lovers of comics was established in 1962 and published one of the first journals in the field and the first major exhibition of comic books, *Comics and Narrative Figuration*, was held at the Louvre in 1967. The exhibition catalogue is still considered to be one of the most important publications about comics.

From 1968, American underground comics started to be translated and published on a regular basis and these introduced a new sense of artistic freedom and subject matter into Europe. All these factors combined with the revolutionary influence of SF magazine *Metal Hurlant* (1975) – which offered readers superb artistic techniques, as well as erotic content and innovative storylines – formed part of a dynamic background to the first edition of *FIBD* in 1974. Whilst humour and comic books for children were dominant, the organisers also included events of specific interest to adults in the official programme. Thus in 1976 it hosted a debate on the value of comic books and during the fifth festival in 1979 another debate on freedom of expression which achieved important media impact and contributed to the abolition of censorship in France in 1983 (Cannet, 1993). As the first era of *FIBD* ended, the festival could reflect that its main goals had been achieved.

Across the channel in the UK, public radio and television provided comedy writers and performers with a platform to display their talents and access to an audience impossible through live work alone. Allied with the emergence of a more youth oriented cultural offer in Europe and North America in the 1950s and 60s, comedians began to enjoy a higher profile. In the 1990s comedy in the UK was described as 'the new rock and roll' (Fleming, 2013), a phrase that reflected its influence on how we were beginning to see ourselves and others.

In 1994, perhaps sensing this zeitgeist, Arts Management students at De Montfort University in Leicester proposed a comedy festival as their final year project. This reflected their interest in promoting comedy within a range of venues as part of a programme that followed a format that was becoming familiar to audiences – the urban, multi venue festival. In the UK this model was established in 1947 with the *Edinburgh International Festival* (*EIF*) and *Edinburgh Fringe Festival* (*EFF*). Comedy, however, was little represented outside of the *EFF* until the *Leicester Comedy Festival* (known as *Dave's Leicester Comedy Festival* since 2011, when the UK TV channel Dave became its main sponsor) in 1994.

Globally, *LCF* was not the first of its kind; *Just for Laughs* in Montreal had launched in 1983 and *Melbourne International Comedy Festival* in 1987. The *Cat Laughs Festival* in Kilkenny, Ireland started in 1995 and each year more are established so that today many towns will feature a bespoke comedy festival, or include comedy as a significant aspect of a multi-disciplinary festival. The demand for comedy festivals shows little sign of abating.

But the future of many of these festivals remains fragile in terms of their artistic and/or long term financial sustainability despite the emergence of high profile sponsors such as Dave and Sky (Sky has sponsored the *Cat Laughs Festival* since 2013). In this regard *FIBD* is different in that its future, after 43 years, seems more secure. But *FIBD* has experienced its own troubles with respect to sponsors and partners, some of whom have had considerable influence, not through being a named sponsor, but through being members of the Administrative Council.

Achieving a sustainable future is a goal that most festival organisers would prioritise, but achieving that does not come easily; many festivals do not make it past one or two editions. Such early death is a feature of life cycle theory. Adizes' (2004) model recognises several phases in an organisation's growth and development and expresses these as an outcome of four management functions: Purpose, Administration, Entrepreneurialism and Integration.

| Management role | Key function | Questions asked |
|---|---|---|
| Purpose | Effective/functional/short run | What are we going to do? |
| Administration | Efficient/systematised/short run | How will we do it? |
| Entrepreneurial | Effective/proactive/long run | What is needed? |
| Integration | Efficient/organic/long run | Who will do it, who for, who with? |

**Figure 16.1:** Adizes' Four management functions (adapted from Adizes, 2015)

Of these the most challenging is commonly that of 'integration' and this is the aspect that we will focus upon in this chapter.

Festivals are often set up by enthusiasts who have some knowledge of an aspect of the arts, such as Groux et al. with *FIBD*, so the entrepreneurial function is a strong feature of many new festivals. Organisers will also have a clear (if narrow) sense of their aims and may also have some management competence, i.e. they may understand how to run organisations and events. However, what is often more challenging is to identify clearly the target markets and how to meet their needs both as potential partners and consumers/audiences.

Adizes (2015) argues that organisations follow a predictable lifecycle from courtship to death with recognisable strengths and problems at each stage. The Prime phase is the optimal position on the lifecycle. He describes this as follows:

> the organization finally achieves a balance between control and flexibility. Prime is actually not a single point on the lifecycle curve. Instead, it is best represented by a segment of the curve that includes both growing and aging conditions. This is because flexibility and self-control are incompatible and there is no stable equilibrium. Sometimes the Prime organization is more flexible than controllable, and sometimes it's not flexible enough. (Adizes, 2015)

Relating this to the two key organisations selected for this chapter we can make a series of observations, beginning with *FIBD*.

> A truly remarkable event, every January the entire town becomes a shrine to comics, with every available space given over to exhibitions, talks and guest appearances from fashionable *auteurs*. With the attendant media razzmatazz (the event is covered by nationwide TV), Angoulême's reputation as 'The Cannes of comics' is not far off the mark (Sabin, 1993: 197).

This description summarises a key feature of *FIBD* which is the distinctive balance it has developed between its programme for readers and professionals, between its artistic and commercial goals, and its overall diversity. But it took 40 years to reach this level of maturity and along the way there were many ups and downs in the festival's history, including periods when its future was uncertain. These included abrupt and traumatic changes of the festival's directors; difficult relationships with Angoulême's mayor and local government about control of the festival's direction; and occasional financial problems and difficult partnerships with private businesses, also related to the festival's development. No matter how much all of the parties involved wish the festival to succeed, the power struggles have persisted, and determining the balance between survival and artistic excellence was and still is omnipresent.

A turning point for it was the festival's ability to engage with a wider set of aims than those that inspired its establishment. For example, as it moved beyond its first editions there were many cultural factors and intellectual discussions that gave it a nudge in different directions, and these have ensured that the festival in Angoulême now performs an important role in the comics industry and specifically in France.

A feature of the history of both *FIBD* and *DLCF* is that the forms with which they worked have not enjoyed high status in the eyes of cultural policy makers and the public. In *FIBD's* case, an additional challenge is that for most of its history comics were not commonly viewed as 'serious', and only the work of a limited number of artists was seen as important. From the beginning of the 20th century, publishers sought to engage with a new market through lowering the age of their target market. Comics were adapted to the taste of children in their form and narratives but with the same humorous intent. According to Sabin (1993, 2001) by 1914 most comic books were aimed at children and that remained so until the 1960s when a new wave of comics for an adult readership appeared.

However, in France and francophone speaking areas comic strips are called *bande dessinée*, 'drawn strips', a term that does not imply humour in the same way as the English term does, and this may account for the more liberal attitude which has existed there. Another important feature of francophone comics is the popularity of the physical format of the *album*, which resemble formal books more than the standard comics format sold through newsagents. Perhaps more importantly, the albums were available through public libraries, which gave comics respectability and authority in France. The first publication of this kind came out in 1930, *The Adventures of Tintin*. This format was soon adopted in France as the standard form preferred by both publishers and readers and became popular in the rest of the Western world only with the rise of the graphic novel in 1980s (e.g. *A Contract with God* (1978) by Will Eisner; *V for Vendetta* (1989) by Alan Moore). France also had a well-regulated system for guaranteeing authors' rights and ensuring they retained ownership of their characters, so that comic book authors were able to earn a living from their work. Reprints of popular works helped to establish a star system (Sabin, 1993), which was an important factor in enabling the festival's organisers to have the impact that they have had, as *FIBD* became an important place for fans to meet their favourite author.

The festival has not been dominated by humour-based comics, but was able to engage with other factors of importance to the wider industry of authors and publishers. During the 1980s the festival became one of the main lobbyists for the inclusion of comics in national cultural policy and public sector funding. From 1982 till 1985 several ministerial and one presidential visit to the festival demonstrated that comic books had acquired a distinctive place in the cultural programme of Mitterrand's socialist government.

*FIBD*'s focus moved beyond the festival in 1977 when it established a research centre, which has now developed into the *La Cité internationale de la bande dessinée et de l'image* (Citebd, 2015). Alongside this, a project for a comics gallery in the Museum of Angoulême in 1980 was a starting point for the establishment of The Museum of Comics which, in 2009, finally moved into its own building. With the opening of the National Centre for the Comics and Image in 1990, the festival became more international (especially Asian) in its remit, and adopted a more professional, business-oriented strategy with education and training among its main aims. In 1997 the Charante Department, the town of Angoulême and the Chamber of Commerce and Industry created the Syndicat Mixte du Pôle Image Magelis (SMPI) in order to guide the development of this important, regional project. SMPI presently incorporates 90 companies working in the image industry, 20 animation studios and three sound studios. Citebd and SMPI between them support, complement and coordinate the actions of the many players now based in Angoulême, which includes *FIBD* itself. In 2001 the festival initiated a programme dedicated to children and to young talents, which was designed to nurture the young audience without which no festival can have a sustainable future. The area now offers eight programmes in local schools and colleges which provide students with opportunities to develop their skills in a range of disciplines (comics, animation, sound, video games), and from high school through to a Masters programme. The festival now also promotes a year-round programme of exhibitions, lectures and co-curated programmes, some with its long term collaborator, the Pompidou Centre in Paris.

Due to the festival's influence and high profile, Angoulême has become the city where the most important institutions related to comics are now established and through the 1990s the whole region developed as a centre for an image-based industry. The city which gave initial support to the festival is now regarded as a global centre for comics and its festival operates as a catalyst in a range of comic book related activity not just as a focus for readers and collectors.

Referring back to Adizes' model, *FIBD* ticks all the boxes for an organisation in the prime phase and in particular for how its scope has developed to deliver a festival and organisation that has depth and breadth in respect of its aims, and with whom and for whom it works – the *integration* function. Could this serve as a potential blueprint for other festivals?

In February 2015, *DLCF* delivered its 21st festival and whilst stand-up comedy is a significant feature of its programme, it too has shown that an ability to engage with a wider set of aims and objectives is critical to long term sustainability. In its early years the festival focused upon developing a network of venues and promoters through which the festival could be extended, with the festival itself providing a structure within which to nurture and promote its concept and programme. *DLCF* has never had the financial resources to curate and deliver the festival alone, but working through its network it has developed a comedy festival that has become one of the key cultural events in the city and one of the biggest in the UK. In recent years *DLCF's* programme has been extended and in 2015 it ran for 19 days with over 640 events in 47 venues attracting paying audiences of over 75,000. In 1994, its first edition ran for seven days, and the programme consisted of 40 acts in 23 venues and attracted an audience of 5,000.

But the financial issue that limits its capacity to curate the festival has been a stimulus to diversification in its activities outside the festival period. These activities, whilst linked to its experience of events management, reflect the benefit of its participation in a wide range of networks through which, for example, it has "become a specialist arts and health organisation. Committed to using a range of creative techniques to convey important health messages" (DLCF, 2015).

From 2002 it has worked with organisations such as the UNISON trades union to pioneer innovative work related to men's health, teenage pregnancy and mental health. In terms of 'integration', it is programmes like this that enable the festival to be a year-round organisation with a permanent office and five staff. Its website provides a fuller examination of its work in these areas, which in 2015 included a project aimed at breaking down isolation and contributing to improving participants' overall health and well-being. 'Sing Leicestershire' formed a choir from 300 participants that performed during the festival, including some from the deaf and blind communities.

These programmes make up the 'Make Me Happy' programme which, together with *Dave's Leicester Comedy Festival*, are strands of the parent company, Big Difference Company's (BDC) work. Geoff Rowe, the CEO of BDC, said that as well as the festival, BDC aimed: "to engage with people, to bring people together, to allow them to enjoy themselves and also to make a long lasting difference for themselves and their communities" (Caine, 2015).

An outcome of this analysis is to focus attention on governance and management and the volunteer trustees/directors whose role it is to advise the organisation on strategic matters and long term developments, more than day to day issues. BDC is a risk-oriented organisation and its history reveals occasions when the risks taken exceeded the organisation's capacities and competence to manage them. However, it has been at such times that the roots of the festival within the local community, the strategic value attached to the festival by public authorities and its capacity to deliver projects across the arts, cultural and social policy agendas has enabled it to work its way out of difficulty.

Environmental scanning is part of the tool kit for survival and both *FIBD* and *DLCF* show the value of this in terms of how they connect to the wider industry of which they are a part. *FIBD* at the present time is an essential component of comics publishing industry in France, with a global perspective too. *DLCF* has also built on its local connections to create a network of partners which is providing something distinctive for the city and county, which in turn provides the festival with a sustainable future, albeit one that is still fraught with challenge.

In this context two recent articles by the journalist David Lister illustrate other dimensions to this discussion. Writing about the summer festivals in Edinburgh and specifically the *Edinburgh International Festival* and *Edinburgh Festival Fringe* he drew attention to two important features that are also a challenge in terms of the integration function (Lister, 2015a, 2015b) and specifically "for whom and with whom" the festival experience is curated.

First, the impact of a festival on its audiences. The legacy of a festival is more difficult to deliver when the beneficiaries of its programme, its audiences, are frequently not people with whom the festival has a long term relationship through which to understand and sustain their engagement and deliver longer term impact. Despite this, many publicly funded festivals may feel under pressure to deliver measurable outcomes, equivalent to those of a building based organisation. In the case of *DLCF*, its community programme has attracted positive comment from many sources including *The Times* which stated: "They've become much more than a comedy festival. They've also been able to project comedy as a vehicle for strong community and social messages" (DLCF, 2015).

This programme therefore provides *DLCF* with evidence of its impacts at a social level whilst annual research of audiences reveals data about its economic impacts on and benefits to the local economy. After 40 years, the impacts of *FIBD* are such that it now stands as an important example of a symbiosis of creativity and industry. *FIBD* has managed to influence an array of fields related to comics; what began with a focus on comics for children, art education, research, and heritage protection, now embraces ways of doing business in the cultural industries and includes new approaches to supporting the creativity of young people.

Second, the political content of a festival's programme. This directs attention to a broader feature of festivals, the extent to which they seek to be a mirror to society and not just, as Adorno and Bernstein (1991) might describe them, a distraction from life. Adorno's critique is not one that is commonly applied to festivals but at a time when pressure has been increasing on public expenditure on the arts it is perhaps appropriate to ask whether focusing more on their potential for enabling collective social and political change, through the praxis of liminality, might help a festival to secure its long term future.

Comedy is one artform in which a political perspective is a significant feature of the work of many comics' authors and stand-up comedians. However, the extent to which this is integrated into a festival programme may be a reflection of whether the programmer seeks to deliver more than a good night out. A festival of comics or stand-up comedy is a time/place where awkward and challenging ideas and material can be presented. However, if public subsidy becomes more limited through perceptions that festivals can or should be self-financing, this may lead those programming such events to adopt a lower risk approach in which popularity and financial prudence take precedence over other factors, e.g. political content.

This introduces the final aspect of this discussion: the capacity of a festival to deliver liminal or liminoid experiences for their audiences/participants. Van Gennep (1962), Sutton-Smith (1972) and Turner (1974) were amongst the first to describe the potency of special events in individual and community life as part of 'rites of passage'. These are events which carry important social and community meaning for those who participate, and in which participation is compulsory, e.g. confirmation, a sacred rite of initiation in several Christian denominations which is required if a believer wishes to develop their relationship with their faith and their community; and other sacred festivals, which the photo-journalist Jeremy Hunter (2002) has documented so well. Rites of passage are a formal transition consisting of distinct phases which Turner described as pre-liminal, liminal and post-liminal and through which the participant achieves a change in their social status.

Some arts festivals have by virtue of their longevity acquired some of these qualities, e.g. *Bayreuth Festival*, the *Burning Man Festival*, the *Edinburgh Fringe* and *International Festivals, Glastonbury Festival, Carnival* in Rio de Janeiro, *Venice Biennale.* Those who participate as artists or audience invest huge importance in these and other festivals as places/times of significant personal discovery and development. However, because attendance at these festivals is not a formal requirement for personal progress in a particular society (recommended perhaps but not compulsory) the impacts of these events are grouped under the category of liminoid.

## Conclusions

Research into festivals has revealed that they provide a range of benefits for audiences, some of which are life changing experiences. What is presently less clear is how strong the causal relationship is between the programme and any life changing experiences; as opposed to more incidental outcomes such as the conversations that Lister (2015a) describes that take place in the bars and restaurants of Edinburgh during August. Festivals' research is expanding our understanding of this aspect of integration. Recent published work, e.g. the book of collected essays edited by Newbold et al (2015) also reveals that resolving the challenges of integration is crucial if a festival is to withstand the effects of festivalisation (Négrier, 2015), to develop the communities of interest that will sustain them (Fletcher, Norton, Koprivšek, and Silvanto, all 2015) and to achieve a high level of integration of a festival into the daily life of a community, even when the festival is not on (Winkelhorn, 2015).

Similar features and outcomes are observable at *FIBD* and *DLCF*. The challenge is to retain the flexibility required for them to continue to innovate and retain a subtle focus on challenging their audiences through giving them a fuller, liminoid experience, i.e. one that is a product of how the festival has been programmed and in which the programme is more than a reflection of the industry with which it is associated.

Achieving this, whilst also remaining financially solvent, is possibly the major challenge for all festivals that aim to be more than one-off or time limited.

This chapter has taken two festivals that share some common heritage in the comedy industry to explore some factors that may contribute to a festival having a long term future. Short introductions to both festivals have been mapped against the work of Adizes on life cycles of organisations and the challenge of becoming financially sustainable expressed in terms of the need for organisations to develop a close link with its communities of interest.

Both *FIBD* and *DLCF* have changed and developed through the nature of their local connections and their wider links into the humour/comedy industry. They have both survived for significant periods of time, have demonstrable legacies and have established themselves as part of their respective industries. This could however be a double-edged sword, as this brings with it a perception that these are festivals that can be financially self-sufficient, or in the case of *DLCF* may lack the artistic credentials to attract significant amounts of public authority support. The inevitable and understandable need to deliver financial more than artistic goals may be a limiting factor in terms of the festivals' ability to currently provide the sorts of liminoid experience for their audiences that is often associated with the festivals sector.

## Bibliography

Adizes, I. (2004) *Managing Corporate Life Cycles*. Santa Barbara, CA: Adizes Institute Publishing.

Adizes, I. (2015) *The Adizes Corporate Lifecycle: Prime*. Available from: http://www.adizes.com/prime/, accessed August 2015.

Adorno, T., and Bernstein, J. (eds.) (1991) *The Culture Industry: Selected essays on mass culture.* London: Routledge.

Barker, M. (1989) *Comics: Ideology, power and the critics.* Manchester: Manchester University Press.

Caine, S. (2015) *EP25 – Geoff Rowe – Founder of Dave's Leicester Comedy Festival* available at Ask the Industry podcast: http://simoncaine.co.uk/ATI/GeoffRowe, accessed 30 August 2015.

Cannet, H. (1993) *Angoulême: Le grand vingtième*. Angoulême: P.Q.R & Charente Libre.

Couperie, P., Horn, M., Destefanis, P., Fransois, E., Moliterni, C. and Gassiot-Talbot, G. (1974) *A History of Comic Strip*. New York: Crown Publisher.

Crociani-Windland, L. (2011) *Festivals, Affect and Identity*, London: Anthem Press.

DLCF (2015) *Make Me Happy*, available at: www.comedy-festival.co.uk, accessed August 2015

Eisner, W. (1978) *A Contract with God*, New York: Norton.

FIBD (2015) *History*, available from: www.bdangouleme.com, accessed August 2015.

Filippini, H., Glénat, J., Sadoul, N. and Varende, Y. (1980) *Histoire de la bande dessinée en France et en Belgique: Des origines à nos jours*, Paris:Glenat.

Fleming, J. (2013) *Revealed: who actually said that 'comedy is the new rock-n-roll'*, available at: So it goes: John Fleming's blog, accessed April 2015 at https://thejohnfleming.wordpress.com/2013/11/29.

Fletcher, R. (2015) Festivals of Transition: Greenlight Festival, Leicester, in C. Newbold, C. Maughan, J. Jordan, and F. Bianchini (eds.) *Focus on Festivals: Contemporary European Case Studies and Perspectives* (eds.), Oxford: Goodfellow.

Groux, F. and Mardikian, J. (eds.) (2012) *Au-delà de la BanDe! 1974-2013, comment le Festival a changé Angoulême*. Angoulême: Association Entre Dans la Bande.

Hunter, J. (2002) *Sacred Festivals*. London: MQ Publications.

Jeffries, S. (2014) The science of comedy: can humour make the world a better place? in *The Guardian*, 11 February 2014.

Koprivšek, N. (2015) *Mladi levi* Festival – Reflections and Memories, in C. Newbold, C. Maughan, J. Jordan, and F. Bianchini (eds.) *Focus on Festivals: Contemporary European case studies and perspectives* (eds.), Oxford: Goodfellow.

La Cité internationale de la bande dessinée et de l'image. (2015) History, available from: www.citebd.org, accessed August 2015.

Lister, D. (2015a) The real glory of the Edinburgh Festival is off the stage, in *The i*, 17 August 2015.

Lister, D. (2015b) Politics is sadly absent from the Edinburgh Festival, in *The Independent*, 21 August 2015.

Lockyer, S and Pickering, M. (2005) *Beyond a Joke: the limits of humour*, London: Palgrave MacMillan.

Mankoff, R. (2014) Untitled, *The New Yorker*, 27 January 2014 http://www.newyorker.com/from-the-desk-of-bob-mankoff/untitled, accessed April 2015.

McCloud, S. (1994) *Understanding Comics: The Invisible Art*, New York: Harper Perennial.

Moore, A. (1989) *V for Vendetta*, New York: DC Comics

Négrier, E. (2015) Festivalisation: Patterns and limits, in C. Newbold, C. Maughan, J. Jordan, and F. Bianchini (eds.) *Focus on Festivals: Contemporary European Case Studies and Perspectives* (eds.), Oxford: Goodfellow.

Newbold, C., Maughan, C., Jordan, J., and Bianchini, F. (eds.) (2015) *Focus on Festivals: Contemporary European Case Studies and Perspectives*. Oxford: Goodfellow.

Norton, J. (2015) The Diggers' Festival: Organising a community festival with political connotations, in C. Newbold, C. Maughan, J. Jordan, and F. Bianchini (eds.) *Focus on Festivals: Contemporary European Case Studies and Perspectives*, Oxford: Goodfellow.

Sabin, R. (1993) *Adult Comics: An Introduction*, London: Taylor & Francis.

Sabin, R. (2001) *Comics, Comix and Graphic Novels: A History of Comic Art*. London: Phaidon.

Silvanto, S. (2015) How to *Flow*, in C. Newbold, C. Maughan, J. Jordan, and F. Bianchini (eds) *Focus on Festivals: Contemporary European Case Studies and Perspectives*, Oxford: Goodfellow.

Sutton-Smith, B. (1972) Games of Order and Disorder. Paper presented to Symposium on *Forms of Symbolic Inversion*. American Anthropological Association, Toronto, December.

Turner, V.W. (1974) Liminal to liminoid in play, flow, and ritual: An essay in comparative symbology. *Rice University Studies*, **60**(3) 53-92 available from https://scholarship.rice.edu, accessed August 2015.

Van Gennep, A. (1960) *The Rites of Passage*, Chicago: University of Chicago.

Winkelhorn, K. (2015) The Enchanted City: Holstebro Festive Week, in C. Newbold, C. Maughan, J. Jordan, and F. Bianchini (eds.) *Focus on Festivals: Contemporary European Case Studies and Perspectives*, Oxford: Goodfellow.

## Notes

1 The authors thank the editors for their encouragement in the writing of this chapter; Richard Fletcher for his work on the collection and analysis of the research on *DLCF*. The authors also thank the trustees of *DLCF* and *FIBD* for their support of this research. All views expressed are those of the authors.

2 Through out this chapter the word 'comics' is used for drawn and printed works. The word comics is used in order to differentiate it from the word comic (which could be misunderstood as an adjective and is therefore not used in comics theory, unless it really refers to something funny). 'Comedian', 'comedy' or 'stand up comedy' for performed work.

# FOCUS ON WORLD FESTIVALS

## SECTION 3
## USING FESTIVALS· CULTURE and IDENTITY

# Introduction

Chris Newbold

As is apparent in many of the festivals discussed so far in this book, by their very nature festivals evolve and change, their traditions become subject to the scrutiny of modernity, be it fluctuations in the religious climate, political interventions, economic considerations, or simply the demands of health and safety. This section concerns itself with how and why festivals emerge and develop, the forces that drive change and with a consideration of some of the contemporary manifestations of festivals around the world.

The festivals represented in this section reflect events that have a relationship to a sense of cultural identity and cultural purpose. In many cases this is drawn on and developed by public authorities who use the festivals as part of wider social engineering and policy programmes. As we shall see, the degree of autonomy that festivals have in this relationship is often associated with their origins and development. Festivals can emerge organically from traditions, social and cultural experiences and belief systems, but their original genesis is often lost over time and confused by centuries of evolution and change. Festivals can also be the result of the actions of artists, entrepreneurs and motivated individuals who have a vision, a programme, or a belief in the possibility of change they wish to see realised. More recently conceived festivals can be the result of a purposive effort to bring festivals to a place, and the key to a great many of these festivals is that they draw on cultural and festival aesthetics in order to achieve their 'festive' goals. They might also revive, rehabilitate or develop cultural traditions in order to provide a focal point or a brand upon which to hang the event. Here national or local identity can become part of the driver behind a festival's founding and development.

At the root of the discussions in many of the chapters in this section are concerns with festival authenticity; specifically, the role of local and national tourist authorities is noted and interrogated. Quinn (2013) points out that authenticity is a term with a long history in both social sciences and tourism studies, Getz reminds us that authenticity is "a difficult concept open to many interpretations"(1994: 425). Quinn states:

> Very often festivals and events of a traditional nature are constructed and represented by tourism producers as being the embodiment of authenticity. Traditional events are revived, repackaged, modified and refashioned, while new traditions are invented to attract tourist audiences (2013: 1).

There are two dimensions to this debate, as represented in this section of the book: first that tourists and visitors are not being exploited by some form of fakery of cultural traditions; and second that the local people do not feel that their heritage is being displayed inauthentically in order to attract 'outsiders'. Local people are often keen that their traditions are passed on to their youngsters, or that through festivals their younger generations get an opportunity to be involved in their lived heritage. It is important though to recognise that the search for authenticity may well be as elusive as the search for any kind of golden age. Many of the case studies in this book, as well as in *Focus on Festivals* (Newbold et al., 2015), demonstrate the evolutionary nature of festivals; they develop and change, adapting to outside forces as well as local changes, such that a discussion of authenticity in the context of many contemporary festivals may well be illusory.

The first chapter in this section provides an example of perhaps the purest anthropological form of traditional festivals. The chapter is about the Nawuri *Guinea Corn Festival* in Ghana called *Kayuji*. It illustrates a festival that is clearly traditional and deeply engrained in the community and its real life experiences. Through the festival Samual Ntewusu discusses the role of food, drink, land and deities in the daily life of the Nawuris. Guinea corn, the focus of the festival, is celebrated as it plays such a central role in the lives of the Nawuris. In essence it is a harvesting festival, but at its core it provides a sense of historical continuity and is an embodiment of Nawuri social, religious and economic identity.

Arkotong Longkumer (Chapter 18) discusses how the *Hornbill Festival* in north-east India was instituted primarily as a cultural event by the government of Nagaland. This was in order to attract tourists, and also to bring together the different Naga tribes. It has now become a brand, presenting and fixing the Naga tribes peoples' identity as somehow exotic for tourist voyeurs, creating tensions with the lived reality of the inhabitants. For Longkumer the tensions come from the festival itself, which struggles to articulate the lived Naga culture within this manufactured form that is representing them.

Not a manufactured festival, but a traditional one that has been moulded and branded, the *Songkran Festival* or *Water Festival* in Thailand discussed in Chapter 19 illustrates how the national tourist authority has, over a long period of time, played a leading role in the development and promotion of the festival. The case study illustrates how that very success has led to a number of unforeseen consequences, which the same authority is now in the process of trying to reverse by re-emphasising traditional cultural aspects of the festival. A surprising dimension of the perceived tourism marketing success is that others in South East Asia are attempting to borrow the *Songkran* format, creating a situation in which Thailand has explored its intellectual property rights in relation to traditional cultural activities. The *Songkran Festival* can be seen as a 'driven' festival with traditional roots, where the main driver has been the demands of tourism and its concomitant economic impact.

Newbold and Xiang in Chapter 20 examine the role of national and local government in what they call the 'rehabilitation of festivals' in China. Here they argue that traditional Chinese festivals fared badly during the period of the Cultural Revolution. However, since the economic reforms of Deng Xiaoping, festivals have been rehabilitated by the government and re-directed towards economic growth and the emerging tourist industry. Taking the city of Lianyungang as their example, they examine the revival of traditional festivals such as the *Dragon Boat Festival*, alongside the development of new festivals by the municipal government. With the opening up of China, the arrival of the western festival calendar led to fears of the loss of Chinese cultural identity and traditions. The political will to defend Chinese traditional national cultural identity has resulted in the supporting of traditional festivals that had once been chided for their localism, backwardness and focus on gods, princes, emperors and superstitions. Two aspects of traditional festivals come out strongly in this chapter: first, the emphasis on traditional foodstuffs associated with each festival, second the role of traditional medicine alongside festivals, and the link of both of these to seasonality and the 'turns' of the natural world.

Florianne Gaber is also interested in festivals in totalitarian societies. She looks at the role of street art festivals in countries where criticism and debates are either forbidden or inconceivable in public spaces. In Chapter 21 she discusses street festivals in Iran, Belarus, Morocco and Kuwait. For Gaber, street festivals help people to experiment with new ways of behaving, and to feel stronger towards unjust authorities by allowing artists to play with and challenge the rules. Festival organisers and artists using the streets and venues to challenge powerful forces and respond to social crisis is also the theme of Chapter 22. Here Paolo Vignolo examines the *Iberoamerican Threatre Festival of Bogotá* and, in particular, the role of its founder and inspiration Fanny Mikey. As an act of faith in Colombia, the festival's development is charted against the backdrop of Colombia's ongoing internal strife and war. Through theatrical manifestations actors and artists dramatised a kind of collective catharsis, and reflected and opposed the climate of violence and death.

Festivals which challenge perceptions of death are also the focus of Chapters 23 and 24. In the first chapter Emily Bradfield discusses *Dia de los Muertos* (*Day of the Dead*) as a celebration that mixes Spanish Catholic traditions with ancient Aztec rituals and looks at how the festival itself, as well as its aesthetic imagery of the *Calaveras*, have begun to spread outside the borders of Mexico and the festival's cultural and historic origin. She attributes the exuberant nature of the festival and its celebration of death to Mexican national characteristic, but also finds similar festivities represented in different cultures around the world. Rachel Bowditch (Chapter 24) looks at the *Tucson All Souls Procession* and shows how the procession, founded in 1990, is a hybrid festival inspired by *All Souls' Day* and *Dia de los Muertos* that provides a public space for mourning, with a community altar and personal altars forming the focal point for communal sharing and healing. In 2002 the procession became a national focal point for remembering and mourning the victims of the 9/11 attacks, giving the festival a public purpose as well as a personal one. She highlights, too, the role of social media in sharing symbolic images of mourning and the memorialisation. Iconographic imagery is central then to both of these festivals, not only in the aesthetics of the event itself, but also in its dissemination in the aftermath of the festival.

In Chapter 25 Robyn Archer argues that in order to discover authenticity we must go off the beaten track. She recounts her experiences and delight in discovering such festivals as the *Torres Strait Island Festival* in Australasia, *Celtic Colours* in Canada, the *Reykjavik Festival* in Iceland, and the *IF* festival in Indonesia. Her main discussion is of the *Garma Festival of Traditional Culture* in Australia's Northern Territory, an invitation-only festival set on the traditional land of the Yolgnu people that combines traditional and modern dance, art and music, with education workshops and discussion of Aboriginal issues such as land rights. For Archer these festivals are founded on pilgrimage and defined by place.

At the other end of the scale, both in terms of its content and its location is the *Parkes Elvis Festival* in New South Wales. In Chapter 26 Schlenker, Foley and Carroll-Dwyer examine a festival dedicated to one of the twentieth century's global celebrities, the 'King of Rock and Roll' Elvis Presley, in what they describe as an otherwise unremarkable town with no connection to the late superstar. They examine both the social and economic impact of the festival with a particular focus on the boost to tourism. In terms of motivations for attendance they found that the festival generated a sense of community, and that fun and play were the key factors, ranking higher than being an Elvis fan. For O'Grady (2015) festival play is associated with;

> having fun, messing around, cutting loose, making believe, experimenting, imagining, becoming someone else, creating something else and, ultimately, learning how to be with other people in the present moment through improvised sociabilities (2015: 150).

For Mumford, play and culture are indistinguishable, with playful rituals providing the social cement that is necessary for communal existence (Mumford 1967).

In the final chapter, Milla Riggio examines *Carnival* and the festive culture of the twin Island Republic of Trinidad and Tobago. Here too, play, to 'play mas' as Riggio sees it, has become a metaphor for how '*Carnival* people' live their lives. In the 'islands of celebration' Riggio focuses on three main festivals, *Ramleela/Ramdilla*, *Hosay* and *Carnival*. *Ramleela/Ramdilla* and *Hosay* emerge from the largest group in the Trinidadian population, the Indo-Trinidadians. They reflect the cultural heritage of this population, although they have been 'Trinibagoed' and as she points out during *Hosay* everyone in the Islands becomes Muslim for the duration of the celebration. The only national carnival in the region, the *Trinidad and Tobago Carnival* affirms a sense of place and belonging to the *Carnival* people both nationally and locally. Competition is essential to *Carnival.* It has three governing divisions – calypso/soca, pan/steel drum and mas. Resistance and subversion are also key to understanding its heritage and contemporary manifestation. The story Riggio tells is of cross-cultural fertilisation of the festivals and events in Trinidad and Tobago, and it is these that all contribute to the identity of the *Carnival* people.

The chapters in this section are eclectic and breathlessly globetrotting. Each tells the story of the uses festivals are put to in their own particular context. Each has a deep connection to their community, although the uses might be contested by the differing stakeholders, such as in *Songkran* in Thailand, and different readings of the event itself might emerge, as in the *Hornbill Festival* in Nagaland and measures of success may also be debated, as in the *Parkes Elvis Festival.* However, celebration and festivity are at the heart of all of them, whether it be the harvest of the Guinea Corn in Ghana, the Monkey King story in Lianyungang, survival in Bogotá, death and commemoration in Mexico and Tucson, or simply being one of the carnival people in Trinidad and Tobago.

## Bibliography

Getz, D. (1994) Event tourism and the authenticity dilemma, in W. F. Theobald (ed.) *Global Tourism*, Oxford: Butterworth Heinemann.

Mumford, L. (1967) *The Myth of the Machine.* London: Secker and Warburg.

Newbold, C., Maughan, C., Jordan, J., and Bianchini, F. (eds.) (2015) *Focus on Festivals: contemporary European case studies and perspectives.* Oxford: Goodfellow.

O'Grady, A. (2015) Alternative playwords: Psytrance festivals, deep play and creative zones of transcendence, in. G. McKay (ed.) *The Pop Festival: history, music, media, culture.* London: Bloomsbury, 149-164.

Quinn, B. (2013) *Key Concepts in Event Management,* London: Sage.

# 17 'Appealing for Grace': The *Guinea Corn Festival* of the Nawuris of Northern Ghana[1]

Samuel Aniegye Ntewusu

## Introduction

Festivals are recurrent celebrations and often with ritual events and meanings. Festivals reveal something of the identity, values and world views of the community or ethnic group that celebrates them (Szabó, 2015). Festive occasions involve local residents and visitors. In Ghana, there are several festivals celebrated by different ethnic groups. For example the people of Accra, the capital of Ghana, celebrate the *Homowo* festival, which is a festival that literally 'hoots at hunger'. The festival was initiated following a bumper harvest after years of famine and hunger. The people of Akropong, Akwapim in the eastern region of Ghana celebrate the *Odwira* festival. It is a festival that enables the people to purify ancestral stools[2] and spiritually cleanse the towns and villages in and around Akropong. In the same way the people of Cape Coast also celebrate the *Fetu Afahye* festival, which is a multi-purpose festival that marks cleansing of the people of Cape Coast from a plague in pre-colonial times. The festival also celebrates an abundant harvest of fish from the sea and offers the opportunity for the people in the area to thank the seventy-seven deities of the Cape Coast for their protection over the years (Opoku 1970).

The Ewe people of Anlo, in the Volta Region of Ghana, celebrate a festival called *Hogbetsotso*. It is a migration festival that tells the story of the escape of a group of Ewes from one of their tyrannical rulers, King Agokoli. The Dagomba people of the Northern Region celebrate the *Bugum* or fire festival. Local traditions provide two explanations for the festival. The first credits the origin of the festival to the Prophet Noah whose Ark docked on Mount Ararat. Local historians claim that after the floods the occupants of the Ark came out with torches to find their way out and around. The second version indicates that at a point in the history of the Dagomba people a king lost his son. The king assembled his warriors who composed a search party. They finally found the son in the night sleeping under a tree. Because they managed to find him using torches made from grass, the king decreed that every year the event should be celebrated with torches made from grass.

Beside these traditional festivals, there are other specially created ones, like the state instituted *National Festival of Art and Culture* (*NAFAC*) and the *Pan-African Festival of Art and Culture* (*PANAFEST*), that are specially organised to showcase aspects of the country's historical and cultural heritage to the world. From what has been narrated so far, it is evident that Ghana is quite active when it comes to the celebration of festivals. But just how different is the Nawuri *Guinea Corn Festival*? I attempt to answer this question by first giving a brief history of the Nawuri people. I shall proceed to give a descriptive account of the *Guinea Corn Festival* after which I give an analysis of all the events that take place in the course of the festival.

## A brief history of the Nawuri people

The Nawuri are part of the larger Guan group in Ghana. Guans are believed to be the first settlers in modern day Ghana. They are scattered across eight of the ten regions in Ghana. Guans speak distinct languages that are different from the major languages in Ghana. However, some of these Guan languages are influenced by major languages, depending on where a particular Guan tribe is located. Guans in the Volta Region include Kraakye/Krachi, Akpafu/Lolobi, Buem, Nkonya, Likpe, Logba and Anum-Boso. In the central region we have the Effutu, Awutu and Senya in Winneba and Bawjiase areas. There are Larteh and Kyerepong in the Eastern region. The Gonja, Nawuri, Nchumburu and Mpre people in the Northern and Brong Ahafo regions. Some indigenes of Kpeshie in Greater Accra also claim Guan ancestry.

The Nawuris are concentrated in the present day Northern Region, where they have Balai, Bladjai, Kabonwuli, Katiejeli, Kitari, Kpandai Nkanchina, Awuratu, Tampoai and Gyiman as their settlements. There are Nawuris also in the Volta Region and can be found in a town called Njari. The Nawuri are predominantly farmers, hunters and fishermen. Crops grown by Nawuris include yam, guinea corn, maize, cassava, groundnuts, aubergines, tomatoes, beans, okra and pepper.

One question that is worth asking is why, out of these several crops, guinea corn was and still is selected for celebration through a festival?[3] This chapter answers this question by arguing that it is because guinea corn plays an important role in the social, economic and ritual life of the people.

## *The Guinea Corn Festival (Kayuji)*: A description

The Nawuri word *Kayuji* literally translates as 'guinea corn eating'. For the Nawuris the *Guinea Corn Festival* marks the end as well as the beginning of the year. As a result the festival focuses on the land, the environment, the deities and the ancestors. *The Guinea Corn Festival* is also concerned with the development of society, therefore, during the festivities rituals are performed to ensure the progress of everybody in the community through the New Year. As it marks the end of the year, in former times a ban was imposed on any form of celebration for a month. At the physical level the ban was to allow for the processing of the guinea corn that will be used to prepare the guinea corn beer – *ayuu nta* popularly called *pito*. At the spiritual level the prohibition also enables Nawuris to be at peace with nature and ancestors.

There is a traditional officer called *Kulondiwura* who keeps the ritual calendar and will remind the Kankpe shrine priest, called the *Eseipu,* as well as clan and lineage heads, chiefs and the general public when the time of the festival is approaching. Usually the time of the festival is calculated to fall on a special day called *Kikpaa*. Kikpaa is a seven week calendar of the Nawuris and the last day of the seventh week is Kikpaa which is considered very sacred for Nawuris. Usually the festival falls within November or December. A few weeks before the festival, hunters go to hunt for antelopes. The meat from the game is smoked and pieces preserved for the festival.

Three weeks before the festival the Kankpe priest goes through a number of rituals to cleanse himself and the general community from pollution. While these background activities are going on, clan heads also perform some spiritual rites to curtail the adverse effect of enemies on clan members. Elders also within this period go into spiritual consultation with diviners to find out whether some abominable acts have been committed and at the same time appealing to individuals who have committed various crimes to come out for the right pacification and sacrifices to be performed.

A week before the appointed day, women start the preparation of the local beer, *pito*. The preparation of *pito* involves soaking guinea corn in water for two days, followed by malting, and allowing them to sit for five days in the basket or on the floor. The malted grains are milled and mixed with water and boiled. The resulting mash is allowed to cool and later filtered through a fine mesh basket. The filtrate thus obtained is allowed to stand overnight until it assumes a slightly sour flavour following which it is boiled to a concentrate. A starter from the previous brew trapped in a kind of fibre locally called *bilide* is added to the cooled concentrate which is again allowed to ferment overnight. *Pito* is thus obtained. The product varies in colour and could be dark brown or golden-yellow. The taste also varies from sweet to bitter and contains lactic acid, sugars, amino acids, some vitamins and proteins with 2-3% alcohol (Ekundayo, 1969).

According to the ritual calendar of the festival, the day that the *pito* is ready for drinking should coincide with the day of celebration. On that day the traditional office holder selects young boys and girls, preferably virgins, and send them to the stream to fetch water around 4 a.m. They carry the water in gourds and dress in white calico with clay marks on their arms, legs and forehead. In the meantime, women assemble in the house of the Kankpe shrine priest to grind or pound the fresh guinea corn into floor. The pounding and grinding is supposed to coincide with the bringing of the water from the stream. Once the water is brought, it is used to prepare soup and also a special food called *kikari*. The soup normally contains the lumps of smoked meat from the antelopes that were killed by the hunters the previous weeks. *Kikari* is prepared by pouring freshly milled or pounded guinea corn into boiling water. This is stirred for about forty minutes or one hour until a sticky substance, which is similar in texture to Tuo Zafi or T.Z (literally 'very hot', a thick porridge) is obtained.

The food is served in calabashes. Usually the calabashes number about forty and each calabash is marked with two white and red lines. The lines are not crossed. This is significant because in Nawuri culture anything that is crossed is a negation and since during the festival what is needed is progress the marks must be straight. Also, to serve the food in a calabash is of ritual importance. Ritually, each calabash signifies wholeness of life. As it represents a complete life, eating in it is a way of symbolically ensuring that one lives throughout the year.

Some of the food is served to family and clan heads. The one served to family and clan heads are normally in small calabashes with the food in bigger calabashes reserved for the Kankpe shrine. Once the food is served to clan heads, everyone is permitted to 'eat the new guinea corn'. 'Eating guinea corn' has a much broader implication and goes beyond the physical food that has been prepared. It shows that the ban on eating the fresh guinea corn has been lifted and from then on people could use the guinea corn for any purpose that they want. Among the Nawuris it is used to prepare over six different kinds of dishes and also significant for spiritual offerings, where the raw guinea corn seeds are mixed with kola nuts and placed by roads and bush paths to pacify unknown spirits that are perceived to be causing havoc in their lives. In most cases people still want to wait till the final rites are performed at the Kankpe shrine before they eat the food.

As the food is being served, the hair of the Kankpe priest is shaved, leaving a small portion in front or on the side of the head. In Nawuri such a hair style is called *wiliba*. The shaving of the hair is very significant. The Kankpe priest shaves the hair only once a year and only during the *Guinea Corn Festival*. Shaving of the hair means shaving off the past and preparing for the New Year, which is exemplified by the new hair that will grow on the head of the Kankpe priest. At the same time the small portion of hair signifies transition and continuity. Hence in the rituals surrounding the hair of the Kankpe priest, one can analyse how the festival represents both the old and the new year. Wiliba is also of symbolic essence. *Wiliba* in Nawuri means 'hard core' or 'resilience'. And so the hair cut of the Kankpe priest serves as reminder to the community of their resilience throughout the year. It is important to mention that both the preparation of the food and the shaving of the hair of the Kankpe priest are punctuated with singing of war and hunting songs and recital of appellations, especially in praise of past and present hunters and brave men.

The second aspect of the festival has to do with the Kankpe shrine. Kankpe is a shrine for a clan in Balai called Kabisu and it is situated in a big grove about one mile to the north-east of Balai. Initially the clan lived in an area called Kowato about one mile south-east of Kpandai and very close to present day Mbowurai. As a result of the discovery of this deity the Kabisu clan decided to move to the place where the shrine is located today and name it Kankpe which means to 'migrate or move to'.

The priest leads the way to the shrine and the rest follow him in a single file. As he approaches the grove that houses the shrine he begins chanting words and praises to the deity. When he arrives he instructs the youth to take brooms and sweep around after which he takes his seat. He takes a calabash containing freshly grind millet called *along*. He puts water in it and stirs it for about five minutes then pours libation with it, after which he pours everything on the Kankpe mound. Second he takes a calabash with the food – *kikari* – then he cuts smaller pieces and put it on the Kankpe mound. After that he pours some of the *pito* into a calabash and offers libation. In the offering of *along* and *kikari* the prayers are usually short but it is in offering *pito* that he really intensifies his prayers. This is indicative of the importance of the local beer in ritual prayers involving the priest, deities and ancestors.

After the libation the remainder of the food is sent into a small hut/room which houses additional objects related to the shrine. The same prayers are repeated there after which the food is brought out again and served to the other five smaller deities dotted about twenty metres away from the main Kankpe shrine. The five small deities are consulted for specific needs. The first is for protection, the second for fame, the third for success, the fourth for re/production and the fifth for victory both in war and over enemies. After the offering of food and drinks to the smaller deities, the priest returns to the big mound. It is at that moment that those who consulted the Kankpe deity for specific needs or solutions to problems the previous year come forward in a single file to thank the deity for answered prayers. Some show appreciation by donating money or bringing goats, sheep or cows to the shrine.

After that, those who have particular concerns or needs for the incoming year also come forward and the priest equally will put their request before the deity. This would have taken the time to about 2 p.m. The priest makes sacrifices of fowls, goats and sheep, which would mostly have been provided by those whose requests the previous year were granted or others who have already pledged to give to the deity the aforementioned animals to facilitate or ensure a quick solution to their problems.

After the sacrifice, the animals are roasted or cooked and served to all present. When everyone is served with the roasted or cooked meat, some pito which has been reserved all this while is mixed with sand. The sand is used to make cross marks on the foreheads of the people who went to the shrine. Portions of the sand are also carried away in fresh leaves to be used for the same purpose at home. It is important to point out how in the case of the food, two straight marks are made and yet with the sand it is a cross. The issue is that the sand is supposed to negate bad luck. In Nawuri cosmological belief system bad luck and sicknesses are caused by spirits that inhabit the head. One can only negate the power of the spirits by physically putting the cross sign on the forehead.

After the 'anointing' session, the Kankpe priest declares all rituals related to the festival completed. The priest is escorted from the shrine through the thick forest to the village. But just before the Kankpe priest and his elders enter the village, hunters meet them halfway with songs. Some of the hunters fire musketry and at the same time brandish animal horns, jaws, tails, skins and skulls as trophies. Women join again to chant out appellations. The whole village leads the Kankpe priest to his house. The rest continue to a popular dance arena in the village where the hunters' or brave peoples' dance (Kakpancha and Enyinawo) is performed. As the dance is performed, the *pito* that has been brewed for the purpose of the festival is brought out and served to both indigenes and visitors, free of charge. As the drink is being served the greeting changes from *antire* or *anulaa* that is good afternoon or good evening to *ye anu kosu pupoe,* meaning 'and our new year' for which the response is *ebuare eti anisu ko su pupoe,* 'May God add us another new year'. Thus marking the end of the *Guinea Corn Festival.*

## Analysis

Festivals in Ghana are multi-dimensional. The religious, political, social and artistic are combined into a unique performance (Odotei, 2002). From what has been narrated above, the *Guinea Corn Festival* provides a lot of analytical insights. The Kankpe shrine is the focus around which activities involving the festival are organised. The religious and spiritual elements are important binding factors in the festival. First, the fasting enables the priest to be in a very pure state of mind and to transcend the physical realm to be able to access the kind of knowledge and wisdom that is needed to conduct spiritual activities in the incoming year without failure. Second, fasting brings the traditional priest closer to the ancestors and the deities. Third, fasting by the Kankpe priest is also historical. There was a time in the history of the people where there was no food and it therefore became difficult to celebrate the festival. Oral historians indicate that Nawuris had to go and dig through the holes of ants to get some of the seeds stored by ants to grow again. That year there was no *pito* and no *kikari* food. The fasting therefore reminds the whole community of that event. The sad experience of lack of food vis-a-vis the festival is perfectly re-enacted in the shrine with the use of crushed millet, *along* in pouring libation first before the food and *pito*. It is said that the year of famine compelled the then priest to use millet instead of guinea corn to pour libation. This tradition has been continued to date. Due to the sacredness of it, it is a taboo to plant millet in the entire Nawuriland as the millet reminds them of the drought and famine. The millet that is used for the rites is usually brought from neighbouring Nanumbaland.

Usually guinea corn that is used for the ceremony, both for the food and *pito*, does not go through any kind of modern machinery or grinding mill or ball mill but instead the grinding is done on a stone or pounded in a wooden mortar and pestle. The simple reason is that when the priest commences fasting he does not taste any kind of crop on a farm containing guinea corn until he celebrates the festival. Any mixture of any kind from any grinding mill means pollution or contamination. Contamination is highly possible since the grinding mills are public and anyone can send any product for grinding.

But besides contamination, a much deeper analysis would reveal that the utilisation of this kind of traditional technology enables the Nawuris to remember their past, a period where there were no grinding mills. Going back to grinding on stone is also an educative period as the younger generation are able to learn and appreciate the early or previous ways by which their forbears lived. In fact it is during this occasion that children and young adults come to try their hands at traditional modes of grinding the guinea corn. One observation that has been made over the years is that the pounding, grinding and cooking sessions during the festival usually attract more people, both indigenous and visitors. One obvious conclusion is that the festival offers many participants the opportunity to learn old and traditional ways of life which are quite exceptional or different from the present.

The festival also confers social prestige on hunters, drummers and singers, who are associated with events during the festival. Drumming, singing and firing of musketry are indicative of their occupation as hunters and their bravery in wars that were fought in an attempt to protect their land and deities from enemies. Hunting remains the most important occupation among Nawuris. For them shooting an elephant, a lion, leopards, and antelope among others add to one's social status. In fact there are several appellations that go along with each animal that has been shot. This explains why they carry along tails, jaws, horns and skins as trophies during the festival. Flourishing such trophies allows society to publicly see and judge the achievement of individual hunters and also appreciate their rich cultural heritage.

*The Guinea Corn Festival* is not free from economics and entrepreneurship. *Pito* brewing is an important economic activity of women in the Nawuri area. It is an industry entirely operated by women. Until the *Guinea Corn Festival* is celebrated women are not allowed to brew *pito* with the newly harvested crop. They can do so with the old stock that they have. The reason for not preparing the *pito* with the new crop until the festival is celebrated is that it would lead to contamination of the land and the deities. It is in order to obtain permission to be able to brew *pito* that drinking beer from the new guinea corn is an integral part of the festival (Henryk Zimon, 1990).

It must be emphasised that without *pito* a number of social, religious and economic activities would grind to a halt. *Pito* plays an important role in the lives of Nawuris. As an economic activity almost every Nawuri woman is taught how to brew *pito*. Almost all members of the Nawuri society drink it. It plays an important leisure role. When farmers return from farm they normally retire under trees and drink *pito*. It is here that traditional musicians compete for fame by singing praises to entertain prominent customers at the drinking place. Patrons who are touched by the praises dish out money to the praise singers who shower more accolades on them raising their status higher on the social ladder, most often to the point of exaggeration.

*Pito* is used to pour libation at every occasion – marriage, naming ceremonies, funerals and festivals. Indeed, it is mandatory for clan and family heads to perform sacrifices of animals to clan and family deities, but that must be preceded with libation using *pito*. It however needs to be pointed out that the utilisation of *pito* for such ceremonies is not limited to Nawuris alone but is very common among most ethnic groups in the northern part of Ghana as well as the coastal people. The only difference is that among the coastal people, especially among the Ga, maize is used instead of sorghum or guinea corn in the brewing of beer, which the Ga of the Accra region called *ŋmãda*.

## Conclusions

It is clear that there is a symbiotic relationship between the festival and the brewery industry. Women participate actively in the festival because it facilitates the lifting of the ban on the use of new guinea corn which will enable them engage in their brewery as it is an important source of employment for the women. On the other hand the men are also interested in the *pito* brewed by the women because it enables them perform their ritual functions. From the discussions, it is evident that the festival is periodic but its core function is as an embodiment of Nawuri social, religious and economic identity and historical continuity.

Essentially one could regard the *Guinea Corn Festival* as a harvest festival associated with the harvesting season that is around November and December. The timing of the celebration to coincide with harvesting is indicative of the importance of the crop in the life of Nawuris. The festival in a general sense shows the relationship between the Nawuri and their land and deities. But the fundamental need throughout the festival is the 'appeal for divine grace' through the prayers offered by the Kankpe traditional priest. The contents of the prayers covers all spheres of life and all needs felt by the participants be they individuals or the whole community. The prayers express thanksgiving, promises and often specific goals some of which include fecundity, abundance of food, prosperity, health, rain, peace and social harmony. The cardinal value of the Nawuri lies in a life which is continuously sanctified, renewed and multiplied and for them such a life can only be achieved by celebrating or participating in the *Guinea Corn Festival* every year.

# Bibliography


Akyeampong, E. and Ntewusu, S. A. (2014) Rum, Gin and Maize: Deities and Ritual Change in the Gold Coast during the Atlantic Era (16th century to 1850), in *Afriques: Débats, méthodes et terrains d'histoire*, **5**(3).

Ekundayo, J. A. (2007) The production of pito, a Nigerian fermented beverage, in *International Journal of Food Science and Technology*, **4**(3), 217 - 255.

Kirby, J. P. (2006) Ethnic conflicts and democratization, new paths: Toward equilibrium in Northern Ghana, in *Transactions of the Historical Society of Ghana*, New Series, **10**.

Odotei, I. K. ( 2002) Festivals in Ghana: Continuity, transformation and politicisation of tradition. *Transactions of the Historical Society of Ghana*. New Series, **6**.

Opoku, A. A. (1970) *Festivals of Ghana: Past and Present*, Accra: Ghana Publishing Corporation.

Szabó, J. Z, (2015) Festivals, conformity and socialisation, in C. Newbold, C. Maughan, J. Jordan, F. Bianchini (eds.) *Focus on Festivals: Contemporary European case studies and perspectives*, 40-45. Oxford: Goodfellow.

Zimon, H. (1990) Guinea Corn harvest rituals Among the Konkomba of Northern Ghana, in, *Studia Ethnologica*, **2**, 207 - 217.


# Notes

1 In this article guinea corn means sorghum. Sorghum is known under a variety of names such as great millet and guinea corn in West Africa, kafir corn in South Africa, dura in Sudan, mtama in eastern Africa, jowar in India and kaoliang in China and milo grain in the United States of America.

2 Enstoolment is the process of appointing a tribal leader. A stool used by a powerful ancestor is considered to retain much of that person's power, even after death, and will be kept and revered.

3 The Nawuri have two major festivals that is the *Yam* and the *Guinea Corn Festival*. For discussions on the *Yam Festival* of the Nawuris see: Akyeampong and Ntewusu (2014).

# 18 Visualising National Life: The *Hornbill Festival* as Culture and Politics

Arkotong Longkumer

## Introduction

The global circulation of images has become a powerful tool in representing the visual richness of cultures around the world. It has made the annual *Hornbill Festival* in North-east India a product that acts as a brand. The plethora of visual images – tribal people in their traditional clothes, scenic representation of landscapes, and tourist information on how to reach Nagaland to attend the festival – have fixed the identities of the Nagas of India in such a compelling and exotic manner that it resembles a kind of modern primitivism, a getaway from the decadent and uncultured world, to a place that still preserves these pristine habitats for cultural and tourist voyeurs.

This chapter will suggest that in order to appreciate the festival one has to take into account the different levels of what I shall call the 'performance of identity'. First, the festival celebrates the creation of Nagaland in 1963 as a state in India after years of civil and military unrest in the region. Second, while the political situation remains unresolved, the festival is an attempt to project a distinct Naga identity that correlates with notions of indigenous peoples' rhetoric of 'preservation of culture' and 'self-determination' as the cornerstone of national identity. While these different forces are at play in the global arena of indigeneity, the *Hornbill Festival* also functions as a contested site of culture. On the one hand, it plays on representations of exoticism from colonial ethnography found in glossy coffee-table books and adventure tourism materials. On the other hand, the festival itself is struggling to articulate a Naga culture that represents the lived reality of present day Nagas. Tension arises from displaying a manufactured, but nonetheless real, culture that is dependent on the political economy of global markets. It is in these tensions that we can come to understand the evolving nature of culture and all its manifest contradictions.

I highlight three categories of performance articulated by Askew (2002,) drawn from various cultural theorists to underscore the focus on performance. First, performance is an active engagement of all in attendance and not a product that is controlled solely by the performers and transmitted for audience reception. Second, performance is a "renewable action without clear origin or end" – it is *performative* (Butler 1997: 40; italics mine). Finally, there is a resonance between performance and the active construction of social life (Askew 2002: 23). Therefore, it is within the framework of 'cultural performance' that the anthropologist David Guss attempts to analyse festivals in a wider spectrum that negotiates the presence of meaning. This is how Guss articulates this view:

> Meaning, it became clear, was not something that simply resided in an ideal model (or 'text') waiting to be released. It was something that was created with each performance, and to understand it meant comprehending the entire context in which it was produced. It also meant recognizing that this context was continually changing and that festivals were being readily deployed to meet these changes (2000: 7).

Borrowing the idea from Milton Singer's work in India, Guss sees cultural performances as a socio-political reality in praxis that is performed both for an audience and for the performers themselves. Through the power of cultural performances, new social imaginaries are produced that unite a people together and evoke a common symbol for a nation. These points similarly reverberate with Askew's earlier observations regarding performance as a dynamic interplay of forces between the actors, the audiences and the social reality it fosters; as *performative*. This theoretical intervention is useful for this essay's analysis of the *Hornbill Festival*, particularly if one is to view it as a 'performance of identity'. Before we examine this in detail, some context is required.

## 'The Mongolian Fringe'

The *Hornbill Festival* has become an international event in the last 10 years, held annually in the first week of December (usually 1-7th; in 2014 it was extended to 10 days). Nagaland is in the eastern Himalayas and is part of a region of India that is known as the 'Northeast'. It consists of eight states – Arunachal Pradesh, Assam, Manipur, Meghalaya, Mizoram, Nagaland, Sikkim, and Tripura. Roughly ninety percent of its borders are with international countries – China, Bangladesh, Bhutan, Burma and Nepal. In fact there is a small corridor of 27 km – called the 'chicken neck' – that connects the region to 'mainland India'. This tenuous geographical anomaly has cultivated a feeling of isolation and alienation in the region from the other parts of India both politically and culturally.

Borrowing the notion of 'The Mongolian Fringe' from an official paper written by the Foreign Secretary Olaf Caroe to the British Indian Government in 1940, the political scientist Sanjib Baruah suggests that this term captures the "divide between Mongolians and inhabitants of 'India proper'." (Baruah 2013: 82). Partly due to this geographical and cultural fact, together with the haphazard administration by the British since the mid-19th century and with the introduction of Christianity to this region by American and European missionaries, the region captures a complex array of variables. Any integration with India since its independence from the British in 1947 has highlighted these protean factors to the extent that it remains a thorn in the side of the Indian nation-state. The dizzying mixture of factors brought about many vibrant nationalistic movements in the region that disputed the incorporation of the region into India. This has led to military and civil unrest spanning over 60 years and has made the region one of the most militarised in the continent.

Indeed, to counter these claims of an intransigent periphery unable to integrate with mainland India, Prime Minister Narendra Modi rallied his PR team in utilising his visit to the *Hornbill Festival* in 2014 to great effect. The photograph of Modi dressed in Naga outfit when attending the festival was recycled in government advertising and in the media as far away as Mumbai "suggesting a clear public strategy of performing national unity — of taming the recalcitrant frontier" (McDui-Ra, forthcoming).

## Land of festivals

There are numerous festivals all over India and throughout the year. Some prominent ones are like *Diwali* (the festival of lights), *Holi* (the festival of colours), *Durga Puja* (after the deity), *Eid al-Fitr* (festival of breaking of fast for Muslims), *Pongal* and *Onam* (harvest festivals) and *Christmas*. There are also the different and diverse regional, religious and cultural festivals all over India. Some of these festivals are older while others are newer. The *Hornbill Festival* is in the latter category. It was instituted primarily as a cultural event by the Government of Nagaland to give audiences a pan-Naga experience. Nagaland of course has many other smaller festivals associated with each of the sixteen tribes. Therefore, in a way, although the *Hornbill Festival* is promoted primarily as a state festival, over the years it has become a global event that merits closer analysis.

## The spirit of the festival

December in Nagaland is tourist season. Driving up from the city of Dimapur airport to Kohima takes roughly around 3 hours and the journey into the hills is an arduous one. Once in Kohima, the capital of Nagaland, the streets are buzzing with activity. Numerous billboard signs advertising the festival provide a colourful and rich background to the normally muted social scene in Kohima.

The date of the *Hornbill Festival* is associated with two significant factors. First, the festival is to celebrate Indian statehood. Nagaland was formed when the moderate elites of the Naga nationalist movement, the Nagaland People's Convention (NPC), arrived at a compromise with the Government of India in 1963 regarding a home for the Nagas. Thus, Nagaland was inaugurated as the sixteenth state of the Indian Union on the first of December 1963. The second culminating factor that made the festival possible was the ceasefire signed between the Government of India and the largest of the nationalist group, National Socialist Council of Nagalim (Isak-Muivah) in 1997, which carved a politically neutral space where peace and reconciliation between the various actors could ensue.[1]

It is not clear who initiated the idea for the *Hornbill Festival*. One prominent artist that I know claimed that it was he who came up with the idea of the festival, after the renowned Hornbill bird that is central to Naga folklore and whose feathers are used in most dances. The festival touches on the theme of preservation of Naga culture, without realising that its colourful performances equally participate in the endangerment of the Hornbill bird, whose feathers are so prized that utilising plastic ones is seen as 'inauthentic'. The irony is that the timbre of culture cannot be sustained without the violence it perpetuates.

The other story is associated with the United Nations celebration of the first International Decade of the World's Indigenous People between 1995-2004. According to a prominent Naga human rights activist, Neingulo Krome, they organised an event called Naga week, where amidst the most difficult period in Nagaland when there was incessant violence due to clashes amongst the different Naga nationalists and between the Indian security forces, the Nagaland People's Movement for Human Rights (NPMHR) and the Naga Students Federation (NSF) called for a lull in violence. The event was celebratory and emotional but also a show of solidarity amongst the different Naga peoples from all over Northeast India and Western Burma, that visualised – through the performativity of culture – the sovereignty of the Naga people. This is what Krome told me:

> One way the *Hornbill Festival* is good is that it is keeping traditions alive – the other negative aspect is that it is corrupting indigenous life. Without the real intention of indigeneity, it has become a commercial enterprise. If we want to have our indigenousness, then let's have it in its original form. *Hornbill* is a copycat of what we originally did in 1995 along with the NSF from December 1-5. There we asked each and every Naga tribe to come and construct their original Naga house in the Kohima local ground. During this time there was a lot of factional killing amongst the different nationalist groups, but when we said that we are partnering with the United Nations, then the nationalists stopped the violence. It was a very significant moment for us because during that week we all pulled a stone (a traditional ceremony practised by some Nagas). The eastern Nagas such as the Yimchungru and Khiamniungan, who never pulled stones, participated in the event. When the stone couldn't be pulled faster then the tribes exchanged places…The stone moved faster as if there was some 'spirit' (laughter). During that time all the Naga tribes participated, nowadays only the sixteen official tribes participate. At that time twenty seven Naga tribes came – Manipur, Assam and Burma (though they came as Konyak and Khiamniungan otherwise to come openly as Burmese Naga would have been unacceptable to the Indian government).

For Krome, the festival, at least in its first form, was firmly associated with the indigenous peoples movement and what it means to be 'indigenous', a term that is both celebrated and dogged with controversy. But in the Naga case, indigeneity is often associated with ties to land, tradition and custom and, importantly, with sovereignty and national self-determination. So in a way, the Naga week celebration consolidated these abiding concerns into a larger 'Naga' festival that married the best of all worlds, at least according to the UN standard of celebration indigenous life in all its richness – cultural, political and social.

## Kisama and the globalisation of the *Hornbill Festival*

The festival became a truly global event when the Government under the Chief Minister Neiphiu Rio shifted the festival to its current location in Kisama. Kisama is around 10 kilometres away from Kohima. This land was acquired by the State Government of Nagaland and was gradually developed over the years into Kisama Heritage Village.

A large amphitheatre is the focus for the main programme of events, with traditional Naga *morungs* (dormitories) and stalls encircled around it. Events normally start at 9am and go on until dusk. The opening ceremony itself is a grand event. Usually all the official dignitaries are present – from the Governor, to the state Chief Minister and also important national politicians. In 2014 it was the Prime Minister of India, Narendra Modi, who inaugurated it.

Usually, the *Hornbill Festival* begins with a traditional Naga chant or, on some occasions, a blessing led by a Christian pastor. Alongside state officials, there is also a large seating area for the Indian military establishment and their families. Many of them live in nearby military camps and the *Hornbill Festival* is an informal space away from their isolated bastions. By day these men guard the check-posts and patrol the area with their machine guns and by night they want to be included in the party. Indeed, this awkward mix of different audiences at the festival reflects the socio-political situation in Nagaland itself.

Due to the space created by this new venue, the festival is able to include not only the various performances but also foster an entrepreneurial spirit by allowing local traders to sell their goods. It has expanded to include a variety of activities like fashion shows, car rallies, book festival, rock shows, horticultural stalls and exhibitions, and a children's carnival. All of these mini-events were consolidated into one space. Kisama Heritage Village has two amphitheatres, various stalls that serve local food and drink and a Bamboo Pavilion that sells local produce (like jam, pickles), handicrafts and handlooms. The circulation of these artefacts has made Naga products popular all over the world, making Nagaland better known than many of the other Northeast states of India.

The main focus of the festival though is the large amphitheatre where all traditional performances happen.

All of the sixteen Naga tribes are given a slot to perform their dances, songs, and narrate stories. All the performers, each morning, proceed from their *morungs*, or dormitories, to the seating area of the amphitheatre where they each have 20-30 minutes performance slots. For 10 days the ritual repeats like clockwork. This is partly to allow the different tourists who visit the venue on and off an opportunity to watch these cultural performances in one site. Once the performance finishes in the amphitheatre, each of the tribal performers go to their traditional *morung*, or dormitory, accompanied by their respective songs or chants. *Morungs* are an important feature of Naga society. It was the place where young people were trained in the art of war, weaving, dance, customs and traditions and was a very significant and stable institution until the advent of Christianity. Now these *morungs* are largely cultural heritage sites that perform different functions. For instance, they are used for tribal council meetings and for other festive occasions to accommodate large groups of people.

**Figure 18.1:** Site of main performances (Photograph by Akummeren Jamir)

The *morungs* at Kisama are organised according to where each of the tribes in Nagaland live. In other words, the spatial symmetry of the *morungs* represents the geographical locality of the tribes, so the southern Nagas occupy the bottom while the northern and eastern Nagas at the top. Each *morung* is an attempt to represent the unique characteristics and culture of the tribe. Some have elaborate carvings while others are plain and simple. Here tourists can visit each *morung*, interact with the performers, take photographs and also taste tribal delicacies sold at the *morung*. On occasion, the performers burst out in dance or song. For instance, a couple of the eastern tribes draw a lot of attention due to the fact that they appear more 'wild' in their dress and also because they are renowned for their use of an indigenous muzzle loaded gun during their dances, distinguishing their performance from that of the other tribes.

For many local visitors, however, these performances are not always their main concern. It is the food and 'hanging out' that is of interest to them. People exchange gossip and news about which *morung* serves the best food and which serves the best rice-beer, a locally brewed alcoholic drink. Kisama itself is a place for the youth to meet and have a good time. Facebook entries before the festival are rife with comments such as 'see you at the HBF', and it allows friends scattered across India to come together during this event.

## Audiences in the festival

Tourists and visitors can generally be classified into three groups. First, there are the local visitors from the area or from other parts of the state. This is the largest group of visitors regardless of its obvious tourist focus. Many of them attend parts of the festival and others come to enjoy food and meet up with different friends. The youth in particular come to the festival site in the evenings for the bonfires and to have a good time drinking the local rice-beer. Many of the younger people that I interacted with often complained about the lack of opportunities for them in Kohima town and the *Hornbill Festival* is one place where they can 'let their hair down'. It is also a safe haven, well protected by the various security personnel. In towns, particularly at night, it is unsafe for these kinds of social activities.

One view is that the festival is for the Nagas. Khekiye Sema, the Commissioner for Tourism, Art, and Culture, said that the festival is primarily for the younger generation because Naga culture is going through a sort of 'amnesia' (interview 2007). This is where the festival provides a forum: Naga culture becomes an educational tool. It is meant to highlight to the younger generation the value of traditions and customs from dance and songs to clothes, to food, drink, and ornaments. There are many school visits to the festival. The idea is to show the next generation the 'traditions', allowing them to appreciate and see them. Younger villagers remarked that participating in the festival itself meant rehearsing with elders the specific dance steps and songs that they were unaware of and made them more familiar with tradition. Sema said, "we are preserving continuity with tradition and must appreciate that with the changes in the world, we must also preserve our distinctiveness" (Longkumer 2015: 57). In another way, these forms of preservation and performances are important for the Naga community – performers and the audience as well. It helps other Nagas to visualize Naga culture in all its diversity, and to witness the strength of one Naga nation. A group of performers from the Pochury tribe from eastern Nagaland in 2007 said that they came to the festival to participate in the larger notion of 'Naganess' and to interact and visualize the 'Naga people as one' – that was their primary focus even though there are hardships associated with their journey to the festival. For many, without any Government funding, it is difficult to come; for others small subsidies are not adequate for their visit from afar and they have to depend on clan or village members in towns to house and support them. This idea of 'Naganess' encapsulates what Askew, Butler, and Guss regard as the performativity of culture. In this sense, the *Hornbill Festival* provides the space for the construction of this culture and the social life it demonstrates.

The second group are the national visitors – those who come from nearby states in the Northeast and from as far-flung as Delhi, Mumbai, Bangalore and Kolkata. One group of tourists that I interacted with in 2012 were from South India in Bangalore. They were part of a large photography club. They had, they explained, been expecting 'the exotic' on their visit but once they arrived in Nagaland they realised that it was not all 'tribal' but that Nagaland is very modern. But the point of contact and influence for them were travelogues and coffee-table books produced by photographers/anthropologists and having seen the pictures of Nagaland, this sparked their curiosity. Many of the Indian tourists are largely unaware of the nationalist movement amongst the Nagas.

The third group are the international tourists who come to the festival with differing agendas and expectations. Some attend the festival as 'cultural tourists' and go festival hopping. A German couple I met told me that they recently attended a similar festival in Papua New Guinea and were on their way to Bhutan when they heard about the *Hornbill Festival*. Many are cultural tourists and also avid photographers. I met a number of international tourists from England. I got talking to Johnny, who ran an adventure travel agency. He told me that the reason he came here was because of the reputation of the *Hornbill Festival*. For him the festival celebrates 'authentic' Naga culture and is an expression of 'national identity'. He was sceptical, like his fellow traveller, Mike, about what constitutes 'authenticity'. For Mike, he was not interested in debates concerning what is 'authentic' but was of the view that the *Hornbill Festival* is the 'real deal' in terms of experiencing Naga culture.

This is a statement that is echoed by some tourists but not all. An Indian journalist, Pradeep, told me in 2007 that he travels all over India to experience the different festivals. He noted that *Hornbill Festival* is a major innovation – and he is not interested whether it is 'authentic'. Rather he appreciates the spontaneity of the dances and the creativity that is present in the festival. For example, some may remark that the costumes and dress people are wearing are not 'genuine' – but that is not the point, remarks Pradeep. All people, regardless of one's locality, forget certain practices but then make adaptations. For Pradeep, that is enough. Indeed, these kinds of changes, or adaptation of culture, are not unique to the Nagas; it is happening to all societies as they move from one cultural form to another. The question is: why focus solely on preserving this past, rather than celebrating how it evolves?

The question of the 'authentic' Naga culture seems to be prevalent amongst some tourists. Johan, for example, from the Netherlands, said that for him the *Hornbill Festival* is about experiencing 'real' Naga culture. The festival in itself offered little diversity in this regard, he said, and instead it was life outside Kisama that was more interesting. Remote villages in eastern Nagaland offered more authenticity due to a certain vision of what 'Naga culture' is for Johan – does semi-nakedness, lack of electricity and thatched roofs signify this (Longkumer 2015: 59)? Sabina, similarly, was of the view that the *Hornbill Festival* was extremely 'managed'. From her experience of attending festivals in Thailand, she noted how they were more spontaneous and less efficient and organised. For her, going to remote areas like eastern Nagaland had more resonance with her image of what a 'Naga' should be like, rather than a choreographed version of it in Kisama. There was one underlying comment from many of the tourists visiting the festival: that theirs was a jarring experience in terms of their popular image of India with that of the Northeast of India and Nagaland. Nagaland for many of them felt more like Southeast Asia – Thailand and Burma being two popular associations. This in a way plays into the Nagas' sense of difference from that of the Indian nation-state and also helps popularise the national position.

## Materiality, tradition, and Christianity

There is a growing tension about what kind of 'culture' is emerging in the development of the *Hornbill Festival*. As I have noted, there are numerous performances happening throughout that display a particular kind of activity – whether typically traditional performance, or the more modern variety like fashion shows and rock concerts. Christianity here is an important aspect, particularly due to its overarching presence in Nagaland – a state that is comprised of nearly 95 percent of Baptist Christians. What this means in reality is that the festival for some Christians is an abomination – free flowing liquor, sexual promiscuity that the festival reportedly encourages, and the wanton reviving of traditional culture that sometimes clashes with the competing thought system of Christianity. In 2007, there was a public performance of reconstruction of pre-Christian rituals of divination involving the sacrifice of a chicken. The graphic performance was an attempt to give a glimpse of traditional Naga ritual, now of course abandoned due to the advent of Christianity. Although it was a public spectacle presented as parody, it did not sit well with the Christian public. In fact, many of the Baptist leaders told me that the *Hornbill Festival* is destroying the fabric of Naga culture given its clashes with the church. In 2012 therefore a cross was erected on top of the Kisama Heritage Village to signify that this is a Christian village and when I attended the festival again in 2014, a small chapel had been built in Kisama. This was to provide pastoral support but also to act as a symbol: that Christianity is part and parcel of the landscape.

Although the majority Baptist Christian population does not condemn the *Hornbill Festival*, some tensions are evident when it comes to representing 'traditional culture' alongside Christianity. A more visceral example of this tension occurred during my research in Mopungchuket village, in Mokokchung district of Nagaland, centred on the construction of a tourist village. The Christians there were claiming that traditional symbols, represented on woodcarvings, were diabolical and opposed the ethos of puritan Christianity. The 'traditional past' was viewed as 'heathenism' and resurrecting these symbols could in turn welcome these 'ancient' spirits back. However, the new tourism has to evoke the sentiments of exoticism through its association with 'traditional culture'.

One of the village residents, Akang, told me in December 2011 that "Western tourists have great interest in the woodcarvings and they want to sleep in thatched huts, wanting to photograph only those with traditional hair styles, tattoos, necklaces, loincloths – and not really interested in people wearing shirts and trousers." Some village residents, Akang said, are wary of these woodcarvings because they represent the 'evil past'. This is because, aside from being Christian, some of the residents (particularly the older generation) still remember the days when such pre-Christian symbols were destroyed by the religious fervour that engulfed entire villages. The oppositional rhetoric implied by these worldviews is rooted in the larger fabric of tradition. For pre-Christian Nagas, these woodcarvings were efficacious and tied within a specific ritual context; for Christian Nagas, these works represent 'ominous idols' (Benjamin 1999: 216-18). The revitalisation of these activities is largely to do with the space that the *Hornbill Festival* has created. It has fostered, for some, a positive path that encourages the appreciation of traditional Naga culture. More broadly, it has created a local economy aware of the market potential for Naga artefacts, clothing and handicrafts that many say does not clash with Christianity. With the revival of culture, initiated largely by the *Hornbill Festival,* debates over traditional Naga culture and its relationship with Christianity have spilled over into other arenas. This shows that Naga culture, like all societies, is constantly evolving.

## Conclusion

What began as an exercise to generate more tourists and to bring together the different Naga tribes from all over Nagaland has become a global event that encompasses a variety of activities. Its popularity has meant that not only does it attract people from all over the world, but it has also gained an international reputation as a travel destination. For instance, during the *Edinburgh Military Tattoo* in the summer of 2014, Naga traditional performers were invited for the month long celebration by the producer Brigadier David Allfrey.[2] Unlike the usual military focus, the Naga group's focus was on cultural performance (in the press they were seen as a 'folkloric group'). *The Edinburgh Tattoo* became a reality for the

Nagas because Brigadier Allfrey was invited to the *Hornbill Festival* in 2013. During this time, it was suggested to Allfrey by the then Chief Minister of Nagaland, Neiphiu Rio, that giving a platform to the Nagas would popularise the *Hornbill Festival* further and also provide an opportunity to the Nagas travelling to Edinburgh to have a 'dynamic impact on Naga society' upon their return. According to Gugs Chishi, the leader of the Naga contingent to Edinburgh, it was not simply about being good ambassadors and encouraging tourists to come to the *Hornbill Festival*. Gugs noticed that his performers' "mind-set had changed" since the day they arrived; they began to adopt "the concept of thinking like Nagas first before one's own tribal identity". This kind of national identity was affirmed during their Scottish visit not only at a personal level, but also as one nation to another. Their visit came at a time when Scotland was considering its own national identity in the build up to the referendum in September 2014. Indeed, one of the *Tattoo* organisers even highlighted the common ground for Scottish and Naga nationalistic movements. Could it be that the performance of culture present in the *Hornbill Festival* exposes a deep abiding concern for human freedom that can be understood around the globe?

Flying in the face of classic theories on nationalism that assumed a congruence between the political, national and the cultural aspects of the nation-state (Gellner 1983) and the development of a nation as a cultural construct premised primarily on 'print capitalism' (Anderson 1991), it is more likely that the variations of nationalism emerge within specific cultural contexts that highlight their highly negotiated internal dynamics. Thus I have shown that the emergence of a Naga national culture is very much premised on the performativity of social identities that not only negotiate the distinctiveness of identity, but how the *Hornbill Festival* is increasingly viewed within the framework of indigenous peoples' rhetoric of belonging. Not all Nagas have this singular vision, nor do all express these sentiments unequivocally, but there is engagement at a popular level – from the various tourists attending the festival to the Nagas themselves – that the visualisation of Naga culture affirms the view that there is something that can be called a Naga national culture.

## Bibliography

Anderson, B. (1990) *Imagined Communities: Reflections on the Origins and Spread of Nationalism*, London: Verso Books.

Askew, K. (2002) *Performing the Nation: Swahili Music and Cultural Politics in Tanzania*, Chicago: University of Chicago Press.

Baruah, S. (2013) India: The Mongolian Fringe, in *Himal Southasian*, **26**(1), 82-6.

Butler, J. (1997) *Excitable Speech: A Politics of the Performative*, London: Routledge.

Gellner, E. (1983) *Nations and Nationalism*, Ithaca: Cornell University Press.

Guss, D. M. (2000) *The Festive State: Race, Ethnicity, and Nationalism as Cultural Performance*, Berkeley: University of California Press.

Longkumer, A. (2015) As our ancestors once lived: Representation, performance and constructing a national culture amongst the Nagas of India, in *Himalaya*, **35**(1), 51-64.

Longkumer, A. (2013) Who sings for the Hornbill?: the performance and politics of culture in Nagaland, Northeast India, in *The South Asianist*, **2**(2), 87–96.

McDui-Ra, D. (In Press) *Debating Race in Contemporary India*, London: Palgrave Macmillan.

## Notes

1. D. Kikon, Operation Hornbill Festival 2004: http://www.india-seminar.com/2005/550/550%20dolly%20kikon.htm, 2005 (accessed 16th April 2012).
2. My thanks to Setuomenuo Ao for sharing her interview notes with the Naga performers in Edinburgh, 2014.

# 19 The World's Largest Water Fight, or the Battle for the Soul of a Festival: *Songkran* in Thailand and South East Asia

Chris Newbold

## Introduction

The *Songkran Festival* in Thailand, although not an indigenous festival, has become the most popular one in the region with tourists, which is why people around the world have assumed that it was originally from Thailand. Traditionally it is a time for reunions, house cleaning and Buddhist rituals and observances, however, it is water that is at the heart of *Songkran*. Water is celebrated as a blessing and is given as a sign of respect; festival participants sprinkle, splash or douse each other with water as an act of cleansing and good wishes. Traditionally in Thailand *Din Sor Pong* (white powder) or coloured powders are smeared on the celebrants' faces, representing the sins of the past which can then be washed away by the water pitched at them by close relatives, friends or other revellers. This traditional lunar new year festival is celebrated by many of the bordering countries including Cambodia, Myanmar, Laos and Yunnan Province China where the new year festival is variously known as *Chaul Chnam Thumey* in Cambodia, *Thingyuan* in Myanmar, and *Pbee Mai Lao* in Laos. For the Dai people in the Dehong area of southern Yunnan Province of China it is called *Shangkran* or *Shangjian*, pointing to its common Buddhist roots with *Songkran* in Thailand. As we shall see, the festival has become an important tourist attraction for these countries, but nowhere is it more exuberantly celebrated and enthusiastically marketed than in Thailand.

This chapter[1] will explore the origins and meanings of the *Songkran Festival* itself; it will look at the development of the festival and discuss how its adherence has changed over the decades particularly as tourism has become a major industry for Thailand and other countries in the region. We consider the role of the Tourism Authority of Thailand (TAT) in promoting and developing this festival in order to attract mass tourism. As with many 'cultural' festivals, we shall see how *Songkran* has gone through a process of secularisation, with the 'main event' now being characterised as a 'water fight'. We will also examine the issues that this festival and its growth have had for Thailand and the region. In particular we look at the debates surrounding the health and safety of the three to five day long festival, and some of the issues that emerge in a country torn between, on the one hand, its desire to attract mass tourism and, on the other, to defend its cultural identity and integrity.

## The *Songkran Festival*

*Songkran* is the Thai form of the Sanskrit *sankranta,* meaning passage or change. In the lunar calendar there are twelve songkrans in a year, the April passage of the sun is called Maha Songkran, or major passage as the sun leaves Pisces and enters Aries at the beginning of the lunar new year. Traditionally its timing was based on the lunar calendar, *Songkran* is now a fixed three day festival in Thailand, and runs from the 13th to the 15th of April, although in some areas especially in the North of Thailand it can last the week. *Songkran* has its origins in this area, especially around Chiang Mai, one of eight of Thailand's Northern Provinces that were once part of the ancient Lanna Kingdom that borders Yunnan Province China, Myanmar and Laos.

The original emphasis of *Songkran* celebrations were based on the Buddhist cultural inheritance of the region and many of the events were centred around the temples or wats. In a ceremony called *song nam phra* statues of Buddha are cleansed with fragrant water in order to bring good luck and prosperity in the forthcoming year. Originally it was this water that was gathered in small silver bowls as it ran off the statues; this 'blessed' water would then be used to splash relatives on their shoulders and bring good luck for the coming year. The water would also be poured onto the hands of monks in a ceremony called *rod nam dam hua.*

Buddhist merit-making *tham bun,* is a key element of the festival, and part of the ritual in Bangkok is to visit nine sacred wats (nine is a lucky number for the Thais). Building sand pagodas or *stupa* in the wats is called *chedi sai* and this is another form of merit-making as it returns sand to the wat which has been removed on visitor's feet over the previous year. Also the builders will leave money on their pagodas and buy candles, joss sticks and flowers from the wat in order to decorate their pagodas. Other forms of merit making during *Songkran* days were the releasing of fish and birds. Fish were particularly important in the low lying central region of the country, as during the rainy season these flooded areas had encouraged fish to spawn, but when the drought arrived fry were trapped in diminishing water pools, and releasing them into rivers not only gained great merit, but also helped to guarantee next season's supply (Rajadhon, 1956). The other key aspect of the *Songkran Festival* holiday is the familial traditions. Families travel for re-unions to their relatives in ancestral regions and towns, the elders are respected and ancestors remembered.

The traditional three days of the festival are clearly delineated, the first day *Wan Sungkran Long* marks the passing of the year, Buddha statues are brought out from the wats, and escorted down the streets in parades, houses are swept and the old year is seen out with fireworks and fire crackers. The second day *Wan Nao,* new year's eve, is the day for building the sand pagodas, and preparing for the religious ceremonies of the third day. Food preparation also takes place on *Wan Nao*. These first two days have been secularised by the Thai government and given the designation the *National Day for Older Persons* and Thailand's *Family Day*. The third day *Wan Paya Wan* is the day for respecting elders and monks, for the washing of the Buddhas and for the water sprinkling.

As we have seen, the use of water symbolises the washing away of bad luck from the previous year. Traditionally water would be sprinkled or a small silver bowl poured over family or close friends, the modern festive derivation now includes live elephants, buckets, hose pipes and water blasters, and the targets are anybody and everybody.

Wei Liming talking about the *Water-Splashing Festival* in Yunnan China observes that:

> There is a 'gentle' way and a 'rough' way of water splashing. The gentle way is to dip flower stems in water and sprinkle each other in blessing. The rough way involves people using bowls and buckets to soak each other. The more you are soaked, the happier and luckier you will be in the New Year (2011: 120).

Alden Lauzon observes:

> as a foreigner witnessing the event for the first time the search for the traditional aspect of this festival required diligent efforts. For those who have not witnessed this event their access is mostly via the advertisements provided by TAT as published in the print media, both local and international.... The event has been transformed into a water splashing contest; just like other purportedly sacred festivities, a more secular emphasis has gained popular support (2010: 62).

The Thai sense of *sanuk,* meaning fun, is often portrayed as being at the heart of the modern derivation of the *Songkran Festival*. As Porananond and Robinson say:

> The *Songkran* would seem to conform to a more carnivalesque event than was ever intended, providing an opening for Thai communities to break momentarily from their normative social order (2008: 320).

Clearly the nature of the *Songkran Festival* has changed. A Western writer in Thailand in 1967 observed only that, "this is an ancient northern custom which takes place in the middle of April, when for three or four days there are parades and carnivals and dancing of the Ramwong, and during which provincial beauty queens are chosen" (Davies, 1967: 75). There is no mention of water fights here.

Modern tourist guides almost across the board highlight the 'water fight' aspects of the festival, with the *Rough Guide* referring to "an excuse for a national water fight" (2011: 14), *Dream Trip Thailand* informs its readers that *Songkran* is "celebrated with more gusto in Chiang Mai than anywhere else. Boisterous water-throwing directed particularly at farangs: expect to be soaked to the skin for the entire four days" (Footprint, 2013: 101), and *The Lonely Planet* tells its readers that, "the Thai New Year is a no-holds-barred countrywide water fight that has to be seen to be believed" (2014: 23).

## *Songkran* and tourism

With the early establishment of a Tourist Authority in Thailand (TAT) in 1960, and a number of high profile campaigns, 'Visit Thailand Year' (1980 and 1987), 'Amazing Thailand' (1998), 'Unseen Thailand' (2003), and 'Discover Thainess' (2015), the important role that tourism has in the Thai economy is clear. The development of international offices in United States, Japan, Singapore, London and across European capitals played a major role in driving these campaigns home to an international market. Marketing from the very beginning was TAT's most important activity (Lauzon, 2010) and one of its first promotions was of Chiang Mai (in 1977), where the *Songkran Festival* was, as we have seen, the most important event on the Lanna calendar, as Porananond and Robinson state:

> The *Songkran Festival* remained a key attraction. The infrastructure developed steadily to cater for influxes of general interest tourists, who came not only for the *Songkran Festival* in April but also for *Loy Krathong Festival* held in November in Chiang Mai [and across the wider region] (2008: 316).

The 'backpacker' tourist in the Far East began to be recognised as a major phenomenon in the 1990s (Huang, 2008), particularly being draw to Chiang Mai where, they "began to participate directly in the festivities rather than merely observing" (Porananond and Robinson, 2008: 317). The key date for Lauzon in TAT's marketing of *Songkran* comes in 2004 when, "TAT embarked on a 70 million Baht marketing blitz to promote the *Songkran Festival*" (2010: 61).

The trajectory that *Songkran* was on is clearly recognised by Porananond and Robinson (2008), who identified three periods of development for the festival. For them, the 1950s through to the 1970s saw the festival becoming more participatory and organised, involving new practices with events such as processions and beauty pageants. They also note that it was during this period that *Songkran* began to expand out to fill more public spaces, building capacity and an 'expectation for tourists'. The commercial inroads made during this period expanded rapidly through to the 1990s with the increased involvement of local government and TAT. They observed that the Thai infrastructure developed along with the growth of international tourists. In the period from the 1990s Porananond and Robinson observe not only a shift from the private to the public nature of the festival, and a change in the economic emphasis of the festival, but it is at this point that they address some 'key' changes in the practices of *Songkran*, in particular the change from placid water throwing to industrial water-fights, accompanied by loud music and large pickup trucks transporting water tanks for the continual throwing of water. For them though the core practices are clearly still identifiable, as they say:

> It appears that the 'tradition' of the contemporary *Songkran Festival*, effectively a product of the 1950s, is secure precisely because it has continually been reinvented in the light of tourist audiences. Tourism as a mark of modernisation has enabled the festival to attempt to bring together (and protect) traditional cultural values with a need for economic development (2008: 320).

A pivotal turning point in this development can perhaps be seen with the *Grand Lanna Civilisation Songkran Festival* organised by TAT in 2004 in Chiang Mai. This 'mega festival' as Porananond and Robinson called it, had all the trappings of a national and regional culture and heritage celebration attracting both domestic and foreign tourists. TAT now also hold the 'official' *Songkran Festival* called the *Bangkok Songkran Splendours Festival*, which has an opening ceremony, shows, displays and a Miss Songkran competition, where the emphasis is on the cultural aspects of *Songkran*. Both of these can be seen as in part an attempt by TAT, to bring the cultural element of *Songkran* back to the fore. However the economic importance of *Songkran* to the tourist industry remains the driving force.

In 2015 the Ministry of Tourism and Sport announced that 470,000 foreign tourists attended the *Songkran Festival*, an increase of 39 percent from the previous year, with the income from tourism during the five days of the festival 9th – 13th April being 7.5 billion Baht (National News Bureau of Thailand, 2015a). In 2012 the TAT had estimated tourism revenue at 4.6 billion Bhat.

## *Songkran* and its issues

As we have seen, the *Songkran Festival* has developed from being a low key family celebration based around the 'local' wat, to being an internationally known event where the attraction is taking part in the world's 'biggest water fight'. This explosion in size and intensity has naturally brought with it a number of issues, both imported and indigenous. Amongst the key management issues are road safety, drink driving, pickpocketing, drug dealing, and sexual harassment. The fundamental ingredient of the festival itself, water, is sometimes an issue, in that excessive use of water in the celebrations is officially discouraged in times of shortage and drought. Another water related issue is the squirting of polluted water, causing bacterial infections in eyes, ears and throat and dysentery, especially in Chiang Mai, where water is taken from the city moat, which is the centre of celebrations there.

The modern derivation of *Songkran* is controversial with many government and authority figures who are unhappy with Thailand's reputation as the "hub of the water party with booze and a high death toll" (Prommin Kantiya, Director of the Accident Prevention Network [Bangkok Post, 2014a]). Where a heady mix of heavy alcohol consumption, frenzied water fighting, with anyone as a target and an anti-helmet wearing attitude prevails, inevitably you get the festival period described as 'seven days of danger'. In 2015 there were 3,373 road accidents, 364 people died and 3,559 were injured (The Nation, 2015). Motor cycles are historically involved in 80% of accidents, with the majority involving people between the ages of 20 and 49. Siviroj et al state that:

> During *Songkran* holidays motorcycles were the major cause of road traffic accidents [76.6%] and the most common causes identified included alcohol and not wearing a helmet [98.4%] (2012: 3288).

More generally they comment that "the daily fatalities during the *Songkran Festival* rise up to 84 and 95 persons per day, compared with an average of 34 persons per day in the non-festival period" (2012: 3288). Siviroj et al.'s recommendations are media campaigns for road safety and the tightening of the law. Lauzon noted that few young people heeded the warnings. One declared "I don't care if the police arrest me for not wearing a helmet. The measure doesn't make sense and I won't follow it" (2010: 62). Lauzon understands this attitude as being symptomatic of what he sees as two divergent types of celebration, the subdued 'official' way favoured by state and city agencies, and the more populist water-splashing kind favoured by young people. He interprets this "either as the degradation of an otherwise solemn occasion, or the reclaiming or negotiating of the event by certain groups, like the youth, in order to assert their identity" (2010: 62). Clearly a generational divide is evident, with older generations vacating Bangkok during the festivities to visit traditional home areas or relatives out of the city, leaving the streets to the raucous and exuberant celebrations. There is some evidence that the major incidents of trouble occur in the main tourist areas where mass crowds gather such as Chiang Mai, or the main routes in Bangkok the Silom Road and Khao San Road. Promminn Kantiya of the APN is supporting the zoning of *Songkran* celebrations, into designated pedestrian areas where the sale of alcohol is banned.

> Each area of each province will have to determine the specific area of their town for the *Songkran* celebration. People can only splash the water in one specific zone with supervision by local officials (Bangkok Post, 2014a).

The Bangkok Metropolitan Administration has banned alcohol in places where *Songkran* celebrations are taking place, whilst the Khao San district of Bangkok tried to ban powders in 2015, for blocking sewers, and as it was believed to be used by some revellers as an excuse to 'touch' members of the opposite sex, constituting potential sexual harassment.

Thailand's Moral Promotion Centre Director Sin Suesuan, has stated that *Songkran's* high accident rates is caused by alcohol, unsafe driving, disputes and sexual assault. In response to many of the issues that have arisen the Centre has this year (2015) published seven values for safety during *Songkran*:

1. **Discipline**: Follow the rules underlined by society, such as traffic laws, safe driving within the speed limit, avoid crosscutting others. When using public transport we must stand in line.
2. **Be Patient**: Avoid gambling, and tolerate anger from those who are drunk and others to avoid potential fights.
3. **Kindness**: Show kindness help and support one another.
4. **Giving**: Be sharing, be giving, and be helpful to others and the society, like offering seats to elders.
5. **Responsibility**: Know one's duties in society to guarantee the safety of others, e.g. bus drivers.
6. **Consciousness**: Know what one's actions may lead to; not drinking while or before driving.
7. **Caution**: Be careful in everything that we do, don't do anything that may harm or injure yourself or others. (National News Bureau of Thailand, 2015b).

A military coup on the 22nd May 2014 led to General Prayuth Chan-ocha becoming Head of Government leading the National Council for Peace and Order, the declared aim of the coup was to restore peace and to morally renew Thailand. Clearly as we have seen, the image of Thailand abroad is a major concern to the authorities and renewed attempts to subdue some of the excesses of *Songkran* celebrations can be seen as part of this process while at the same time maintaining the draw of the event to the all-important tourist market.

## *Songkran:* Thailand and Singapore

Not only is the new government keen to morally renew *Songkran*, it is also jealous in its protection of the festival as being part of Thailand's cultural heritage, and as one of its major tourist events. Singapore was not part of the Lanna Kingdom in ancient times and does not necessarily have the same cultural inheritance as Thailand and the Greater Mekong sub-region. Thus the recent development of a *Songkran* event in Singapore was treated with some suspicion by the Thai authorities, believing that the reason that Singapore celebrates *Songkran* is purely a gimmick to attract tourists, possibly to the detriment of the Thailand's own tourism at this time. April is a slow time of year for tourism in Singapore, so in 2013 The Singapore Tourist Board (STB) licenced its first *Songkran Festival*.

The STB sees 'place-making' initiatives such as festivals as important to its tourism development in Singapore, thus the event was heavily marketed and publicised. Thailand's *Songkran* tends to dominate the regional tourism at that time of year. Tourists were perceived to have changed their holiday plans to Singapore instead of Thailand, including some Thai people who wanted a new celebration experience. The '*Celebrate Songkran 2014*' festival which was held on April the 12th and 13th fell foul of the national campaign in Singapore to conserve water that year, thus, the event was unable to have any major water-based activities; the very core of *Songkran*. The emphasis of the event was on the Thai origins of *Songkran*, with Thai sports, music and food central to the activities. Apart from its concern about the potential loss of revenue, TAT reasoned that how the *Songkran Festival* was organised in Singapore detracted from the authenticity of the celebration of Thai tradition and culture. The key to this controversy has been that the event was conducted without the sponsorship and involvement of either local Thai communities or the Thai authorities. *Songkran* events and celebration have been held across Singapore in previous years, associated with the embassy, Thai Buddhist temples, Thai students and the general Thai community in Singapore's Golden Mile (Little Thailand District); this new turn was established by private companies with a profit motive, and deemed to be associated with the STB.

Thailand's Cultural Surveillance Bureau director Yupa Taweewattana-boworn is reported to have said that "Singapore is using the festival to promote tourism without acknowledging the value of the traditions behind *Songkran*", she went on to say that "*Songkran* is not just about splashing water for fun, but is aimed at strengthening relationships between family members and communities" (Intathep, 2014). Vilaiwan Twichasri, Governor for Tourism Products and Promotions at TAT said she would consult to see if intellectual copyright protected traditional cultural activities based on traditional Thai arts and culture and festivals such as *Songkran* and *Loy Krathong* (Bangkok Post, 2014b). Although threats to sue have receded, this was clearly a sensitive issue that touched a raw nerve in Thailand and could have potentially affected the relationship between the two countries.

# Conclusions

The *Songkran Festival* provides an intriguing example of a traditional regional festival, that as we have seen has been developed and exploited by one country as to some extent its own cultural property, and particular aspects of that festival have come to dominate the public perception of the event, both nationally and internationally. The role of the Tourist Authority of Thailand has been really interesting in that it first rolled out and encouraged the emphasis on the water splashing aspects of the festival and indeed encouraged tourist participation and then tried to draw back and re-emphasise the 'cultural' and 'traditional' aspects and re-position tourists as mere voyeurs of cultural events.

The exuberance with which the festival is celebrated is clearly proving problematic for the authorities, particularly the military regime with its pledge to morally renew Thailand. The practical aspect of road deaths during this period must make *Songkran* the most dangerous festival in the world, the social order dimension, with alcohol abuse, and sexual harassment clearly make the festival an unpleasant experience for many, with a concomitant perceived exodus of older people from Bangkok during the *Songkran* period. Zoning appears to be the preferred response to some of these issues, but this may well serve only to concentrate and ghettoise the festival, clearly changing the very heart of the celebration itself. Indeed, three versions of *Songkran* may emerge or have already emerged from this, the culturally based 'performance festival' preferred by TAT, the quiet home/family based 'traditional' festival for the Thais themselves, and the zoned 'water fight' festival so attractive to young Thais and backpackers alike.

The recent online book publication aimed at the tourist market, *Songkran* (2015) by Khiew Wan Wongsawat epitomises this struggle over the future shape of *Songkran* in Thailand, where his emphasis is on the 'correct' and 'traditional' way to celebrate the *Songkran festival*, placing great value on tradition, continuity and the exotic. For tourist boards like TAT these are the cornerstones of their marketing endeavour and their various international campaigns over the years. As we have seen, the cultural values of the *Songkran* experience have been changed, both by what the overseas visitors are looking for, as well as what the Thai people, particularly Thai youth, are looking for from *Songkran*, but also in the development of the festival from the 1950s, not least by TAT themselves. The decisions on promoting and marketing, certain aspects and destinations for the celebration of the *Songkran Festival* have themselves led to a cultural event that has outgrown its origins. Indeed, in developing and encouraging *Songkran* to be the festival it is now in order to attract tourists, has the TAT and the Ministry of Tourism and Sport unleashed a genie it is now struggling to put back in the bottle?

## Bibliography

Bangkok Post (2014a) Lawless culture takes its toll, in *Bangkok Post* http://www.bangkokpost.com/lite/news/404724/lawless-culture-takes-its-toll accessed 22/09/2015

Bangkok Post (2014b) Songkran in Singapore, in *Bangkok Post Stories* http://ww.bangkokpost.com/learning/learning-from-news/400635/songkran-in-singapore accessed 22/09/2015.

Davies, D (1967) *Thailand: The Rice Bowl of Asia*, London: Frederick Muller.

Footprint (2013) *Dream Trip Thailand*, Footprint Publications.

Huang, F. Y. (2008) Western and Asian Backpackers in Taiwan: Behaviour, motivation and cultural diversity, in J. Cochrane, (ed.), *Asian Tourism: Growth and change*, Oxford: Elsevier.

Intathep, I. (2014) TAT considers legal action over Singapore Songkran, in *Bangkok Post* (19th March 2014).

Lauzon, A, W. Q. (2010) *Songkran* and Chiang Mai Tours: Interfacing tourism, the state and local culture, in *Ritsumeikan Journal of Asia Pacific Studies*, **28**, August 2010, Ritsumeikan Centre for Asian Pacific Studies.

Liming, W (2011) *Chinese Festivals*, Cambridge: Cambridge University Press.

Lonely Planet (2014) *Vietnam, Cambodia, Laos & Northern Thailand*, Lonely Planet Publications

National News Bureau Of Thailand (2015a) 7 Values for safety during *Songkran* holiday, in *National News Bureau Of Thailand* (7th April 2015) http://thainews.prd.go.th/website_e/news/news_detail/WNSOC5804070010049 accessed 22/09/2015

National News Bureau of Thailand (2015b) PM lauds Thais for being good host to foreigners during *Songkran*, in *National News Bureau Of Thailand* (14th April 2015) http://thainews.prd.go.th/website_e/news/news_detail/WNSOC5804150010001 accessed 22/09/2015

Porananond, P., and Robinson, M. (2008) Modernity and the evolution of a festive tourism tradition: The *Songkran Festival* in Chiang Mai, Thailand, in *Asian Tourism: Growth and change*, J. Cochrane, (ed.), Oxford: Elsevier.

Rajadhon, P. A. (1956) *Loy Krathong and Songkran Festival*. (4th edition)Thailand Culture Series no.5. Bangkok: The National Culture Institute.

Rough Guide (2011) *The Rough Guide to Thailand's Beaches and Islands*, Rough Guide Publications.

Siviroj, P., Peltzer, K., Pengpid, S., and Morarit, S. (2012) Helmet use and associated factors among Thai motorcyclists during Songkran Festival, in *International Journal of Environmental Research and Public Health*, **9**(9).

The Nation (2015) Road toll exceeds last year's figures, in *The Nation*, http://www.nationmultimedia.com/national/Road-toll-exceeds-last-years-figures-30258126.html, accessed 10/12/15.

Wongsawat, K. W. (2015) *Songkran*, Lulu online Publishing.

## Notes

1 I would like to acknowledge the help of Mareeya Chanurai for her assistance in the direction this chapter has taken and in the early research in Thailand.

# 20 China: Rehabilitating Festivals

Chris Newbold and Meng Xiang

## Introduction

It is to be expected that in a country with a five thousand year history, 56 different ethnic groups, and a population of 1.4 billion people, festivals will play a major part in both modern and traditional cultural life in China. Understandably a great many festivals have come and gone, most others have evolved and changed over the centuries, the combination of religious influences, cultural differences and political and economic changes across a vast nation has given China a huge range of festive traditions. Many of these festivals such as *Lantern Festivals, Dragon Boat Festivals* and *Chinese New Year* are well known and have been exported around the globe as Chinese diaspora have moved and settled. A great many festivals in China are related to their ethnic and regional origins and are hence little known in other parts of the country let alone across the world. As we shall see, an important factor in understanding festivals in contemporary China is the arrival of the Western events calendar, where *Christmas Day, Valentine's Day*, and *Halloween*, have come to be the significant dates in the year for the younger urban population, inevitably driven by the demands of commercialism and the media.

This chapter will discuss the extent to which what we identify as the five dominant configurations of festivals in contemporary China reflect and illustrate the tensions that exemplify modern China, that is, between tradition, Westernisation and economic growth. In examining contemporary festivals in China, five clear and distinct types emerge. First, there are the traditional festivals deeply rooted in the rural culture, Chinese historical traditions, and the Chinese Luna calendar; the *Spring Dragon Festival*, the *Ullam-bana Festival*, the *Double Nine Festival* are but a few examples. Second, there are the music festivals, the generational signifier of outward looking modern Chinese youth; the *Strawberry Festival*, the *Midi Festival* and the *Orange Isle Music Festival*. Third, as we have already mentioned above, there are the 'new' Western influenced celebrations. Fourth, there are the political festivals which are designed to reaffirm guiding political and moral principles in China; *International Labour Day, Women's Day, National Day*. Fifth, there are the economic oriented festivals and events allied to economic investment and growth plans, tourism and the MICE industries (Meetings, Incentives, Conferences and Exhibitions): *The Great Festival of Creativity Shanghai, Kunming International Cultural Tourism Festival, Lianyungang Silk Road International Logistics Expo, Tianjin Food Expo* etc. The latter festival type is often tied to the first in terms of the use of traditional festival performances (music, dance) and festival aesthetics in order to attract tourists, businessmen and organisations, and to bring business, investment and economic impact to an area.

It would be impossible in a brief chapter such as this to scratch the surface of festivals in China as a whole, however, in choosing the case study of Lianyungang in Jiangsu Province we can begin to discuss some of the themes through looking at an ancient city that is now at the very heart of China's economic development plans, and thus examine the role of festivals in a modern Chinese city and its region. This chapter will examine the range of festivals in the city; it will look at their development and role; and it will relate this to primary research carried out with a sample of fifty members of the festival audience in Lianyungang. First though, we will begin by looking at the key debate concerning festivals in modern China, that of the place and role of traditional festivals.

## The debate over traditional festivals in China

During a large part of the second half of the twentieth century the three key aspects of what makes festivals work, localism (which was subsumed under a centralised national identity), traditional culture and the freedom to travel, were all disapproved of or actively suppressed in China (Sofield and Li, 1988; Arlt, 2008). Internal tourism under Communist rule was seen as "a wasteful and bourgeois practice" (Arlt, 2008), and the rush to modernisation meant that anything associated with the past needed to be purged (Clark, 2008). Jasper Becker quotes an old Beijinger who grew up before 1949:

> at *Spring Festival* there were many rituals – the offering to the Kitchen God, the blessing of the God of Wealth... Now, it is just eating and drinking, just showing off... Still it is better than the 1970s ... then *Spring Festival* lasted a day and people prided themselves on how little they ate or drank (2000: 182).

Throughout Mao Zedong's leadership of the Chinese Communist Party (CCP), and in particular during the Cultural Revolution (1966 – 1976) the doctrine of 'totalistic iconoclasm' meant that 'living cultural heritage' was to be purged and replaced with the new 'Chinese socialist culture'. For traditional festivals to survive, they needed to conform to the eight 'revolutionary' or 'model' performances (*yangbanxi*) that were allowed. Celebrations of gods, emperors, imperialist lackeys and superstitions of all kinds were to be replaced by the proletarian line, where heroic workers, peasants and soldiers were the models to be recognised, emulated and celebrated. As Paul Clark states in his authoritative work on the culture in the Cultural Revolution:

> Modelling was not confined to the performing areas. Other forms of creative art were also, at one stage or other during the Cultural Revolution years, expected to incorporate the spirit of the model performances (2008: 74).

Performance festivals associated with these models were permitted, particularly of the model operas, and regional festival success for performers could lead to national level festival performances in Beijing.

The only festival that really survived was *Chunjie, The Spring Festival* (*New Year Festival*), which continued as the main public event as Paul Clark stated:

> Throughout the period people were given a day or days off work, made dumplings, and families gathered together. Separated couples got together, perhaps for the only time each year or one of two times. As mentioned in my book, new operas and films were often launched around the holiday, and familiar operas etc. shown in 'festivals' (e.g. of model performances, or some other genre), (correspondence with author 2015).

Our research indicates that quiet, private festival observance continued, but was subdued, family-based, and unsanctioned – not supported by the authorities. Special festival food, where available, would be eaten. During *Qingming* the visiting of family memorials still took place, and graves were still swept, but without making great play of it. Although as Professor Clark reminded us, "in 1976 disgruntled young people in Beijing chose the *Qingming Festival* (5 April) to commemorate the passing in January of Premier Zhou Enlai and contrast his alleged enlightened leadership with that of what became the Gang of Four" (correspondence with author 2015).

The aftermath of the Cultural Revolution and the reforms started by Deng Xiaoping led to some relaxing of the pressures on both minority and traditional cultures; the recovery of the local, the authentic, the folk and diversity of Chinese historical and social experience began to take place (Clark, 2008). David Bonavia, chief Beijing correspondent for *The Times*, writing in 1981 observed:

> Social customs and festivals are coming alive again with colour and spluttering fireworks… Old customs associated with such traditional festivals as the *Chinese New Year*, the *Moon Festival* and *Lantern Festivals* are being revived with their special food recipes and delicacies rooted in ancient religious beliefs (1981: 12 – 13).

The new 'open door' policy of Deng Xiaoping saw one and a half million tourists visiting China by 1986 (Gittings, 1989: 223), thus tourism far from being prohibited was now actively encouraged, and this had a rejuvenating effect on festivals, as Sofield and Li state:

> Once tourism became an accepted form of economic activity in China after 1978, it almost automatically encompassed and pursued heritage in all its manifestations, from built heritage to cultural festivals to traditional lifestyles (1988: 367).

There has been official support for the re-invigorating of a festival tradition in China since 2004 when the then Vice Minister of Culture Zhou called on Chinese youth to uphold traditional festivals in the light of the "encroaching values and lifestyles of developed countries". He observed, "young people are keen on foreign festivals, while traditional festivals, which are full of diverse cultural connotations, are increasingly being left out in the cold" (reported in *China Today*, July 2004). These comments were made on the back of a combined Ministry of Culture and Ministry of Finance project to protect Chinese ethnic and folk culture, started in 2003. A couple of years later, the *China Daily* was lamenting the decline of the *Qixi Festival* (or *Double Seven Festival*, the Chinese Lovers Day) in the face of the encroaching Western *Valentine's Day*:

> Young people are showing less interest in traditional culture as symbolised by these festivals (*Dragon Boat Festival*, *Mid-Autumn Festival*, and *Qixi Festival*). Even if all traditional festivals are finally made legal, the risk of them becoming purely formalised celebrations with little meaning is not removed. If the younger generation fails to identify with the cultural significance of these holidays, there is little that can be done.

Addressing this question and the idea of festivals as carriers of traditional Chinese culture, Wang et al. (2014) identify a number of key issues facing traditional festivals in modern China:

- Lack of core modern values
- Loss of emotional experience identity
- Missing of traditional folk arts
- Confusion around the application of festival symbols
- Popularity of Western festival culture

Traditional festivals are linked to agrarian customs and rituals and an understanding of the relationship between human beings and nature which is no longer the lived experience of most Chinese people, hence these festivals contain no modern values which people can relate to. A loss of emotional experience identity occurs, for Wang et al., when people can no longer understand the cultural connotations and cannot join in with them due to modern living, thus, observing the moon during the *Mid-autumn Festival* is difficult for people living in smog-filled high-rise cities. Traditional folk arts that supported these festivals were seen during the Cultural Revolution as 'backward sectors' and socialist collective ownership was imposed. Many traditional skills such as Dragon Boat building are dying out and those skills being lost over time. Key festival symbols have been lost or confused in recent times. For Wang et al., primary amongst these is the loss of the 24 cycle Chinese Lunar Calendar (upon which festival dates were set) in 1912 when the Gregorian calendar was adopted, causing confusion as the translation of dates year to year was no longer fixed but in constant flux. They also see traditional festive symbols becoming commercialised and the themes that were attached to specific festivals being applied to other and unconnected events, so the Chinese patriotism of the *Dragon Boat Festival* has been grafted onto the *Tomb Sweeping Festival,* with the worship not of ancestors but of heroes of the revolution. Finally, Western festival culture with its globalised festival industry, economic strength and imitation of Chinese festivals has meant that festivals such as *Valentine's Day* have replaced the *Qixi Festival,* and chocolates and roses have replaced seven-hole needle threading. Becker observes how many Chinese have 'abandoned their traditional sweets, such as mooncakes passed around at the *Autumn Moon Festival,* and began to buy chocolate' (2000: 190). The emphasis now is on 'holiday' rather than celebration, as Wang et al. state:

> Nowadays people still spend the holidays, but mostly they are just superficial, only a few cultural symbols like festival souvenir, festival food and festive entertainments which can bring about economic benefits can get some attention in the social environment dominated by consumption market, whereas the profound inherent spirits, emotions and cultural connections are often intentionally or unintentionally ignored (2014: 56).

Our own research this year has shown how the older generation in Lianyungang echo these fears about the young losing sight of their traditional culture, talking about the *Journey to the West Festival,* one lady noted that, "It is a good way to help the youth to know more about Chinese traditional culture".

In 2009 the Chinese Ministry of Culture placed two festivals on the UNESCO list of the Intangible Cultural Heritage of Humanity, the *Qiang New Year Festival* of Sichuan Province, and the *Dragon Boat Festival,* and in doing so made a number of commitments to financial support, safeguarding measures, documenting, and educational activities (UNESCO, 2015). Interestingly in their application to UNESCO the Ministry identify "declining interest in Qiang heritage amongst the young and the impact of outside cultures" as being key factors putting the festival at risk (UNESCO, 2015). Another indication of the change in official support for festivals and their role in contemporary China is the increase in national holidays from 11 in 2008 to 27 in 2015, with festivals such as *Chinese New Year, Ching Ming Festival, Dragon Boat Festival, Mid-Autumn Festival* and *Chung Yeung Festival* being clearly prominent.

As we shall see shortly it is not just the upholding and rejuvenating of traditional festivals that mark the contemporary approach to festivals in China, but also the development of new festivals, and festive activity. It is clear from the research that the traditional festivals have been reintegrated into Chinese national culture, although they remain in large part home- and family-based celebrations.

## Lianyungang, industry and tourism

Lianyungang is a prefecture-level coastal city and logistics centre on the Yellow Sea, which is in the north-east of Jiangsu province. Lianyungang has a long history from the Xia and Shang Dynasties (2000 BC). To Westerners it was known as Haichow (Island in the Ocean) for many centuries and was one of the first ports to be opened up to foreign traders in the seventeenth century.

For centuries Lianyungang has played an important role in Chinese development related to the economy and the various 'open door' trade policies. One of the original 1858 Treaty Ports, in 1984 Lianyungang was selected as one of the fourteen Opening Port Cities (OPC), the main bases for international trade into and out of China. Of key importance to contemporary Lianyungang is the development of the One Belt One Road (OBOR) strategy announced by Chinese President Xi Jinping in 2013. The strategy has two elements to it, the Silk Road Economic Belt (SREB) and the Maritime Silk Road (MSR). The belt stretches from China's coastal ports via the 'string of pearls' (international ports) to central Asia and Europe. The latter is particularly important to Lianyungang as its tradition as a sea port and its vital connections to the outside world now mean that it is a central part of the OBOR plan, especially in connecting China to the ASEAN countries. Lianyungang is also at the Eastern end of the Eurasian land bridge, so it also occupies a key role on the SREB.

In order to boost international attention to this development plan, 2015 was declared the Year of Silk Road Tourism. Lianyungang, central to both the MSR and the SREB, clearly has an important cultural role to play, as well as its economic one. The main tourist features of the city and district of Lianyungang can be described in four words: sea, antiquity, mystery and peacefulness. Sea is its core competitive advantage, as one of China's biggest container ports. Lianyungang's tourism also starts from the sea; it is a beach resort, with Lian Island and the scenic environment moving from the coast up to Huaguo Mountain being its main attractions. The meaning of 'antiquity' is that the area dates back to the stone-age. In Kongwangshan it has one of the earliest images of the Buddha, and Sun Yua Palace dates back to the Tang Dynasty (618 -907 AD). 'Mysterious' is used to describe Huaguo Mountain itself, the Water Curtain Cave and the Lingquan Spring that is believed to lead to the Dragon King's Palace. The last word, 'peaceful', represents the environment of Lianyungang, especially the views of the harbour, sea and mountain. In all, there are fourteen scenic resorts and around 116 beauty spots in Lianyungang. The air quality of Lianyungang is also one of best amongst Chinese cities. All these elements combine to attract tourists.

There are clearly a number of dynamics at play here which combine to make Lianyungang an illustrative case study of the role of festivals in contemporary China. Firstly the drive to economic development, has meant that Lianyungang is perfectly placed to play a major role in the OROB policy, its already well established tourism industry, plus the re-emergence of support for 'traditional festivals' discussed earlier in the chapter, with the emphasis on using tradition and traditional images and themes to attract tourism and business, all work together to make up the whole cultural environment and offering.

## The festivals of Lianyungang

At the turn of the millennium the Lianyungang Municipal Government established the growth of tourism as one of its main economic objectives, looking to develop experience and expertise, and to 'vigorously' expand the domestic tourism market into a growing international one. Correspondingly, there has also been a growth in the development of festivals which are held in Lianyungang and its region, and the economic and cultural impacts of tourism have become a much larger part of the city's economy.

The key festivals are *The Lianyungang Dragon Boat Festival, The Journey to the West Cultural Festival,* and *The Summer of Lianyungang Festival.* The first we discuss is the *Dragon Boat Festival,* a traditional festival with a long history deep in the roots of ancient China. The second, the *Journey to the West Festival,* is a recent invention, that revolves around the evocation of the Monkey story from ancient Chinese literature that has been developed to utilise Lianyungang's connection to this story as the 'Monkey King's hometown'. The *Summer of Lianyungang Festival* is a key local and regional festival designed to showcase Lianyungang's cultural and physical attributes, and to develop the tourism potential of the city and district.

Before discussing these three festivals as the main case studies in our research, it is worth emphasising that although these festivals are emblematic of China's new approach to festivals, they are not the whole story of the festival activity in Lianyungang. Other festivals in the Lianyungang administrative zone reflect the very specific nature of parts of the area, such as the multi-art form based *Magnolia Festival,* set around the four ancient magnolia trees in the Donglei District, which celebrates the traditions and varieties of the magnolia. The *Donghai Crystal Festival* held since 1991 celebrates Donghai as the capital of China's crystal production. It combines arts performance, exhibitions, crystal seminars and a crystal market, and attracts both tourists and representatives of the crystal industry. The *Haizhou Lantern Festival,* like all traditional *Chinese Lantern Festivals* marks the end of the *Spring Festival* (*Chinese New Year Festival*), on the fifteenth day of the first lunar month. Haizhou is the old district of Lianyungang and the festival attracts both local and regional tourists.

Our research in Lianyungang has shown that many of the 'traditional' Chinese festivals such as *Qingming* (tomb-sweeping), *Qixi Festival* (Double seven Festival), are observed within the family, or between individuals, not as officially, or nationally sanctioned festivals.

All of these festivals contribute to the notion of Lianyungang as a 'city with festivals', like so many others in China, which are aiming to build a tourist strand to their economic development as well as defend a notion of cultural heritage manifested in their folk, regional and Chinese identity.

## The *Dragon Boat Festival*

As one of China's traditional festivals, the *Dragon Boat Festival* is one of the most ubiquitous of the Han nationality tradition. The *Dragon Boat Festival* is held on the fifth day of the fifth month (lunar calendar) annually, and usually covers three days of celebration with only one being an official holiday. The festival is often associated with the story of the suicide of Qu Yuan, a third century BC statesman, who drowned in the Miluo River, and commemorates the frantic race to search for his body. The festival is held in order to show respect to Qu Yuan, and the story teaches people about the Chinese spirit, to be loyal, respectful of elders and ancestors, benevolent and righteous. As part of this search for the body of Qu Yuan, the rescuers threw rice into the water to distract the fishes from his body. Traditionally the key event of the festival is the dragon boat racing re-enacting the attempted retrieval of Qu's body. Zongzi (traditional Chinese rice-pudding) is also part of the festival, recalling the rice thrown into the river; it is made at home and eaten as the traditional food.

It is probably the case that the festival predates this event and may originally have been held as part of the summer solstice celebrations where it was believed the yin and the yang collide. The belief was that the yang (spring into summer) began to lose its power around this time as the yin (autumn into winter) was in the ascendancy. The power of the yin begins to increase and the festival comes at a point in the year when the evil spirits that bring diseases need to be warded off, thus people's houses are cleansed and protected by hanging herbs such as mugwort and calamus around doors and windows. Specially prepared wine is also drunk and sprinkled around the house. These also ward off the five poisonous creatures, the snake, scorpion, toad, gecko and centipede. The *Dragon Boat Festival,* also known as the *Health Festival* which may endorse its older origins, is linked, like so many festivals, to seasonality; the weather becomes hotter and May is the month when insects emerge and bring diseases, especially mosquitos in Lianyungang. There are some special folk activities in Lianyungang which link to the *Dragon Boat/Health Festival* in this period, thus people will use some folk prescriptions to keep healthy. The time of the *Dragon Boat Festival* is good for dietary therapy. Thus, these traditional medical ideas become part of the many traditional ways to celebrate this festival in Lianyungang, key among these are:

- People will put wormwood into the bath, then take a shower with the water to help the body become healthy and keep away some skin diseases.

- According to the ideas of traditional Chinese medical science, the belly button and the anus are the most sensitive areas of the body. Using bezoar on these areas can kill bad insects and help avoid diseases.
- Eat goose eggs, radish pickled with black sugar and five special foods. Radish will be matured during this festival, so local people will use it to make a dish which can help joint health. The five special foods are eel, yellow croaker, cucumber, salted duck eggs and Shaoxing wine. All these foods are good for health and the effect will be best during festival time, so this tradition has been kept.
- Wear perfumed sachets with seven coloured threads around them (again to ward against insects).

The dragon boat racing itself takes place on the East Yan He river in the city, and is held between different teams and different levels of ability. As dragon boat racing is now an official sport in China, there are different levels, national, provincial and city. The races held during the festival are city level. So what started with an informal festival activity in 2008 became part of the formal sporting calendar, and is now very much a competitive activity. Consequently this aspect of the festival is organised as part of the sporting competition by the dragon boat racing authorities. The *Dragon Boat Festival* then combines a focus on family, the home, health and the historic and patriotic celebration of Qu Yuan. The focus in Lianyungang is on the home and family with spectatorship of the Dragon Boat races on the river being approached as a sporting event.

## The *Journey to the West* and *Summer of Lianyungang Festivals*

There are two key annual festivals organised by the Lianyungang Municipal Government. The first, the *Journey to the West Cultural Festival* builds on pre-existing and proven local historical and mythological attractions, the second *Summer of Lianyungang Festival*, draws on the city's marine attributes and its arts and cultural products.

The *Journey to the West Festival* began in 2010 and runs from September to October every year. Based around the sixteenth century Chinese classic novel of the same name, the *Journey to the West Cultural Festival* clearly aims to attract the tourist market both internally and externally. The reason for the festival being held here is that Lianyungang is where Cheng'en Wu wrote the book. The idea for the book also has its origins in the city; in the tale, the Monkey King is born out of a rock on Huaguo Mountain and later he chooses the Water Curtain Caves as his home. The festival was started and is run by the municipal government, with the aim of providing a platform for visitors to learn more about the novel, *Journey to the West*, and as a focal point for celebrating the story and its connections with Lianyungang. One respondent said the festival helped her to recall a childhood memory of the story. It thus has an educative and, at the same time, a promotional function, drawing on an internationally known story to attract local, national and international visitors, indeed providing a brand for Lianyungang to develop its tourism identity around.

In the first year of the festival, the events focused on promoting the local area, and establishing the festival as a major local event, but also with potentially a national and international audience. The municipal government wanted to promote the festival widely, so there was a big investment in a spectacular opening ceremony and also a re-reading of the novel, and these became the two main events. In subsequent years the festival has attracted 'headline acts' and well-known artists came to do displays around the theme of *Journey to the West*.

By 2013, the events featured in the festival had become more diverse. Because of the new One Belt and One Road policy, more visitors from outside the area came to the city and this has influenced the content of the festival. The cultural content of this festival is no longer only limited to local reference points but is combined with other cultural references, both nationally and internationally. Because of this the festival has grown as more events have been included in the programme. There is a strong family audience with respondents saying the festival gave "chances for families to be together". For some members of the older generation, attending a festival like this was a new experience.

Through this festival, local tourism has grown, and there is clearly an element of local pride in the *Journey to the West* connection. Research showed that those audience members who had come from outside the area were either on business in Lianyungang, or were tourists. This festival then has become the characteristic event of Lianyungang.

*The Summer of Lianyungang Festival* is the key festival aimed at promoting local culture and maximising the existing tourism potential of Lianyungang. The festival started in July 1997 on Dao beach, with an opening ceremony encompassing land, sea and air. A key event harking to the Journey to the West story was the 'Golden Monkey welcomes guests' pageant. Locally supplied elements included the Donghai County Ganyu Drum team, a local Dragon Dance team performance, the Liandao fishing boats and the Qingdao Sailing school. The climax was a skydiving exhibition by the National Parachuting Team.

The 2014 *Summer of Lianyungang Festival* took place in the 30,000 seat Lianyungang Metro Seagull Square stadium, and had as its theme the 'Silk Road co-operation with Jiangsu coastal development', bringing together the main focus of the municipal government on tourist development, exhibition development, and trade. Three key elements were: strengthening the linkages between the city and the counties; developing internal and external trade links; and attracting domestic and foreign friends to come over. Traditional Chinese entertainments such as fireworks, dance and acrobatics, combined with 3D technology and laser shows to visually demonstrate the themes of the event. Other activities during the season included concerts, a food festival, and a *Chinese Painting Biennale*.

## Conclusions

As we have seen, the fortunes of contemporary festivals in China are inextricably tied to that of tourism and thence to the economy, but also the political will to defend Chinese traditional culture and identity. What is also true and mirrored in our research is that as the greater economy grows and people get richer they have more money to spend on festive activity. As one of our respondents indicated, when she was young, "the events during festivals were not so many, when people are not rich enough all they need to think is the cost of daily lives", however some traditional customs are always there, "people just try to make them high quality, for example, the content of Zongzi may be different because meat is expensive during a hard time".

Festivals (particularly traditional festivals) fared badly during the period of the Cultural Revolution, being regional, historical, based on custom and superstition. The drive to revive them has only really emerged with the turn of the millennium and the economic/tourism motive, combined with the defence against the arrival of the Western events calendar. Indeed the movement of traditional festivals in the twentieth century from very public affairs to them being private, quiet, family occasions has not been reversed to any great extent, with the exception of the *Chinese New Year*. The link between festivity and health in traditional Chinese festivals is an interesting one, and as we saw linked to the realities of the season and the turn of the natural world.

Clearly the Lianyungang municipal government is keen to develop and promote its natural and cultural advantages in terms of tourist activity, its two key festivals *Lianyungang Summer* and *Journey to the West Cultural Festival*, are at the forefront of this endeavour as are its trade expos such as this year's *Silk Road International Logistics Expo*. For the people of Lianyungang these provide entertainments as we have seen, and build on the area's cultural connections, bringing in tourists and being used as a focus for entertaining visiting businesses. Clearly festivals and their roles have been rehabilitated in contemporary China. The reinvigorating of traditional festivals is important when combined with the growing number of national holidays, meaning families can spend more time together, a precious commodity in an economically progressive China.

## Bibliography

Arlt, W. G. (2008) Chinese Tourists in 'Elsewhereland': Behaviour and perceptions of mainland Chinese tourists at different destinations, in J. Cochrane (ed.) *Asian Tourism: Growth and Change*, Oxford: Elsevier. 134–144.

Becker, J. (2000) *The Chinese*, London: John Murray.

Bonavia, D. (1981) *The Chinese: A portrait*, London: Allen Lane

China Daily (2005) Festivals are Lifeblood of Traditional Culture, in *China Daily*, 12 August 2005.

China Today (2004) Remembering Traditional Chinese Festivals, in *China Today*, July 2004.

Clark, P. (2008) *The Chinese Cultural Revolution: A History*, Cambridge: Cambridge University Press

Fu, Y., Long, P., and Thomas, R. (2015) Diaspora community festivals and tourism, in C. Newbold, C. Maughan, J. Jordan, and F. Bianchini, *Focus on Festivals: Contemporary European Case Studies and Perspectives*, Oxford: Goodfellow.

Gittings, J. (1989) *China Changes Face: The road from revolution 1949 - 1989*, Oxford: Oxford University Press.

Huang, S. (1991) Chinese traditional festivals, in *Journal of Popular Culture*, Winter 1991, **25**(3), 163–180.

Liming, W. (2011) *Chinese Festivals*, Cambridge: Cambridge University Press.

Pleskacheuskaya, I. (2004) Chinese festivals: Keeping traditions alive, *China Today*, January.

Sofield, T. H. B., and Li, F. M. S. (1988) Tourism development and cultural policies in China, in *Annals of Tourism Research*, **25**(2), 362–392.

UNESCO (2015) www.unesco.org/culture/ich/index.php?1g=en&pg=00011&RL=00225, accessed 03/09/2015

Wang, J., Tang, X., Pang, Y., and Duan, W. (2014) Analysis on modern anomie situation of Chinese Traditional Festivals, in *Asian Culture and History*, **6**(2) Toronto: Canadian Centre of Science and Education, 56–63.

Yeh, C-L. (2009) Politicizing Chinese New Year Festivals: Cold War politics transnational conflicts, and Chinese America, in Ross, M. H. (ed.) *Culture and Belonging in Divided Societies: Contestation and symbolic landscapes*, Philadelphia: University of Pennsylvania Press.

# 21 Festivals that Change Lives

Floriane Gaber

## Introduction

There are countries in the world where 'freedom' and 'democracy' don't have the same meaning as in our western European countries, especially in the street or in what is called 'public space'. Even so, in some of these countries, street art festivals exist and they can change the life of the artists and of the population. Jürgen Habermas, in *The Structural Transformation of the Public Sphere* (1962), has defined this term. According to him, the bourgeois public sphere (which appeared in the 18th century) is the place between private individuals and government authorities in which people can meet and have critical debates about public matters. Whether debates are about culture, habits or law, in the countries discussed in this chapter (Iran, Belarus, Morocco and Kuwait), this barely happens. Critical debate is forbidden or simply inconceivable.

## Street art festivals

If one considers that Thespis on his chariot was the first actor and that his performances in the streets of ancient Greece led to the creation of tragedy, street art performances are several thousand years old. One can also mention the Middle Ages performances on the parvis, pavements or in public squares, and the acrobats and ropewalkers travelling from one city to another, following the merchants in the fairs. But what is considered as street art performances nowadays dates from the late 60s, early 70s, and appeared in the United States, then in United Kingdom and France (Gaber, 2009). At that time societies were shaken by social conflict and large demonstrations in favour of racial and sexual minorities, or peace in Vietnam flooded out into the avenues. Artists would play music, carry huge puppets, revive *commedia dell'arte*, etc. alongside the protestors.

In France, the phenomenon has increased too, so that today there are 1100 street companies and 300 festivals dedicated to street performances. But in the pioneers' time, it was not always easy to perform on the sidewalks. It was (and still is) forbidden to perform outdoor if 'causing a breach on the peace' in France and, except in festival time, the artists would be arrested by the police. It is one of the reasons why today artistic performances can hardly be found in the street outside festival times. Festival organisers themselves have to ask permission to cause a breach on the peace 'under control'. If an artist decides to perform the same act the day after the end of festival, on the same corner in the same city, he may get a penalty because he has got no permission from the mayor (who's in charge of public order). In the country of 'Freedom, Equality and Brotherhood', citizens are not allowed to do anything they want wherever they want.

In Europe, laws about the use of public space are different in each country, but still it is permitted to perform and to organise a festival if one gets the proper authorisation. *Aurillac's Festival*, one of the biggest for street art in France, celebrated its 30th birthday in August 2015. Nowadays local authorities rarely prevent artists from organising an event and people are used to watching shows in the streets, in the frame of festivals occurring in the city one morning and disappearing a couple of days later. But there are countries where it is not so, in which artists and organisers still have to struggle to be allowed to perform in so-called 'public space' or to address social or political issues.

## Street art festivals in Iran

Recent changes in the geopolitical sphere might seem to have opened the gates and helped Iran renew relations with foreign countries. Despite this, what can be done and said in the street or in public space is strictly controlled by the authorities. But as it was the case in former Soviet Union satellite countries, artists find ways to show themselves on the sidewalks and develop very creative ways of weaving a subtext into their performances. They never address an issue head on, they pretend just to tell a traditional tale, or a story situated in another time or another country.

In Iran, 250 street companies get subsidies from the Ministry of Culture and Religious Affairs, so do 10 street festivals organised in the regions and in the capital. To be allowed to perform, a company must submit their text or project to a national committee that will give the authorisation or not. For festivals, the national committee keeps an eye on the programme and decides which plays can be performed or not. In this context, street arts in Iran are extremely diverse, as they use all the old tricks that artists have been using for centuries, in all countries, to elude censorship, and at the same time they try to develop experimental forms for the same purpose. Their goal is not only to express themselves, but to give the population the opportunity to see that it is possible to 'resist', pretending to accept the rules but indeed twisting them, on stage as in everyday life.

The street companies address the many different topics with which the people are strongly concerned, and most of the time they denounce the behaviour of the authorities regarding these issues. For example, when an actor plays his solo show about drug addiction, he of course supports the national fight against this huge problem, but his props are made of all the needles and material he has found in the park of the city where he's performing and, thus, one can understand that he is accusing the mayor and health services of not finding proper solutions to overcome this plague. The audience, pressing up on the sidewalk, can't believe their eyes when the actor chooses one of the spectators and offers him a syringe. Is it for real or not? Some of them hesitate, don't know, but all of them are facing the problem of drug addiction, in its worst aspect, in the flow of their daily life. They'll probably look at junkies in a different way when they meet one.

The same principle can be seen when a company performs a play about the distress of farmers in Northern Iran, about women's situation in the countryside, and the 'droit de seigneur' that still exists in remote areas. They pretend to tell a story inspired by a tale: "Once upon a time, there was a female farmer struggling to keep her land, against wild boars and against the lord keen to rape her and seize her farm..." Indeed the company denounces the behaviour of the state and the big industrial farms that ruin the smaller ones, and the way that women are treated almost as having no social rights. At the end, the female farmer (of the story) commits suicide and her house is destroyed by the boars. Nobody can be indifferent: what solutions could be found to create a different outcome in real life, for farmers or for women?

## Belarus is not Russia

One remembers movies with the Cold War as a backdrop: spies and plain clothes policemen are everywhere; nobody dares to speak frankly in public or even in private spaces, and people disappear all of a sudden, and some of them never to return. Nowadays, there are still plain clothes policemen merging into the crowd in Russia (as well as in France in big demonstrations or events) and 'causing a breach on the peace' is more than ever a sword of Damocles. But Russia and Belarus treat street performances in a different way. *Archangelsk Festival*, takes place in the streets, on the riverside, in the squares, and people are free to come and go, as the artists are free to play and walkabout as they want. Run by Victor Panov's company for decades in Archangel, a remote city in the north of European Russia, this is a noteworthy exception as most the street festivals in Russia are 'under control'. Neither the audience nor the artists are allowed to stay and walk in the streets of the cities where the events take place. In Saint Petersburg and Moscow, the main street festivals are organised in a big park, whose gates are supervised by police and security guards.

In Perm, the *White Nights Festival* is even worse for the street artists. Just at the foot of the cityhall, the big empty square that used to be a slum before the old buildings were torn down, is perfect for the large military demonstrations. That's where the *White Nights Festival* takes place. Indeed, each summer the local authorities build tall fences and security gates supervised by bodyguards. In this enclosure, the people and the artists are 'free' to move, but it is strictly forbidden to put a toe on the sidewalk. If the police catch them, the artists and the artistic director find themselves with big problems (that's what happened when the Slovenian company Kjud Ljud performed their *Pink People* show out of the fences). One can say that Perm has (re)invented 'open air indoor' street arts.

Belarus street festivals don't work like this. Especially in Minsk, the capital, where the government has placed towers overlooking the city, 'causing a breach on the peace' is to be considered seriously. The laws are strict and censorship is not an empty word. How do the organisers of festivals play with the rules? Each big city in Belarus celebrates the building of the city day, the end of the Second World War, Independence, etc. Those days, the city councils organise military demonstrations in the streets. In Minsk, the organisers of the Street Theatre Forum have asked permission to organise a 'cultural demonstration' on the same day, on other streets in the city, and they got it!

How come that these young artists dared to ask for permission? A couple of years ago, Kjud Ljud (the same company that 'escaped' from the enclosure in Perm) had been invited by the big and very official indoor theatre festival in Minsk. They had proposed to run a workshop, and of course this workshop would take place in the street. According to a young Belarussian actress, when she heard that they would go and rehearse in the open air, she thought: "I'm dead. I'll be caught and thrown into jail." She hardly dared to put a toe on the square, full of fear, on the lookout for the policemen. But after one or two minutes, the policemen staying on the corner, watching but not running onto the actors to arrest them, she could breathe, and says: "This minute has changed my life", just because she knew that "It is possible" while she had always thought that it was not.

Performing in the street in Minsk is giving the opportunity to the people to experiment with this feeling of freedom, of just being able to enjoy a performance in the public space, in the middle of a crowd, and this performance not being a military demonstration and yourself not being obliged to be there on pain of big trouble. This simple feeling can help people overcome the weight of being under control in all aspects of everyday life.

## Street arts in Maghreb and Middle East

Morocco and Kuwait are two Southern countries where the weather can be very hot. In the first one, the sun helps people living outdoors, being curious and enjoying every new proposal, especially if it would be an artistic one. In the second country, the 45 to 50 degrees Celsius push the wealthy people to spend most of their time in their air-conditioned cars, never mingling with the poorer migrant workers. So too the 'expats' in Morocco, a former French protectorate.

In order to have the different types of people meeting, the *Earth Event*, in Kuwait, uses a very simple strategy: ambassadors, local wealthy or middle class people, expats, students, etc., are invited, be it formally or informally (via social networks, having children decorating the site, or involving volunteers who may invite their relatives). The event is an open air night-show, organised as a journey through different places, with several acts. When the audience arrives at the front gate, each person is assigned to a group, and each group is given a colour and asked to follow the 'shepherd' wearing a shirt of that colour. In each group, there is a mixture of ambassadors, expats, wealthy or middle-class people, students, children and workers and they attend the acts together, sharing these particular moments and experiences. Such communal activity is not common in Kuwait. First of all because street performances are very new in the country because of the heat; but also because they never mingle with the other classes or groups in the population. But the surprise of attending such a show, in such conditions, lets all of them be more open minded than they are in their daily life and, at the end, for the finale, when the whole audience gathers together, it's even stronger. This event gives people an opportunity to experiment with "living together or alongside" the other members of the community, and to erase the social gaps, albeit for a short moment. But this moment could become a habit the more the people attend street events like this.

In Morocco, for ten years, *Awaln'art Festival* has been bringing street shows everywhere in the country, from small villages around Marrakech to big cities like Casablanca, Agadir and of course on Jeema El Fna, the Marrakesh square famous for its traditional storytellers and snake charmers. In these different contexts, the choice of the type of performance is crucial to the acceptance of new forms of arts in a country full a rich and age-old traditions. But moreover shows in the street can address social modern issues, like the situation of women in Maghreban society. Denouncing head-on the way some of them are brutally treated would be ineffective, but presenting, in the public space, an act in which two acrobats mimic a love story full of tenderness and of respect can open the eyes and the mind of men as well and women and, who knows, change their life or the lives of their children.

That's what street arts are about, everywhere in the world, in different kinds of contexts. They help people reconsider their way of life, their relation to their fellow citizens, to their relatives, and sometimes to themselves. They help people feel stronger towards unjust authorities and give them the opportunity to experiment with new ways of behaving, safely thanks to the artists and the organisers who know how to play with the rules when critical debates about public matters are not allowed.

## Bibliography

Dacheux, E. (2008) *L'Espace public*, Paris: CNRS Editions.

Habermas, J. (1978) *L'Espace public*, 1st edn 1962, Paris: Payot.

Gaber, F. (2009) *Comment* ça *commença*, Paris: Ici et là.

Gaber, F. (2015) The unintended consequence of festivals, in C. Newbold, C. Maughan, J. Jordan, and F. Bianchini, *Focus on Festivals: Contemporary European case studies and perspectives*. Oxford: Goodfellow., 191-200.

# 22 A Holy Week Carnival? The *Iberoamerican Theater Festival of Bogotá*[1]

Paolo Vignolo

## Introduction

This chapter explores the entangled relations of a contemporary and post-traditional festival with a much older festive substrate associated with *Holy Week* and *Carnival*. In this sense it is not intended as a systematic study of the *Iberoamerican Theater Festival of Bogotá (ITFB)*, much less as a summary of its more than two decade long history. My more modest goal is to read this festival as a material and rhetorical *dispositif* arising in response to a social crisis (Castro Gómez, 2011), closely related to what I have called elsewhere regimes of festive alteration (Vignolo, 2015: 138-159):

1 The *fiesta-bonanza*, distinguished by excess and associated with human, territorial, and resource exploitation on the frontier of capitalist expansion (Braudel, 2002; Taussig, 1980: xii).

2 the *fiesta-revolution*, dominated by the trope of inversion and aiming to undermine the status quo, disrupt the social order, and scramble established dichotomies (Bakhtin, 1984; Eco, 1984).

3 The *fiesta-passion*, where the ritual sacrifice of a savior figure provides the community with a chance to separate from the conflicts that threaten its unity, through the trope of transfiguration. (Girard 1977; Esposito, 2003).

Intertwined, superimposed, and interarticulated, they encompass practically all the festive events of the last 30 years in Colombia, and it would be possible to trace their genealogy back to colonial times (Vignolo, 2015: 139).

## Prelude: "I want my funeral to be a real carnival"

Theater notable Fanny Mikey, the legendary founder of the *Iberoamerican Theater Festival of Bogotá*, died on August 16, 2008. Her wake was held in the Colombian Capitol Building in the style of a great state funeral, the first time that such an honor had been accorded to any person of her profession. Thousands of people waited for hours to bid their final farewell to this Argentine woman from a Lithuanian Jewish family, who had once explained that "I am very proud of my country, which is Colombia. One is born in the place of one's choosing." (Mikey, 2007). On the solemn occasion of her wake, held in a chamber more frequently used to honor the country's founders and great heroes of the Republic, the red wig for which she was known was placed atop the coffin, creating an iconic image that is used today on posters, parades and even in national stamps.

In keeping with her last wishes, the city government moved a salsa festival then in progress to the Plaza de Bolívar in front of the Capitol, turning her funeral solemnities into a "an all-out carnival and celebration". "She was very clear on this," said her son Daniel Álvarez (2008) to the media, "when I go," she said, "I don't want mourning. No, nothing like that... I just want them to bring Joe Arroyo... and I want them to dance, because life goes on." Actress Margarita Ortega (2008) added, "Luckily, Fanny got her way as always. She even turned her own leave-taking into a great festival."

## Act I: the struggle between Carnival and Lent (1988-1994)

Indeed, a great festival is the reason for Fanny's huge popularity. The personal charisma of its founder has without a doubt played a central role in making the *Iberoamerican Theater Festival of Bogotá* one of the premier theater events in the world. Fanny brought together a consuming passion for the theater – which gave her credibility and influence in the profession – with an extraordinary talent for entrepreneurship that she applied tenaciously and effectively to a pursuit as apparently unprofitable as the performing arts. The context of her efforts, however, was decisive in her success. In 1988, Bogotá was a city on the verge of collapse, brought on by paroxysms of violence between the traditional political elite and the *nouveau riche* of the cocaine boom. For the first time since the 1940s the ongoing war in Colombia had burst into the urban environment with a wave of bombings, kidnappings, and targeted killings. Ramiro Osorio (2014), co-director with Fanny Mikey of the *FITB* in its first four years, remembers:

> That may have been the most difficult time of the war with drug traffickers, and we opted for culture as an agent of peace in response to the terror we felt as a result of the mafias' violent attempt to assert their control over society. It was an opportunity to open a new window, to let some fresh air into this country, and give people a chance to dialogue with the cultures of the outside world.

The very idea of holding an international theater festival in the midst of this situation struck some as absurd and quixotic. But that was precisely what made it such a powerful and seductive challenge.

### An act of faith in Colombia

The first of the festivals was called 'An act of faith in Colombia'. No finer name could have been found, for it was profound yet appealed to common sense.

Above all it evoked a miracle, an epiphany, a passion that could generate a collective resurrection.

Fundamental to this idea was the risky decision for the festival to coincide with *Holy Week*. The organizers chose this week for practical reasons above all: fewer people are working, the city is quieter, and hotel occupancy is down. Nonetheless, the symbolism was huge.

The proposal met with fierce opposition from the Catholic hierarchy from the Archbishop down, to whom it was sacrilege for a theater festival to coincide with the celebration of Easter. The festive tradition in Bogotá still revolved around a liturgical calendar whose most important events were the *Procession of Corpus Christi*, the *Christmas novena*, and *Holy Week*.

The very idea that carnivalesque parades would compete with the processions of the *Via Crucis*, that crowds would throng to theaters rather than churches, that loud applause would be heard in place of solemn prayer, and that the Passion of Christ would not be the most important dramatic representation in that holiest of weeks simply outraged those ultraconservatives who had still not reconciled to living in a modern metropolis that no longer conformed to the parochial ways of the small city they once knew. As arguments grew more pointed, the atmosphere darkened and anonymous threats were received.

On the fourth day of the festival, a bomb exploded in the National Theater during a performance. The explosion devastated the hall, the dressing rooms, the offices, and the rest rooms. Luckily there were no deaths and only one minor injury among the actors and the 450 people in attendance. Asked for comment by the news media, Fanny Mikey simply said "God is with us" (Dorado, 2000: 127).

Unexpectedly, what could have been a tragedy resulted in a massive outpouring of support for the festival. All the Colombian and international theater groups that were present decided to stay on, and the public reflected their determination, refusing to be intimidated. The audience that was in the theater on the day of the explosion even returned for a rescheduled performance on the next day. In her memoirs, Fanny remembers the following day:

> The first call was at 7:30 in the morning; it was from President Barco. "Fanny," he said… "I want you to know that I'm with you." … later in the morning I was in the office when at about 11:00 a man called saying he would talk only to me. "I'm the lawyer for the extraditables," which at that time was a way to refer to the leaders of drug cartels like Pablo Escobar, Rodríguez Gacha, all of them together… Anyway, their lawyer says to me that "We wanted to let you know that it wasn't us and if you need any help or anything we're here for you." The guerrillas called the same day, so sweet, to tell me that they were with us too, and that they hadn't planted the bomb either (Dorado, 2000: 127-128).

The government, the cartel, the paramilitaries, the guerrillas.... For once – and maybe for the only time – every armed group in the complex Colombian war of the 1980s agreed on one thing: they were in solidarity with a theater festival! The act of faith had truly generated a miracle.

## The retaking of the palace

The festival was scheduled to culminate with a final performance in the city's Plaza de Bolívar, in front of the country's most important cathedral. A Catalan theater company called Els Comediants was to present a show called *The Demons*, inspired by the grotesque imaginary of medieval carnivals. This had been one of the primary motivations for the Church's harsh criticism of the *FITB*.

To Colombians, though, the site of this performance had an even greater symbolic importance. The work was to be performed directly in front of the heavily damaged facade of what had been the Palace of Justice. Other than public prosecutors, no one had entered the ruins of this building for three years, since the M-19 guerrilla group had seized it in broad daylight, taking hostage 350 people who were inside, including most of the members of the Supreme Court. The army intervened with tanks and destroyed the building, killing 98 people inside, including both guerrillas and their hostages. 11 people brought out alive by the military were subsequently tortured and disappeared. This series of events have come to be known as the taking and retaking of the Palace of Justice. (Valbuena García, 2015: 29-89)

The third taking of the building was intended to be festive, but as the threats continued, and despite impressive security measures, the situation was tense. The members of the theater troupe were anxious. Nonetheless, public attendance was massive, greater than had ever been seen for a night-time performance in the city. Between 60,000 and 100,000 people poured into the plaza.

It was a landmark experience for Colombians to see the Palace of Justice in flames once again, with loud fireworks, diabolical figures hanging from rooftops, and the public square bursting at the seams with the enormous crowd. It was a cathartic first theatrical representation of an enduring trauma in the country's collective memory. At the same it also became an act of resistance against those who would spread terror with the use of bombs, and an unprecedented act of citizen participation for a population clamoring to reclaim the streets and squares of the capital city. At the end of the show, the crowd joined their voices in singing the national anthem.

## The world on a stage

In this sense, the 'act of faith' expressed a collective pride, long trampled and frustrated in a Colombia that seemed to have strayed off course in its own national project. Some among the audience may have recognized in the name a literary reference to a story by Jorge Luis Borges (1998: 9) in which a Norwegian woman asks the protagonist what it means to be Colombian, and he replies cryptically, "I don't know. It is an act of faith." Beyond literary references, though, to the great majority of the hundreds of thousands who attended the *FITB* in its first year, daring to going out on the street and fill the theaters despite the horrendous traffic, the muggings, and the blackouts was courageous, an expression of active citizenship. The public in Bogotá received the festival works with a contagious enthusiasm, a festive ardor that infected even the visiting artists. It was the other face of the palpable anguish felt in the city day to day.

The incipient economic opening of those years was accompanied by a collective hunger to open the country in other ways: to other people, other places, and other cultures. There was a custom (which persists) of referring to cultural products based on their country of origin, which produced among spectators the illusion that they were travelling the world while seated in a theater. For this audience in the early 1990s, the festival represented a virtual Theatrum Mundi, a cartography of the international dramatic arts.

Like Argentinean art critic Marta Traba in the 1960s, Fanny Mikey brought new winds of globalized modernity to the fervid but still very inward looking world of Colombian theater.

> "Before the FITB, the most modern things to come through Bogotá were Zarzuela and ballet–classical and Spanish", recalls Ana Marta de Pizarro, the current festival director (Fernández-Santos, Elsa, 2014). Ricardo Camacho, director of *Teatro Libre*, is unequivocal in stating that the festival deparochialized Colombian and Latin American theater. "Theater people who could not leave the country were completely marginalized, condemned to inventing what was already invented." (Lozano,1998)

In some cases, the internationalization of artistic itineraries had lasting effects. For example, Mano Chau and his group Mano Negra came to the country just for the festival but stayed for more than a year in order to develop the project The Train of Ice and Fire, a visionary project that traced the route of an abandoned train line between Santa Marta and Bogotá (Chao, 2010).

The *FITB* also provided an invaluable platform for other groups. For example, the National University's Research Workshop on the Dramatic Image, which I belonged to at that time, projected its work internationally under the name Theater of the Senses.

## Act II: a secular passion (1995-2002)

In the second half of 1990s, the longstanding guerrilla insurgency became much more visible to the urban public. There was a significant military buildup; armed paramilitaries multiplied and consolidated a national structure. The conflict intensified and there was a dramatic increase in the frequency of massacres, mass displacements, assassinations, and targeted disappearances, leading to widespread fear, uncertainty, and terror (CODHES, 2009: 3; Vignolo and Murillo, 2012: 602).[2]

At the same time, Colombia was beginning to feel the effects of its worst economic crisis in recent history. Nevertheless, the *Theater Festival* continued to experience increasing success. This may seem surprising, since boom and bust cycles theoretically affect first and foremost those sectors that can be considered luxuries, and theater in particular. How can we explain this apparent paradox?

## Our daily theater

A first response may have to do with what was happening in Bogotá. While these were Colombia's most terrible years, it was a time of social peace and positive urban transformation in the capital city, thanks in part to the innovative cultural policies of Mayor Antanas Mockus, whose governing program prioritized what he called 'citizenship culture.'

Mockus's citizenship education campaigns included putting mimes on the street to direct traffic, painting black stars where there had been traffic accidents, and decreeing a 'women's night' for women to go out and enjoy themselves while men stayed home. These practices turned the city upside down and continue to be studied internationally for their implications about the relation between art and politics (Lennard, 1997: 45; Sommer, 2005: 261-276; Vignolo, 2006; Dundjerovic and Navarro Bateman, 2006; Tognato, 2015).

Beyond Mockus's dramatic inclinations and his talent for performance, his administration promoted the use of public spaces, contributing decisively to the image of Bogotá as a city where public culture marked a path to social change (Mockus, 2001: 1-2). Massive outdoor events flourished for the first time in the city's history, first among them the annual *Rock in the Park*, perhaps the largest free event of its kind in Latin America. The free rock festival was soon followed by other popular cultural events including street-theater parades (*comparsas*), nights when city streets are ceded to cyclists, hip-hop, jazz and opera festivals, and more.

Naturally this paradigm change favored the *FITB*, which had in fact pioneered these kind of activities. At the same time, though, the proliferation of free cultural events in public spaces deprived the Festival of its exceptional nature. No longer a bold demand for cultural and citizenship rights, the *FITB* was now but one more cultural event among a wide and expanding range of them, and like any of the others it had to compete for resources and visibility.

The 1994 return of Els Comediants may be the episode that best illustrates how things had changed between the heroic days of the Festival's origins and the pragmatism of these new times. Invited once again to celebrate the closing of the Festival in the Plaza de Bolívar, the Catalan company confronted a new and unexpected obstacle, based not on Church ostracism or threats from extreme rightists, but on city policy. Mayor Mockus had set the reduction of violent deaths as an absolute priority for his administration and in this context had prohibited the use of fireworks, which were traditionally used in great quantities for both public and private celebrations (Null Value, 2015). Mockus stubbornly resisted the pleas of *FITB* organizers for an exception, and finally Els Comediants presented a toned-down finale without flames or fireworks of any kind.

Antanas Mockus was a peculiar alter ego and an unusual competitor for Fanny Mickey. The festival queen, who was a clown seeking to make theater an everyday experience, found herself negotiating with the new mayor– a jester who sought to theatricalize daily life.

## From an act of faith to a pact of confidence

It soon became clear that in order to remain viable the *FITB* would have to transform its act of faith in Colombia into a pact of confidence in Bogotá. This was reflected in its finances. While at first the Festival lost money and barely managed to survive with support from the National Theater Foundation from which it had emerged, it gradually broke even and its scope and size grew steadily.

The *FITB's* autonomous management and its stable and increasingly experienced workforce contributed crucially to its internal consolidation. Beginning in 1996 it even began to produce its own Colombian theatrical works. The naming of Ramiro Osorio as Minister of Culture was also helpful, but the decisive factors were its practices of advance sales and sponsorships.

One thing that makes the *FITB* unique is its unusual form of independent financing. Even today, almost 50% of its total budget is raised at the box office, something practically unheard of for an event of its size (Ruíz, Barrios y Valderrama, 2013: 129). Bogotá's middle class was hungry for cultural options, and the supply was still unequal to rising expectations. People thronged to fill theater seats, including those of works not ordinarily expected to attract large audiences. Whether it was Shakespeare in Bulgarian, a performance of Japanese Butoh, Vietnamese puppets, or Canadian contemporary dance, the important thing was to go to the theater at some point during the two weeks of the festival.

The successful policy of advance sales, frequently in the form of packages that admit the purchaser to a variety of performances throughout *Holy Week*, provided the cash flow needed to guarantee the presence of international companies. The willingness of the audience to purchase tickets to experience unfamiliar genres points to their confidence in the aesthetic criteria of the organizers and to their sense of belonging, which makes the festival a collective ritual that no one wants to relinquish.

The other aspect of this pact of confidence with the city had to do with the strategy of "a small hat passed around to many sponsors", in the words of Ruíz, Barrios, and Valderrama The hat was passed from small business to small business and government office to government office, many of which were able to contribute. This was an important task for Fanny Mickey personally, because "the sponsors gave to Fanny, not to the Festival" (2013: 122).

As described by Ocampo (1998), Colombian capitalists have historically sought out profits associated with volatile boom cycles, infrequently reinvesting in the country. The festival, in contrast, has increasingly positioned itself as emblematic of a bourgeoisie that has staked its interests on the viability of Bogotá, both as an audience of citizen-consumers who subsidize the project with their purchase of season tickets, and as citizen-producers who sponsor the event. Far now from its quixotic origins, the *Iberoamerican Festival* had become the largest cultural enterprise in the country.

## A Vanity Fair?

In its first ten years, the *FITB* redefined the *Holy Week* experience for many in Bogotá, introducing a worldly context that favored civic over ecclesiastic rituals, and even introducing a secular analogue to the deeply religious Passion play. As the festival grows and is institutionalized, however, both its intimate connection to the sacred and its festive and irreverent nature are ever less evident.

The festival's flirtation with religious elements such as faith, sanctity, and the miraculous suggested a return to the roots. Associating a theatrical series with the Catholic Easter is an implicit reconnection to some of the deepest and most potent antecedents of Western theater such as mystery plays, *auto sacramentales*, and representations of the Passion of Christ.

The other important antecedent was the street performance. From the very beginning, Fanny Mickey knew how to attract prominent figures in the street theater movement, one of the most active and fervent manifestations of the Colombian arts scene. Juan Carlos Moyano, director of *Teatro Tierra*, recalls that his group and others like it had been prohibited from using public spaces until the 1980s. Many artists of his generation engaged in a covert struggle to take back the streets for public performance in the face of the military's repressive measures (Red capital de teatro callejero, 2004; Vignolo, 2006)

Given this recent history, street performers were enthusiastic participants in the first years of the *FITB*, contributing in important ways to its development of a popular festive event. Since the mid-1990s, though, relations between the festival and the most politicized proponents of experimental theater have grown tense (Duque Mesa, 2004: 420).

As with any theater event of renown, the *FITB* now has a fringe version. In one sense this brings it prestige, but at the same time it reflects the distance between the festival and the historical Colombian theater community that is most engaged with the national political agenda and that is best known internationally. This generated dangerous divisions. According to Klaić: "The worst mistake festivals can make is to neglect the artists in their immediate vicinity while reaching out to those in far-flung places" (2005: 149, also in Newbold et al 2015: 166). As a result, many artists no longer felt that they were involved in a common project with the *FITB*, and their relationships with the festival organization became more instrumental and opportunistic (Négrier, 2015: 23).

## Act III: one candle for God and another for the Devil (2003-8)

The February 2002 collapse of the Pastrana government's peace process with FARC guerrillas and the war on terrorism adopted as a new geopolitical strategy worldwide after September 11, 2001 paved the way for the rise of a rightist strongman in the person of Álvaro Uribe, then governor of the department of Antioquia (Palacios Rozo, 2012, 165-167 & 189).

Uribe won the presidency promoting 'democratic security'. He promised "a strong hand and a big heart" to restore order and authority throughout the country, assuring the military defeat of the leftist guerrillas (his strong hand) but open to negotiations with rightist paramilitaries known as the United Self-defense Forces of Colombia (his big heart) (Vignolo and Murillo, 2012: 601-602).

The new president achieved great popularity accompanied by a wave of neo-nationalism exemplified by two media campaigns. The first, under the slogan 'Live Colombia: travel it' was designed to promote domestic tourism, and the second, 'Colombia is Passion' was intended to improve the international image of the country.

### Passion for Colombia

The 'Live Colombia' campaign entailed the organization of tourist caravans: surreal processions of vehicles protected by military forces. Tanks, helicopters, and battallions of heavily armed soldiers accompanied tourists' private cars as they traveled to selected domestic destinations. Government officials reconfigured the national identity using a discursive and iconographic repertoire that deployed travel to heritage sites and participation in folkloric activities to reconstruct the country's battered image and restore its allure. Popular festivals, fairs, and carnivals played a special role in this campaign. The tourist caravans were a bizarre amalgam of tourist promotion, the mobilization of patriotic sentiment to support the government and its policies, and organized weekend partying under military protection (Criscione and Vignolo, 2014: 473-517).

The new president achieved great popularity accompanied by a wave of neo-nationalism. Beginning in 2006, the private sector sponsored the 'Colombia is Passion' campaign to sell a more positive image of the country, attract foreign investment, promote international tourism, and stimulate the demand for national exports. The campaign sought to position the word 'passion' and an iconic red heart as the country's new trademarks, associating them with the Colombian people as 'resourceful, hard-working, creative, and happy' (Jaramillo Hoyos, 2009: 345-349).

In a deeper sense the campaign seconded Uribe's 'firm hand, big heart,' inspired anew by the Sacred Heart of the Passion of Christ. In fact, the country had already been officially consecrated to the Sacred Heart in 1903 and 1950, in hopes that a miracle that would staunch the bloodletting of its frequent civil wars. This consecration was reiterated with the adoption of the slogan 'Colombia is Passion,' now in the form of a marketing campaign (Vignolo, 2009: 94-102).

The ambiguous euphoria of patriotism pushed by the state apparatus and big capital impelled the *FITB* to reposition itself once again. As we have seen, one of the profound reasons for which the festival so resonated in the beginning had to do with a reawakening of national pride. Now the 'Live Colombia' and 'Colombia is Passion' campaigns had transcended the festival's 'act of faith in Colombia.'

Passion for the theater was incorporated into a greater passion for the Blood of Christ and for a Colombia once again consecrated to the Sacred Heart. The image of the heroic spectator defying the bombs of the ultra-right to attend the theater was newly embodied in the tourist who defied the guerrillas by travelling the roads of Colombia in military-civilian caravans.

## Act of faith or *auto-de–fe*?

The far right in power set about to reconfigure the Colombian national identity in its own image by means of a hegemonic project that saturated the news and entertainment media, defining friends and enemies and rewriting the nation's official history from its own ideological perspective (Vignolo and Murillo, 2012: 604). Reflecting a politically contradictory tendency, however, Bogotá elected Luis Eduardo (Lucho) Garzón as the first openly leftist mayor in the city's history. With this new political situation the organizers of the festival were faced with a dilemma.

One option was to maintain a critical posture toward the violations of human rights and democratic freedoms that were taking place, in keeping with a well-established tradition of the Colombian and Iberoamerican theater movement. This would mean openly defying the Pax Uribista, defined by historian Marco Palacios (2012: 62) as the combination of Uribe's Policy of Democratic Security with the practices of parapolitcs.[3] The *Alternative Festival* followed the latter course, and despite a chronic lack of funding and endemic disorganization it took on a newly influential role in those years as it served as an artistic sounding board for social movements and victims' associations.

The second option was to embrace the rightist and populist rhetoric of the national government and transform the festival into Bogotá's way station on the tourist caravan, an icon of Colombian neo-nationalism and an exemplar of the Colombia is Passion campaign.

The *FITB* opted for "lighting one candle to God and another to the Devil", assuming a posture of political neutrality and entrepreneurial consolidation. Fanny Mikey and her collaborators felt no affinity for the project of President Uribe, but they never distanced themselves from the government. They ceded this kind of leadership to the Colombian Theater Corporation and its director Patricia Ariza, which did respond to burning questions such as the forced displacement of millions of peasants driven from their land (the Exodus project), gender discrimination and violence against women (the *Festival of Women on Stage*), the denunciation of the army for the false positives scandal[4] (Memory of the Absence) and, and the vindication of historical memory in reconstructing the social fabric (the Antigone Project).

The exclusive, commercial, and elitist aspects of the *FITB* have been accentuated since the beginning of the twenty-first century. Despite the festival's independent programming of politically and poetically radical groups like Mapa Teatro and Matacandelas, it has gradually become an official spectacle enacting the collective catharsis brought on by the ever-present realities of an ongoing war. But this was a catharsis more akin to colonial *autos-da-fe* than to Greek tragedy. Under the watchful eye of an inquisitorial power that underwrote the theatrical manifestation, actors and artists dramatized the sins and guilt of a society wracked by violence and injustice for an audience representing all social strata, sharply distinguished by esthetic preference and economic power.

## A not very festive Festival

The *FITB* resorted to statistics to defend the festival's billing as 'the most important cultural event in Colombia and the largest theater arts festival in the world'. Three important changes went hand in hand with these quantitative superlatives:

1. As a marketing strategy, the *FITB* heralded itself as a world-class theater exposition, establishing the International Showcase of the Performing Arts (*Ventana Internacional de Artes Escénicas*). During the festival, it incorporated outreach events such as training workshops, academic presentations, and talks and demonstrations by performing artists. In order to maximize the crucial economic support of embassies, the festival now highlights the participation of one specially invited country each year.
2. The *FITB* moved many of its presentations to a new 'Theatre City' located at Corferias, a cluster of pavilions usually used for commercial expositions, where for a moderate price ticket-holders get access to a broad range of performances in what resembles a theme park more than an urban public space.

3 The festival changed its strategy for attracting sponsorship. At one time, Fanny Mikey personally made a regular set of rounds asking for contributions. Apart from being an exhausting task, this produced an unstable and unpredictable income stream that led to periodic shortfalls and uncertainty throughout the organization. "We developed various alternatives but eventually reached the conclusion", says Ana Marta Pizarro, "that it would be better to get a few large sponsors" (Ruíz, Barrios, and Valderrama, 2013: 130).

While these three innovations reversed longstanding festival practices, they were successful. Until that time, *FITB* performances had been presented in two very different scenarios, strongly segregated by social strata. Audiences for theater stages largely consisted of the upper middle class while free street performances in low income areas were attended by the working class and the poor. Thinking as an insightful entrepreneur, Fanny Mikey realized that this model excluded a potential market segment made up of middle and lower middle class families, particularly couples with small children who could not afford tickets to theater performances but were afraid to attend free performances due to the dangers of street life and mingling with crowds. The Theater City at Colferias was an ideal venue for a population of citizen-consumers who were more accustomed to enacting public life in shopping malls than in traditional market plazas. (Martín-Barbero, 1981: García-Canclini, 2004) The festival itself was marketed with aggressive new techniques, and its institutional and financial reimagining had diminished its open and festive nature, making it ever more akin to a commercial exposition.

## Epilogue

Predictably, the death of Fanny Mikey gave rise to a number of difficult tensions within the *FITB* that still plague efforts to redefine its foundational project.

One of these tensions arises from a schism in the festival's organizational structure. According to Jordan (2015: 82), quoting Handy (1999), it is common for founders of projects to be "used to having complete decision-making control, to being spiders at the center of the organizational web". In this case, the organizational web sustained damage due to a traumatic separation between the National Theater and the *FITB*. This split not only sundered a united and motivated team of professionals, but provoked a divide between what Négrier (2015: 20) calls the relation between cultural permanence and 'presentism'. The festival program is no longer a reference point for the Colombian theater scene throughout the year, and its capacity to continue establishing a benchmark for the nature of that theater scene has become questionable.

Financing is a second issue. The effort to make the *FITB* an international theater showcase – for example through synergy with the International Society for the

Performing Arts – has not been sufficient to compensate for the deep economic stresses of recent years, and it has even been necessary to add the name of a corporate sponsor to the name of the festival.[5] The funding crisis has developed despite a prolonged mining and oil boom, and one can only wonder what will happen now with the sudden drop in petroleum and raw materials prices. It is not the survival of the festival that is at stake but the ability to revitalize its alliance with the local bourgeoisie.

This brings us to a third important question. Can the *FITB* help stimulate urban regeneration and counteract socio-economic segregation in Bogotá by providing inclusive and affordable access to cultural offerings in the city? Evidence from recent years is mixed. Despite some timid efforts to reestablish public space in the area of the *Centro Internacional* and a few minor initiatives to improve the fabric of urban life, the tendency is disheartening. The festival sells more expensive tickets, produces fewer street performances, and barely coordinates its offerings with the cultural programming of the city government. Rather than concrete proposals for the post-conflict and for social inclusion, there has been generic rhetoric on the desirability of such initiatives, seemingly justifying the criticism of Patricia Ariza: "Big festivals do represent power today, but it is the power of exclusion." (Fernández-Santos, Elsa, 2014).

Finally there is the ambivalent relationship of the festival with old and new forms of nationalism. In this sense, the *FITB's* latest slogan, 'Proudly Colombian,' is disappointing, far from the 'act of faith' that drew so much attention to the event in its early years. In 2013 the festival was declared a manifestation of the 'cultural heritage of the nation'. On the one hand this recognition is welcome. It consolidates the event, anchoring it to long-term cultural policy both rooted in tradition and projected toward the future. On the other hand, it runs the risk of claiming a relationship with the festive traditions of the city by decree, a relationship that is less evident in practice.

From the time of its origins, the outstanding strength of the *FITB* has been its ability to channel the rituals of *Holy Week* and *Carnival* in a contemporary festival, comingling traditional celebrations and highly orchestrated mega events (Waitt, 2008: 513), organic expressions of the community and commercially-driven social phenomena associated with the cultural industry (Giorgi and Sassatelli, 2011: 1-11; Sassatelli, 2015: 28) in ways that had not been seen before.

The funeral of Fanny Mikey briefly revived this intimate connection with the city's festive heritage, which had attenuated with the passing of time. It is too early to tell if with the radical changes that it is currently undergoing the *FITB* will once again resonate with the city's residents or whether its weaknesses will provide an opening for other carnivals, other passions, and other festivals.

# Bibliography

Álvarez, D. (2008) Interview in Funeral de Fanny Mikey fue todo un carnival. *Noticias Uno*, 18/08/2008 available from https://www.youtube.com/watch?v=NQ93lhP0SSc [Accessed 26/10/2015].

Bakhtin, M. (1984) *Rabelais and his World*. Bloomington: Indiana University press.

Borges, J. L. (1998) *El reloj de arena*. Madrid: Alianza, available from http://biblio3.url.edu.gt/Libros/borges/libro_de_arena.pdf [Accessed 26/10/2015].

Castro Gómez, S. (2011). *Historia de la gubernamentalidad*. Bogotá: Siglo del Hombre.

Chao, R. (2010) *The Train of Ice and Fire*. Pontefract: Route.

CODHES (2009) Boletín informativo de la *Consultoría para los Derechos Humanos* y el. *Desplazamiento*, **75**. Bogotá.

Criscione, G. and Vignolo, P. (2013) ¿Del terrorismo al turismo? 'Vive Colombia, viaja por ella' como dispositivo de movilidad, entre conflicto armado y patriomonio cultural, in M. Chaves, M. Montenegro, M. Zambrano (eds.) *El valor del patrimonio: mercado, políticas cuturales y agenciamientos sociales*. Bogotá: ICANH, 2013, 473-517.

Dorado, H. (2000) *Por el placer de vivir: Fanny Mikey. Confesiones de camerino con Humberto Dorado*. Bogotá: Planeta.

Dundjerovic, A. and Navarro Bateman, I. (2006) Antanas Mockus's Theatre for Social Change: Creating Civic Culture in Bogotá, Colombia, in *Research Paper Series*, University of Liverpool.

Duque Mesa, F and Prada Prada, J. (2004) Santigo Garcia: El teatro como Coraje, Bogota. Investigacion Teatral, Guadalupe y Ministerio de Cultura

Eco, U. (1984) The drames of comic 'dreedom' in U. Eco, V. V. Ivanov and M. Rector, *Carnival!* (Thomas A. Sebeok ed.). Berlin Mouton.

Red capital de teatro callejero (2014). Teatro en la calle: ciudad y fiesta, in *Escenario abierto. Revista del teatro de calle*, **3**, Bogotá, julio 2004.

Esposito, R. (2010) *Communitas. The Origin and Destiny of Community*, trans. by Timothy Campbell. Standford: Stanford University Press.

Fernández-Santos, E. (2014) Teatro iberoamericano, entre el carnaval y la resistencia. El País, 11 /04/2014 available from http://cultura.elpais.com/cultura/2014/04/11/actualidad/1397204894_171025.html [Accessed 26/10/2015].

García Canclini, N. (2004) *Culturas híbridas: estrategias para entrar y salir de la modernidad*. México: Grijalbo.

Giorgi, L. and Sassatelli, M. (2011) Introduction, in L. Giorgi, M. Sassatelli and G. Delantly (eds) *Festivals and the Cultural Public Sphere*. London: Routledge, 1-11.

Girard, R. (1977) *Violence and the Sacred*. Trans. Patrick Gregory. Baltimore: John Hopkins University Press.

Handy, C. (1999) *Understanding Organizations*. Middlesex: Penguin.

Jaramillo Hoyos, A. (2009) Ciudadanía con marca registrada, in P. Vignolo (ed.) *Ciudadanías en escena. Performance y derechos culturales en Colombia.* Bogotá: Universidad nacional de Colombia, 345-349

Jordan, J. (2015) Introduction section 2: Leadership and Management, in C. Newbold, C. Maughan, J. Jordan and F. Bianchini. *Focus on Festivals. Contemporary European case studies and perspectives.* Oxford: Goodfellow, 80-87.

Klaić, D. (2005) LIFT Outgrows its festival clothes, in R. De W. Fenton and L. Neal (eds.), *The Turning World*, London: Calouste Gulbenkian Foundation.

Lennard, J. (1997) Mayor of a different mould, in *Americas* (English Edition) March 1997 **49**(2): 40-45.

Lozano, P. (1998) Els Comediants clausura el festival de teatro de Bogotá. El País, 14/04/1998 available from http://elpais.com/diario/1998/04/14/cultura/892504802_850215.html [Accessed 26/10/2015]

Martín-Barbero, J. (1981) Prácticas de comunicación en la cultura popular. Mercados, plazas, cementerios y espacios de ocio, in *Comunicación alternativa y cambio social.* M. Simpson ed. México: UNAM, available from http://es.scribd.com/doc/6334231/Practicas-de-comunicacion-en-la-cultura-popular-mercados-plazas-cementerios-y-espacios-de-ocio [Accessed 26/10/2015].

Mockus, A. (2001) Cultura ciudadana, programa contra la violencia en Santa Fe de Bogotá, Colombia, 1995-1997, in *Estudio Técnico.* Washington D.C.: Banco Interamericano de Desarrollo, available from http://es.scribd.com/doc/63048/Colombia-Cultura-Ciudadana-Experiencia-Bogota [Accessed 26/10/2015]

Mikey, F. (2007) interview, in *Gente*, RCN, 04/04/2010 available from https://www.youtube.com/watch?v=cf3xI3BHdqU [Accessed 26/10/2015]

Négrier, E. (2015) Festivalisation: Patterns and limits, in C. Newbold, C. Maughan, J. Jordan and F. Bianchini. *Focus on Festivals. Contemporary European case studies and perspectives.* Oxford: Goodfellow, 18-27.

Newbold, C., Maughan, C., Jordan, J. and Bianchini, F. (2015) *Focus on Festivals. Contemporary European case studies and perspectives.* Oxford: Goodfellow.

Null Value (2015) Mockus dejó sin luces a Bogotá, in *El Tiempo*, 08/03/2008 available from http://www.eltiempo.com/archivo/documento/MAM-342391 [Accessed 26/10/2015]

Ocampo, J. A. (1998) *Colombia y la economía mundial, 1830-1910.* Bogotá: Fedesarrollo, Colciencias, TM Editores.

Ortega, M. (2008) Interview in Funeral de Fanny Mikey fue todo un carnaval. Noticias Uno, 18 / 08 /2008 available from https://www.youtube.com/watch?v=NQ93lhP0SSc [Accessed 26/10/2015]

Osorio, R. (2014) Interview in *El Festival Iberoamericano de Teatro, un acto de fe en Colombia.* Porta(l) Voz, 27/03/2014 available from http://www.nci.tv/index.php/menuportalvoz/submenu-conversaciones/12402-el-festival-iberoamericano-de-teatro-un-acto-de-fe-en-colombia [Accessed 26/10/2015]

Palacios Rozo, M. (2012) *Violencia pública en Colombia, 1958-2010*. Bogotá: Fondo de Cultura Económica.

Ruíz Gutierrez, J., Barrios Laborda, C. and Valderrama Arias, A. (2013) *El Festival Iberoamericano de Teatro de Bogotá: su gestión en escena*. Bogotá: Universidad de los Andes.

Sassatelli, M. (2015) Festivals, urbanity and the public sphere: Reflections on European festivals, in C. Newbold, C. Maughan, J. Jordan and F. Bianchini. *Focus on Festivals. Contemporary European case studies and perspectives*. Oxford: Goodfellow, 28-39.

Sommer, D. (2005). *Cultural Agency in the Americas*. Durham: Duke University Press.

Taussig, M.J. (1980). *The Devil and Commodity Fetishism in South America*. University of North Carolina Press

Tognato, C. (ed.) (2015) *Cultural Agents Reloaded. The legacy of Antanas Mockus*. Cambridge: Harvard University Press.

Valbuena García, L. (2015) Literaturas de la toma del Palacio de Justicia. La tragedia entre la historia y la literatura. Tesis de Maestría, departamento de Historia. Bogotá: Universidad Nacional de Colombia (unpublished)

Vignolo, P. (2006) La prise de la rue: carnaval et conflict à Bogotá, in *Vie des Idées* (April), 71-82.

Vignolo, P. (2009) Metamorfosis de una pasión, in P. Vignolo, *Ciudadanías en escena. Performance y derechos culturales en Colombia*. Bogotá: Universidad Nacional de Colombia, 94-102.

Vignolo, P. (2015) Vestigios de Fiesta, in *Derechos Humanos y Memoria, revista Errata*, n. 13, 136-159.

Vignolo, P. and Murillo Ramírez, O. (2012) Un arma de doble filo: la espada de Bolívar y el resurgir de los nacionalismos en Colombia y Venezuela, in B. Tovar Zambrano (ed.) *Independencia: historia diversa. 50 años del departamento de Historia (1962-2012)* Bogotá: Universidad Nacional de Colombia, 593-620.

Waitt, G. (2008) Urban festivals. Geographies of hype, helplessness and hope, *Geography Compass*, **2**, 513-537.

## Notes

1 The text has been translated from Spanish to English by Andy Klatt.

2 According to the Consultancy on Human Rights and Displacement (*Consultoría para los Derechos Humanos y el Desplazamiento* - CODHES), 4,628,882 people – almost a million families – were forcibly displaced from their regions in the time period 1985-2008 (CODHES 2009, 3).

3 By 2011, more than 120 recent members of Congress had been investigated for connections to paramilitary groups, and more than 40 had been convicted. About a third of all mayors, governors, and members of Congress had been implicated in some way for these ties.

4 In the false positives scandal, soldiers lured poor young men to distant parts of the country with the promise of work. There they were killed and their bodies presented as guerrillas killed in combat so that these soldiers and their officers could collect rewards for successful 'kills' in the counterinsurgency war.

5 The name of the event now is *Festival Iberoamericano de Teatro de Bogotá* - CLARO.

# 23 *Dia de los Muertos* and its Representation of *Calaveras*

Emily Bradfield

## Introduction

> The word death is not pronounced in New York, Paris or London, because it burns the lips. The Mexican, by contrast, is familiar with death, jokes about it, caresses it, sleeps with it, celebrates it... it is one of his most favourite toys and his most steadfast love. True, there is perhaps as much fear in his attitude as in that of others, but at least death is not hidden away... (Paz, 1967, in Sayer, 2009: 105)

While every country has its own festivals and celebrations, each deeply rooted in the country's culture, none does so more vibrantly than Mexico's festival of *Dia de los Muertos* (*Day of the Dead*), which dates back to the Aztec belief in life as part of the wider cycle of existence (Weiss, 2010). Celebrated on *All Saints'* and *All Souls'* days at the start of November, Mexico's festival is significantly different from other countries' celebrations, such as the perhaps more familiar Westernised, secular celebration of *Halloween*. Although festivities vary from region to region across Mexico, it seems that *remembrance* remains central to the festival, during which the living "honour the souls of the departed with gifts of food and flowers" (Sayer, 2009: 12).

Far from being a sombre affair, *Dia de los Muertos* is a time for celebration mixing Spanish Catholic traditions with ancient Aztec rituals, it is "quite the reverse of morbid; it is a period full of life, colour and festival" (Carmichael and Sayer, 1991: 7). By contrast, Western Catholic countries continue to honour more traditional practice of *All Saints' Day*, a national holiday in many Catholic countries, including Spain, where *Todos los Santos* remains as one of the country's most celebrated religious festivals and *All Souls' Day*, on which ancient customs of decorating graves and praying for the dead are still observed (Catholic Culture, 2015).

## Celebrating the dead

Almost every culture has a belief that the dead should be honoured and across the globe different religions and communities have been remembering the deceased for centuries. *Lemuralia*, a ritual to free one's house of spirits, dates back to ancient Rome. In Hindu tradition people remember the deceased through offerings of food as part of *Pitru Paksha* (Fortnight of the Ancestors). Similarly, the Chinese celebrate *Qingming* (Ancestors' Day), a national holiday on which families visit relatives' tombs to clean them and provide offerings of food and tea; and *Ghost Festival*, during which spirits are invited to visit their living descendants, in a solemn attempt to ease the suffering of the deceased (McDonald, 2013).

However, while these festivals bear some resemblance to Westernised traditions of remembrance, there are countries other than Mexico which seemingly 'celebrate' death; *Bon Festival* in Japan, commemorates the dead with fireworks, feasting and dance, and *Chuseok* in Korea and *Gaijatra* in Tibet are both light-hearted celebrations. In Madagascar local people have a stronger sense of obligation towards the deceased, demonstrated by the importance placed on death and funeral customs amongst the ethnically diverse Malagasy people. The ritual of exhumation and reburial is of great importance in most regions, but for the Merina people, the most dominant ethnic group, time and effort is prioritised for *Famadihana* (Turning of the Bones). In this festival, tombs are opened, corpses removed and wrapped in silk, then carried around the tomb to live music by the family of the deceased (Metcalf and Huntingdon, 1991).

While such festivals cannot be discounted in providing a wider context, there seems to be something extraordinary about *Dia de los Muertos* festivities, which "are central to life in Mexico" (Paz, 1967, in Sayer, 2009: 25). There remains something intriguing about *Dia de los Muertos,* in particular, the associated imagery of grinning skeletons (McDonald, 2013). Perhaps this is due to the inherent culture which sees Mexicans "obstinately refuse to take death seriously" (Rogers 2002: 146). Rather, through their obsession with skull and skeleton motifs the paths of life and death "intersect in a visual way, as they do nowhere else" (ibid: 146). This relationship of Mexican culture with death goes back to the indigenous Nahua peoples who saw the skull as a symbolic of life. *Dia de los Muertos* is an example of the mischievous osmosis of Aztec masks and modern sugar skulls "with its armies of skeletons and hollow-eyed, grimacing skulls" (Geoffroy-Schneiter and Wharry, 2006: 154).

## Death in the Mexican imagination

In a short film commissioned by the Wellcome Trust, Lupe Velaquez, a Mexican living in the UK, described how in his childhood *Dia de los Muertos* was "something amazing which moved [him]" (Velaquez, 2011). Even whilst living on the streets, the day was special, decorating the hut where he lived with other street kids with pieces of string and coloured fabric they had found. They were alone without their parents, but the festival brought them together. He saw this as a form of being creative. In the UK, Velaquez celebrates differently by explaining the festival to friends and preparing food and candles. "It is important to understand that one day we will be part of this death and they will celebrate us... As Mexicans, death is always present" (Velaquez, 2011).

Rather than mourning the passing of the deceased, celebration of life, with its associated colourful representations of *calaveras* (skulls), seems inherent to Mexican culture, with departed relatives returning to join in the festivities. Traditional Catholic *All Souls' Day* cemetery visits and prayer are embellished with colourfully decorated graves and home altars laden with offerings of food for the deceased. These rituals indicate a fusion with the Aztec custom of providing offerings to the goddess *Mictecacihuatl* (Lady of the Dead) in memory of children and adults who had died (Weiss, 2010).

An interesting parallel can be drawn here between *Dia de los Muertos* and the Malagasy festival *Famadihana,* also known as 'Dance with the Dead', in that both celebrations involve a transformation of sorts, which allows the dead to return to experience the joys of life once more. Also interesting to note is both festivals' divergence from traditional Catholic practice of praying for the souls of the dead to aid their journey from purgatory into heaven. In an altogether more lively affair, these 'death celebrations' offer the chance to party with the dead, a concept which has been criticised by the Catholic Church.

Criticism has however recently been on the decline as *Famadihana* becomes viewed more as a 'cultural' celebration rather than a religious festival (Holloway, 2014). Nevertheless, according to Metcalf and Huntingdon (1991), it is the centrality of death in Malagasy systems of religion, economics and social prestige that appears to "deprive them of that sense of abnormality and near indecency" (ibid: 110) that most Western cultures feel towards death and again leads to comparison with Mexican culture. In regions where indigenous culture are especially strong, celebrations may last longer, including celebrations for the souls of dead children, infants who have died before baptism and may even be preceded by festivities for adults who have died in accidents or violence (Sayer, 2009).

## Mexican folk art

*Dia de los Muertos* arts and crafts vary across the regions throughout Mexico, with small country villages placing more emphasis on flowers and food. By contrast, urban areas are a site for rich celebration, with vibrant skeletons and sugar skulls, traditional puppets and museum *ofrendas* (offerings) designed by contemporary artists and curators. Production of these crafts is usually the work of local people, who have passed the skills down the generations, and have become art forms in their own right. Felipe Linares, an artist from Mexico City who makes painted papier mâché figures for the festival, says "I inherited my calling from my father. Right from the start I like the craft of papier-mâché. It is an important Mexican tradition and I want to keep it alive – that is my motivation. It is very important to me that people are pleased with what I make." (cited in Baker, 1996)

The Linares family have been creating papier-mâché figures for over a hundred years, since Don Pedro, Felipe's father started producing *cartoneria,* traditional objects created specifically to last only for the length of the festivities (Kongdon and Hallmark, 2002). The objects are created using paper and wheat-flour paste, which are then painted in bright colours to create *alebrije*, strange magical creatures from Oaxaca. However, the Linares family have become most well known for their three-dimensional *calaveras* which are used in *Dia de los Muertos* celebratons. Leonardo, Pedro's grandson, and his father, Felipe, continue the family tradition of creating these three-dimensional figures for the festival (Sayer, 2009).

Local people even bake special bread for the festival named *Pan de Muerto* (Bread of the Dead), a sweet dough shaped into human forms that represent *animas*, souls of the dead. While special dishes associated with *All Saints' Day* are also prepared in Spain, including roasted chestnuts, almond cakes and *huesos de santo* (Saint's bones) made from marzipan, eggs and sugar syrup, their customs of remembrance seem to lack the vitality of the colourful festivities adopted in Mexican culture (Spanish Fiestas, 2015). Coloured banners, candle holders made by specialist potters and archways decorated with Mexican marigolds, the flower of the dead, add to the festivities which, according to Octavio Paz, Mexican poet "...are central to life in Mexico. Fiestas are our sole luxury... What is important is to go out, open up, get drunk on noise, people, colours. Mexico is in fiesta." (Paz, 1967, in Sayer, 2009: 25)

The preparations, which may start weeks or even months in advance, are extensive, even for simple ceremonies, with cloths for wrapping food being woven or embroidered and perishable goods being "deployed with ingenuity and skill" (Sayer, 2009:16). Works are often unsigned and can be sold far from the place of origin. By contrast, in *Famadihana* the act of preparing the bodies with anointed silk cloth forms the basis of the celebration, an opportunity for family to come together to prepare ancestral corpses for the party. Bodies are then returned to their tombs the following morning, buried with gifts of money and alcohol, and laid upside-down to "close the cycle of life and death" (Holloway, 2014).

Conversely, according to Sayer, in Mexico, it is the "output of these 'anonymous' creators which gives the festival its unique character and visual power"(2009: 119) and, again, makes *Dia de los Muertos* unique. Given the Catholic origins of Mexican festivities, it is not unsurprising to find similarities in the *Fallas* fiesta of Valencia, which also involves months of work to construct papier-mâché *ninots*, figures that are burnt in celebration of the end of winter (Spanish Fiestas, 2015). Indeed, celebrations in the Christian calendar such as *Carnival* and *Mardi Gras*, entail extensive preparation, yet *Dia de los Muertos* stands out from these celebrations of spring and rebirth, through its integral theme of death, where skulls and skeletons "mimic the living and disport themselves in a mocking modern dance of death" (Carmichael and Sayer, 1991: 9).

## *Alfeñique* (sugar paste skulls)

Given the ancient Mexican belief that death signified a stage in a constant cycle of life, celebrations in the central valleys of Oaxaca, where indigenous culture is at its strongest, remain undiminished. Mixquic, or 'City of the Dead', south of Mexico City, celebrates with a funeral procession, while Toluca is famed for its *alfeñique* (sugar paste skulls). The city of Oaxaca comes alive with a "special beauty of flowers, food, creativity and folklore" which has evolved in recent years into a more commercial event, with a Best Altar competition organised by the local council.

In spite of this commercialisation, the unique craftsmanship of *calaveras* or *alfeñique* production remains at the heart of local culture. Consuelo Garcia Urrutia, from Toluca, says, "I learnt the skill from my mother; she learnt it from her mother, and so on for generations." While maintaining traditional craftsmanship, Wenceslao Rivas Contreras, aged 71, aimed to keep ahead in his trade by creating new models of sugar skulls each year, based on new ideas (Carmichael and Sayer, 1991: 108-110).

In spite of the iconic association of the sugar figures and skulls with *Dia de los Muertos*, the origin of this craft is unclear. Perhaps the earliest reference to sugar figures comes from writings of Francisco de Ajofrin, who described the scene of colourful stalls with crowds of people selling *alfeñique* and figures of the dead, he witnessed on arriving in Mexico City in 1763. In a letter written in 1841, Scottish born Fanny Calderon de la Barca describes numerous booths filled with sugar skulls "temptingly ranged in grinning rows", with women crying out "Skulls, niñas, skulls!" (Carmichael and Sayer, 1991: 51).

While stalls in Toluca continue to sell *alfeñique*, traditional ideas have evolved. Toy-makers at markets in Oaxaca, Puebla and Mexico City have started to sell humorous toy coffins, cardboard skeletons and painted clay caricature skeletons mimicking everyday activities. While in pre-Hispanic times human skulls were kept as trophies in honour of certain gods, skulls have also long been a symbol of death within Western Christianity, therefore *alfeñique* could have Catholic origins as well. For Nutini, their survival as part of the cult of the dead rests in a fusion of pre-Hispanic Mexican and Spanish Catholic symbolism (Carmichael and Sayer, 1991).

# Representations of *calaveras*

In addition to traditional offerings of flowers and food, lights, sugar skulls and colourful banners play a significant part in the visual power of the festival, all somehow inextricably linked to death. *Dia de los Muertos* incorporates colourful, visual representations of *calaveras* in a jovial manner. "...death is an excellent visual motif, allowing the juxtaposition of contrasting blocks of black and white, finely defined contours, bold dynamic arrangements of elongated cylindrical shapes placed at striking angles, intricate formations of bones." (Rivera, 1958, in Rotherstein, 1989: 187) "From Teotihuacan jade funerary masks, to delightful sugar or papier mâché skeletons... Mexican art has always flirted with the world of the dead." (Geoffroy-Schneiter & Wharry, 2006: 60) In the late 1960s the art form's influence spread when Mexican American art student Chaz Bojorquez began experimenting with symbols and signs in the underground sewerage tunnels in Los Angeles. His *Senor Suerte* (Mr Luck), a stylised skull has influenced generations of graffiti artists (Dowling, 2011).

Skeletons made of cardboard, clay or papier-mâché and dressed as musicians, office workers or drinkers, provide a humorous vehicle for social comment, while painted sugar skulls are an edible reminder of our mortality and demonstrate the cultural relationship with death (Sayer, 2009). *La Catrina: Tribute to Jose Posada,* an exhibition held in the United States, told the story of *La Catrina*; created by the Mexican printmaker, Jose Guadalupe Posada; made popular by Diego Rivera, the Mexican muralist; and which continues to influence contemporary art around the world. In Posada's work "Death makes a fool of all of us, regardless of socio-economic status", and reminds us that we all must die (American Museum of Ceramic Art, 2014). Interestingly, Posada's workshop was close to the Aztec temple of Tenochitilan, and consequently it could be said that his use of *calaveras* brought ancient reminders of death into modern Mexican art (Rotherstein, 1989).

Posada's influence on the Mexican mural painting of the 1920s comes to a pinnacle in Diego Rivera's *Dream of a Sunday Afternoon at Alameda Park*. The mural shows Posada, arm in arm with *La Catrina,* holding hands with Rivera depicted as a young boy, with Rivera's wife, Frida Kahlo, standing behind. For Rivera, Posada's engravings had "the essential, lasting expressive qualities that constitute true art" (Rivera, 1958, in Rotherstein, 1989: 187), while *La Catrina* has become a "ubiquitous symbol in Mexican art and culture" (Ades et al, 2009: 54). Rivera's own relationship with mortality was integral to his psyche: "If you look around my studio, you will see Deaths everywhere, Deaths of every size and colour." (Rivera, 1920, quoted by Weiss, 2010)

Furthermore, *La Catrina* has become the symbolic icon of *Dia de los Muertos* and Posada's legacy continues to live on in contemporary papier-mâché skeleton figures and puppets, such as those by the Linares family, Analee Fuentes and Saulo Moreno (Carmichael and Sayer, 1991). Fuentes, who creates *Dia de los Muertos* inspired work, highlights the "strong element of humour" in her work, based on Posada's belief that "regardless of wealth and class, we all die" (Notman, 2013). For Moreno:

> Life and Death are the eternal duality. In Mexico we never tire of representing death. When I was a child, I played with skulls and skeletons... When we die, our bodies decompose: they feed the earth and are reborn. We are all part of this constant cycle of death and regeneration. (Moreno, cited by Carmichael and Sayer, 1991: 125).

The Mexican attitude towards death, seen in celebrations of *Dia de los Muertos* makes a usually difficult subject accessible to everyone. A free festival at the British Museum in October 2015 brought Mexican art and performance to London in a multi-sensory experience incorporating incense, light, music and representations of *calavera* throughout the museum. Learning to cope with mortality has, in the Western world, traditionally been symbolised through 'memento mori' and 'vanitas', as "a moral metaphor for vanity as the curse of modern life" (Dowling, 2011: 137). However, the so called Mexican "cult of the dead" is gradually becoming absorbed into Western cultures as the skull has emerged as "one of the most recognizable symbols of today's contemporary visual landscape... an emblem for the human consciousness... through which to explore our fascination with the transience of life, death and the human soul." (Dowling, 2011: 7)

1,500 local extras made-up in traditional *calavera* face paint provide the backdrop in the opening sequence of the latest James Bond film, *Spectre*, set to be "the most visually-exciting opening to a Bond ever". Director Sam Mendes said "I wanted the audience to be dropped right into the middle of a very, very specific, very heady, rich environment. It's the Day of the Dead, everywhere you look there's colour and detail and life." Make-up artist for the film, Naomi Donne, said "I felt strongly that the Day of the Dead is intrinsically Mexican and I didn't want to take it over." (Ranscombe, 2015).

Damien Hirst readily acknowledges his connection with Mexico and the Mexican attitude towards death "I think that the way that I deal with death is a bit Mexican. In England people hide or shy away from death and ideas about it, whereas Mexicans seem to walk hand in hand with it... I came to Mexico and I thought [my work] really fits in here." (Hirst, quoted by Tuckman, 2005) Indeed, in sketches for *For the Love of God* (2007), one of Hirst's most important works, he noted beside a sketch of the diamond skull "like that Mexican skull with the turquoise on it" (Hirst et al, 2007). In discussions with Galguera, whilst in Mexico, Hirst referred to these Aztec skulls as a source of inspiration. Galguera (2012) describes Hirst's longstanding infatuation with Mexico being based on its interest in death. "There is no other country in the world that treats death in the majestic way Mexico does."

In an interview for Tate (2012), Hirst described how "Every art work that's ever interested [him] is about death." When designing *For the Love of God* he thought;

> What's the maximum you can pit against death, and then, you know, diamonds came to light. Because we're dealing with death, which is so negative, it has to be entirely positive......it has to be ridiculous in its perfection. It has a kind of quietness, a kind of transcendent feel, that it's sort of mesmerising and optimistic... (Hirst, 2012).

According to Dowling the skull has "evolved from its spiritual and religious origins to become an icon for a post-modern society... which has straddled the worlds of music, fashion, art and popular culture." (2011: 7) However, while the skull has appeared "throughout the myth and legend of human culture there seems, in Mexico, to be a unique attitude to death that has encapsulated the imaginations of people across the world" (ibid: 7). But it is also apparent that the colour and vibrancy of the symbolism behind this festival and Mexican art has played a crucial role in the survival of the skull as "the ultimate symbol of life, death and human experience" (ibid: 137).

## Conclusions

Perhaps it is the deep rooted history of the significance of Aztec belief of the cycle of life and death, topped with the manner in which the Mexicans embrace the celebration of death with colour and vibrancy, which has led to the universal intrigue surrounding the festival. Over the decades Posada's images of "death personified as a skeleton that gets drunk, picks fights, sheds tears and dances for joy" (Rivera, 1958, in Rotherstein, 1989; 187) have provided a pathway for trans-cultural artists to access the "playful familiarity and proximity to death" practised in Mexico (Weiss, 2010). *Dia de los Muertos* is a festival that welcomes the souls of the dead to return and participate with the living in joyous and colourful celebrations.

For Mexicans, death is regarded as an equalizer, for rich and poor, powerful and weak; seen in the work of Posada, whose vivid, lively skeletons with grinning faces, accompanied by satirical verses, have been used to enliven the festivities for decades. At the core of the festivities are the arts and crafts passed down from generation to generation. Local communities remain true to ancient traditions of celebrating the souls of the deceased and the cycle of life and death through maintaining skills in craftsmanship (Notman, 2013).

Although the colourful rituals around *Dias de los Muertos* are restricted to the festival, representations of *calaveras,* the availability of folk art, and the Mexican view of death, have become clearly integrated into Mexican identity and in more recent years have started to creep into Western culture as well. The notion that *Dia de los Muertos* events are becoming popular across the world demonstrates the influence that the festival and Mexican attitude to death have had, even across cultures. "It's part of your daily life. People die and you're going to die too" (Torres, in Notman, 2013). This good humour towards death clearly shines through in the art and colour of *Dia de los Muertos* and makes the cultural meaning of the festival an inspiration to cultures around the world. Rather than mourning those who have passed away, the festival can be seen as an elaborate celebration of life.

## Bibliography

Ades, D., McClean-Cameron, A., Campbell, L. and McDonald, M. (2009). *Revolution on paper*, Austin: University of Texas Press.

American Museum of Ceramic Art (2014). *La Catrina: Tribute to Jose Posada - American Museum of Ceramic Art*. Available at: http://www.amoca.org/la-catrina, accessed 15 Feb. 2015.

Baker, C. (1996) *Gallery of Modern Art Glasgow - The First Years*, London: Scala Books.

Carmicahel, E. and Sayer, C, (1991) *The Skeleton at the Feast. The Day of the Dead in Mexico*, London: British Museum Press.

Catholic Culture (2015) *Catholic Recipe: Panes de Muertos*. Available from: http://www.catholicculture.org/culture/liturgicalyear/recipes/view.cfm?id=1380&repos=3&subrepos=4&searchid=1507042, accessed 06 March 2015.

Congdon, K., and Hallmark, K. (2002) *Artists from Latin American Cultures: A Biographical Dictionary*, London: Greenwood.

Dowling, F. (2011) *The Book of Skulls*, London: Laurence King Publishing.

Galguera, H. (2012). Sugar skulls and sacrifice: Damien Hirst and Mexico's death culture in pictures. *Guardian*. Available at: http://www.theguardian.com/artanddesign/gallery/2012/apr/19/damien-hirst-mexico-death-in-pictures, accessed 19 Apr. 2015.

Geoffroy-Schneiter, B. and Wharry, D. (2006) *Primal arts*, New York: Assouline.

Hirst, D. (2012) *TateShots: Damien Hirst, For the Love of God*. [video] London: Tate. Available at: http://www.tate.org.uk/context-comment/video/tateshots-damien-hirst-love-god, accessed 19 Apr. 2015.

Hirst, D., Fuchs, R., and Beard, J. (2007). *For the Love of God*, London: Other Criteria/White Cube.

Holloway, A. (2014) *Turning of the bones and the Madagascar dance with the dead*. Available from: http://www.ancient-origins.net/ancient-places-africa/turning-bones-and-madagascar-dance-dead-001346, accessed 06 March 2015.

Kasprzak, E. (2012) Day of the Dead: From Mexico City to London Town. *BBC News*. Available from: http://www.bbc.co.uk, accessed 11 February 2015.

McDonald, C. (2013) *10 Festivals that honor the dead*. Listverse, 19th Jan. [weblog] Available from: http://listverse.com/2013/01/19/10-festivals-that-honor-the-dead/, accessed 07 March 2015.

Metcalf, P. and Huntingdon, R. (1991) *Celebrations of Death. The Anthropology of Murtuary Ritual*, 2nd edition. Cambridge: Cambridge University Press.

Notman, A. (2013) *Dia de los Muertos: Behind the misunderstood and misappropriated Mexican holiday*. Available from: http://www.eugeneweekly.com/20131017/lead-story/dia-de-los-muertos, accessed 15 February 2015.

Paz, O. (1967) *The Labyrinth of Solitude: A dramatic Portrait of the Mexican Mind*, trans. London: Lysander Kemp, Penguin Press.

Ranscombe, S. (2015) Bond make-up artist Naomi Donne on making up 1,500 SPECTRE extras, *The Telegraph*, 7 October. Available from http://www.telegraph.co.uk/beauty/make-up/bond-spectre-make-up-artist-naomi-donne/, accessed 23 October 2015

Reuters (2007) *FACTBOX: The Day of the Dead's global spread*. Available from: http://www.reuters.com/article/2007/11/01/us-dayofdead-idUSN0142516020071101, accessed 15 February 2015.

Rogers, N. (2002) *Halloween: From Pagan Ritual to Party Night*, Oxford: Oxford University Press.

Rotherstein, J. (1989) *Posada: Messenger of Mortality*, London: Redstone Press.

Sayer, C. (2009) *Fiesta: Days of the dead and other Mexican festivals*, London: British Museum Press, London.

Spanish Fiestas (2015) *All Saints Days Spain. Dia de Todos los Santos*. Available from: http://www.spanish-fiestas.com/festivals/all-saints-days/, accessed 06 March 2015.

Tate (2012) *TateShots: Damien Hirst, For the Love of God*. Available at: http://www.tate.org.uk/context-comment/video/tateshots-damien-hirst-love-god, accessed 19 Apr. 2015.

Tuckman, J. (2005). The bell tolls for Hirst's tried and tested work. Guardian. [online] Available at: http://www.theguardian.com/world/2005/oct/24/artsnews.mexico, accessed 19/03/15.

Velaquez, L. (2011) *When the Souls Arrive: Reclaiming the dead*. [video] Available at: http://www.d-aep.org/portfolio/when-the-souls-arrive-reclaiming-the-dead/, accessed 2 May 2015.

Weiss, A. (2010) Why Mexicans celebrate the Day of the Dead, *The Guardian*, 2nd Nov. Available from: http://www.theguardian.com, accessed 11 February 2015.

# 24 Commemorating the Ancestors: Performances of Death at the *Tucson All Souls' Procession*

Rachel Bowditch

## Introduction

At dusk close to 100,000 people clad in black and white face paint and hand-made costumes emerge from all directions marching along a two-mile procession route from Hotel Congress in Tucson, Arizona to the finale site carrying puppets, banners, effigies, floats and posters with photographs of the dead of all shapes and sizes. Crowds of people line the streets; however unlike the *Macy's Day Thanksgiving Parade* and other official processions, there are no street barriers separating those marching in the procession and those observing; the lines are porous and blurred. Participants move fluidly in and out of the procession between spectating and marching: dancing, drumming and walking. There is no clear distinction between sidewalk and street; between official performers and spectators—everyone is a participant. There is a somber sense of excitement and anticipation. A large-scale sculptural urn assisted by guardians from the performance troupe Flam Chen weaves through the dense crowd collecting hand-written prayers and offerings from passersby. *Day of the Dead* motifs of black and white skeletons, flowers, and masks dominate the visual landscape mixed with a fusion of hybrid imagery that evokes death, memory and celebration.

Suspended weightlessly above a crowd of fire-lit faces, a figure moves gracefully without a safety net, wrapping her body in aerial silks tethered to helium balloon clusters. Stilted figures in ornate hand-constructed costumes twirl fire to the thundering beating drum. Costumed figures scale the metal tower with torches to light the large paper mache urn, which is filled with the prayers of the entire community. Flames lick up the sides of the urn transforming it into a ball of raging fire; the crowd cheers as they watch their prayers ascend into the darkness. This ritual burning of the urn signifies the culminating act of the *Tucson All Souls' Procession*. Flam Chen, pyrotechnic performance troupe from Tucson and Many Mouths One Stomach, the organizers of the event, stage a fire aerial performance followed by the symbolic burning of the urn filled with the community's prayers and wishes.

Since the founding of the *Tucson All Souls' Procession*, occurring annually the first Sunday of November, it has grown from a small group of friends to over 100,000 participants in 2014. Several aspects of the event—the history and evolution of the procession, the tentative relationship with the city of Tucson, the personal and community altars, the ritual of burning of the urn and the finale—serve as powerful modes of community healing. They act as a vehicle for what procession organizers Nadia Hagen and Paul Weir call 'festal culture,' creating a necessary space to process trauma and create a sense of community identity.[1]

## History of the procession

The procession, founded in 1990 by local artist Susan Johnson, is loosely inspired by practices surrounding *All Souls' Day* and *Día de Los Muertos*, both celebrated widely across the Americas. The procession began as a personal healing ritual and gesture of grieving for Johnson's father. In an interview with Erin White at the *Arizona Daily Star*, she stated, "*All Souls' Day* is one of the oldest holidays celebrated in the world. [...] I wanted to create an artists' parade, not just a celebration of one culture. The merging of art forms with the heaviness of death became a very beautiful thing. It brought down a lot of barriers between the different cultures" (2006). After the first procession, Johnson says, she felt transformed: "It opened up my heart and let me connect with things that were frightening to me. [...] The parade is a really powerful vehicle to express anger and rage constructively. To create and use your own creation—it is transforming" (in White 2006). Recruiting performers and friends from the downtown Tucson arts scene, she organized a three-day invitation-only event to commemorate her father. Johnson made masks and costumes in her studio with friends and the evening culminated in an intimate procession of about 20 people wandering through the streets of Downtown Tucson. The response to the early processions was overwhelming and she received over 250 letters thanking her and asking how they could be involved the following year. For the first several years, the procession was relatively small, with at most a few hundred people, mainly from the downtown art crowd. At the end, everyone would gather around a bonfire to tell stories of loved ones. Local artists started hosting mask-making workshops and spent weeks making puppets, costumes and floats, and inviting the community to participate free-of-charge. For the next eight years, Johnson organized the procession and workshops; in 1998 she passed the organizational reins over to Nadia Hagen, founder of the fire performance troupe Flam Chen. Hagen had stumbled across the procession in its third year, quite by accident, when out riding her bicycle at 2:00 A.M. She recalls that everyone was dressed up and pushing decorated shopping carts—what she refers to as 'insta-floats,' complete with generators for lights and music (Hagen 2010).

By 1997 the crowds had started spilling onto the streets, which consequently had to be closed for safety reasons. As the procession continued to expand Hagen quickly realized she needed an infrastructure to manage the event and formed an umbrella nonprofit organization, Many Mouths One Stomach, to fiscally manage and organize the event. Soon after, Hagen became the artistic director and Paul Weir, her husband and Flam Chen's technical director, became a central organizer and the procession's technical director, taking the finale to new heights of innovation and spectacle. While a small group of organizers manages the event, it takes over 280 volunteers approximately 2,500 hours to run the procession. While no one receives a full-time salary, a few organizers and artists receive a small stipend, between $100 and $500. As Hagen realizes, "None of the stipends are remotely close the amount of time that people put in" (Hagen 2010).

The procession continued to grow exponentially each year through word of mouth, viral marketing and fliers posted around downtown Tucson, doubling in size each year—by 2001, more than 2,000 people were participating and by 2009 the procession had grown to 30,000. Weir sees attendance at the parade as a process of initiation: people show up with their lawn chairs, but soon realize that they can participate by wearing a costume and walking in the procession. Next year, ideally, they are converted and fully participate (Weir 2010).

## Festival palimpsest

The *Tucson All Souls' Procession* could be seen as a unique hybrid festival that is suspended between *All Souls' Day* and *Día de los Muertos* celebrations as well as bearing a striking resemblance to the ancient pagan festival *Samhain*, signifying the end of summer and the completion of the harvest, marking the transition of the seasons (Cosman 1981). As Jack Santino in *Halloween and Other Festivals of Death* points out, the ancient celebration of *Samhain* could be considered the prehistory of modern *Halloween* (1994: xiv). He notes how *Samhain* was widely practiced in ancient Ireland, which converted to Christianity in A.D. 300-400 (xv). The practice of grafting Christian festivals onto ancient festivals was a way to ease conversion. According to Santino, "the early church adapted and accommodated the traditional religious beliefs and practices of those it sought to convert. Many of the festivals and holidays we enjoy have resulted from this policy and were derived in some part from already existing festivals and celebrations" (xvi), creating what he calls a "palimpsest of festival culture" (xvi).

*Samhain*, the Celtic New Year, was celebrated on 31 October and 1 November, the last day of the previous year, and became identified with death (Santino 1994: xv). The Celts believed that the spirits of the dead returned to earth on that night to cause mischief and chaos. On this night, the boundaries between the living and the dead were blurred. During *Samhain*, bonfires were lit to guide the spirits and people wore costumes and masks dressing as spirits, witches, and ghosts (xv). Around the end of the first millennium, the Catholic Church fought to extinguish these pagan rites by appropriating the practices and renaming the celebration to honor the dead: *All Souls' Day* was known as *All-Hallowsmas* and 31 October was *All Hallowed's Eve* or Hallow'e'en.

When the Spanish conquistadors arrived in the New World in the 16th century, they brought the Christian *All Souls' Day* with them. As Valeria Menard notes, by the time the Spaniards arrived, the Aztecs already had in place a complex system of festivals dedicated to death (2000: 149). The ancient indigenous peoples of Mexico (Purepecha, Nahua, Aztec, Totonac and Otomí) had their own elaborate festivals dedicated to the dead, with a month-long festival—in honor of the lord of death, Mictlantecuhtli and his consort Mictlancíhuatl, the goddess of death (Carmichael 1992: 25). The Spanish appropriated indigenous practices and grafted them onto their Christian *All Souls'* festival, resulting in a yet another syncretic fusion and hybrid festival what is known today as *Día de los Muerto* or *Day of the Dead*, which merged aspects of both European and Aztec beliefs and customs (Palfrey 1995).

Traces of festivals, such as *Day of the Dead*, *All Souls' Day* and *Halloween* are evident in the *Tucson All Souls'* as cultural palimpsests, products of continuously shifting worlds, resonating with what Arjun Appardurai has termed "diasporic public spheres"[7] (Appadurai 1996: 22). Through these diasporic public festive performances, the layers of encounter are rendered visible and brought to the surface. These festivals create an alternative public sphere for communication making both tradition and the contemporary moment "pervasive, vital, ongoing, and highly visible" (Jasper and Turner 1994: 149).

## Staging national trauma after 9/11

As it has evolved over two decades, the *All Souls' Procession* has become Tucson's unofficial signature cultural event. According to Weir, the event gained this iconic status in 2002 after the pivotal procession commemorating 9/11. While there have always been subtle political undercurrents, the procession in 2001 served as a public platform for processing national trauma. For Weir, the wars in Iraq and Afghanistan aided in solidifying and unifying the procession around a larger public purpose beyond individual mourning. According to Ann Kaplan in *Trauma Culture*, there are varying degrees of trauma and it is important to distinguish between personal trauma and collective trauma (2005: 1–2). For the majority of Americans, trauma is experienced on a regular basis through the media, with such traumatic images as the tsunami in Southeast Asia, the devastation of Hurricane Katrina and the harrowing earthquakes in Haiti and Japan. On September 11, 2001, U.S. citizens in New York, Washington DC and Shanksville, PA, experienced tragedy first hand, while the rest of the nation encountered mediated versions of the event, replayed over and over again on every news channel (ibid: 2). Kaplan identifies this phenomenon as 'secondary' or 'vicarious' trauma (ibid: 20). She argues that viewers of the media, "like therapists working with trauma victims, are often vicariously traumatized. [...] Vicarious traumatization may be an inevitable part of sharing what others have suffered, but it too can have socially productive aspects in specific contexts" (ibid: 21–22). She coined the term "empty empathy" in analyzing the function of war photographs in relation to viewers and how the repetition of traumatic images produces a numbing effect (ibid: 21-22). She explores how people can "move beyond sharing trauma and engage in 'witnessing', a stance that has public meaning or importance and transcends individual empathic or vicarious suffering to produce community" (ibid: 22–23). As Kaplan notes, the trauma of 9/11 created a new collective subject and a civic cohesiveness that had not been experienced before (ibid: 22–23). Through mediated images of 9/11, temporary publics were formed around the national trauma to produce collective spaces of healing. *The Tucson All Souls' Procession* was one such space. As Kaplan states, "Complex interconnections between individual and cultural trauma—such that, indeed, where the 'self' begins and cultural reactions end may seem impossible to determine. [...] Short-lived but real creation of new public-sphere communities as specific crises are 'translated' from group to group." (ibid: 2)

In the aftermath of 9/11, the need to transform personal trauma into collective trauma was seen in public gatherings such as the *All Souls' Procession*, where spontaneous public memorials sprang up around the city—the street transformed into a fertile space to process collective trauma (ibid: 12). However, as Kaplan points out, "It gradually became clear that national ideology was hard at work shaping how the traumatic event was to be perceived." (ibid: 13) The national tragedy was quickly co-opted by politicians and others who, overnight, translated the tears of trauma into a nationalist cry for war and revenge. This tragedy formed two publics, the one portrayed by the media and the other public that was silenced and manipulated (ibid: 13).

In 2001, the procession offered an alternative civic space for the public to express their dissent against the call for war. It was a safe haven for people to witness others who also felt alienated and frustrated with what they saw in the media. Just by virtue of going out on the street, donning a costume and mask, and being present with others was an affirmation of a different set of values than those being propagated by the media and by the government. The gathering of bodies *en masse* in the streets forged a positive healing community space to remember those killed during the attacks and heal the personal and national wounds, building a powerful sense of collective and individual agency. Since 9/11, the collective space of mourning has continued to remain a vital outlet for the community to process trauma and grief.

## The *Ancestor's Project*: from personal to community mourning

Several important parts of the *All Souls'* event take place the night before the main procession: the personal altars vigil, coordinated for many years by former Flam Chen performer Alysa Volpe; the community altar, coordinated by Susan Johnson; and the *Procession of Little Angels*—their version of the *Día de Los Angelitos*. This parade to honor children who have died comes at the end of a full day of children's workshops and performances at the downtown Joel D. Valdez Main Library Plaza. Johnson's community altar is one large evolving memorial where the entire community can add a memento, photograph or candle, whereas the personal altars are created by individuals and dedicated to specific people. The personal altar vigil begins around noon and ends at midnight, and most people stay for the entire vigil, sharing stories and anecdotes of loved ones. Personal altars have been part of the *Tucson All Souls' Day* commemorations from the beginning, but in 2006, the organizers provided a space for people to set up personal altars in front of the downtown library.

Altars vary from person to person; many contain photographs of the deceased, votive candles, poems, sometimes fruit and food. Some are erected just once; others reappear each year. These personal altars allow people to extend that healing process and share it in a public, communal way. It provides a healing network where people grieving can be around others who are also suffering a loss. For Volpe, the personal altars capture the essence of what the procession is all about.

Another altar of sorts is on display throughout the procession. Established in 2005, the *Ancestors' Project* is a visual public memorial that is often projected directly above the personal altars and on other civic buildings around Tucson along the procession route. By going to the *All Souls'* website, the public can upload images of their ancestors onto an online portal, which receives an average of 200 photos each year. Originally, these images were processed and colorized with sepia tones to give them an antiquated appearance by multimedia artist Adam Cooper-Terán, director of the *Ancestor's Project* until 2009, but due to the volume, they are now projected as they are received in a slide-show format. Cooper-Terán has observed how emotional people get when they see their relatives projected onto a public building: "It totally transforms people and they are so grateful. The act is so powerful. [...] It stirs up dialogue. There are always stories that come out of these types of public gatherings when people start coming together with the intent to mourn or celebrate someone who passed" (interview 2010). For several years, the images were projected onto the City Court building at Sixth Avenue and Bennington, in storefronts along Congress Street, along Stone Avenue and at the finale site.

## Forging 'imaginary' mourning communities

In *Media and Ritual: Death, Community and Everyday Life (2013)* Johanna Sumiala asks how we understand ritual in a constantly shifting transnational environment? She observes how in contemporary society the line between 'producer' and 'consumer' is increasingly blurred; the traditional hierarchical role of the media is subverted transforming a passive consumer into an active agent through social media. In a public memorial of death, like the *Tucson All Souls' Procession*, social media is far more pervasive than the mainstream media. A plethora of electronic devices flood the visual landscape capturing the event from multiple perspectives and vantage points, which instantly circulate via social media networks like Facebook, Twitter and YouTube. As grassroots reporters sprout up via social media networks, counter-narratives enter into the conversation vying for a piece of the 'attention economy' transforming the passive consumer into an active agent in the visual economy of image and meaning making.

The media serves a ritual function in constructing what Sumiala calls a "dramaturgy of grief" by disseminating symbolic images of mourning and memorialization that facilitate the grieving process. Mediatized death rituals, according to her, manage public emotion and bring community together through symbolic communication such as lighting candles and placing flowers on community altars. Sumiala notes a significant paradigm shift occurring across the globe—the emergence of fragmented imaginary online communities whose boundaries are porous and constantly shifting. She argues that a close reading of these mediatized death rituals within this shifting landscape offers an important glimpse into our current moment and provides a deeper understanding of our selves and the diverse, imaginary communities we belong to—the *Tucson All Souls' Procession* is evidence of this. The procession brings disparate communities together forging a momentary communitas. This temporary mourning community is reinforced via multiple social media networks.

What does the *All Souls' Day Procession* mean for the community of Tucson; what function does it serve? For Cooper-Terán the procession fulfills the public's need to mourn. Another central organizer, Matt Cotten of Tucson Puppetworks, emphasizes that the procession is very different from *Halloween*, "I think that's why this has gotten so big because people yearn for a ritualistic way to celebrate death and mourn people they've lost" (Bodfield 2003). Weir believes that people gravitated towards the event because there are so few opportunities to mourn in the US: "There's not a lot of room in Western culture for grieving in an exalted way—to express your emotions and your grief. It serves the role of festal culture. *Festal* is this very archaic word that references the core human need for celebration" (in White 2006). Festive events such as the *All Souls' Procession* are temporary, efficacious and transformative, evoking real life changes producing a meaningful public forum to collectively mourn and celebrate the dead outside of official mainstream culture.

## Bibliography


Anderson, B. (2006) *Imagined Communities: Reflections on the Origin and Spread of Nationalism,* New York: Verso Books.

Appadurai, A. (1996) *Modernity at Large: Cultural Dimensions of Globalization.* Minneapolis: University of Minnesota Press.

Bodfield, R. (2003) Revelers' puppets tell personal stories: Tucson's all souls spectacle, in *The Arizona Daily Star* 2 October.

Bowditch, R. (2016) Mourning En Masse: Tucson's All Souls' Day Procession, in *Performing Utopia.* London: Seagull Books.

Brandes, S. (2006) *Skulls to the Living, Bread to the Dead,* New Jersey: Wiley-Blackwell Publishing.

Carmichael, E. (1992) *The Skeleton at the Feast: The Day of the Dead in Mexico,* Texas: University of Texas Press.

Cooper-Terán, A. (2010) Interview with author. Tucson, Arizona. 10 May.

Cosman, M. P. (1981) *Medieval Holiday and Festivals: Calendar of Celebrations.* New York: Charles Scribner's Sons.

Hagen, N. (2010) Interview with author. Tucson, Arizona. 10 May.

Jasper, P. and Turner, K. (1994) Day of the Dead: The Tex-Mex tradition, in J. Santino (ed.), *Halloween and Other Festivals of Death and Life,* Tennessee: University of Tennessee

Kaplan, A. (2005) *Trauma Culture: The Politics of Terror and Loss in Media and Literature,* New Jersey: Rutgers University Press.

Marchi, R. (1994) El Día de los Muertos in the USA: Cultural ritual as political communication, in J. Santino (ed.) *Halloween and Other Festivals of Death and Life,* Tennessee: University of Tennessee.

Marchi, R. (2009) *Day of the Dead in the USA, The Migration and Transformation of a Cultural Phenomenon,* New Brunswick: Rutgers University Press.

Menard, V. (2000) *The Latino Holiday Book: From Cinco de Mayo to Día de los Muertos. The Celebrations and Traditions* of Hispanic Americas. New York: Marlowe and Company.

Palfrey, D. H. (1995) Day of the Dead, Available at: http://www.mexconnect.com/articles/1972-november-2-the-day-of-the-dead (accessed 13 October 2010).

Santino, J. (ed.) (1994) *Halloween and Other Festivals of Death and Life,* Tennessee: University of Tennessee.

Santino, J. (2006) *Spontaneous Shrines and the Public Memorialization of Death,* London: Palgrave.

Sumiala, J. (2013) *Media and Ritual: Death, Community and Everyday Life,* London: Routledge.

Turner, K. (1999) *Beautiful Necessity: The Art and Meaning of Women's Altars,* London: Thames and Hudson.

Volpe, A. (2010) Interview with author. Tucson, Arizona. 11 May.

Weir, P. (2010) Interview with author. Tucson, Arizona, 10 May.

White, E. (2006) All Souls Procession, in *Arizona Tucson Daily Star* 5 November. http://www.highbeam.com/doc/1G1-153859362.html

## Notes

1 Segments of this chapter have appeared in 'Mourning En Masse: *Tucson's All Souls' Day Procession*,' by Rachel Bowditch. *Performing Utopia*. London: Seagull Books. Forthcoming.

# 25 Off the Beaten Track

## Robyn Archer

One of the key elements of success in any festival is its authenticity. This is often more easily achieved in generically specific celebrations of dance, theatre, opera, food, film – anything where the context allows for a deep exploration of the genre, rather than the cherry-picking approach which a large multi-arts festival demands. But authenticity can also be achieved through a serious engagement of the host city, town or region. There are festivals whose programs, at first sight, live and breathe a sense of place: you want to be there, to experience a program which will allow you to understand the cultural depth of a place. Many religious festivals demand pilgrimage, and those arts festivals that necessitate getting you off the beaten track already have a head start in generating excitement and devotion.

This isn't a travel pitch, but the business of getting there, arriving and grabbing as much as you can while you're there, including serious engagement with the local culture and creating the possibility of collaboration or exchange, is central to the experience. You don't go to these places to slow down, but to be informed and re-invigorated by a socio-geographic and cultural environment which you may never have expected to discover.

East Arnhem Land sits at the top of Australia's Northern Territory. It is the traditional land of the Yolgnu people who have been there for tens of thousands of years. Each year, the *GARMA* festival takes place on this land. Attendance is by invitation only, though that can be extended to you by application. Its defining agenda is Indigenous cultural exchange.

The land itself is remarkable. The festival is held at the top of an escarpment which looks out onto the plains and coastline below. The easiest way to get there is to fly to Nullumbuy, and then be driven to the site. In the temperate night, it is an inspiration to feel more than a thousand people at rest, and at peace, in small silver tents pitched beneath slender grey-green gum trees. Sound idyllic? It is, especially since the mix of people all sleeping together here are young and old, Indigenous and non-Indigenous Australians from all over the continent, plus international guests, all displaying a diversity of occupations – teachers, artists, singers, bankers, politicians, social workers, film stars, architects and more. One of the reasons for applications to take part in this festival is that you have to have a purpose for being there.

Lest you get the impression that this is not an arts festival, I can list who was there and what was on the program, but it's significant that the mix of panels and workshops about health, education, resources, and land rights sits alongside concerts, dance, visual art and film in a way which says a lot about the place of the arts in Australian Aboriginal and Torres Strait Islander culture. Traditionally, rock and land art would have recorded things to do with seasons, hunting and gathering, ceremony, law, and unique incidents or encounters. 'Installations' and 'costume' are still created for ceremony around important gatherings, deaths, and law (when young men are initiated), and song and dance are part of all this.

While the seamlessness of art and life is no longer so ideally realised in the daily life of all communities, at *GARMA* you feel it intensely. The hot days are filled with moderated conversations on a wide range of topics. I sat in on one which showed how new technologies were assisting teaching in this region: one senior Aboriginal woman showed a film of her teaching on a pristine beach, talking to students online from the very location which was central to the lesson. Through its daily conversations and activities, *GARMA* provides a platform for learning about Yolgnu culture and life in this environment.

Food is provided three times a day in a communal dining area, and the outdoor gallery sits right at the edge of the escarpment. Contemplation of art on the trail, and huge vistas beyond, recharges you for more brainfood. In the evening, the arts dominate. Within view of my tent was an inflatable screen, which showed Indigenous films every night. Further from the quiet tent city was a main stage. A highlight concert featured Mandawuy Yunipingu, legendary leader of the rock band Yothu Yindi. The opening welcome saw Mandawuy sitting next to the then federal Minister for the Arts Peter Garrett, lead singer of Midnight Oil. On the concert night this was a rare re-gathering of Yothu Yindi, and the band's succession plans were evident in a group of young Yolgnu kids hip-hopping and breakdancing out front on stage. The program that night, under the clear northern sky and its spectacle of stars, also featured one of Australia's finest singer-songwriters Archie Roach and his equally gifted partner in life and song, Ruby Hunter.

The night became even more special in retrospect because Ruby passed away not so long afterwards. It was the last chance we had to see them on stage together, and for me the last chance to see and hear either, as Mandawuy was not well and passed away a few years later. In retrospect, it underscored one of the most urgent issues for Australia: how to close the gap between the health and average life expectation of an Indigenous Australian versus a non-Indigenous Australian. Mandawuy and Ruby were highly respected elders, high achievers in the world of music, inspiration to so many, yet they died many years earlier than they should have. This is exactly why *GARMA* has not only music and dance on the program, but health and education. They are not separate matters in these communities: one without the other is out of kilter with the realities of twenty-first century life. Mandawuy died at Yirrkala on 2 June 2013: he was 57. Ruby died February 2010: she was 55. As I write, I learn that the philosopher Peter Singer will take part in a debate in which he will argue that philanthropy should now not support the arts, but instead be directed to people in need. I feel sure that *GARMA* shows the divide is not as clear as that, and for many people facing dire challenges, the arts are still a vital component of daily life.

Amidst such a feast of knowledge and culture there were a couple of even more memorable moments.

A number of awards were to be presented, including an OAM (Member of the Order of Australia) to Dr Raymattja Marika (posthumously as she had died a few months earlier, at 49) and a medal to Gary Marika. Given that these investitures normally happen in the heritage confines of a State government house, or Government House in Canberra, the dry red-earth setting of an open performance/sports ground was something different. The then Administrator of the North Territory sat at one end with his wife, community members and officials, and at the other end gathered a large contingent of young and old Yolgnu dancers who advanced in their customary forward and retreat manner to the accompaniment of singing, clap sticks and Yidaki, the instrument commonly known as didgeridoo. There is immense strength in the form and, as it advanced, the dancers painted with traditional markings and wearing traditional costume and decoration, one felt the full weight of the presence of white Australia and the representative of its sovereign Queen in the Northern Territory. I have referenced a YouTube clip[1] which covers some of this very investiture – and other clips which cover the exciting (I don't use the word lightly) dances which you see at *GARMA*.[2, 3, 4, 5]

Pilgrimage is very much part of the experience at *GARMA*, and central to most of the festivals I talk about here. While the multi-genre international festivals of capital cities offer us all the joy of the arts, and I have had the privilege to direct many editions of these, it's the lesser-known festivals, defined by place, which often hold greater riches for me. Unless the artistic director or curatorial team of one of these larger festivals is ever mindful of the host city, the experience can sometimes be – "I could see this anywhere in any major city festival". While that is unlikely to apply to the majority of the local audience, who have few opportunities to travel to other cities in their country, or internationally, it is different for those of us who have privileged mobility. Even so, for those who deliberately embark on cultural tourism, especially those who live in a city which has an international arts festival, I wonder if choosing something off the beaten track – which can only be experienced in that place – is a better option than just replicating the festival experience in another major city. Everyone wants to experience *Edinburgh* or *Avignon*, and *Aix*, but has East Arnhem Land ever occurred to them?

While we're in the same part of the world, there's also the *Torres Strait Island Festival*. This used to happen every year on different islands in the Torres Strait Island group, but now usually on Thursday Island which is where I encountered it. Again, the pilgrimage is central to the experience. I flew to Darwin, and then took a smaller plane to Thursday Island, but participants come from all over the Torres Strait by tiny planes, helicopters and watercraft large and small. The Torres Strait separates the very top of Australia's York Peninsula and the southernmost part of Papua New Guinea. There are some two hundred and seventy islands whose peoples traded with Papua New Guinea, mainland Australia, and the Macassans of Indonesia way before British occupation.

The festival is held over three days and is more a time for meeting and sharing culture, than to provide a spectacle for visitors, but you're lucky to be there as an observer and, as with *GARMA*, there's ample opportunity to learn about this remarkable place and its people. The major activity is a series of presentations from the separate islands. These are large group dances, accompanied by, mainly, elders who sit and sing with musicians. The dances are divided into women's, men's, girls' and boys' groups, and the variety of dance, song, costume and headdress is staggering. The long back-to-back series can induce a trance-like state, assisted by the long form drone-like singing. Amidst this continuo, there are frequent surprises, such as the tall adults from Saibai Island who dance with bows and arrows, as do the juniors, and there's little anywhere to match this warriors' performance save perhaps the Maori *haka*. These performances also mark the clear differences between Torres Strait Islander culture and that of Aboriginal Australia (See Youtube clip).[6]

Australian Aboriginal and Torres Strait Islander cultures can now be observed in many Australian festivals dedicated only to those cultures. But these rich cultures can also be found in many other festivals, small and large. If we move down the east coast from Cape York, we reach the southeastern part of Queensland, and there a young festival is engaging with its location in ways previously unimagined.

*BLEACH* expresses the authentic personality of the Gold Coast as an arts festival. Its very name conjures the hairdos of the sixties' "blond-headed stompy-wompy real gone surfer boys"[7] as it embraces coastal/hinterland life in this region. That includes creating platforms for Indigenous artists and stories, and contributes to changing perceptions from Meter Maids (bikini-clad beach babes who used to fill the parking meters for free) and Ladies Who Lunch, to Indigenous matriarchs and young female entrepreneurs and all-age artists. The 2015 edition commissioned a project around the Aboriginal mullet story – a story of fishing and sharing: manifested as a huge lit-from-the-inside fish borne by six strong carriers, the story was shared by local elders to festival audiences. There's a future project being discussed about 'the first lifesaver', who was Aboriginal. While proud of the Gold Coast's history as the place where twentieth century surf lifesaving was born, the festival can point to earlier origins through this project.

*BLEACH 2015* also looked to the Coast's history as party-town with the *Inaugural Social Dance Affair.* Held in the charmingly old fashioned Tugun Progress Hall, this was a project to remember social dancing in the region, especially the Gold

Coast's original hokey-pokey, and included not only demonstration dancing by locals, but invited the audience up on multiple occasions for that winning social tool, the Progressive Barn Dance. This edition of *BLEACH* also included a live surf movie, as a hot surf-music band played loud on the beach, and surfers, including one very impressive 8-year-old girl, made their elegant dance-like moves out in the surf to the music they could hear. Past editions (this festival is only four years old) have also included a varied visual arts homage to *The Fibro Coast* and those fabulous shacks, and the future includes being part of an international strategy which I am devising to connect the Gold Coast with surfing cultures directly across the Pacific. Bred in the southern Gold Coast, this festival is now growing to embrace the whole of the Gold Coast, including the hinterland, but will always connect directly to this part of the continent. Here's a serious arts festival, willing to take creative risks in form and content, in the midst of a beautiful coastal and green hinterland environment. The pilgrimage is a bit less of an adventure than those I've already mentioned; directly to the Gold Coast airport, a fifty minute freeway drive from Brisbane airport, or a nine hour drive (or three day amble) up the coast from Sydney through beautiful country and coastland.

Before moving away from Australia, it's worth going way south to a tiny fishing village called Port Fairy, on the south coast of Victoria, three hours' drive from Melbourne, or six hours from Adelaide via the legendary Coonawarra wine producing region. With its inlets, watercraft of all sizes, and old dark bluestone cottages, this part of Australia is clearly different from the tropical north. There has been a popular folk festival here for many years. But while the folk community travels from all over Australia to participate in March, the end of winter is celebrated there with the *Port Fairy Spring Musical Festival*. Devoted audiences trek between various small halls and venues to hear recitals and concerts of more formal music from the so-called classical repertoire, along with new music and cabaret.

It's the appropriateness that charms. It's a small place, with generally small intimate music in small venues: you walk to everything, except perhaps your accommodation which, if you're lucky enough, is across the inlet and overlooking the rolling waves of the southern ocean. All this contributes to the pleasure of hearing music in this remote locale. Australia has a number of such well-curated music festivals –two of them, *Huntingdon* and *Coriole*, in small vineyards, and one, the *Townsville Chamber Music* Festival back up in tropical Townsville. For fans of the classical repertoire, these festivals appeal through their programs, but also very much because of these places which are off the beaten track. That they are all smaller places, and therefore relatively quiet, is significant. While our recital and concert halls in major cities are acoustically treated to keep the noise of the metropolis or megalopolis out, in these places there's a continuum of quiet outside too. It makes for good listening.

To the west of Australia, across the Indian ocean, we come to South Africa and there, through a flight to Johannesburg and then a smaller flight to Port Elizabeth, a drive gets you to Grahamstown and a festival with orthodox multi-genre international bones. But there's also a real taste of the locale too. This festival has the odd symphonic offering, but the music program is overwhelmingly African, as is theatre and dance, and provides an excellent opportunity to hear and see a diverse program of arts from a number of countries on the continent. It was the place where I first saw the work of Brett Baily – in a fantastic old two-storey wooden barn which our Australian Occupational Health and Safety laws would have ruled out as a venue. There was risk everywhere at that time, and it looks like the festival continues to support artists working outside the orthodox.

To the east of Australia we land in the Americas, and across the continent on the east coast of Canada I discovered *Celtic Colours*, during which one of the highest risks is falling in love with the landscape, and never wanting to leave. The pilgrimage required a flight to Halifax Nova Scotia, and then a drive into the beautiful country of Cape Breton. With a fair dose of the Celt in my genetic background, I've always had a passion for fiddles and mandolin, and this festival, held in Cape Breton's glorious autumn, showcases the Celtic music traditions which have been upheld and modified there for centuries. This isn't a festival of traditional Celtic music alone, but one which celebrates the way the traditions have developed in the hands of the people who live here. You have to have a car as the concerts are held throughout the cape, but that allows for much autumn indulgence. What I loved was not just the music itself, the exquisite skills in instrumental and vocal music, and the use of small halls throughout the region, but the fact that whole family lines were recognized for their maintenance and translation of these musical traditions. The festival introduced me to a lot of music and musicians I had never heard or heard of, and sated me in the lust for autumn colours and smells.

Further east, and a bit more northerly, you hit the *Reykjavik Festival* – another which has the international multi-arts format, but definitely relies very much on the local, especially contemporary, scene. We're all aware of the successes of Bjork and Sigur Ross, but since then the festival has supported a rich line of equally adventurous contemporary music makers. This cultural snapshot happens in the midst of Iceland's extraordinary landscape and history.

And so, from the concrete, to the conceptual. There are two festivals which are outstanding for the fact that one appeared never to happen, and one which really didn't happen.

Marion Pastor Roces is a Philippine academic, curator and activist whose specialist knowledge is in Asian textiles. She once spoke about a festival to which she was very privileged to be invited. Arriving in the village, she was ushered into a hut, with other women, and remained there throughout the night. Whatever happened overnight was only to be experienced first-hand by the men of the village: all the women were indoors. Marion said she could hear things happening throughout the night – people moving about, up and down the village, the sound of ceremony. But in the morning, there was absolutely no trace that anything had happened at all. She drew a parallel with certain textiles that may appear to have an aberration in the weave, seen by potential buyers as a fault. In fact, the aberration is intentional and has ceremonial significance. Just because we don't see it, it doesn't mean it doesn't happen, or is not there.

The tendency to 'assume' is a common practice of audiences for art, festival making included. While every part of a festival needs to be worth its weight, in case an audience member can only afford the time, transport or ticket price to see only one thing, it may be that an assumption is made about the quality, tone, mood or aesthetics of the whole festival on the basis of that one experience. My own approach to curating a festival is to ensure that every part, every work, is worth the time and ticket price, but at the same time ensuring that the more you see, the deeper the experience. Immersion will allow you to see the connection between the many elements, and offer the opportunity to create your own interweaving links. Nothing delights a festival director more than to be made aware of a connection which they had not seen or anticipated: it demonstrates the ferment which has arisen from a strongly curated program. This signals the energy that is arising from the alchemy of the elements, and can take the form of creative thinking, constructive analysis, aesthetic links, new collaborations in prospect, and new connections between artists and companies. The festival turns out to be not just a series of unrelated shows or activities: all the work put into building programmatic complexity, often hidden, has been rewarded in an equally deep and complex response.

*IF* was the title of Jakarts 2008 festival in Indonesia. There's a very detailed thick volume (coffee table dimensions), which describes the program in detail. According to this lush guide, globally eminent artists conducted orchestras, great theatre-makers gathered together, and the work of great artists was exhibited. In pre-festival promotion, the festival boasted works by world-famous painters such as Andy Warhol, Van Gogh and Leonardo da Vinci. "The JakArt festival, established in 2001, would also feature world-class music concerts, including a performance by the New York Philharmonic Orchestra" (The Jakarta Post, 2008). While buses did go to the airport to greet and transport the eminent guests, there were none to greet, and never had been. While there were real performances in the festival, most of a more modest, nevertheless interesting, nature, JakArt founder, pianist Ary Sutedja explained in the Jakarta Post:

> "(Part of the program) is an imaginary festival, included as part of JakArt2008. We dream that someday Jakarta will become a city of culture, Ary, co-founder of the festival," said during a visit to *The Jakarta Post* last week. She said imagination, fantasy and dreams are probably the only luxuries left amid the difficulties of life, which was why the event organizers

> put together a catalogue of their "dream" exhibits and performances for the festival (The Jakarta Post, 2008).

That much of it remained imaginary didn't matter: the catalogue made a memorable statement, still potent, about the differences between resources for festivals in different countries at different times. We would do well not to make too many assumptions about the capacity of those whose imagination is only limited by the lack of resources. In this case, the lack of government funding inspired a triumph of imagination over limitation. JakArts made this statement:

> JakArt@2008 examines the role and contribution of the politician and the bureaucrat, the businessman, the corporate world, the foundation, the cultural institution, the festival, and the individual: the citizen, the artist, the intellectual, in shaping today's and tomorrow's world. Because in today's world everything has been turned upside-down: the corrupt are busy fighting corruption, the immoral are proposing and imposing ethics, the fundamentalists and the intolerant are promoting tolerance, and the unjust promoting justice. And, that is what JakArt@2008 is built around.
>
> *IF*: *The Imaginary Festival* is a collaboration of many real imaginary, real, and imaginary real artists (from all the disciplines of the Arts) intellectuals, critics, promoters, producers, sponsors, volunteers, audiences... *IF* is a contemporary art piece designed to entangle and disentangle the seemingly contradictory threads that so dominate our life; to explore and question our perceptions and their limitations; to expose and promote the power of imagination; to unveil and discover alternative realities while critically examining our society and the realities currently available; to inspire and foster a collective fantasy laced with imagination that if subscribed to and sustained for long enough can in itself become a new collective reality.
>
> This year our motto was: Reality begins where Fantasy ends. (Jakart, 2015)

Imagination is at the heart of new festivals too. Until the first edition happens, new festivals are also imaginary. I love the feeling of great energy and enthusiasm for a new festival: small or large, there's a compelling vision and a passion to make it happen. As I write, there is something brewing in Hong Kong in East Kowloon. We are all aware of the huge development in West Kowloon where the site for the West Kowloon Cultural District has been imaginatively used during development for pop-up stages, exhibitions and festivals. But there's energy in the rapidly changing East Kowloon too, where one woman's passion for doing something for the local residents may well result in a significant new festival. Watch that space.

And keep an eye out for something that may soon emerge in the Caribbean. Jacques Martial (former President of Parc La Villette in Paris) was recently appointed President of Memorial ACTe, a new museum in Guadeloupe. While the museum has been dedicated to the remembrance of slavery, Jacques Martial is planning an active program for Memorial ACTe, and this will surely include thinking about a new festival for this region. It is currently as hidden as the festival Marion Pastor Roces heard but could not see, and as imaginary as JakArt's *IF* in 2008, but we should celebrate these creative eruptions and the energies they release. Festivals are not always just pragmatic aggregations of art and culture, nor simply commercially successful marketing umbrellas. As their early evolutions almost always attest, many festivals all over the world have their own altruistic beginnings and often amount to much more than the mere sum of the parts.

## Bibliography

Jakart (2015) If Indonesian Fantasy Imaginary Festival, at http://www.jakart.info/jakart@2008/if.htm, accessed 10/12/15

The Jakarta Post (2008) Ary Sutedja: offering imaginary, real arts fest, in The Jakarta Post, http://www.thejakartapost.com/news/2008/07/31/ary-sutedja-offering-imaginary-real-arts-fest.html# accessed 10/12/15

## Notes

1 https://www.youtube.com/watch?v=vmIk5c4Ga4o - Investiture

2 https://www.youtube.com/watch?v=zD2eG3iqRR0 - Red Flag dance

3 https://www.youtube.com/watch?v=E-dFNlyh10Q - dance and song

4 https://www.youtube.com/watch?v=199WRUghECw - 2012 with Jack narrating

5 https://www.youtube.com/watch?v=I8qP62ZjoEA - dance and music

6 https://www.youtube.com/watch?v=gz7-R7bDRDY Thursday Island Cultural Festival 2012

7 Title of a 1964 chart hit by Australian singer *Little Pattie*

# 26 The *Parkes Elvis Festival*: Attendee and Host Community Perspectives

Katie Schlenker, Carmel Foley and Eve Carroll-Dwyer

## Introduction

Each year, up to 20,000 people descend upon the rural town of Parkes, 365km west of Sydney, to attend the *Parkes Elvis Festival*. Initiated in 1993 by a group of locals who were Elvis Presley fans, the annual festival has grown from the humble beginnings of a one-day event with a few hundred attendees to a five day festival.

In a bid to assist the festival organisers to understand the impacts of the Parkes Elvis Festival on both attendees and the host community, researchers designed a set of survey instruments to deliver a comprehensive evaluation of the social and economic impacts of the festival. Research was carried out in 2010 and separate surveys were conducted for festival organisers, attendees and local residents. After a brief explanation of the festival, and the man it is inspired by, this chapter explores the methods used to collect data before outlining the results. The results are divided into two key sections, attendees' perceptions, and host community perceptions.

First we profile the demographics, motivations and experience of festival attendees. Second, we profile the perceptions of the host community with respect to both the economic and social impacts of the festival. The surveys demonstrate the overwhelming goodwill and enthusiasm for the festival, by both the host community and attendees. Results show that the festival attracts a mix of first time and repeat visitors, and that many of the returning attendees do so to catch up with friends made at previous festivals. For residents, regardless of whether they attend or not, the large majority understand the economic, tourism and community benefits generated by the festival.

## Elvis and the *Parkes Elvis Festival*

Known as the 'King of Rock and Roll', Elvis Aaron Presley was born in Tupelo Mississippi, in 1935 and became one of the most influential and celebrated singer/

entertainers of the 20th century. His momentous career lasted over 20 years, and ended with his premature death at the age of 42. Elvis's career spanned both music and film and will be forever associated with the rise and evolution of Rock n' Roll. The festival is timed to coincide with Elvis' birthday (January 8th) and includes a multitude of Elvis impersonators who provide official featured showcases, as well as the more informal busking Elvises. Alongside the musical entertainment there are over 120 activities spread throughout the town of Parkes, each inspired by various facets of Elvis' career. Popular activities include a street parade, vintage car exhibition, rock and roll dancing, a poets' breakfast – where odes to Elvis can be delivered – market stalls, a Miss Priscilla dinner (honouring Elvis's wife, Priscilla Presley, and with a new 'Miss Priscilla' being crowned each year), an interdenominational gospel service and a mass renewal of wedding vows (http://www.parkeselvisfestival.com.au/).

**Figure 26.1:** Elvis impersonator at the *Parkes Elvis Festival.* © Parkes Elvis Festival

The whole town of Parkes embraces the theme with a range of business operators getting involved. The main shopping streets are festooned and retailers take up the festival theme, decorating their shop windows for example, 'Love me Tender lamb chops at $10.99 a kilo!' (Jonson, et al. forthcoming). Loud speakers and buskers line the streets and a jovial ambiance radiates throughout the, otherwise quiet, country town. A key feature that fortifies the spirit, and eccentricity, of the event is that attendees are not simply spectators at the festival – they also participate and take an active role as they dress up in outfits inspired by Elvis, be it his music, movies or the rock n' roll era. Individuals address their fellow participants/entertainers as if they are real characters. Thousands of Elvises and

Pricillas walk the streets engaging with each other, and their 'fans' in full character in an otherwise unremarkable, Australian rural town.

As a region whose main economic staple is farming, and is otherwise best known for its CSIRO satellite dish (featured in the classic Australian movie *The Dish*, released in 2000), Parkes does not hold any obvious connections to music, or indeed Elvis himself. Despite the festival's unconventionality, its growth and sustained success attracted sponsorship from companies such as CountryLink, Coca Cola, Clubs NSW, Rex Regional Express, Anderson First National Real Estate (Foley et al., 2011). Parkes has become widely known as the 'Elvis Capital of Australia' and the festival has become a major event in the New South Wales regional calendar. The overwhelming success of this regional event, and its largely favourable perception amongst both attendees and the host community, means that it serves as a beneficial case study.

## Survey method

Two surveys were conducted to access both the attendees' perspective and the perspective of locals regarding the festival during the 2010 *CountryLink Parkes Elvis Festival*. A team of five researchers surveyed attendees on-site at the festival using a three page paper-based questionnaire. Some 371 festival attendees completed the questionnaire over the three-day period. The poll was conducted on a purely random basis, with no quota sampling applied. Both visitors and Parkes residents were interviewed. A 'next person past' method was used in approaching respondents. When approaching a couple or group, researchers asked one person to nominate himself/herself as the person to complete the interview.

The host community was surveyed two weeks after the festival using a random fixed line phone poll of 403 Parkes residents aged 18 years and over. Respondents were selected at random from a commercial database of 3,137 residential telephone numbers within the 2870 postcode, with no quota sampling applied. Potential respondents were screened to ensure they were aged 18 or over and had heard of the *Parkes Elvis Festival*. The survey time varied from 8 to 29 minutes, with an average of 12.8 minutes. Response rate was satisfactory, with approximately 48% of the eligible households contacted agreeing to participate.

## Attendee perspectives

The attendee survey demonstrated the key demographics of those who attended the *Parkes Elvis Festival* in 2010 (see Figure 26.2). Over half of all respondents resided in regional New South Wales. One quarter of the respondents were from its capital, Sydney and 15% were from interstate or overseas. 16% of attendees were from the local area.

| Gender | |
|---|---|
| Male | 36% |
| Female | 64% |
| **Age** | |
| 18-24 | 2% |
| 25-34 | 3% |
| 35-44 | 11% |
| 45-54 | 27% |
| 55-64 | 37% |
| 65+ | 20% |

| Place of Residence (n=371) | |
|---|---|
| Regional NSW | 53% |
| Sydney | 17% |
| Parkes | 16% |
| State of Queensland | 6% |
| State of Victoria | 5% |
| Other | 4% |
| **First time visiting the Festival** (n=369) | |
| No | 53% |
| Yes | 47% |
| **First time visiting Parkes?** (n=314) | |
| No | 58% |
| Yes | 42% |

**Figure 26.2:** *Parkes Elvis Festival* attendee profile

## Who came?

The *Parkes Elvis Festival* attracts an older demographic, with 84% aged over 45 years of age and 57% aged over 55. This is not surprising considering that Elvis was a music idol of the baby-boomer generation who are represented in these age groups. Additionally, retirees have the time for leisure pursuits and, in general, have the financial means to travel. Only 2% of attendees surveyed were aged between 18-24, 3% aged between 25-34 and 11% aged 35-44. This demographic configuration poses a major concern for festival visitor numbers over the longer term as the baby boomer generation recedes.

Of those surveyed, over two-thirds were female. Retirees provided the largest group of attendees (24%), as can be expected given the older demographic profile of all attendees. The remaining attendees had a wide variety of occupations with the second largest percentages after retirees listed as houseworker (8%) and health care worker (8%), followed by office/administration (6%), teacher/trainer (6%), manager (4%), farmer (4%) and business director/entrepreneur (4%). Ministers, bankers, accountants, scientists and members of the military were also present, amongst others. Ultimately, aside from the large portion of retirees, the attendees came from a diverse range of professional backgrounds and sectors.

## How did they get there?

The official mode of transport for the event was the 'Elvis Express', a Country Link train that leaves from Sydney's Central Station and travels directly to Parkes. The train ticket is a package deal that includes entertainment while on board, a souvenir programme and unlimited shuttle bus transportation within Parkes throughout the festival. While only 7% travelled to the festival on the train, it's an integral part of the event with the train's arrival at Parkes station signalling the start of the festivities. The excitement builds from the time its guests step on board (usually already in costume), singing and dancing their way to Parkes where they are greeted with much fanfare upon their arrival. The vast majority of visitors (83%) travel to the event by car and, once in Parkes, made their way around town by walking (78%).

## Accommodation

With the festival resulting in a short-term boost to the population of Parkes, a variety of types of accommodation are used by visitors. 18% stayed with friends or relatives, 17% camped or stayed in caravans and motorhomes, 15% were hosted in local homes, 15% were accommodated in motels, hotels and cabins within Parkes, with another 13% staying in a motel or hotel outside of Parkes. Finally, 10% camped/caravanned at the Parkes showground.

## How many days they attended the festival

Those interviewed were asked how many days they expected to attend the festival. A sizeable proportion of visitors (32%) were planning to spend three days attending the festival, with a further 36% spending four days or more. Some stayed for shorter periods, with 15% for one day and 17% staying for two days.

## What they spent

Average (estimated) expenditure for festival goers was $256 (AUD) per person overall (includes local attendees), and $280 (AUD) per head for visitors to Parkes. This implies a total contribution from the festival in excess of $3 million (AUD). Main items of expenditure were event tickets, accommodation, meals, other entertainment, transport and personal services. Average per head spend on Elvis and/or festival merchandise was $81 (AUD). With expenditure in New South Wales outside of Parkes Shire at $688 (AUD) per person, the flow-on effect of the festival to other parts of regional NSW was quite high.

## Motivation for coming to the *Parkes Elvis Festival*

Attendees were asked to rate ten motivations for attending the festival on a scale from 1-10, where 1 was 'Extremely unimportant' and 10 was 'Extremely important'. The major motivation was to 'play and have fun' (mean 8.52), closely followed by 'the music/entertainment' (8.51) and 'to escape from one's everyday routine' (8.0). The desire to 'experience a sense of community' (7.29) also ranked strongly. Interestingly these motivations all ranked higher than what would, on face value, be the most obvious motivation – that of being a fan of Elvis (7.02).

These results demonstrate the importance that 'play' has in fuelling the success of an event such as the *Parkes Elvis Festival*. Indeed one interviewer notes that when surveyed participants were asked if their motivation was to 'play and have fun' their faces would light up and they would say 'oh yeah! ... That one (that 'play and have fun' option)! That is what I'm doing!' Jonson et al (forthcoming) argue that the importance of 'play' in the festival's success has significance in how events and leisure are conceptualised on a broader scale. In the context of a postmodern environment where leisure is often regarded as depthless and potentially meaningless, spurred by notions of its inauthenticity, the *Parkes Elvis Festival* is a remarkable exception. By providing a playful space in which attendees can immerse themselves, the festival provides meaningful opportunities for socialisation and community bonding (Jonson et al, forthcoming).

When the motivation of 'play' is blended with notions of 'escaping the everyday', the attraction of the event becomes clear. With adoring 'fans' lining up to 'kiss Elvis', the element of 'play' provided a socially sanctioned opportunity to break standard boundaries. With many attendees dressing up in costume, the festival gives people permission to be playful and to get involved. In turn this built a sense of sociability and community, forging bonds between otherwise diverse individuals. The festival appealed to a wider audience than simply the Elvis fan base and provided a unique and inclusive experience, embraced by the vast majority of attendees.

Of those who attended the festival, 47% had been to the festival before, while 42% were visiting the town for the first time. All but 2% had travelled to Parkes specifically for the festival. The high level of repeat visitation reflects the overwhelmingly positive experience of attendees. One third were attending their second festival, while a loyal following of 7% had attended 15 or more.

Having explored the demographics and motivations of those who attended the *Parkes Elvis Festival*, we now turn our attention to the perception of the host community, a large proportion of whom also attended the festival.

## Host community perspectives

Of the survey respondents, 60% had lived in Parkes for 20 years or more and thus prior to the founding of the festival. 69% of the respondents were female. All were over the age of 18 with 13% being 18-35 years of age, 24% were 36-50, 33% were aged 51-65 and the remaining 30% were over 65years old. 71% of respondents had attended the 2010 festival and 85% had attended in previous years.

The host community survey explored residents' perceptions of the social and economic impacts of the festival. The festival was for the most part a source of great pride and fondness for local residents. Many of the respondents stated that they wanted the festival to continue in the future and get 'bigger and better' and when asked for a word to describe the festival the most popular word was 'great!'.

## Economic effects

Festivals of one kind or another play an important role in the economic and social development of regional communities. Festivals are generally seen as increasing economic activity and creating new jobs resulting from the net increase in demand for goods and services they generate. The attendee survey indicated that the expenditure injected into Parkes Shire as a result of the festival exceeded $3 million (AUD). This expenditure equates to sales revenues of local businesses in respect of ticket sales, accommodation, meals, other entertainment, transport and personal services. In an unprompted question, respondents listed benefits to the economy (51%) and impacts on tourism flows (36%) as the two major positive impacts of the festival. One respondent remarked upon the positive impact of the festival and how "it brings so much outside money into the district… the fact that we are able to double the population in one weekend has a huge positive impact upon the whole town." Another claimed that because Parkes is a rural town, the place can get "very sad after Christmas and the shops get poor". The *Elvis Festival* (in the second week of January) "boosts the economy back up and provides a lovely and happy atmosphere". Underlying the economic benefits accruing from such an event, more than one-third of respondents said that they had worked extra hours as a result of the festival. Comments demonstrated that the festival was perceived as a positive stimulus for employment and skills creation. Certain concerns were evident, however. One respondent argued that growth of the festival had potentially cut out the ability of some local community members to participate. He complained that his wife used to have a stall but as the event has become more commercial, many of the smaller stallholders can no longer afford to rent a stall space. Another stated simply that the festival only benefits a certain number of businesses.

Over the longer term, increased tourism flows to Parkes as a result of hosting the festival can lead to growth of existing businesses, the establishment of new ones, and the development of a more skilled workforce. There is evidence that the hosting of successful festivals is associated with increased business confidence (the business counterpart to increased civic pride), inducing greater business activity including increased business investment, and induced construction and development expenditure (Jago et al., 2003; Newbold et al., 2015). Organisers may wish to find ways to ensure that more businesses, both small and large, can benefit from the festival.

## Social impacts

While the *Parkes Elvis Festival* was a boost to tourism and the economy of the region, much of the fondness that it generated was directed towards the positive impacts it had in terms of building a sense of community and bringing people together. As a rural town with some economic disadvantage, and, at the time of the survey, in the midst of a drought, there was an overwhelming sense that the festival provided a morale boost for locals, even providing them with a "reason to get out of bed for the weekend". It provided the local residents with an escape from their everyday lives, just as it provided the visitors with the opportunity to escape theirs. One respondent perhaps summed it up the best stating: "if (the festival) wasn't held, it would be a big hole – people would miss it".

Locals viewed the access to entertainment very positively, with 97% stating that this was one of the key impacts the festival provided to the local community. Another key impact, with 94% in agreement, was that the festival provided locals with the opportunity to meet new people, and 93% enjoyed a shared experience with friends and family. Factors of social isolation were able to be overcome as the festival provided a means to bond with strangers, as well as drawing a large group of new people to the otherwise relatively isolated town. The festival was also perceived to raise local spirits, with comments such as "I love people at festival time – the festival is so good for the community", and "the festival is good for community spirit and brings people together". These comments demonstrate how the festival was perceived to help provide a means of social connection and create a sense of community within the town.

The festival also relies on local involvement. While most are likely to simply attend and to enjoy the jovial spirit, 10% of respondents worked as volunteers. A further 6% opened their homes to visitors in the 'home hosting' programme and 60% said they would consider doing so in the future. This community involvement helps the festival to continue, providing a source of volunteer labour and helping alleviate the difficulty of accommodating such large numbers of event tourists. The community support provides a backbone to the festival, both in terms of providing a welcoming environment for the festivities to successfully take place as well as the practicality of running the event.

Nearly every respondent agreed that the festival enhanced Parkes' reputation (98%), and 91% said it increased the sense of pride that locals felt towards their town. There was also a clear sense that it helps raise awareness of Parkes and it was frequently mentioned that the festival "put Parkes on the map". A resident explained that when they visited Western Australia (a state on the opposite side of the country to New South Wales) they were amazed that so many people knew of the festival. The fact that it was not just a regional or national reputation also proved exciting, with one local proudly commenting about how they were told by a German visitor that out of all the Elvis festivals she had been to overseas, the *Parkes Elvis Festival* was the best.

While the majority of responses were overwhelmingly positive in their attitudes toward the social impacts of the festival, there were limited concerns regarding some negative impacts upon the local community. For example, 11% complained that the festival increased rowdy behaviour, yet 72% said this was not a problem and 17% remained unsure. There was slightly less consensus regarding concern that the festival encouraged excessive drinking and/or drug use with 16% agreeing that this was a problem, 52% said it was not and 33% remained unsure.

A more common concern was that the festival did not appropriately provide for people with disabilities. For example, the main entertainment area, Cooke Park proved difficult for wheelchair access. Others complained that some events were too crowded and therefore overwhelming for some people with autism or the elderly. Respondents suggested a few smaller events be included to cater for these special needs. Given that the festival attracts an ageing demographic, the need to cater for those with mobility, sight, hearing and other age-related disabilities is even more pressing. Accessible pathways around event and accommodation venues, and accessible transportation and facilities are areas that need further attention (Darcy and Harris, 2003). An additional concern that arose was that the festival had become too big for Parkes to accommodate/handle. Some respondents suggested it may need to move to a nearby larger town such as Dubbo or Forbes, while others strongly argued against this stating "the festival is great for Parkes, I hope Dubbo does not steal it!"

## Conclusions

Clearly the festival has the support of the community. Given the importance of community support and involvement for any such event to be sustainable over time (Small, 2007; Schlenker et al., 2010) we can have confidence that the *Parkes Elvis Festival* will continue to attract visitors into the future. This case study has highlighted the benefits such a festival provides to the town of Parkes – it provides a space for visitors and locals alike to escape the everyday, to bond and to build community ties. The festival provides a unique product, one that does not have an obvious connection to its geographic location. Despite the lack of any tangible connection between Parkes and Elvis, the festival is an overwhelming success and continues to grow. In large part, this is due to its ability to embrace its eccentricity and to provide an inclusive space and a sociable environment.

For the festival to continue to deliver net benefits to locals, however, a number of issues need to be explored. One issue involves the economic effects of the festival, specifically the impacts on local income and employment. To date no economic impact study of the festival has been undertaken. As noted above, expenditure measures alone do not inform decision makers of the effects of the festival on the wider economy (Edwards et al., 2014). More research also needs to be undertaken to determine the role that the *Parkes Elvis Festival* can play in the destination branding of Parkes Shire and the extent to which it can be used to support the tourism marketing effort. To date no surveys targeted at business operators have been undertaken, despite their potential to generate very useful 'supply side' information on operator attitudes and strategies to maximise the economic effects of the festival. Gaps exist also in our understanding of the role played by professional performers and artists in the festival's success. Stakeholder support for any such festival should never be taken for granted by organisers and is essential for its future performance.

As a final comment, the community plays an important role in ensuring successful implementation of events such as the *Parkes Elvis Festival,* particularly in respect of provision of hospitality and visitor safety and security. Hospitality relates not only to the provision of accommodation, food and beverage but also to the perceived friendliness of the local population and community attitudes towards visitors. While the perceived social effects are overwhelmingly positive at the present time, it is essential that festival convenors monitor community attitudes over time. The greater that local involvement is in the development of an event, the more likely residents are to feel a sense of 'ownership' of that event. Local participation in festival planning can help to forge business linkages between tourism activity and other, formal and informal, activity in the community to secure a vibrant and sustainable future for the *Parkes Elvis Festival.*

# Bibliography

Darcy, S., and Harris, R. (2003) Inclusive and accessible special event planning: An Australian perspective, in *Event Management: An International Journal,* **8**(1), 39-47.

Edwards, D. C., Schlenker, K., Foley, C. T., Hergesell, A., and Dwyer, A. (2014). Evaluating the economic contribution of a large indoor entertainment venues: an inscope expenditure study, in *Event Management: An International Journal,* **18**(4), 407-420.

Foley, C., Schlenker, K., and Schweinsberg, S. C. (2011) Triple-Bottom-Line event evaluation and the 2010 CountryLink Parkes Elvis Festival, in J. Allen, W. O'Toole, R. Harris, and I. McDonnell (eds.), *Festival and Special Event Management,* Milton, Queensland: John Wiley and Sons Australia, 511-515.

Getz, D. (2010) The nature and scope of festival studies, in *International Journal of Event Management Research,* **5**(1), 1-47.

Jago, L., Chalip, L., Brown, G., Mules, T., and Ali, S. (2003) Building events into destination branding: Insights from experts, in *Event Management: An International Journal,* **8**(1), 3-14.

Jonson, P., Small, J., Foley, C., and Schlenker, K. (forthcoming) All shook up at the Parkes Elvis Festival: The role of play in events, *Event Management: An International Journal,* Special issue on 'Event Management and Society'.

Newbold, C., Jordan, J., Bianchini, F., and Maughan, C. (2015) Introduction: Focusing on festivals, in C. Newbold, C. Maughan, J. Jordan, and F. Bianchini (eds.), *Focus on Festivals: Contemporary European Case Studies and Perspectives,* Oxford: Goodfellow, xv-xxvi.

Parkes Elvis Festival. (2015) *Parkes Elvis Festival.* Available: http://www.parkeselvisfestival.com.au/ [Accessed 13 July 2015].

Schlenker, K., Foley, C., and Getz, D. (2010) *Encore Festival and Event Evaluation Kit: Review and Redevelopment,* CRC for Sustainable Tourism, Gold Coast, Queensland, Australia.

Small, K. (2007), Social dimensions of community festivals: an application of factor analysis in the development of the Social Impact Perception (SIP) scale, in *Event Management: An International Journal,* **11**(1-2), 45-55.

# 27 'We have been called Carnival People': The Festive Culture of Trinidad and Tobago

Milla Cozart Riggio

> We have been called *Carnival* people; we live the whole style.... We are about a million and a half, no more than that, making up this twin nation of Trinidad and Tobago. *Carnival* distinguishes us from anybody else I have met, anywhere in the world... [T]his Trinidad *Carnival* is unique. It is part of us, and, like a passport, we go with it everywhere (John Cupid, Stegassy Interview, 1998: 96).

The twin island Republic of Trinidad and Tobago is simultaneously one of the most industrialized Caribbean nations and the home to the region's signature annual *Carnival*, the largest of Trinidad and Tobago's many festivals.[1] Currently the world's leading exporter of ammonia, second leading exporter of methanol and the largest supplier of liquefied natural gas to the United States, Trinidad has a lifestyle, an economy, and a cultural diversity harvested from old world civilizations in Africa, Europe, and Asia – all keyed simultaneously to its industrial energy production and its rich festive calendar. A half dozen miles off the coast of Venezuela, this small island republic is partially defined by what it hovers between: urban and rural communities, a kaleidoscope of ethnicities and races, industrial development and multi-ethnic, multi-religious festive celebrations.

T&T (as the Republic is often known) is poised between the demands of work and play (Riggio, 2004). Central to this lifestyle is *Carnival*, which in the late nineteenth century evolved as an African Emancipation celebration masked within the French Catholic pre-Lenten *Carnaval* ('farewell to the flesh'). Popularly dubbed 'the greatest show on earth'[2] or, ironically, 'the Mecca' of carnival performances, Trinidad *Carnival* coexists with a wide range of ethnic, religious, and secular celebrations.

For 2015, the Trinidad and Tobago government authorized thirteen official holidays. Beginning with January 1, they include *New Year's Day*; the *Spiritual (Shouter) Baptist Liberation Day* on March 30; *Good Friday* and *Easter Monday*, April 3 and 6; *Indian Arrival Day*, May 30; the feast of *Corpus Christi*, June 4; *Labour Day*, June 19; *Eid-Al-Fitr*, Saturday July 18; *Emancipation Day*, August 1; *Independence Day*, August 31; *Republic Day*, September 24; *Divali*, November 11; *Christmas Day*, December 25 and *Boxing Day*, December 26. Of these official holidays, one celebrates the Gregorian New Year, four commemorate historical milestones and eight are religious.

The eight religious holidays represent four different religions: five Christian, one Muslim, one Hindu, one African Baptist. *Good Friday*, *Easter Monday*, and *Corpus Christi* are moveable Christian feasts linked to *Easter*, governed by the intersection of lunar cycles with the spring solstice. *Divali*, a Hindu autumn celebration, is likewise keyed to the intersecting movements of the moon and the sun, in the Hindu months of Asvina and Kartika (corresponding roughly to October and November). *Eid-al-Fitr*, on the first day of the Islamic month of Shawwal culminates the month of fasting during Ramadan; keyed only to the cycles of the moon, Eid in typical Islamic fashion moves throughout the twelve months of the year.

Ethnic and political emancipation is deeply encoded in T&T national history. *Emancipation Day* directly honors the liberation of the enslaved Africans initiated in 1834 (completed in 1838); *Indian Arrival Day* commemorates the arrival of Indians who were brought first in 1845, many against their will, mainly from Northern India, to work the plantations in Trinidad after the African liberation and who now constitute the largest ethnic group in Trinidad. The latest census (2011) reported 1,328,019 residents of Trinidad and Tobago. Of these, in Trinidad, 35.43% report as Indo-Trinidadian, 34.22% Afro-Trinidadian, 7.66% mixed Indo and Afro, 15.16% other ethnic mixtures, with 1.31% split between Caucasian, Portuguese, Syrian/Lebanese, Chinese, Indigenous, and 6.22% not identified. In contrast, Tobago reports more than 85% of Afro-descent (Central Statistical Office, T&T Government, 2012).[3]

*Independence Day*, which in 1962 brought Trinidad's first Prime Minister, Afro-Caribbean, Oxford University PhD Eric Williams to office, celebrates freedom from British colonial rule. *Republic Day* marks the 1976 creation of the Republic of Trinidad and Tobago. Notably *Labour Day*, which in 1973 was declared a holiday, honors the Butler oilfield riots that took place in 1937, led by Tubal Uriah 'Buzz' Butler, a leader in the Oilfield Workers Trade Union and a devout Spiritual Baptist. Spiritual (or Shouter) Baptists were from 1917 to 1951 forbidden to practice their faith. Forty-five years after the ban was lifted, this largely Afro-Trinidadian sect gained its own *Spiritual Baptist Liberation Day* in 1996, ironically granted by the United National Congress government led by Indo-Trinidadian Prime Minister Basdeo Panday, who himself rose to power through his role in the Trinidad Cane Farmers union.

In addition to the thirteen legal holidays, many other festivals enrich the story of cultural cross-fertilization. The First Peoples, whose population was decimated by the arrival of the Spanish, still claim their ancestry as the foundational culture. The most visible concentration of the Kari'ña (formerly known as Caribs) is in the borough of Arima, where their annual *Santa Rosa Festival* is held each August in the Catholic Church. The First Peoples community is led by Chief Ricardo

Bharath Hernandez (probably of mainly Lokono origin) and Queen Jennifer Cassar, the Chief a former deputy Mayor of Arima and the Queen an official in the National *Carnival* Commission, both devoutly Catholic as well as honored leaders of the Santa Rosa First People, as is Cristo Adonis, the community's *payai* (healer; see Adonis).

The First People share with their Afro- and Indo-Caribbean countrymen a profound respect both for the sanctity of the earth and the continuity of the ancestral presence. Orisha feasts are held traditionally from the Yoruban month Igbe (April) through Owaro (November). Yoruban cosmology, which recognizes Olorun as the supreme deity, establishes not only a pantheon of Orishas but also "affectionate filial links between the living and their ancestors [through] sacred masquerade festivals". The ability to reach across the divide between the living and the dead reflects a core feature of T&T identity: the sense that the seen and the unseen, the material and the immaterial, and the past and present are in perpetual balance, sharing in the cosmic song that incorporates death into its festive circle.

> [R]itual sacrifices and the manipulation of reality... simulate the ritual return, on an annual basis and in times of crisis, of ancestors. During these festivals the returning ancestors fraternize with the living, entertaining with songs/chants, graceful dance steps, magical feats, and generously bestowing their blessings on them (Aiyejina and Gibbons: 39).

Together, Afro- and Indo-Trinidadians constitute approximately 80% of the total culture. Concentrated in Central Trinidad, the Hindu community also sustains ancestral legacies. *Divali*, the only official Hindu holiday brightens the waning year with thousands of lighted deyas (clay vessels filled with lighted oil) and enlivens it with the sounds of bursting bamboo and the sight of beautiful Indian women gracing the *Divali* fashion shows, attracting many non-Hindu participants.[4] *Divali* culminates the autumnal play cycles of *Ramleela*, known in the Trinidad vernacular as Ramdilla, a term still used in the Hindu Prachar Kendra, the temple where for the past twelve years a summer camp has prepared children for their fall re-enactment, for which they learn Hindi as well as their own ancestral history (See Figure 27.1).

In a cycle that lasts three to ten nights, *Ramleela/Ramdilla* dramatizes the narrative of sixteenth-century Hindu poet-saint Tulsidas's *Ramcharitamanasa*. Trinidad – with Hindus approximately 24% of its population – presents arguably the largest *Ramleela* outside of India. Approximately 30 venues annually enact the drama of Sri Rama's exile from and return to the throne of Ayodhya. The annual cycle reenacts not only the sacred text but also the experience of Hindus who dwell 'in between' their home in Trinidad and the homeland from which their ancestors were exiled, primarily from Uttar Pradesh and other northern regions close to the ancient city of Ayodhya. The story of exile, thus, both historically and mythically annually enacts their own cultural identity on multiple levels (Riggio, 2010).

**Figure 27.1:** Panchawati (forest) episode at Bal Ramdilla, Hindu Prachar Kendra, Raghunanan Road, Enterprise, Trinidad and and Tobago. Left to right Ravish as Shri Ram, Prashanta as Sita, Jovan as a vanar (monkey) and OM Prakash as Lakshman. 2006. (Photograph by Jeffrey Chock)

In the spring, Hindu celebrations include *Shiv Ratri*, often close to *Carnival*. But *Phagwa*, also known as *Holi-Phagwa*, bridges the last day of Phalguna, the twelfth Hindu month, and the beginning of Chaitra, the first month of the Hindu year. Culminating a season that also honors the birth of Mother Saraswati, the Hindu deity of knowledge and patroness of creative arts, *Phagwa* brings in the Hindu new year with celebrants throwing or using tubes known as *pichakaree* to spray a colorful liquid known as *abeer* over each other. Though not an official national holiday, "as with all observances in our multi-ethnic, multi-religious country, the wider community always gets involved" (*Newsday*, March 2, 2015).

Significantly, *Phagwa* embodies two other features of Trinidad festivals: first, good fun fuels cultural education. *Holi-Phagwa* dramatizes the heroic story of Prahalad, who resisted wild elephants, poisonous snakes and other tortures devised by his wicked father Hiranyakashipu, and ultimately the fire that his wicked Aunt Holika tried to cast him into, only to be burnt herself while he miraculously survived. Second, Trinidad festivals interpenetrate. *Pichakaree*, used to pitch *abir* (*abeer*), is now the name of a new musical form, with a national competition devised by Raviji to give Hindu youths an alternative to *Carnival* competitions – calypso, soca, and the well-established hybrid form *soca chutney* (chatney) – that occur also during the spring.

Despite the differential between Hindus and Muslims (Muslims about 5-6% of the overall population), Trinidad contains over 100 mosques (masjids) and organizations, including an Islamic Academy founded by a female doctor, the late Dr. Joan Kasim. The one official Muslim holiday, *Eid-al-Fitr* breaks the Ramadan fast in mainly private dinners. Drawing a larger public audience and controversial in a way *Eid* is not is *Hosay*, the event that first took me to Trinidad in 1991. This nominally Shi'i festival further – astonishingly – illustrates the interpenetration of festive traditions in a nation characterized by a contradictory cultural rhythm: that which is and that which is not often cohabit.

*Hosay* is itself contested. Imported into Trinidad from India in the nineteenth century by indentured workers, it commemorates the event that marks the schism between the Sunnis and Shi'is – the assassination of Hussein Ibn Ali, the grandson of Mohammad, his brother Hasan, his sons and followers on the plain of Karbala (outside Baghdad), in the Islamic year 61AH (680 CE).[5]

This siege occurred reportedly over the first ten days of the month of Muharram, the first month in the Islamic calendar, culminating on Ashura, the tenth day, with the death of Hussein himself. As one of the holiest of events in the Shi'i year, the celebration of Ashura worldwide has been the locus of sometimes massive attacks by Sunni extremists on Shi'i worshippers. Even in Trinidad *Hosay* is repudiated by some 'orthodox' Muslims.[8] Moreover, though the celebrants of *Hosay* follow strict rituals of abstinence that reflect their piety, the Trinidad processions, celebrated in the streets, attract large, often noisy beer-drinking crowds. Thus, despite the core of devotion, *Hosay* has been criticized in terms that also characterize attacks on *Carnival* – for profaning a sacred occasion.

**Figure 27.2:** Bis-Ali Hosay performs on the Western Main Road on the final evening of *Hosay* celebrations in St James, January 19, 2008. The front bass drummer is Jamaal Bisnath. (Photograph by Mark Lyndersay)

Trinidad *Hosay* is centered on a month of drumming and building preparation, accompanied by fasting and abstinence. Three nights and one day of funereal processions culminate the celebration: on the first night flags are carried, on the second small tadjehs or tombs honoring Hasan, and on the third night and on Ashura, the following day, large tadjehs reincarnate the tomb of Hussein, accompanied by tassa drums that play four different beats (Korom, and Riggio, 2007; see Figure 27.2). The crucial aspect of *Hosay* here, however, is how a nominally Islamic occasion not only engages others but in the South is organized by Hindus (with a few Christians). The how and why of that is key to the nature of T&T festive culture. In the southern fishing village of Cedros, the patriarch of the Ganpat family, when asked why Hindus were so involved, said simply, "It's easy. We become Muslims for a month" (Riggio, 1992).

Beyond the fascinating implications of this idea, *Hosay* parallels *Ramleela/Ramdilla* in recalling the homeland of India. Several *Hosay* families claim to have carried a bucket of Indian soil on the *Fatel* Razack, the first ship to bring indentured workers to Trinidad in 1845. At each *Hosay* celebration site, particularly in Cedros where *Hosay* is still partially identified with sugar plantations, this soil becomes part of a consecrated 'chowk', around which prayers are said and where the commemorative objects – the flags, small Hasan tadjehs, and massive Hussein tadjehs – are consecrated on successive nights after being moved into yards from building sheds known as Imambarra. Though ostensibly a relic of the plain of Karbala, the soil carried from India has mythically been moved from chowk to chowk, an emblem of the homeland. The religious ceremony has become entangled in ancestral legacies manifest in the new home.

In the broader sense, *Hosay* reflects the levels of cross-celebration that characterize the T&T festive calendar, the intermingling of Afro-, Indo- and other ancestries, of Islam, Hinduism, Christianity and Afro-based religions in the context of public celebration, and the push and pull between simultaneously denouncing and celebrating an event that, despite protests, draws large crowds in a festive atmosphere. In doing that, it also reflects the challenge that the kaleidoscopic blend of religions, races and places of origin presents in this largely diasporic, quintessentially Caribbean nation. T&T festivals encode the process of becoming Caribbean, while also enacting and kinesthetically recalling memories of the ancestral homeland – sustaining traditions within a context of cross-cultural communal sharing.

Nowhere is this composite function of T&T festivals more evident than in the largest non-official holiday of them all: *Carnival*. Also a legacy of the nineteenth century, Trinidad (and, more recently, Tobago)[8] *Carnival* evolved as a festival that assimilated the Catholic French pre-Lenten celebration into post-emancipation celebrations of Afro-Trinidadians that had shifted (perhaps as early as 1848) from August 1 to *Carnival* Monday and Tuesday, the only two days that Afro-Trinidadians were allowed to 'mask' (see Liverpool 2001: 220-222; Hill, 30;

Cowley, 19-21; Brereton, 2004: 57). Having participated in *Carnival* from early on, Afro-Trinidadians incorporated festive traditions from their own background, including full body masking, 'playing royal,' the embodiment of 'moko jumbies' – African-derived stilt-walking spirits crossing the porous boundaries between the physical and immaterial worlds (See Amegago, Ensfelder, Hill, Liverpool, 1998 and 2001, Riggio, 1998 and 2015).

In its twentieth and twenty first century history, this inclusive festival has incorporated Chinese, Portuguese, Syrian, emphatically Indo-Trinidadian and other elements – singers, mas (masquerade) band organizers, forms of music, mas characters such as Chinese dragons, and even a large figure of Buddha[8] (see Chang, Sankeralli, Riggio and Gibbons). As well as incorporating festive modes from its cultures of origin, *Carnival* is by its very nature embedded in the history of the nation itself; its many traditional characters recall the degradation of enslavement;[9] its incorporation of both calypso (and its musical heirs soca, rapso, soca chutney) and pan (steel drums) link it to the T&T Emancipation story (see Green and Sher, Henry, Honore, Phillips, Brereton 2004).

One of the three largest pre-Lenten *Carnivals* in the Americas (matched only by Brazil and New Orleans), Trinidad has perhaps the only truly national *Carnival*. Even in Brazil, *Carnival* changes character from Rio de Janeiro to Bahia. However, throughout T&T, *Carnival* has the same three governing divisions – calypso/soca, pan/steel drum and mas, both traditional and modern. Moreover, *Carnival* participants tend to 'carry' their performances across the island of Trinidad and to and from Tobago, with Port of Spain regarded as the 'Mecca' of all performances, but with San Fernando also central, Tobago an increasing locus, and village or borough carnivals spread across the islands.

Despite its national status, those who participate in *Carnival* also have a strong sense of the local – of the village or borough from which they come. From Paramin Mountain to Penal to Scarborough (Tobago), or even from the Port of Spain suburb Woodbrook, where property is still leased from one large estate, to nearby Belmont with its tiny winding streets and sometimes hidden houses or in the Picadilly area 'behind the bridge' where the festival is said to have developed through nineteenth century clashes, *Carnival* affirms the sense of place, both nationally and locally (Riggio, 1998: 16-17).

The biggest *Trinidad Carnival* celebrations take place in the week leading up to *Ash Wednesday*, with the final five days before Lent an indivisible *Carnival* package. *Carnival* celebration begins on those five days with a re-enactment 'behind the bridge' in Picadilly of an 1881 pre-dawn clash on Duke Street, known as the Canboulay Riots, which pitted massed stickfighters from across Trinidad against the police led by Barbadian (Bajan) Captain Arthur Baker, who had been brought in by the British. Though Baker won the 1881 battle, he lost the war, and many historians point to these and smaller clashes in 1884 as turning points in the Afro-

Trinidadian emergence as the primary *Carnival* force (see Brereton 2004; Liverpool, Elder, Hall 1998; see Funk for a description of the re-enactment).

On Friday afternoon a traditional character competition winds through the streets of Port of Spain, to end in Woodford Square. Friday night brings the Soca Monarch finals and usually the semi-finals of the massive King and Queen costume competition. Saturday all day is *Children's Carnival* in Port of Spain, many thousands of costumed children moving through the streets in large and small mas bands, passing through the same four or five judging venues where their elders will follow on *Carnival* Tuesday. Saturday night is the Panorama Finals, the highlight of the *Carnival* season for many, in which both large and middle sized steel bands compete for the national Panorama titles. Sunday afternoon traditional *Carnival* characters compete in Victoria Square; Sunday night brings Dimanche Gras, a large production that usually includes the finals of the Kings and Queens and also of the Calypso Monarch competition.

The final two days of *Carnival* begin with Jouvay (derived from the French patois term 'jour overt' or break of day), a welcome to the dawn mud-masking street revel. Monday dawn also brings what is known as the pan 'bomb' clash. *Carnival Monday* mas, in the afternoon in Port of Spain and San Fernando, is a cool, fairly low keyed playing of mas that anticipates the much more elaborate *Carnival Tuesday*.[10] *Carnival Monday* is also a day when the regional carnivals flourish – in Arima, for instance, or in Caripichaima, which in 2007 commemorated its 50th year of *Carnival Monday* mas celebration, organized by the Indo-Trinidadian family of B. M. Singh and his daughters Jill and Sue. From the beginning, territory and place were central. Even today stickfighters, still primarily Afro-Trinidadian, or the whip-cracking Indo-Trindadian jab jabs will not fight those from the same gayelle (fighting ring) or region (See Riggio, 1998: 17).

On *Carnival Tuesday* the streets are transformed by the untold thousands, 85% of whom are now women, who take over the city in their 'pretty Mas' costumes, these days often decried by many as nothing but 'bikinis and beads'. Large mas bands can have as many as 8,000 members (minimally 1,000 to qualify), but there are also medium sized bands, small bands, and now mini bands competitions.

*Carnival Tuesday* mas happens across T&T, but on this day Port of Spain, followed by San Fernando, is central. The mas bands may form anywhere in either city, but like the children's bands, in Port of Spain they must pass through several judging venues. Interspersed between the bands of various sizes emphasizing the 'high' and 'low' of this celebration will be some individual competitors– Midnight Robbers and other traditional characters – and very tiny groups of white-faced minstrels, along with pansides on trucks, and so forth[11]. The large bands will be accompanied by multiple 18 wheel flatbed trucks that hold their music, their liquid refreshments and food, followed by the necessary porta-potties. Tuesday evening brings 'last lap', a steel band cool down centered in the borough of St.

James. Then, precisely at the stroke of midnight, police vans shut the celebrations down. *Carnival* is over and, by the dawn of *Ash Wednesday*, the city has been swept clean of the physical debris, with the Catholics ready for their ashes and 30,000 or more heading for a relaxing day on the beach.

**Figure 27.3:** 'The Midnight Robber,' performed by Peter Samuel, Jr., from the mas presentation Danse Macabre, by Minshall (Trinidad *Carnival*, 1980). (Photograph by Norton Studios)

For all its massive density, the final five days of *Carnival* do not, however, tell the *T&T Carnival* story. Preceding and surrounding these events are a plethora of other competitions and fetes. The *Carnival* season spans the time between *Three Kings Day* (January 6) and *Ash Wednesday*, but it lasts all year. Because *Carnival* has become so closely tied in the public imagination with the identity of the island, its aura and its activities linger beyond itself. Indeed, 'to play one's mas' or 'make mas' – a term heavily influenced by *Carnival* masman Peter Minshall (Minshall, 1998) – has become a metaphor for the way the '*Carnival* people' live their lives.

Trinidad *Carnival*, itself a diasporic event, now it has a diaspora of its own – having been 'carried' not only across the nation but internationally to dozens of locations throughout the Caribbean, North America, Europe, Asia, and even Australia. Those who 'come back home' to *Carnival* constitute much of Trinidad's tourist trade, and they often include non-Trinidadians who have found in the celebration a link to their own disparate identities – whether from Jamaica or Japan. To begin to understand the draw of this massive spectacle, it is necessary to see it in the context of its emergence from the horrors of enslavement.

If competition is essential to *Carnival*, resistance is no less basic to the celebration, fueling the dialectic between vagabondage and respectability that *Carnival* enacts (Riggio, 1998, 2004). During the nineteenth-century, the newspapers of Trinidad often identified the street *Carnival* as 'an annual abomination' or 'a diabolical festival' that would be worthwhile once it had crawled 'out of the Afric mud'

(Hill, 1997: 17, Riggio, 1998: 16; see also Cowley passim). At each point *Carnival* 'vagabonds' have provided much of the energy of resistance and subversion: the jamettes – those literally 'beyond the boundary' — often associated with the African presence in 19th century *Carnival*, Canboulay stickfighters of the kind who clashed with police in 1881 and 1884. When African drums were banned, tamboo bamboo drums were developed. Made from bamboo poles, with holes strategically placed along the poles, tamboo drums make a distinctive percussive sound when beaten with sticks or stamped on the ground. But when simply carried they are not so easily identified as drums. Following the Second World War, pan – the only acoustic instrument invented in the 20th century – emerged and was initially despised, though now celebrated as the national instrument. In each phase of *Carnival* development, the marginal has moved into the mainstream, while another powerful force protecting its newly defined territory has – until now – moved onto the scene.

By far the largest celebration in T&T, *Carnival*, thus, encapsulates the festive ethos of this island nation. It is essentially contradictory: not an official holiday and, yet, every school, every bank and most businesses that do not directly cater to carnival participants are closed at least for *Carnival* Monday and Tuesday (and often for the previous Friday as well). *Carnival* is widely celebrated but also denounced by many, particularly evangelical Christians, some Hindus and Muslims, and others, as profane. And yet, those who denounce it often take their children to beaches or community centers for an alternative celebration of their own; thus, in their own resistant way, they celebrate the carnival period, if not *Carnival* itself.

Moreover, like other celebrations, it serves as a kind of essential multi- and intercultural festive school. Its huge *Children's Carnival* celebrations, with many school 'jump-ups', engage children nationwide, from ages as young as one or two, often accompanied by parents who encourage them and sometimes push their strollers or carry their costumes through the heat, as they enact (often without knowing it) their historical legacies.

Beyond that, *Carnival* – like the many other festivals – embodies one final, crucial function as a stabilizing force in this Caribbean nation. Of course, this island republic is hardly a utopian oasis. There are reported incidents of personal, often domestic violence, with some terrifyingly high profile disappearances and deaths. Partly fueled by an increasing link to the flow of South American drugs and a growing urban gang scene, crime has increased since I first visited Trinidad for *Hosay* in 1991 and began seriously to study *Carnival* in 1995.

Nevertheless, Trinidad and Tobago remain more politically and socially stable than even they often realize in the midst of increasing fears. Police, though at times ineffective or corrupt, do not threaten with their massive presence. The wall-to-wall crowds at *Carnival* seem governed largely by internalized principles of decorum. Following a 2001 election that failed to establish a governing majority, the republic survived for almost a year without a legitimately elected government. In 2011 this two-island republic maintained its composure throughout a declared State of Emergency while sporadic 'curfew parties' simply began before and broke up after the 11 pm – 4 am curfew established in selected regions.

In 1990, Islamic Jamaat-al-Muslimeen led by Yasin Abu Bakr attempted a political coup that resulted in 24 deaths and a brief takeover of the government. The coup did not destabilize T&T, but it did appear quickly in its mythology. Calypsonians sang about it in large numbers, sometimes mournfully but always optimistically, lamenting the social inequality on which the coup was blamed but, in the words of Calypsonian Cro Cro, affirming 'We are still the best' as 'Trinbago's flag is still flying high'. The coup had occurred during *Hosay*. In a 1991 lyrical dirge called 'Hoosay', *Carnival* superstar David Rudder not only linked the 'bloody asphalt' of the coup to the festival it had interrupted, but he also circled back to a massacre of *Hosay* worshippers in 1884, led by Police Captain Baker of the Canboulay riots of 1881 and 1884. By bringing *Hosay* into the *Carnival* frame, Rudder reminded the 80% of T&T population who claim India and Africa as their ancestral homeland of their essential kinship, encompassing national tragedy in a rhythm that is cathartic and healing but grounded in the toughest realities of life:

> the drums were silent but somehow the rhythm continues, the night that they say the martyrs died….Oh how we dance

Calypso's power is primarily embedded in its social criticism, satirizing everything from government, racial prejudice, and ethnic stereotypes to gender and sexual repression, with some fairly heavy hits at international issues. Fortified through this and other traditions, recently including the Hindu musical competition known as *Pichakaaree*, T&T has been able historically to absorb a high degree of political tension and racial conflict.

*Trinidad Carnival*, however, is far from entirely satirical and subversive. It is also magnificently beautiful. As a festival, it transforms emblems of past degradation into celebratory modes, not to hide, disguise, or escape the pain of history, but to honor and sustain survival. This happens in many forms in T&T, but the most spectacular transformations occur in the *Carnival* mas Bands of the Year. Such have always incorporated the African notion of 'playing royal' (see Hill, Cowley, and Liverpool). But in the second half of the twentieth century, significant designers like Carlisle Chang, George Bailey, Wayne Berkeley, and Stephen Derek have brought splendor to the streets of Port of Spain in bands that range thematically from history to mythology to ecology and beyond.

Chief among the masters is masman artist Peter Minshall, creator of opening and closing ceremonies for three Olympics, whose mas bands, since he first designed and made the Hummingbird for his twelve-year-old adopted sister at his mother's insistence in 1974, have been the glory of the nation. Minshall brings this introduction to the festive culture and '*Carnival* People' of T&T full circle. Mr.

Minsh, as he is affectionately known, has consistently managed the dual function of sharply critiquing the nation he so deeply loves (Minshall, 2013) and creating entirely new artistic forms as vehicles into which to pour social but also cosmic vision. For Minshall, making mas is a sacred act – through it all, he prays for and with his people, defying the charges of profanity (see cover image).

To be called '*Carnival* People' goes far beyond *Carnival*. It engages the many strands of this complex culture in celebrations that are central to the identity formation of both individuals and groups. However, the dialectic that has for two centuries sustained this rhythm is engaged in yet again a new struggle. Current attempts to alter the basic nature of T&T culture – to dispossess street vendors, enclose and air-condition malls, and most of all to harness the festive energies in the service of state economic interests – amounts to a battle for the soul of the nation (Minshall 2013).

It is true that calls for *Carnival* to 'clean up' its act have co-existed with the festival from the beginning, sounded recurrently throughout the late 19th century, echoed, for instance, in Eric Williams's attempts in 1962 to sanction the festival as the signature of the new nation, if only it could clean up and clean out the vagabonds. Thus, the risk that the 'rough beast' – the energy of resistance and the dialectic of vagabondage and respectability so crucial to this festive culture – will be tamed by the governing infrastructure or, even more, by money-driven commercial interests, and that the healthy dialectic will consequently collapse is not new (see Burke). The forces that would have T&T emulate its 'powerful' allies to the North may in this vacuum seriously threaten the core of the republic's distinctive identity by misunderstanding both its source and its power, resulting ironically in greater national fragmentation, manifest in widening racial and ethnic divisions, and no doubt partly fuelling the increase in crime, which *Carnival* itself, through pan and other means, had in the past helped to curb.

In attempting to redefine that which is unique in this complex, multi-ethnic society, Trinidad and Tobago may find that the real threat is not, in fact, the festive culture, but the forces that would expand the nation's air-conditioned, multiplex, but inevitably minor presence on the economically driven 'world stage'. What the 'modern' world needs is perhaps not a bigger and more threatening set of powerful machines. At a time when globalization is accompanied by ever increasing local tribalization worldwide, Syl Lowhar's 1965 poetic exhortation still has value:

> Power is not enough to make us strong
> The heart must also sing the human song.

In its songs, its many dances, but also its stabilizing festive culture, T&T has the power to manifest potentially redemptive energy, embedded in its sense of community and even its utopian dreams at a time when, harnessed, they might seriously impact the global conversation. Its *Carnival* People, who are also the

*First Nation, Divali, Ramdilla, Phagwa, Eid, Hosay, Spiritual Baptist* and *Orisha* people – the Hindus, Muslims, Christians, and many others who cohabit in this Southernmost Caribbean island nation – offer life-affirming voices to be heard.

# Bibliography

Adonis, C. with Ferreira, J. (2012) Amerindian Languages in Trinidad and Tobago. The University of the West Indies St. Augustine Campus: *eSTAN*. April-June 40-45.

Aiyejina, F. and Gibbons, R. (1999) Orisa (Orisha) Tradition in Trinidad. *Caribbean Quarterly,* **45**(4) (December 1999), 35-50.

Amegago, M. (2013) Interrogating the roots, elements and crossovers of the Caribbean *Carnival*: A case of West African celebrations, in C. Innis et al, (eds.) *Carnival: Theory and Practice.* Trenton, NJ: Africa World Press, 25-34.

Brereton, B. (2004) The Trinidad *Carnival* in the Nineteenth Century, in M. C. Riggio, *Carnival: Culture in Action – The Trinidad Experience.* London: Routledge, 53-63.

Brereton, B. (1982) *History of Modern Trinidad: 1783-1962.* London: Heineman.

Burke, S. D. (2013) Policing the people's festival: State policy and the Trinidad carnival complex, in C. Innis et al, (eds.) *Carnival: Theory and Practice.* Trenton, NJ: Africa World Press, 107-125.

Chang, C. (2004) Chinese in Trinidad *Carnival,* in M. C. Riggio, *Carnival: Culture in Action – The Trinidad Experience.* London: Routledge, 85-90.

Chulov, M. (2014) *The Guardian.* 3 November.

Chelkowski, P. (1979) *Ta'ziyeh: Ritual and Drama in Iran. New York:* New York University Press.

Cowley, J. (1999) *Carnival, Canboulay, and Calypso: Traditions in the Making.* Cambridge: Cambridge University Press.

Crowley, D. (1988) The Traditional Masques of *Carnival,* in G. A. Besson (ed.), T*rinidad Carnival,* Port of Spain: Paria, 42–90. (Rpt of original 1956 publication).

Delano, P., and Riggio, M. C. (eds.) (2008) *In Trinidad: Photographs by Pablo Delano.* Kingston: Randle Publishing Co.

Elder, J. D. (1998) Cannes Brûlée, in M. C. Riggio, *Trinidad and Tobago Carnival. The Drama Review, Special Expanded Edition.* Fall, 1998. **48**(3) 38-43.

Ensfelder, S. (2013) The African heritage in Trinidad *Carnival*: From cultural resistance to identity formation in Earl Lovelace's *The Dragon Can't Dance,* in C. Innis et al, *Carnival: Theory and Practice,* Trenton: Africa World Press. 53-62.

Funk, R. Rituals of Resistance: the Canboulay riots re-enactment, in *Caribbean Beat,* Issue 108. http://caribbean-beat.com/issue-108/rituals-resistance#ixzz3hPOHcjGm

Gibbons, R. (2015) Personal Communication with Rawle Gibbons, August 12.

Green, G., and Sher, P. (eds.) (2007) *Trinidad Carnival: The Cultural Politics of a Transnational Festival.* Bloomington: University of Indiana Press.

Hall, T. (1998) They want to see George Band: Tobago Mas according to George Leacock, an Interview by Tony Hall, in M. C. Riggio, *Trinidad and Tobago Carnival. The Drama Review, Special Expanded Edition.* Fall, 1998. **48**(3), 44-53.

Hall, T. (1998) The legacy of George Bailey, in M. C. Riggio *Trinidad and Tobago Carnival. The Drama Review, Special Expanded Edition.* Fall, 1998. **48**(3), 172-173.

Hall, T. (1998) Lennox Pierre, an interview by Tony Hall, in M. C. Riggio *Trinidad and Tobago Carnival. The Drama Review, Special Expanded Edition.* Fall, 1998. **48**(3), 41.

Henry, J. (2013) *Carnival*/Masquerade in Trinidad: Resistance through Performance, in C. Innis et al, *Carnival: Theory and Practice.* Trenton, NJ: Africa World Press. 65-78.

Hill, E. (1997) *The Trinidad Carnival.* Austin Texas: The University of Texas Press, 1972. Paperback edition, London: New Beacon Books.

Honore, B. (1988) The Midnight Robber: Master of Metaphor, Baron of Bombast, in M. C. Riggio, *Trinidad and Tobago Carnival. The Drama Review, Special Expanded Edition.* Fall, 1998. **48**(3) 124-131.

Innis, C., Rutherford, A., and Bogar, B. (eds.) (2013) *Carnival: Theory and Practice.* Trenton, NJ: Africa World Press.

Korom, F. (2003) *Hosay Trinidad: Muharram Performances in an Indo-Caribbean Diaspora.* Philadelphia: University of Pennsylvania Press.

Liverpool, H. (1998) Origins of rituals and customs in the Trinidad *Carnival*: African or European? in M. C. Riggio, *Trinidad and Tobago Carnival. The Drama Review, Special Expanded Edition.* Fall, 1998. **48**(3), 24-37.

Liverpool, H. (2001) *Rituals of Power and Rebellion: The Carnival Tradition in Trinidad And Tobago, 1763-1962.* Research Associates School Times Publications and Frontline Distribution International.

Millette, J. (1970) *The Genesis of Crown Colony Government: Trinidad, 1783-1810.* Trinidad: Moko Enterprises.

Ministry of Planning and Sustainable Development Central Stastical Office. *Trinidad and Tobago 2011 Population and Housing Census Demographic Report.* Port of Spain: Government of Trinidad and Tobago, Central Statistical Office, 2012. Online.

Minshall, P. (1998) A Voice to add to the Song of the Universe, an interview by Richard Schechner and Milla C. Riggio, in M. C. Riggio, *Trinidad and Tobago Carnival. The Drama Review, Special Expanded Edition.* Fall, 1998. **48**(3), 170-93.

Minshall, P. (2013) Nignorance and enwhitenment, in C. Innis et al *Carnival: Theory and Practice.* Trenton, NJ: Africa World Press.

Newsday (2015) Sights of Chowtaal Sammelan, Port of Spain: *Newsday.* March 2, 2015. Np. Online.

Phillips, E. (2013) The Politial Calypso: A sociolinguistic process in conflict transformation, in C. Innis, et al, *Carnival: Theory and Practice.* Trenton, NJ: Africa World Press.

Riggio, M. C. (1992) Interview with Mr. Ganpat, Cedros.

Riggio, M. C. (1994) *Ta'ziyeh* in Exile: Transformations in a Persian tradition, in *Comparative Drama*, 28 (Spring, 1994) 115-140. Rpt. Johann Christoph Bürgel und Stephan Guth, *Gesellschaftlicher Umbruch im Zeitgenössischen Drama der Islamischen Welt*, Stuttgart, Steiner, 1997, 235-258.

Riggio, M. C. (ed.) (1998) *Trinidad and Tobago Carnival. The Drama Review, Special Expanded Edition*. Fall, 1998. **48**(3), (T159).

Riggio, M. C. (1998) Resistance and Identity: *Carnival* in Trinidad and Tobago, in M. C. Riggio, *Trinidad and Tobago Carnival. The Drama Review, Special Expanded Edition*. Fall, 1998. **48**(3), 7-23.

Riggio, M. C. (2004) 'Play Mas' – Play me, Play we, in M. C. Riggio *Carnival: Culture in Action – The Trinidad Experience*, London: Routledge, 93-108.

Riggio, M. C. (2004) The *Carnival* story: Then and now, in M. C. Riggio, *Carnival: Culture in Action – The Trinidad Experience*, London: Routledge, 39-47.

Riggio, M. C. (2004) Time out or Time in: The urban dialectic of carnival, in M. C. Riggio *Carnival: Culture in Action – The Trinidad Experience*, London: Routledge, 13-30.

Riggio, M. C. (ed.) (2004) *Carnival: Culture in Action – The Trinidad Experience*, London: Routledge.

Riggio, Milla Cozart. (2007) 'For the sake of Allah and all humanity': A jihaji journey into Trinidad, in S. Rastegar and A. Vanzan,(eds), *Muraqqa'e Sharqi: Studies in Honor of Peter Chelkowski*. Repubblica San Marino: AIEP, 2007. 145–162.

Riggio, M. C. (2010) Performing in the lap and at the feet of god: Ramleela in Trinidad, 2006-2008, in *The Drama Review (TDR)*, **54**(1), 2010. 106-149.

Riggio, M. C., and Gibbons, R. (2015) 'Pay de Devil, Jab Jab': Festive devils in Trinidad *Carnival*, in M. C. Riggio, A. Marino, and P. Vignolo, (eds.) *Festive Devils of the Americas*, India: Seagull Books, Distributed by the University of Chicago Press, 189-220.

Sankeralli, B. (2004) Indian presence in *Carnival*, in M. C. Riggio, *Carnival: Culture in Action – The Trinidad Experience*, London: Routledge, 76-84.

Stegassy, R. (1998) Interview with John Cupid, in M. C. Riggio *Trinidad and Tobago Carnival. The Drama Review, Special Expanded Edition*. Fall, 1998. **48**(3), 96-107.

Walsh, M. (1998) Jouvay Mornin' with the Merry Darceuils: A small neighborhood band on carnival morning, in M. C. Riggio, *Trinidad and Tobago Carnival. The Drama Review, Special Expanded Edition*. Fall, 1998. **48**(3), 132-146.

Walsh, M. (2004) The Blue Devils of Paramin: Tradition and improvisation in a village carnival band, in M. C. Riggio, *Carnival: Culture in Action – The Trinidad Experience*, London: Routledge, 146-156.

## Notes

1 Separated from Venezuela by the Gulf of Paria, Trinidad is the southernmost Caribbean island, 1,864 square miles. Trinidad has many boroughs and two cities: Port of Spain, the capital on the northwest coast, and San Fernando, 42 miles due south. More rural Tobago, 20 miles northeast of Trinidad, is 116 square miles, with the southern coastal town of Scarborough as its capital.

Spain claimed Trinidad until 1797 when the Spanish Governor Don José María Chacón surrendered to British General Sir Ralph Abercrombie. Trinidad's population had swelled from roughly 1,000 in the 1770s to more than 18,000 because of the Cedula of Population, which in 1783 offered free land to any Roman Catholic settler who would swear allegiance to the Spanish crown (32 acres per planter and 16 acres per slave). African and 'free coloured' planters were given exactly half as much land. During the period of the French Revolution, French Creole planters from Martinique and other islands took advantage of this offer so that by the time Spain surrendered Trinidad, 80% of its population were French-speaking planters and their enslaved labor. The Treaty of Amiens in 1802 between England and France ceded Trinidad to the British, who governed both Trinidad and Tobago as crown colonies until they won independence on 31 August 1962 (For Crown Colony government, see Millette). First allied by the British in 1889, with Tobago established as a ward of Trinidad, the islands officially became the Republic of Trinidad and Tobago in 1976. (Expanded from Riggio, 'Resistance and Identity,' 1998, p. 7; for demographic information, see www.indexmundi.com/trinidad_and_tobago/demographics)

2 See, for instance, http://www.gotrinidadandtobago.com/trinidad/carnival/ or Hill, who calls *Trinidad Carnival* 'undoubtedly the greatest annual theatrical spectacle of all time' (p. 3).

3 Allied as a Republic, Trinidad and Tobago have separate histories; Tobago is much smaller, more rural, with a more developed tourist trade. Both Trinidad and Tobago are prime destinations for bird watchers. Tobago still has its own House of Assembly. Tobago's primary annual festival, the *Heritage Festival*, takes place each year in July. Tobago also has goat races on *Easter Monday*. This paper will concentrate on festivals that are primarily (if not entirely) Trinidadian.

4 During *Divali* in the early years of this century, I discovered on Independence Square, Trinidad, the name YMCA (Young Mens Christian Association) spelled out in an array of lighted deyas.

5 See Korom, Chelkowski, Riggio 1994 & 2007, for a more detailed discussion of the many forms these celebrations take across the world.

6 Muharram, the first month in the Islamic calendar, ushers in the Muslim New Year and is celebrated by all Muslims. However, for Shi'i it is also a month of mourning, commemorating the deaths of Karbala. The assassination of Hussein and his family is the event that, more than any other, both historically and theologically, separate what are now known as Shi's [or Shi'ites] and Sunnis. The resistance to the festival in Trinidad is calm in comparison to the violence that occurs in India and, even more, in Iraq.

7 See Tony Hall, Interview with George Leacock, 1998. Ordinarily, assumed to have begun in Tobago in the 1940s, Leacock placed the earliest introduction to Tobago in the 1920s, for which he assumed credit.

8 In Carapichaima in 2000, photographer Pablo Delano found a replica of Buddha in the *Carnival* processions, followed by a Chinese dragon. (See Delano and Riggio, p.112 and Riggio, 2004, illus. 7.8, p. 105)

9 Such characters include Midnight Robbers, boastful outlaws who are always avenging an ancestor, the many forms of devil (jab molassi, jab jabs, dragon bands), Fancy and Bad Behavior Sailors, among many others, all with ties to the periods of enslavement and colonialism. (Crowley, Cowley, Riggio, 1998 & 2004, Riggio & Gibbons, 2015, Honore, Walsh 2004)

10 There are at times bands that play only on *Carnival Monday* in Port of Spain, as for instance the 2014 "Miss Miles Woman of the World," brought by Peter Minshall and Tony Hall, focusing on a tragically famous whistle blower of the 1960s, the band derived from a prizewinning one woman play by Tony Hall of the same name.

11 See Walsh 1998 for a description of an experience with one small *Carnival Tuesday* band.

# A Author index

# S Subject Index